ECGs MADE EASY

Barbara Aehlert, RN, BSPA

Southwest EMS Education, Inc.
Phoenix, Arizona, and Pursley, Texas

THIRD EDITION

MOSBY JEMS

ELSEVIER

MOSBY
ELSEVIER

11830 Westline Industrial Drive
St. Louis, Missouri 63146

ECGs MADE EASY, THIRD EDITION
Copyright © 2006, 2002, 1995 by Mosby, Inc.

ISBN-13: 978-0-323-03969-7
ISBN-10: 0-323-03969-3

Notice

ISBN-13: 978-0-323-03969-7
ISBN-10: 0-323-03969-3

Executive Editor: Linda Honeycutt
Developmental Editor: Katherine Tomber
Publishing Services Manager: Julie Eddy
Senior Project Manager: Joy Moore
Designer: Kathi Gosche

Working together to grow
libraries in developing countries

www.elsevier.com | www.bookaid.org | www.sabre.org

ELSEVIER   BOOK AID
International   Sabre Foundation

Printed in Canada

Last digit is the print number: 9 8 7 6 5 4 3 2

For Maryalice Witzel, Jeanne Shepard, and Paul Honeywell
Three extraordinary friends and instructors who share the same values
regarding teaching as I do.

Preface to the Third Edition

ECGs Made Easy is designed for use by paramedic, nursing, and medical students; ECG monitor technicians; nurses; and other allied health personnel working in emergency departments, critical care units, postanesthesia care units, operating rooms, and telemetry units who wish to master the skill of basic ECG recognition. This book may be used alone or as part of a formal course of instruction in basic dysrhythmia recognition.

The information presented in this book focuses on the essential information you need to know to interpret ECGs and understand their significance. Each ECG rhythm is described and accompanied by a sample rhythm strip. Possible patient signs and symptoms related to the rhythm and, where appropriate, current recommended treatments for the rhythm are discussed. Additional rhythm strips are provided for practice at the end of each chapter. Answers for each rhythm are provided in the appendix. All rhythm strips shown in this text were recorded in lead II unless otherwise noted.

In the third edition of this book, more practice ECG strips have been added. The Stop & Review exercises at the end of each chapter are self-assessment exercises that allow you to check your learning. These exercises have been expanded and crossword puzzles have been added for additional review.

Every attempt has been made to provide information that is consistent with current literature, including resuscitation guidelines. However, medicine is a dynamic field. Resuscitation guidelines change, new medications and technology are being developed, and medical research is ongoing. As a result, be sure to learn and follow local protocols as defined by your medical advisors.

I hope you find this text helpful. If you have comments or suggestions about how I could improve this text, please visit my web site (http://www.swemsed.com) and drop me a line. I would like to hear from you.

Best regards,

Barbara Aehlert

Acknowledgments

I would like to thank the following individuals:

- Andrew Baird, CEP; James Bratcher; Holly Button, CEP; Gretchen Chalmers, CEP; Thomas Cole, CEP; Brent Haines, CEP; Timothy Klatt, RN; Andrea Legamaro, RN; Bill Loughran, RN; Joe Martinez, CEP; Stephanos Orphanidis, CEP; Captain Jeff Pennington, CEP; Steve Ruehs, CEP; Patty Seneski, RN; Dionne Socie, CEP; Kristina Tellez, CEP; and Fran Wojculewicz, RN, for providing many of the rhythm strips used in this text.

- My developmental editor, Katherine Tomber. Your patience, humor, and understanding have been sincerely appreciated throughout this project.

- The text reviewers. Your thorough review, comments, and suggestions were sincerely appreciated. Areas of this text were rewritten, reorganized, and clarified because of your efforts.

About the Author

Barbara Aehlert is the President and CEO of Southwest EMS Education, Inc., in Phoenix, Arizona, and Pursley, Texas. She has been a registered nurse for more than 25 years with clinical experience in medical/surgical and critical care nursing and, for the past 18 years, prehospital education. As an active instructor, Barbara regularly teaches courses related to the care of the adult cardiac patient and takes a special interest in teaching basic dysrhythmia recognition to nurses and paramedics.

Publisher Acknowledgments

The editors wish to acknowledge the reviewers of the third edition of this book for their invaluable help in developing and fine-tuning the manuscript.

Jeffrey Benes, BS, EMT-P
Benes Consulting Services
Antioch, Illinois

Dennis Edgerly, EMT-P
Paramedic Education Coordinator
HealthONE EMS
Englewood, Colorado

Leslie Hernandez, BS, NREMT-P, LP
Advanced Program Coordinator
Bulverde Spring Branch EMS
Spring Branch, Texas

Joanne McCall, RN, MA, CEN
Educator—Emergency Services
Providence Hospital
Novi, Michigan

Christine McEachin, RN, BSN, CEN, Paramedic/IC
Clinical Nurse Specialist
William Beaumont Hospital—Troy
Troy, Michigan

Contents

3 SINUS MECHANISMS, 86

4 ATRIAL RHYTHMS, 107

5 JUNCTIONAL RHYTHMS, 143

6 VENTRICULAR RHYTHMS, 160

7 ATRIOVENTRICULAR (AV) BLOCKS, 190

8 PACEMAKER RHYTHMS, 211

9 INTRODUCTION TO THE 12-LEAD ECG, 232

10 POST-TEST, 280

APPENDIX, 308

GLOSSARY, 346

CREDITS, 354

INDEX, 360

Anatomy and Physiology

OBJECTIVES

On completion of this chapter, you should be able to:

1. Describe the location of the heart.
2. Distinguish between the apex and base of the heart.
3. Identify and describe the chambers of the heart and the vessels that enter or leave each.
4. Define the terms *atrial kick, chronotropy, inotropy, preload,* and *afterload.*
5. Describe the structure and location of the pericardium, epicardium, myocardium, and endocardium.
6. Name and identify the location of the atrioventricular (AV) and semilunar (SL) valves.
7. Explain how heart sounds are created and their clinical significance.
8. Beginning with the right atrium, describe blood flow through the normal heart and lungs to the systemic circulation.
9. Identify the phases of the cardiac cycle.
10. Name the primary branches and areas of the heart supplied by the right and left coronary arteries.
11. Compare and contrast the effects of sympathetic and parasympathetic stimulation of the heart.
12. Name the primary neurotransmitter of the sympathetic and parasympathetic divisions of the autonomic nervous system.
13. Describe the effects of stimulation of alpha-receptors, beta-1 receptors, beta-2 receptors, and dopaminergic receptors.
14. Identify and define the components of cardiac output.

LOCATION OF THE HEART

The heart is a hollow, muscular organ. It lies in the space between the lungs (**mediastinum**) in the middle of the chest. The heart sits behind the sternum and just above the diaphragm (Figure 1-1). Most of the heart (about two thirds) actually lies to the left of the midline of the sternum. The remaining one third lies to the right of the sternum. The heart is surrounded by

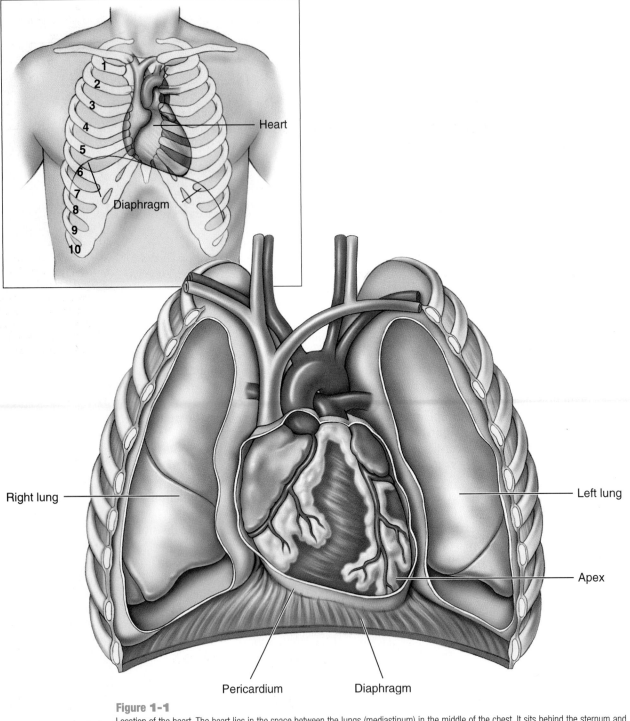

Figure 1-1
Location of the heart. The heart lies in the space between the lungs (mediastinum) in the middle of the chest. It sits behind the sternum and just above the diaphragm.

a double-layered membrane called the **pericardium**. The pericardium's innermost layer is at-tached to the heart muscle. The outermost layer of the pericardium surrounds the roots of the **great vessels** (pulmonary arteries and veins, aorta, superior and inferior vena cavae). The pericardium is attached by ligaments to the diaphragm, spinal column, and other parts of the body. The layers of the pericardium are separated by a thin coating of fluid. This fluid acts as a lubricant, preventing friction as the heart beats.

The base of the heart is its upper portion. It lies at about the level of the second rib. The heart's apex, or lower portion, is formed by the tip of the left ventricle (Figure 1-2). The apex lies just above the diaphragm, between the fifth and sixth ribs, in the midclavicular line. The heart is tilted slightly toward the left in the chest. Thus the anterior surface of the heart is made up mostly of the right ventricle. The heart's inferior surface is formed by both the right and left ventricles, but mostly the left.

> The weight of the heart is approxi-mately 0.45% of a man's body weight and about 0.40% of a woman's.

Size and Shape of the Heart

The adult heart is approximately 5 inches (12 cm) long, 3½ inches (9 cm) wide, and 2½ inches (6 cm) thick. It typically weighs between 250 and 350 g (approximately 11 oz) and is about the size of its owner's fist (Figure 1-3). A person's heart size and weight are influenced by their age, body weight and build, frequency of physical exercise, and heart disease.

HEART CHAMBERS

Atria

The heart is divided into four chambers. The two upper chambers are the right and left **atria**. The atria have thin walls. Their purpose is to *receive* blood. The right atrium receives blood low in oxygen from the following:

- The superior vena cava, which carries blood from the head and upper extremities
- The inferior vena cava, which carries blood from the lower body
- The coronary sinus, which is the largest vein that drains the heart

> Think of the atria as "holding tanks" or "reservoirs" for blood. The wall of the right atrium is about 2 mm thick. The wall of the left atrium is about 3 mm thick.

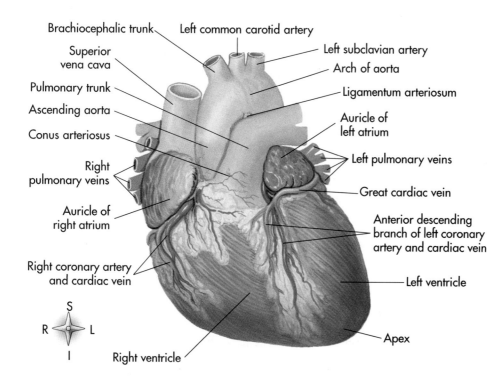

Figure 1-2
Anterior view of the heart and great vessels.

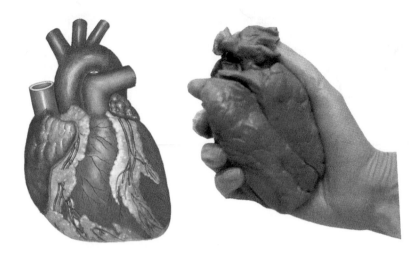

Figure 1-3
The adult heart weighs approximately 250 to 350 g and is about the size of its owner's fist.

The left atrium receives freshly oxygenated blood from the lungs via the right and left pulmonary veins. When the atria contract, blood is pumped through a valve into the ventricles.

Ventricles

The apical impulse is also called the point of maximal impulse (PMI) because it is the site where the heartbeat is most strongly felt.

The two lower chambers of the heart are the right and left ventricles. The walls of the ventricles are much thicker than those of the atria. Their purpose is to *pump* blood. The right ventricle pumps blood to the lungs. The left ventricle pumps blood out to the body. When the left ventricle contracts, it normally produces an impulse that can be felt at the apex of the heart (apical impulse). This occurs because as the left ventricle contracts, it rotates forward. In a normal heart, this causes the apex of the left ventricle to hit the chest wall. You may be able to see the apical impulse in thin individuals.

The outside surface of the heart has grooves called sulci. The coronary arteries and their major branches lie in these grooves. The coronary **sulcus** (groove) encircles the outside of the heart and separates the atria from the ventricles. It contains the coronary blood vessels and epicardial fat.

The right ventricle is approximately 3 to 5 mm thick; the left ventricle is approximately 13 to 15 mm thick.

The right and left sides of the heart are separated by an internal wall of connective tissue called a **septum**. The *interatrial septum* separates the right and left atria. The *interventricular septum* separates the right and left ventricles. The septa separate the heart into two functional pumps. The right atrium and right ventricle make up one pump. The left atrium and left ventricle make up the other (Figure 1-4). The right side of the heart is a low-pressure system. The job of the right side of the heart is to pump unoxygenated (venous) blood to and through the lungs to the left side of the heart. This is called the *pulmonary circulation.*

The left side of the heart is a high-pressure pump. The job of the left heart is to receive oxygenated blood and pump it out to the rest of the body. This is called the *systemic circulation.* Blood is carried from the heart to the organs of the body through arteries, arterioles, and capillaries. Blood is returned to the right heart through venules and veins. The left ventricle is a high-pressure chamber. Its walls are about three times thicker than the right ventricle. This is because the left ventricle must overcome a lot of pressure and resistance from the arteries and contract forcefully in order to pump blood out to the body.

There is normally a continuous flow of blood from the superior and inferior vena cavae into the atria. About 70% of this blood flows directly through the atria and into the ventricles before the atria contract. When the atria contract, an additional 30% is added to filling of the

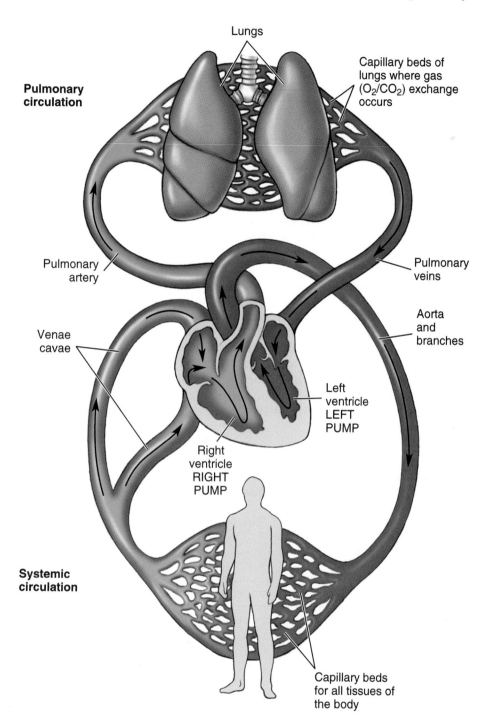

Figure **1-4**
The heart functions as a two-sided pump.

ventricles. This additional contribution of blood resulting from atrial contraction is called **atrial kick**.

Each ventricle holds about 150 mL when it is full. They normally eject about half this volume (70 to 80 mL) with each contraction. **Stroke volume** is the amount of blood ejected from a ventricle with each heartbeat. The *percentage* of blood pumped out of a heart chamber with each contraction is called the **ejection fraction**. Ejection fraction is used as a measure of ventricular function. A normal ejection fraction is more than 50%. A person is said to have impaired ventricular function when the ejection fraction is less than 40%.

LAYERS OF THE HEART

The walls of the heart are made up of three tissue layers: the endocardium, myocardium, and epicardium (Table 1-1). The heart's innermost layer is the endocardium. The **endocardium** is a thin, smooth layer of epithelium and connective tissue that lines the heart's inner chambers, valves, chordae tendineae, and papillary muscles. It is continuous with the innermost layer (tunica intima) of the arteries, veins, and capillaries of the body. This creates a continuous, closed circulatory system (Figure 1-5).

The **myocardium** (middle layer) is a thick, muscular layer that consists of cardiac muscle fibers (cells) responsible for the pumping action of the heart. The myocardium is subdivided into two areas. The innermost half of the myocardium is called the subendocardial area because it lies below. The outermost half is called the subepicardial area. The muscle fibers of the myocardium are separated by connective tissues that have a rich supply of capillaries and nerve fibers.

We already mentioned that the thickness of the myocardium varies from one heart chamber to another. This variation in thickness is related to the amount of resistance that must be overcome to pump blood out of the different chambers. For example, the atria encounter little resistance when pumping blood to the ventricles. As a result, the atria have a thin myocardial layer. On the other hand, the ventricles must pump blood to either the lungs (the job of the right ventricle) or the rest of the body (the job of the left ventricle). So, the ventricles have a much thicker myocardial layer than the atria. The wall of the left ventricle is three times thicker than that of the right because the left ventricle propels blood to most vessels of

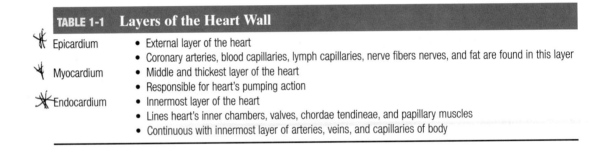

TABLE 1-1	**Layers of the Heart Wall**
Epicardium	• External layer of the heart • Coronary arteries, blood capillaries, lymph capillaries, nerve fibers nerves, and fat are found in this layer
Myocardium	• Middle and thickest layer of the heart • Responsible for heart's pumping action
Endocardium	• Innermost layer of the heart • Lines heart's inner chambers, valves, chordae tendineae, and papillary muscles • Continuous with innermost layer of arteries, veins, and capillaries of body

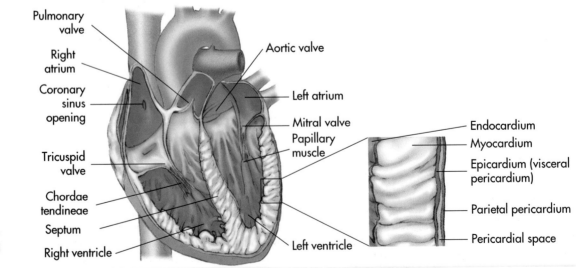

Figure 1-5
Cross-sectional view of the heart wall and tissue layers.

the body. The right ventricle moves blood only through the blood vessels of the lungs to the left atrium.

The heart's outermost layer is called the **epicardium**. The epicardium is continuous with the inner lining of the pericardium at the heart's apex. The epicardium contains blood capillaries, lymph capillaries, nerve fibers, and fat. The main coronary arteries lie on the epicardial surface of the heart. They feed this area first before entering the myocardium and supplying the heart's inner layers with oxygenated blood. **Ischemia** is a decreased supply of oxygenated blood to a body part or organ. The heart's subendocardial area is at the greatest risk of ischemia because of the following:

- This area has a high demand for oxygen.
- This area is fed by the most distal branches of the coronary arteries.

The **pericardium** is a double-walled sac that encloses the heart and helps protect it from trauma and infection. The rough outer layer of the pericardial sac is called the *fibrous parietal pericardium*. It anchors the heart to some of the structures around it, such as the sternum and diaphragm. This helps prevent excessive movement of the heart in the chest with changes in body position. The inner layer, the *serous pericardium*, consists of two layers: parietal and visceral. The parietal layer lines the inside of the fibrous pericardium. The visceral layer (also called the epicardium) adheres to the outside of the heart and forms the outer layer of the heart muscle.

Between the visceral and parietal layers is a space (the pericardial space) that normally contains about 20 mL of serous fluid. This fluid acts as a lubricant, preventing friction as the heart beats. If the pericardium becomes inflamed (pericarditis), more serous fluid is secreted. Pericarditis can be caused by a bacterial or viral infection, rheumatoid arthritis, destruction of the heart muscle in a heart attack, among many other causes. Heart surgery or trauma to the heart, such as a stab wound, can cause a rapid buildup of blood in the pericardial space.

The buildup of excess blood or fluid in the pericardial space compresses the heart. This can affect the heart's ability to relax and fill with blood between heartbeats. If the heart cannot adequately fill with blood, the amount of blood the ventricles can pump out to the body (cardiac output) will be decreased. As a result, the amount of blood returning to the heart is also decreased. These changes can result in a life-threatening condition called *cardiac tamponade*.

The amount of blood or fluid in the pericardial space needed to impair the heart's ability to fill depends on the following:

- The rate at which the accumulation of blood or fluid occurs
- The ability of the pericardium to stretch and accommodate the increased volume of fluid

The rapid buildup of as little as 100 to 150 mL of fluid or blood can be enough to result in signs and symptoms of shock. On the other hand, 1000 mL of fluid may build up over a longer period without any significant effect on the heart's ability to fill. This is because the pericardium accommodates the increased fluid by stretching over time.

The symptoms of cardiac tamponade can be relieved by removing the excess fluid from the pericardial sac. **Pericardiocentesis** is a procedure in which a needle is inserted into the pericardial space and the excess fluid is sucked out (aspirated) through the needle. If scarring is the cause of the tamponade, surgery may be necessary to remove the affected area of the pericardium.

CARDIAC MUSCLE

Cardiac muscle is found only in the heart. Cardiac muscle fibers make up the walls of the heart. These fibers have striations, or stripes, similar to that of skeletal muscle. Each muscle fiber is made up of many muscle cells (Figure 1-6, *A*). Each muscle cell is enclosed in a mem-

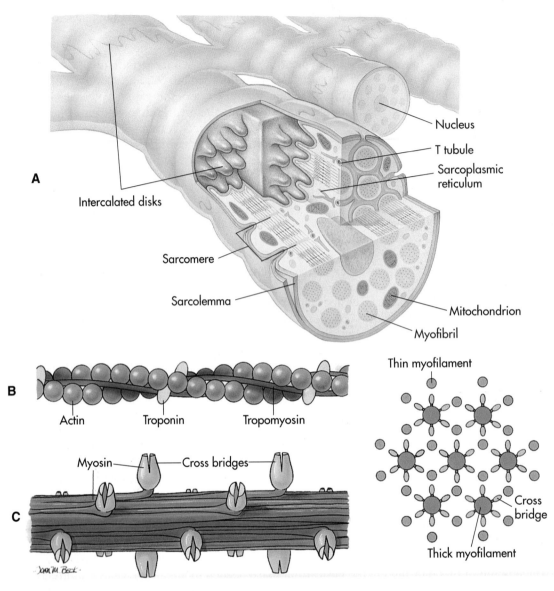

Figure 1-6
A, Cardiac muscle fiber. Unlike other types of muscle fibers, the cardiac muscle fiber is typically branched and forms junctions, called intercalated disks, with adjacent cardiac muscle fibers. **B,** Thin myofilament. **C,** Thick myofilament.

brane called a **sarcolemma**. Within each cell are **mitochondria**, the energy-producing parts of a cell, and hundreds of long, tube-like structures called **myofibrils**. Myofibrils are made up of many **sarcomeres**, the basic protein units responsible for contraction. The process of contraction requires adenosine triphosphate (ATP) for energy. The mitochondria that are interspersed between the myofibrils are important sites of ATP production.

The sarcolemma has holes in it that lead into tubes called T (transverse) tubules. T-tubules are extensions of the cell membrane. Another system of tubules, the **sarcoplasmic reticulum** (SR), stores calcium. Muscle cells need calcium in order to contract. Calcium is moved from the sarcoplasm of the muscle cell into the sarcoplasmic reticulum by means of "pumps" in the sarcoplasmic reticulum.

There are certain places in the cell membrane where sodium (Na+), potassium (K+), and calcium (Ca++) can pass. These openings are called pores or channels. There are specific channels for sodium (sodium channels), potassium (potassium channels), and calcium (calcium channels). When the muscle is relaxed, the calcium channels are closed. As a result, calcium cannot pass through the membrane of the sarcoplasmic reticulum. This results in a high concentration of calcium in the sarcoplasmic reticulum and a low concentration in the sarcoplasm, where the muscle cells (sarcomeres) are found. If the muscle cells don't have calcium available to them, contraction is inhibited (the muscle is relaxed).

T-tubules pass completely through the sarcolemma and go around the muscle cells. The job of the T-tubules is to conduct impulses from the cell's surface (sarcolemma) down into the cell to the sarcoplasmic reticulum. When an impulse travels along the membrane of the sarcoplasmic reticulum, the calcium channels open. Calcium rapidly leaves the sarcoplasmic reticulum and enters the sarcoplasm. The muscle cells are then stimulated to contract.

Much of the calcium that enters the cell's sarcoplasm comes from the interstitial fluid surrounding the cardiac muscle cells through the T-tubules. This is important because without the extra calcium from the T-tubules, the strength of a cardiac muscle contraction would be considerably reduced. Thus the force of cardiac muscle contraction depends largely on the concentration of calcium ions in the extracellular fluid.

Each sarcomere is composed of thin filaments and thick filaments. The thin filaments are made up of actin and actin-binding proteins. Actin-binding proteins include tropomyosin and troponin-T, troponin-C, and troponin-I, among others. The thick filaments are made up of hundreds of myosin molecules. Contraction occurs when the muscle is stimulated. Projections on the thin actin filaments (Figure 1-6, *B*) interact with the thick myosin filaments and form crossbridges (Figure 1-6, *C*). The crossbridges use energy (ATP) to bend. This allows the actin filaments to slide over the myosin filaments toward the center of the sarcomere and overlap. This overlap causes shortening of the muscles cells, resulting in contraction. Actin-binding proteins hinder the formation of crossbridges with myosin. When crossbridge formation is hindered, the muscle is relaxed.

> The cardiac muscle cell shortens (contracts) when the actin and myosin filaments slide together.

When myocardial cells die, such as in an acute myocardial infarction (MI), substances in intracardiac cells pass through broken cell membranes and leak into the bloodstream. These substances (called *cardiac markers* or *serum cardiac markers*) include troponin, creatine kinase, and myoglobin. Blood tests are used to measure the presence of these substances in the blood and verify the presence of an infarction. As you have just learned, troponin is a protein present in the heart. If the level of troponin is elevated (positive test), an MI has almost certainly occurred.

Cardiac muscle fibers are long, branching cells that fit together tightly at junctions called *intercalated disks*. The arrangement of these tight-fitting junctions gives an appearance of a **syncytium**, that is, resembling a network of cells with no separation between the individual cells. The intercalated disks fit together in such a way that they form gap junctions. Gap junctions allow cells to communicate with each other. They function as electrical connections and permit the exchange of nutrients, metabolites, ions, and small molecules. As a result, an electrical impulse can be quickly conducted throughout the wall of a heart chamber. This characteristic allows the walls of both atria (likewise, the walls of both ventricles) to contract almost at the same time.

> Gap junctions allow cells to conduct electrical impulses very rapidly.

The heart consists of two syncytiums: atrial and ventricular. The *atrial syncytium* consists of the walls of the right and left atria. The *ventricular syncytium* consists of the walls of the right and left ventricles. Normally, impulses can be conducted only from the atrial syncytium into the ventricular syncytium by means of the atrioventricular (AV) junction. The AV junction is a part of the heart's electrical system. This allows the atria to contract a short time before ventricular contraction.

HEART VALVES

The heart has a skeleton. The skeleton is made up of four rings of thick connective tissue. This tissue surrounds the bases of the pulmonary trunk, aorta, and the heart valves. The heart's skeleton helps form the partitions (septa) that separate the atria from the ventricles. It also provides secure attachments for the valves and chambers of the heart (Figure 1-7).

> The pulmonary trunk begins at the pulmonary valve and divides into the right and left pulmonary arteries.

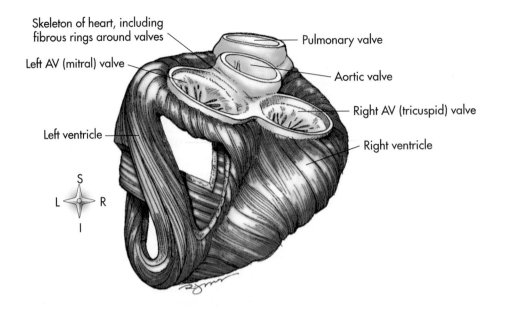

Figure 1-7
The rim of each heart valve is supported by a fibrous structure, called the skeleton of the heart, which encircles all four valves.

TABLE 1-2   Heart Valves

Valve type	Name	Right Heart vs. Left Heart	Location
Atrioventricular (AV)	Tricuspid	Right	Separates right atrium and right ventricle
	Mitral (bicuspid)	Left	Separates left atrium and left ventricle
Semilunar	Pulmonic	Right	Between right ventricle and pulmonary artery
	Aortic	Left	Between left ventricle and aorta

The four valves in the heart make sure blood flows in one direction.

There are four valves in the heart: two sets of atrioventricular (AV) valves and two sets of semilunar (SL) valves (Table 1-2). Their purpose is to make sure blood flows in one direction through the heart's chambers and prevent the backflow of blood.

Atrioventricular Valves

Atrioventricular (AV) valves separate the atria from the ventricles. The two AV valves consist of the following:

- Tough, fibrous rings (annuli fibrosi)
- Flaps (leaflets or cusps) of endocardium
- Chordae tendineae
- Papillary muscles

The mitral valve is so named because it is thought to resemble a mitre (bishop's hat) when open.

The tricuspid valve is the AV valve that lies between the right atrium and right ventricle. It consists of three separate cusps or flaps. It is larger in diameter and thinner than the mitral valve (Figure 1-8). The mitral (or bicuspid) valve has only two cusps. It lies between the left atrium and left ventricle (Figure 1-9).

As the atria fill with blood, the pressure within the atrial chamber rises. This pressure forces the tricuspid and mitral valves open. On the right side of the heart, blood low in oxygen empties into the right ventricle. On the left side of the heart, freshly oxygenated blood empties into the left ventricle. After the atria contract, the pressures in the atria and ventricles equalize, and the tricuspid and mitral valves partially close. The ventricles then contract (systole).

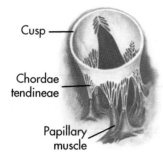

Figure 1-8
The tricuspid valve has three cusps or flaps.

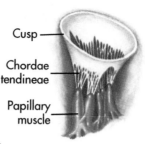

Figure 1-9
The mitral valve has two cusps or flaps.

This causes the pressure within the ventricles to rise sharply. The tricuspid and mitral valves close completely when the pressure within the ventricles exceeds that of the atria.

The **chordae tendineae** are thin strands of connective tissue. On one end, they are attached to the underside of the AV valves. On the other end, they are attached to small mounds of myocardium called *papillary muscles*. Papillary muscles project inward from the lower portion of the ventricular walls. When the ventricles contract and relax, so do the papillary muscles. The papillary muscles adjust their tension on the chordae tendineae, causing them to open and close. For example, when the right ventricle contracts, the papillary muscles of the right ventricle pull on the chordae tendineae. The chordae tendineae stretch, preventing the flaps of the tricuspid valve from bulging back into the right atrium. Thus the chordae tendineae and papillary muscles serve as anchors. Because the chordae tendineae are thin and string-like, they are sometimes called "heart strings."

Semilunar Valves

The pulmonic and aortic valves are **semilunar (SL) valves**. The semilunar valves prevent backflow of blood from the aorta and pulmonary arteries into the ventricles (Figure 1-10). The SL valves have three cusps shaped like half-moons. The openings of the SL valves are smaller than the openings of the AV valves. The flaps of the SL valves are smaller and thicker than the AV valves. Unlike the AV valves, the semilunar valves are not attached to chordae tendineae.

When the ventricles contract, the SL valves open, allowing blood to flow out of the ventricles. When the right ventricle contracts, blood low in oxygen flows through the pulmonic valve into the right and left pulmonary arteries. When the left ventricle contracts, freshly oxygenated blood flows through the aortic valve into the aorta and out to the body. The SL valves close as ventricular contraction ends and the pressure in the pulmonary artery and aorta exceeds that of the ventricles. Closure of the SL valves prevents the backflow of blood into the ventricles. The location of the heart's AV and SL valves is shown in Figure 1-11.

The sinus of Valsalva is a bulge at the base of the aorta formed by the thick leaflets of the aortic valve.

The heart's valves open and close in a specific sequence. This ensures a smooth flow of blood through the heart's chambers. Blood flow through the heart can be hampered if a valve doesn't function properly. Valvular heart disease is the term used to describe a malfunctioning heart valve. Types of valvular heart disease include the following:

- *Valvular stenosis*. If a valve narrows, stiffens, or thickens, the valve is said to be stenosed. The heart must work harder to pump blood through a stenosed valve.
- *Valvular prolapse*. If a valve flap inverts, it is said to prolapse. Prolapse can occur if one valve flap is larger than the other is. It can also occur if the chordae tendineae stretch markedly or rupture.

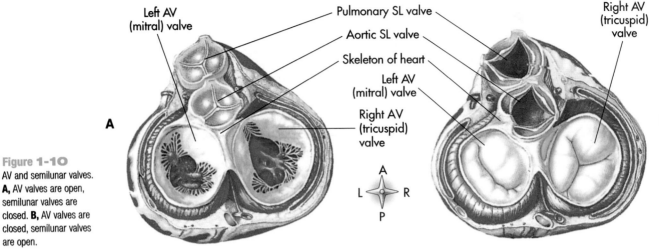

Figure 1-10
AV and semilunar valves. **A,** AV valves are open, semilunar valves are closed. **B,** AV valves are closed, semilunar valves are open.

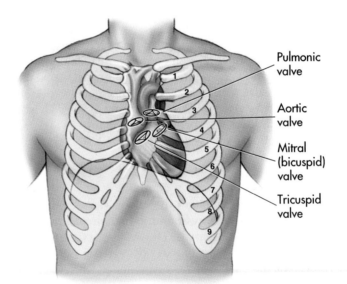

Figure 1-11
Anatomic location of heart valves.

- *Valvular regurgitation.* Blood can flow backward, or regurgitate, if one or more of the heart's valves doesn't close properly. Valvular regurgitation is also known as valvular incompetence or valvular insufficiency.

Think about what might happen if a papillary muscle in the left ventricle were to tear or rupture. The flaps of the mitral valve may not completely close and the valve flap may invert (prolapse). This may result in blood leaking from the left ventricle into the left atrium (regurgitation) during ventricular contraction. Blood flow to the body (cardiac output) would probably be decreased as a result.

HEART SOUNDS

Heart sounds occur because of vibrations in the tissues of the heart caused by the closing of the heart's valves. Vibrations are created as blood flow is suddenly increased or slowed with the contraction and relaxation of the heart chambers and with the opening and closing of the valves.

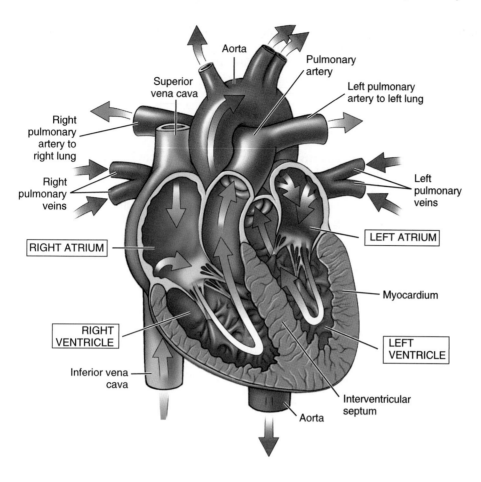

Figure 1-12
Blood flow through the heart.

Normal heart sounds are called S1 and S2. The first heart sound ("lubb") occurs during ventricular contraction when the tricuspid and mitral (AV) valves are closing. The second heart sound ("dupp") occurs during ventricular relaxation when the pulmonic and aortic (SL) valves are closing. A third heart sound is produced by ventricular filling. In persons younger than 40 years of age, the left ventricle normally permits rapid filling. The more rapid the ventricular filling, the greater the likelihood of hearing a third heart sound. A third heart sound heard in persons older than 40 years of age is considered abnormal. An abnormal third heart sound is frequently associated with heart failure. An S1-S2-S3 sequence is called a ventricular gallop or gallop rhythm. It sounds like Ken (S1) –tuck (S2) –y (S3).

S1 = sound one;
S2 = sound two;
S3 = sound three

BLOOD FLOW THROUGH THE HEART

The right atrium receives blood low in oxygen and high in carbon dioxide from the superior and inferior vena cavae and the coronary sinus (Figure 1-12). Blood flows from the right atrium through the tricuspid valve into the right ventricle. When the right ventricle contracts, the tricuspid valve closes. The right ventricle expels the blood through the pulmonic valve into the pulmonary trunk. The pulmonary trunk divides into a right and left pulmonary artery, each of which carries blood to one lung (pulmonary circuit).

The coronary sinus is the largest vein that drains into the heart.

Blood flows through the pulmonary arteries to the lungs (where oxygen and carbon dioxide are exchanged in the pulmonary capillaries) and then to the pulmonary veins. Carbon dioxide is exhaled as the left atrium receives oxygenated blood from the lungs via the four pulmonary veins (two from the right lung and two from the left lung). Blood flows from the left atrium through the mitral (bicuspid) valve into the left ventricle. When the left ventricle contracts, the mitral valve closes. Blood leaves the left ventricle through the aortic valve to the aorta and its branches and is distributed throughout the body (systemic circuit). Blood from

Blood low in oxygen passes through the pulmonary capillaries. There it comes in direct contact with the alveolar-capillary membrane, where oxygen and carbon dioxide are exchanged.

the tissues of the head, neck, and upper extremities is emptied into the superior vena cava. Blood from the lower body is emptied into the inferior vena cava. The superior and inferior vena cavae carry their contents into the right atrium.

CARDIAC CYCLE

In a resting adult, each cardiac cycle lasts approximately 0.8 sec. Atrial systole requires about 0.1 sec. Ventricular systole requires about 0.3 sec. Atrial diastole lasts about 0.7 sec. Ventricular diastole lasts about 0.5 sec during each cardiac cycle. At rest, the rate of blood flow through the cardiovascular system is about 5000 mL/min.

The cardiac cycle refers to a repetitive pumping process that includes all of the events associated with blood flow through the heart. The cycle has two phases for each heart chamber: systole and diastole. **Systole** is the period during which the chamber is contracting and blood is being ejected. Systole includes contraction of both atrial and ventricular muscle. **Diastole** is the period of relaxation during which the chambers are allowed to fill. Both the atria and ventricles have a diastolic phase. The myocardium receives its fresh supply of oxygenated blood during diastole. The cardiac cycle depends on the ability of the cardiac muscle to contract and on the condition of the heart's conduction system. The efficiency of the heart as a pump may be affected by abnormalities of the cardiac muscle, the valves, or the conduction system.

During the cardiac cycle, the pressure within each chamber of the heart rises in systole and falls in diastole. The heart's valves ensure that blood flows in the proper direction. Blood flows from one heart chamber to another if the pressure in the chamber is more than the pressure in the next. These pressure relationships depend on the careful timing of contractions. The heart's conduction system provides the necessary timing of events between atrial and ventricular systole.

Atrial Systole and Diastole

During atrial diastole, blood from the superior and inferior vena cavae and the coronary sinus enters the right atrium. The right atrium fills and distends. This pushes the tricuspid valve open, and the right ventricle fills. The same sequence occurs a split second earlier in the left heart. The left atrium receives blood from the four pulmonary veins (two from the right lung and two from the left lung). The flaps of the mitral valve open as the left atrium fills. This allows blood to flow into the left ventricle.

The ventricles are 70% filled before the atria contract. Contraction of the atria forces additional blood (approximately 30% of the ventricular capacity) into the ventricles (atrial kick). Thus the ventricles become completely filled with blood during atrial systole. During atrial systole, blood does not flow into the atria because the pressure within the atria exceeds venous pressure. The atria then enter a period of atrial diastole, which continues until the start of the next cardiac cycle.

Ventricular Systole and Diastole

Ventricular systole occurs as atrial diastole begins. As the ventricles contract, blood is propelled through the systemic and pulmonary circulation and toward the atria. The SL valves close and the heart then begins a period of ventricular diastole. During ventricular diastole, the ventricles begin to passively fill with blood and both the atria and ventricles are relaxed. The cardiac cycle begins again with atrial systole and the completion of ventricular filling (Figure 1-13).

CORONARY CIRCULATION

At rest, coronary blood flow averages about 250 mL/min. This represents 4% to 5% of the total cardiac output.

The coronary circulation consists of coronary arteries and veins. With normal activity, 65% to 75% of the fresh oxygen in the blood is taken out by the myocardium by means of the coronary arteries. This is the highest removal rate of any tissue during normal activity and one that cannot be significantly improved. Thus the heart can improve its oxygen uptake only by

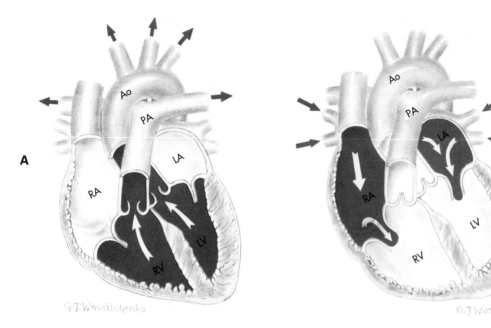

Figure 1-13
Blood flow during systole
(A) and diastole **(B)**.

TABLE 1-3	Possible Causes of Myocardial Ischemia	
Inadequate Oxygen Supply	**Increased Myocardial Oxygen Demand**	
Anemia	Exercise	Cocaine, amphetamines
Hypoxemia	Smoking	Emotional stress
Coronary artery narrowing caused by a clot, vessel spasm, or rapid progression of atherosclerosis	Eating a heavy meal	Hypertension
	Fever	Exposure to cold weather
	Congestive heart failure	Aortic stenosis
	Rapid heart rate	Pheochromocytoma
	Obstructive cardiomyopathy	Thyrotoxicosis

increasing coronary blood flow. With strenuous activity, coronary blood flow can increase significantly to make sure there is an adequate supply of oxygen to the myocardium.

Myocardial ischemia is the result of an imbalance between the metabolic needs (demand) of the heart and the flow of oxygenated blood to it (supply). Ischemia can occur because of increased myocardial oxygen demand (demand ischemia), reduced myocardial oxygen supply (supply ischemia), or both. Supply ischemia results from functional or structural abnormalities in the coronary arteries. For example, spasm of a coronary artery or coronary artery narrowing because of a clot can cause a severe reduction in blood flow and oxygen supply in the area perfused by the vessel. In many cases, ischemia results from both an increase in oxygen demand and a reduction in oxygen supply. Ischemia affects the heart's cells responsible for contraction, as well as those responsible for generation and conduction of electrical impulses. **Angina pectoris** is chest discomfort or other related symptoms caused by myocardial ischemia. Angina is not a disease, but a symptom of myocardial ischemia. Possible causes of myocardial ischemia are shown in Table 1-3.

Coronary Arteries

As you can see, the work of the heart is important. To ensure that it has an adequate blood supply, the heart makes sure to provide itself with a fresh supply of oxygenated blood before supplying the rest of the body. This freshly oxygenated blood is supplied

The coronary arteries encircle the heart like a crown, or corona.

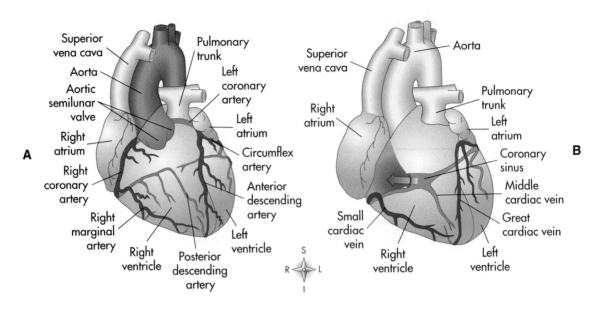

mainly by the branches of two vessels—the right and left coronary arteries. The right and left coronary arteries are the very first branches off the proximal aorta. The openings to these vessels are just beyond the cusps of the aortic SL valve (Figure 1-14). When the heart contracts, blood flow to the tissues of the heart is significantly reduced because the heart's blood vessels are compressed. Thus the coronary arteries fill when the ventricles are relaxed (diastole).

The coronary arteries that run on the surface of the heart are called epicardial coronary arteries.

The main coronary arteries lie on the outer (epicardial) surface of the heart. They branch into progressively smaller vessels, eventually becoming arterioles, and then capillaries. Thus the epicardium has a rich blood supply to draw from. Branches of the main coronary arteries penetrate into the heart's muscle mass and supply the subendocardium with blood. The diameter of these "feeder branches" is much narrower. The tissue supplied by these "feeder branches" gets enough blood and oxygen to survive, but they do not have much extra.

Coronary artery disease is classified as one-, two-, or three-vessel disease.

The three major coronary arteries include the left anterior descending (LAD), left circumflex (LCx), and right coronary arteries (RCA). A person is said to have coronary artery disease (CAD) if there is more than 50% diameter stenosis in one or more of these vessels. Since a myocardial infarction is usually caused by a blocked coronary artery, it is worthwhile to become familiar with the arteries that supply the heart. When myocardial injury or infarction is suspected, an understanding of coronary artery anatomy makes it possible to predict which coronary artery is blocked. Figure 1-15 shows the surfaces of the heart. Note that the posterior surface of the heart is not shown. The areas of the heart supplied by the three major coronary arteries are shown in Table 1-4.

Right Coronary Artery

The right coronary artery (RCA) originates from the right side of the aorta. It travels along the groove between the right atrium and right ventricle. A branch of the RCA supplies the following:

- Right atrium
- Right ventricle
- Inferior surface of the left ventricle in about 85% of individuals
- Posterior surface of the left ventricle in 85%
- Sinoatrial (SA) node in about 60%
- Atrioventricular (AV) node in 85% to 90%

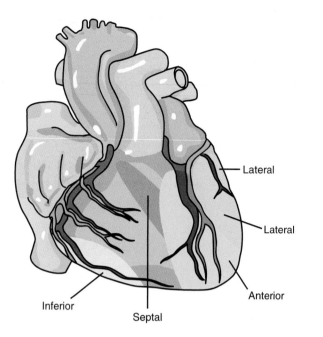

Lateral

Lateral

Anterior

Inferior

Septal

Figure 1-15
Surfaces of the heart. Posterior surface not shown.

TABLE 1-4	Coronary Arteries	
Coronary Artery and its Branches	**Portion of Myocardium Supplied**	**Portion of Conduction System Supplied**
Right		
Posterior descending Right marginal	• Right atrium • Right ventricle • Inferior surface of left ventricle (about 85%)* • Posterior surface of left ventricle (about 85%)*	• SA node (about 60%)* • AV node (85% to 90%)* • Proximal portion of bundle of His • Part of posterior-inferior fascicle of left bundle branch
Left		
Anterior descending	• Anterior surface of left ventricle • Part of lateral surface of left ventricle • Most of the interventricular septum	• Most of right bundle branch • Anterior-superior fascicle of left bundle branch • Part of posterior-inferior fascicle of left bundle branch
Circumflex	• Left atrium • Part of lateral surface of left ventricle • Inferior surface of left ventricle (about 15%)* • Posterior surface of left ventricle (15%)*	• SA node (about 40%)* • AV node (10% to 15%)*

*Percentage of population.

Left Coronary Artery

The left coronary artery (LCA) originates from the left side of the aorta. The first segment of the LCA is called the left main coronary artery. It is approximately the width of a soda straw and less than an inch long. The left main coronary artery supplies oxygenated blood to its two primary branches: the left anterior descending (also called the *anterior interventricular*) artery and the left circumflex artery. These vessels are slightly smaller than the left main coronary artery.

The LAD can be seen on the outer (epicardial) surface on the front of the heart. It travels along the groove that lies between the right and left ventricles (anterior interventricular sulcus)

Blockage of the left main coronary artery has been referred to as the "widow maker" because of its association with sudden death.

toward the heart's apex. In more than 75% of patients, the LAD travels around the apex of the left ventricle and ends along the left ventricle's inferior surface. In the remaining patients, the LAD doesn't reach the inferior surface. Instead, it stops at or before the heart's apex. The major branches of the LAD are the septal and diagonal arteries. The septal branches of the LAD supply blood to the interventricular septum. The LAD supplies blood to the following:

- Anterior surface of left ventricle
- Part of lateral surface of left ventricle
- Most of the interventricular septum

The left circumflex coronary artery circles around the left side of the heart. It is embedded in the epicardium on the back of the heart. The LCx supplies blood to the following:

- Left atrium
- Lateral surface of the left ventricle
- Inferior surface of the left ventricle in about 15% of individuals
- Posterior surface of the left ventricle in 15%
- SA node in about 40%
- AV node in 10% to 15%

Coronary Artery Dominance

In about 85% of people, the right coronary artery forms the posterior descending artery. In the remaining 15% of people, the left circumflex artery forms the posterior descending artery. The coronary artery that forms the posterior descending artery is considered the "dominant" coronary artery. If a branch of the right coronary artery becomes the posterior descending artery, the coronary artery arrangement is described as a *right dominant system*. If the left circumflex coronary artery branches and ends at the posterior descending artery, the coronary artery arrangement is described as a *left dominant system*.

If damage to the posterior wall of the left ventricle is suspected, a cardiac catheterization is usually necessary to determine which coronary artery is involved.

Coronary Veins

The great cardiac vein becomes continuous with the coronary sinus.

The coronary (cardiac) veins travel alongside the arteries. The coronary sinus is the largest vein that drains the heart. It lies in the groove that separates the atria from the ventricles. Blood that has passed through the myocardial capillaries is drained by branches of the cardiac veins that join the coronary sinus.

The coronary sinus receives blood from the great, middle, and small cardiac veins; a vein of the left atrium; and the posterior vein of the left ventricle. The coronary sinus drains into the right atrium. Anterior cardiac veins empty directly into the right atrium.

HEART RATE

The heart is affected by both the sympathetic and parasympathetic divisions of the autonomic nervous system. The sympathetic division prepares the body to function under stress ("fight or flight" response). The parasympathetic division conserves and restores body resources ("feed and breed" or "rest and digest" response). A review of the autonomic nervous system can be found in Table 1-5.

Baroreceptors and Chemoreceptors

Baroreceptors detect changes in blood pressure.

Baroreceptors (pressoreceptors) are specialized nerve tissue (sensors). They are found in the internal carotid arteries and the aortic arch. These sensory receptors detect changes in blood pressure. When they are stimulated, they cause a reflex response in either the sympathetic or

TABLE 1-5   Review of the Autonomic Nervous System

	Sympathetic Division	Parasympathetic Division
General effect	Fight or flight	Conserve resources ("Feed and breed" or "Rest and digest")
Primary neurotransmitter	Norepinephrine	Acetylcholine
Effects of Stimulation		
Abdominal blood vessels	Constriction (alpha receptors)	No effect
Adrenal medulla	Increased secretion of epinephrine	No effect
Bronchioles	Dilation (beta receptors)	Constriction
Blood vessels of skin	Constriction (alpha receptors)	No effect
Blood vessels of skeletal muscle	Dilation (beta receptors)	No effect
Cardiac muscle	Increased rate and strength of contraction (beta receptors)	Decreased rate; decreased strength of atrial contraction, little effect on strength of ventricular contraction
Coronary blood vessels	Constriction (alpha receptors) Dilation (beta receptors)	Dilation

---

Terminology

Chronotropic effect	Inotropic effect
• Refers to a change in heart rate	• Refers to a change in myocardial contractility
• A positive chronotropic effect refers to an increase in heart rate	• A positive inotropic effect results in an increase in myocardial contractility
• A negative chronotropic effect refers to a decrease in heart rate	• A negative inotropic effect results in a decrease in myocardial contractility

---

the parasympathetic divisions of the autonomic nervous system. For example, if the blood pressure decreases, the body will attempt to compensate by:

- Constricting peripheral blood vessels
- Increasing heart rate (**chronotropy**)
- Increasing the force of myocardial contraction (**inotropy**)

These compensatory responses occur because of a response by the sympathetic division. This is called a *sympathetic* or *adrenergic response*. If the blood pressure increases, the body will decrease sympathetic stimulation and increase the response by the parasympathetic division. This is called a *parasympathetic* or *cholinergic response*.

Chemoreceptors in the internal carotid arteries and aortic arch detect changes in the concentration of hydrogen ions (pH), oxygen, and carbon dioxide in the blood. The response to these changes by the autonomic nervous system can be sympathetic or parasympathetic.

Parasympathetic Stimulation

Parasympathetic Receptor Sites

Parasympathetic (inhibitory) nerve fibers supply the SA node, atrial muscle, and the AV junction of the heart by means of the vagus nerves. Acetylcholine is a chemical messenger (neurotransmitter) that is released when parasympathetic nerves are stimulated. Acetylcholine binds to parasympathetic receptors. The two main types of parasympathetic receptors are nicotinic and muscarinic receptors. Nicotinic receptors are located in skeletal muscle. Muscarinic receptors are located in smooth muscle. Parasympathetic stimulation includes the following:

- Slows the rate of discharge of the SA node
- Slows conduction through the AV node

There is little effect on the strength of ventricular contraction because of minimal parasympathetic innervation of these chambers. The net effect of parasympathetic stimulation is slowing of the heart rate.

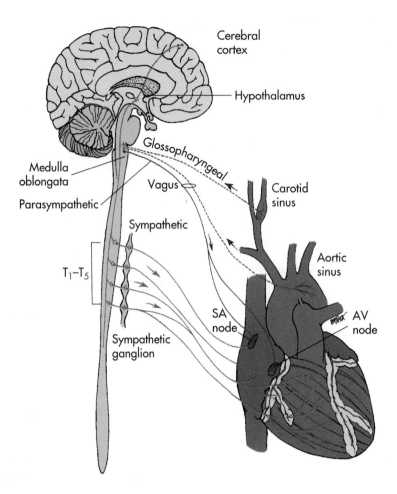

Figure 1-16
Autonomic nervous system innervation of the heart.

- Decreases the strength of atrial contraction
- Can cause a small decrease in the force of ventricular contraction

Sympathetic Stimulation

Norepinephrine is a neurotransmitter.

Sympathetic (accelerator) nerves supply specific areas of the heart's electrical system, atrial muscle, and the ventricular myocardium (Figure 1-16). When sympathetic nerves are stimulated, norepinephrine is released. Remember: the job of the sympathetic division is to prepare the body for emergency or stressful situations. So, the release of norepinephrine results in some very predictable outcomes:

- Increased force of contraction
- Increased heart rate
- Increased blood pressure

Sympathetic Receptor Sites

Sympathetic (adrenergic) receptor sites are divided into alpha-receptors, beta-receptors, and dopaminergic receptors. Dopaminergic receptor sites are located in the coronary arteries and renal, mesenteric, and visceral blood vessels. Stimulation of dopaminergic receptor sites results in dilation.

Remember: Beta-1 receptors affect the heart (you have one heart); beta-2 receptors affect the lungs (you have two lungs).

Different body tissues have different proportions of alpha- and beta-receptors. Stimulation of alpha-receptor sites results in constriction of blood vessels in the skin, cerebral, and **splanchnic** (visceral) circulation. Beta-receptor sites are divided into beta-1 and beta-2. Beta-1 receptors are found in the heart. Stimulation of beta-1 receptors results in an increased heart rate, contractility, and, ultimately, irritability of cardiac cells. Beta-2 receptor sites are found in the

Beta 1 = heart (1 heart)   Beta 2 = lungs (2 lungs)

lungs and skeletal muscle blood vessels. Stimulation of these receptor sites results in dilation of the smooth muscle of the bronchi and blood vessel dilation.

Increases in heart rate shorten all phases of the cardiac cycle. The most important is that the time the heart spends relaxing is less. If the length of time for ventricular relaxation is shortened, there is less time for them to fill adequately with blood. If the ventricles don't have time to fill:

- The amount of blood sent to the coronary arteries is reduced.
- The amount of blood pumped out of the ventricles will decrease (cardiac output).
- Signs of myocardial ischemia may be seen.

When a rapid heart rate occurs with some specific types of abnormal heart rhythms, **vagal maneuvers** may be performed. Vagal maneuvers are methods used to stimulate the vagus nerve. When vagal maneuvers are performed, baroreceptors in the carotid arteries are stimulated in an attempt to slow conduction through the AV node. This should result in slowing of the heart rate. Common vagal maneuvers include asking the patient to cough, try to blow through an occluded straw, or bear down as if having a bowel movement.

Other factors that influence heart rate include electrolyte and hormone levels, medications, stress, anxiety, fear, and body temperature. The heart rate increases when body temperature increases and decreases when body temperature decreases.

THE HEART AS A PUMP

Venous Return

The heart functions as a pump to propel blood through the systemic and pulmonary circulations. As the heart chambers fill with blood, the heart muscle is stretched. The most important factor determining the amount of blood pumped out by the heart is the amount of blood flowing into it from the systemic circulation (**venous return**).

Cardiac Output

Cardiac output is the amount of blood pumped into the aorta each minute by the heart. It is defined as the **stroke volume** (amount of blood ejected from a ventricle with each heartbeat) times the heart rate. In the average adult, normal cardiac output is between 4 and 8 L/min. The cardiac output at rest is about 5 L/min (stroke volume of 70 mL $\times$ a heart rate of 70 bpm).

Because the cardiovascular system is a closed system, the volume of blood leaving one part of the system must equal that entering another part. For example, if the left ventricle normally pumps 5 L/min, the volume flowing through the arteries, capillaries, and veins must equal 5 L/min. Thus the cardiac output of the right ventricle (pulmonary blood flow) is normally equal to that of the left ventricle on a minute-to-minute basis.

Cardiac output may be increased by an increase in heart rate *or* stroke volume. An increase in the force of the heart's contractions (and, subsequently, stroke volume) may occur because of many conditions including the following:

- Norepinephrine and epinephrine release from the adrenal medulla
- Insulin and glucagon release from the pancreas
- Medications, such as calcium, digitalis, dopamine, and dobutamine

A decrease in the force of contraction may result from many conditions including the following:

- Severe hypoxia
- Decreased pH

- Elevated carbon dioxide levels (hypercapnea)
- Medications, such as calcium channel blockers and beta-blockers

Cardiac output varies depending on hormone balance, an individual's activity level and body size, and the body's metabolic needs. Factors that increase cardiac output include increased body metabolism, exercise, and the age and size of the body. Factors that may decrease cardiac output include shock, hypovolemia, and heart failure. Signs and symptoms of decreased cardiac output appear in the ECG Pearl below.

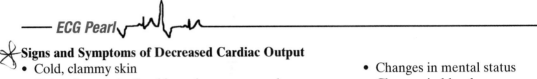

— *ECG Pearl*

Signs and Symptoms of Decreased Cardiac Output
- Cold, clammy skin
- Color changes in the skin and mucous membranes
- Dyspnea
- Orthopnea
- Crackles (rales)

- Changes in mental status
- Changes in blood pressure
- Dysrhythmias
- Fatigue
- Restlessness

Blood Pressure

Tone is a term that may be used when referring to the normal state of balanced tension in body tissues.

The mechanical activity of the heart is reflected by the pulse and blood pressure. Blood pressure is the force exerted by the circulating blood volume on the walls of the arteries. Peripheral vascular resistance is the resistance to the flow of blood determined by blood vessel diameter and the tone of the vascular musculature. Blood pressure is equal to cardiac output times peripheral vascular resistance. Blood pressure is affected by any condition that increases peripheral resistance or cardiac output. Thus an increase in either cardiac output or peripheral resistance will result in an increase in blood pressure. Conversely, a decrease in either will result in a decrease in blood pressure.

Stroke Volume

Preload

Stroke volume is determined by the following:

- The degree of ventricular filling when the heart is relaxed (preload)
- The pressure against which the ventricle must pump (afterload)
- The myocardium's contractile state (contracting or relaxing)

Preload is the force exerted on the walls of the ventricles at the end of diastole. The volume of blood returning to the heart influences preload. More blood returning to the right atrium increases preload. Less blood returning decreases preload.

The Frank-Starling law is named after Frank and Starling, two physiologists.

According to the Frank-Starling law of the heart (Figure 1-17), to a point, the greater the volume of blood in the heart during diastole, the more forceful the cardiac contraction, and the more blood the ventricle will pump (stroke volume). This is important so that the heart can adjust its pumping capacity in response to changes in venous return, such as during exercise. If, however, the ventricle is stretched beyond its physiologic limit, cardiac output may fall because of volume overload and overstretching of the muscle fibers.

Afterload

Afterload is the pressure or resistance against which the ventricles must pump to eject blood. Afterload is influenced by the following:

- Arterial blood pressure
- The ability of the arteries to become stretched (arterial distensibility)
- Arterial resistance

The lower the resistance (lower afterload), the more easily blood can be ejected. Increased afterload (increased resistance) results in increased cardiac workload. Conditions that contribute to increased afterload include increased thickness of the blood viscosity and high blood pressure.

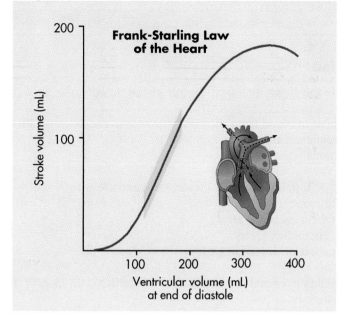

Figure 1-17
Starling's Law of the Heart. The curve represents the relationship between stroke volume and the ventricular volume at the end of diastole. The range of values observed in a typical heart is shaded. Note that if the ventricle has an abnormally large volume at the end of diastole (far right portion of the curve), the stroke volume cannot compensate.

Now that we've discussed heart rate, cardiac output, and stroke volume, let's review an important point. Remember that cardiac output may be increased by an increase in heart rate *or* stroke volume. Consider the following examples:

- A patient has a stroke volume of 80 mL/beat. His heart rate is 70 bpm. Is his cardiac output normal, decreased, or increased? Substitute numbers into the formula you already learned: CO = SV × HR. 5600 mL/min = 80 mL/beat × 70 beats/min. Cardiac output is normally between 4 and 8 L/min. This patient's cardiac output is within normal limits.
- Now, let's see what an increase in heart rate will do. If the patient's heart rate increases to 180 beats/minute and his stroke volume remains at 80 mL/beat, what happens to his cardiac output? Using our formula again (CO = SV × HR) and substituting numbers, we end up with 14,400 mL/min = 80 mL/beat × 180 bpm. This patient's cardiac output is increased.
- What happens to cardiac output if the patient's heart rate is 70 bpm but his stroke volume drops to 50 mL/beat? Using our formula one more time (CO = SV × HR) and substituting numbers, we end up with 3500 mL/min = 50 mL/beat × 70 bpm. This patient's cardiac output is decreased. If the patient's heart rate increased to 90 bpm to try to compensate for his failing pump, what would happen to his cardiac output (4500 mL/min = 50 mL/beat × 90 bpm)? According to our example, the patient's cardiac output would increase—at least temporarily.

S T O P & R E V I E W

Multiple Choice

Identify the letter of the choice that best completes the statement or answers the question.

_B_   1. Movement of blood from the right ventricle to the lungs is called the:
    a. Systemic circulation
    b. Pulmonary circulation

_A_   2. The _____ supplies the right atrium and ventricle with blood.
    a. Right coronary artery
    b. Left main coronary artery
    c. Left circumflex artery
    d. Left anterior descending artery

_____   3. The primary chemical mediator of the sympathetic division of the autonomic nervous system is:
    a. Dopamine
    b. Muscarine
    c. Acetylcholine
    d. Norepinephrine

Completion

Complete each sentence or statement.

4. The _ATRiums_ are the heart chambers that receive blood.

5. The _Ventricles_ are the heart chambers that pump blood.

6. The thick, muscular middle layer of the heart wall that contains the atrial and ventricular muscle fibers necessary for contraction is the _Myocardium_.

Short Answer

7. List three (3) types of sympathetic (adrenergic) receptor sites.
    1. _alpha Receptors_

    2. _Beta Receptors._

    3. _Dopaminergic Receptors_

8. Describe the function of the right atrium of the heart.
Blood from the Superior & inferior vena cava fill the Right atria w/ Oxygen blood, then the atria pumps this to the R Ventricle.

9. Define "atrial kick."
Is the additional 30% of Blood that fills the Ventricles when the atria contract

Matching

a. The pressure or resistance against which the ventricles must pump to eject blood

b. Blood flows from the left atrium through the __ valve into the left ventricle.

c. A negative __ effect refers to a decrease in heart rate.

d. This results when the heart's demand for oxygen exceeds its supply from the coronary circulation.

e. Specialized nerve tissue located in the internal carotid arteries and the aortic arch that detect changes in blood pressure

f. The amount of blood pumped into the aorta each minute by the heart

g. Occlusion of this vessel has been referred to as the "widow maker" because of its association with sudden death.

h. A double-walled sac that encloses the heart and helps protect it from trauma and infection

i. Sensors in the internal carotid arteries and aortic arch that detect changes in the concentration of hydrogen ions (pH), oxygen, and carbon dioxide in the blood

j. A term used when referring to the normal state of balanced tension in body tissues

k. The largest vein that drains the heart

l. Blood flows from the right atrium through the __ valve into the right ventricle.

m. A repetitive pumping process that includes all of the events associated with blood flow through the heart

n. Upper portion of the heart

o. Coronary artery that supplies the SA node and AV node in most of the population.

p. A positive __ effect refers to an increase in myocardial contractility.

___O___ 10. Right coronary artery

___H___ 11. Pericardium

___I___ 12. Chemoreceptors

___P___ 13. Inotropic

___L___ 14. Tricuspid

___A___ 15. Afterload

___N___ 16. Base

___M___ 17. Cardiac cycle

___J___ 18. Tone

___F___ 19. Cardiac output

___C___ 20. Chronotropic

___D___ 21. Myocardial ischemia

___G___ 22. Left main coronary artery

___B___ 23. Mitral (bicuspid)

___E___ 24. Baroreceptors

___K___ 25. Coronary sinus

Label the following coronary arteries:

- Circumflex
- Posterior descending
- Anterior descending
- Marginal
- Right coronary artery
- Left main coronary artery

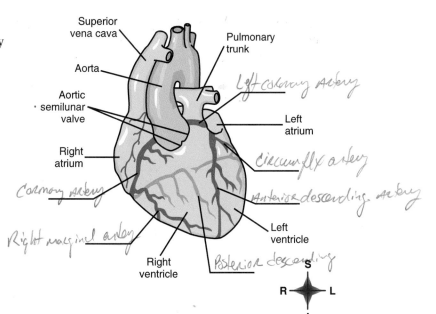

ECG Crossword

Across

2. Sulcus
7. Innermost layer of the heart
9. This electrolyte is very important in cardiac muscle contraction.
10. The heart actually lies to the __ of the midline of the sternum.
11. Partition
13. The myocardial layer of the ventricles is much __ than that of the atria.
17. Inflammation of the pericardium
18. Movement of blood from the left ventricle to the body
22. The bottom (inferior) surface of the heart is also called the __ surface.
23. Elevation of this serum cardiac marker usually means the patient has had a heart attack.
24. This type of heart valve separates the atria from the ventricles.
25. The first heart sound (S1) is the result of closure of the __ valves.
26. Space between the lungs that contains the heart, great vessels, trachea, and esophagus, among other structures

Down

1. When actin and myosin filaments slide together, the cardiac muscle cell __.
3. Striations
4. Lower heart chambers
5. The chordae tendineae are also called __ __.
6. Pulmonary arteries and veins, aorta, superior and inferior vena cavae
8. One of the semilunar valves
12. The percentage of blood pumped out of a heart chamber with each contraction
14. __ __ in myocardial cells function as electrical connections and allow the cells to conduct electrical impulses very rapidly.
15. Upper chambers of the heart
16. The energy-producing parts of a cell
19. The __ septum separates the right and left atria.
20. A buildup of excess blood or fluid in the pericardial space can cause cardiac __.
21. A semilunar valve is shaped like a __.

CHAPTER 2

Basic Electrophysiology

OBJECTIVES

On comlpletion of this chapter, you should be able to:

1. Describe the two basic types of cardiac cells in the heart, where they are found, and their function.
2. Define the terms *membrane potential, threshold potential, action potential, polarization, depolarization, repolarization, augmented lead, bipolar lead,* and *chest lead.*
3. Explain the cardiac action potential and correlate it with the waveforms produced on the ECG.
4. Describe the primary characteristics of cardiac cells.
5. Define the *absolute, relative refractory,* and *supernormal periods* and their locations in the cardiac cycle.
6. Describe the normal sequence of electrical conduction through the heart.
7. Describe the location, function, and (where appropriate) the intrinsic rate of the following structures: SA node, atrioventricular (AV) junction, bundle branches, and Purkinje fibers.
8. Explain the primary mechanisms responsible for producing cardiac dysrhythmias.
9. Explain the purpose and limitations of ECG monitoring.
10. Describe correct electrode positioning and the area of the heart viewed by each lead of a standard 12-lead ECG, lead MCL_1, and MCL_6.
11. Identify the numeric values assigned to the small and large boxes on ECG paper.
12. Define and describe the significance of each of the following as they relate to cardiac electrical activity: *P wave, PR segment, PR interval, QRS complex, ST-segment, T wave, TP-segment, QT interval,* and *U wave.*
13. Define the term artifact and explain methods that may be used to minimize its occurrence.
14. Describe the steps in ECG rhythm strip analysis.

TABLE 2-1 Cardiac Cell Types			
Kinds of Cardiac Cells	Where Found	Primary Function	Primary Property
Myocardial cells	Myocardium	Contraction and relaxation	Contractility
Pacemaker cells	Electrical conduction system	Generation and conduction of electrical impulses	Automaticity Conductivity

TYPES OF CARDIAC CELLS

In general, cardiac cells have either a mechanical (contractile) or an electrical (pacemaker) function. **Myocardial cells** (working or mechanical cells) contain contractile filaments. When these cells are electrically stimulated, these filaments slide together, and the myocardial cell contracts. These myocardial cells form the thin muscular layer of the atrial walls and the thicker muscular layer of the ventricular walls (the myocardium). These cells do not normally generate electrical impulses on their own. They rely on pacemaker cells for this purpose.

Pacemaker cells are specialized cells of the heart's electrical system. They are responsible for spontaneously generating and conducting electrical impulses.

CARDIAC ACTION POTENTIAL

Before we begin a discussion of the cardiac action potential, let's think about how a battery releases energy. A battery has two terminals. One terminal is positive, and the other is negative. Charged particles exert forces on each other. Opposite charges attract. Electrons (negatively charged particles) are produced by a chemical reaction inside the battery. If a wire is connected between the two terminals, the circuit is completed and the stored energy is released. This allows electrons to flow quickly from the negative terminal along the wire to the positive terminal. If no wire is connected between the terminals, the chemical reaction does not take place and there is no current flow. **Current** is the flow of electrical charge from one point to another.

A difference between electrical charges must exist in order for electrical current to be generated.

Separated electrical charges of opposite polarity (positive versus negative) have potential energy. The measurement of this potential energy is called **voltage**. Voltage is measured between two points. In our battery example, the current flow is caused by the voltage, or potential difference, between the two terminals. Voltage is measured in units called volts or millivolts.

Human body fluids contain electrolytes. **Electrolytes** are elements or compounds that break into charged particles (**ions**) when melted or dissolved in water or another solvent. The main electrolytes that affect the function of the heart are sodium ($Na+$), potassium ($K+$), calcium ($Ca++$), and chloride ($Cl-$). Body fluids that contain electrolytes conduct an electric current, in much the same way as the wire in our battery example. Electrolytes move about in body fluids and carry a charge, just as electrons moving along a wire conduct a current. The **action potential** is a five-phase cycle that reflects the difference in the concentration of these charged particles across the cell membrane at any given time.

In the normal heart, electrical activity occurs because of changes that occur in the body's cells.

Polarization

In the body, cells spend a lot of time moving ions back and forth across their cell membranes. As a result, there is normally a slight difference in the concentrations of charged particles across the membranes of cells. Thus, there is potential energy (voltage) because of the imbalance of charged particles. This imbalance makes the cells excitable.

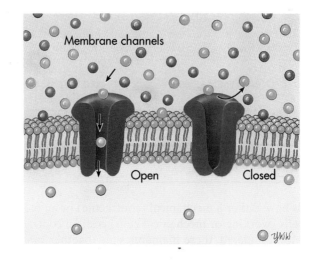

Figure 2-1
Cell membranes contain membrane channels. These channels are pores through which specific ions or other small, water-soluble molecules can cross the cell membrane from outside to inside.

Cell membranes contain pores or channels through which specific electrolytes and other small, water-soluble molecules can cross the cell membrane from outside to inside (Figure 2-1). When a cell is at rest, K+ leaks out of it. Large molecules such as proteins and phosphates remain inside the cell because they are too big to pass easily through the cell membrane. These large molecules carry a negative charge. This results in more negatively charged ions on the inside of the cell. When the inside of a cell is more negative than the outside it is **polarized** (Figure 2-2). The voltage (difference in electrical charges) across the cell membrane is the **membrane potential**. Electrolytes are quickly moved from one side of the cell membrane to the other by means of "pumps." These pumps require energy (ATP). The energy expended by the cells to move electrolytes across the cell membrane creates a flow of current. This flow of current is expressed in volts. Voltage can be measured and appears on an electrocardiogram (ECG) as spikes or waveforms. Thus an ECG is actually a sophisticated voltmeter.

Depolarization

In order for a pacemaker cell to "fire" (produce an impulse), there must be a flow of electrolytes across the cell membrane. When a cell is stimulated, the cell membrane changes and becomes **permeable** to Na+ and K+. Na+ rushes into the cell through Na+ channels. This causes the inside of the cell to become more positive. A spike (waveform) is then recorded on the ECG. The stimulus that alters the electrical charges across the cell membrane may be electrical, mechanical, or chemical.

In our battery example, we learned that when opposite charges come together, energy is released. When the movement of electrolytes changes the electrical charge of the inside of the cell from negative to positive, an impulse is generated. The impulse causes channels to open in the next cell membrane and then the next. The movement of charged particles across a cell membrane causing the inside of the cell to become positive is called **depolarization** (Figure 2-3). Normally, an impulse begins in the pacemaker cells found in the sinoatrial (SA) node of the heart. A chain reaction occurs from cell to cell in the heart's electrical conduction system until all of the cells have been stimulated and depolarized. This chain reaction is called a wave of depolarization. The chain reaction is made possible because of the gap junctions that exist between the cells. Eventually, the impulse is spread from the pacemaker cells to the working myocardial cells. The working myocardial cells contract when they are stimulated. When the atria are stimulated, a P wave is recorded on the ECG. Thus the P wave represents atrial depolarization. When the ventricles are stimulated, a QRS complex is recorded on the ECG. Thus the QRS complex represents ventricular depolarization.

Permeability refers to the ability of a membrane channel to conduct electrolytes once it is open. Threshold is the membrane potential at which the cell membrane becomes more positive.

Before the heart can mechanically contract and pump blood, depolarization must take place. Depolarization occurs because of the movement of Na+ into the cell. Depolarization proceeds from the innermost layer of the heart (endocardium) to the outermost layer (epicardium).

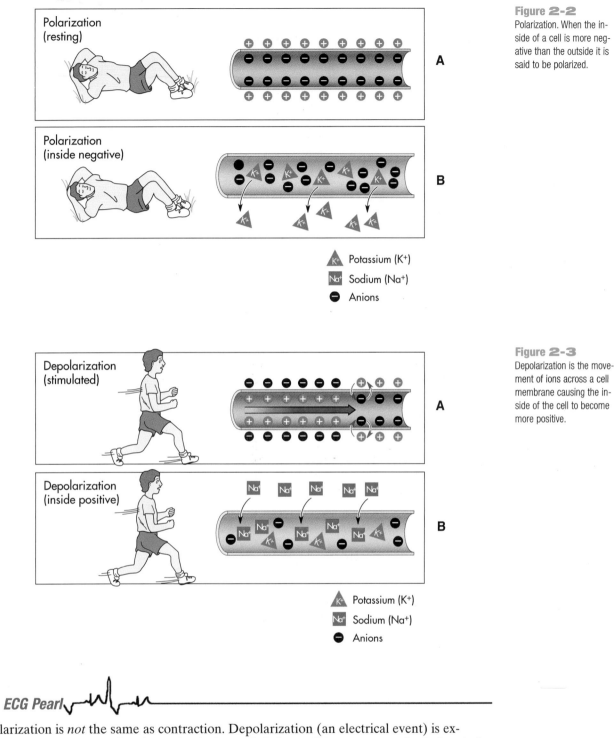

Figure 2-2
Polarization. When the inside of a cell is more negative than the outside it is said to be polarized.

Figure 2-3
Depolarization is the movement of ions across a cell membrane causing the inside of the cell to become more positive.

ECG Pearl

Depolarization is *not* the same as contraction. Depolarization (an electrical event) is expected to result in contraction (a mechanical event). It is possible to see organized electrical activity on the cardiac monitor, yet evaluation of the patient reveals no palpable pulse. This clinical situation is called **pulseless electrical activity** (PEA).

Repolarization

After the cell depolarizes, it quickly begins to recover and restore its electrical charges to normal. The movement of charged particles across a cell membrane in which the inside of the cell is restored to its negative charge is called **repolarization**. The cell stops the flow of Na+ into the cell and allows K+ to leave it. Negatively charged particles are left inside the cell. Thus, the cell

A cell cannot conduct another impulse until repolarization occurs.

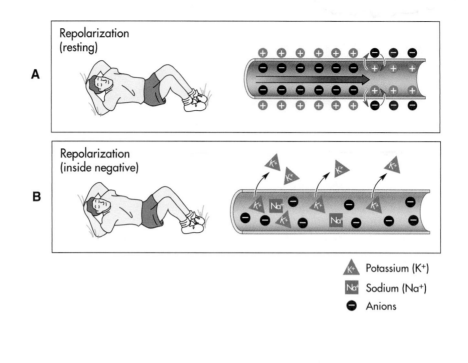

Figure 2-5
Action potential of a ventricular muscle cell.

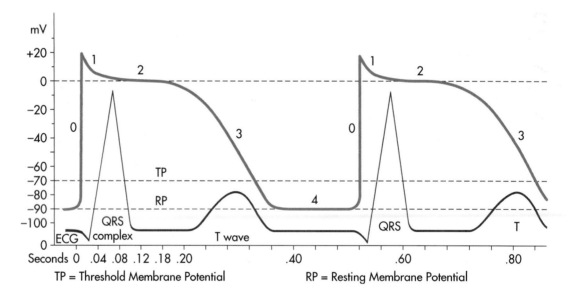

is returned to its resting state (Figure 2-4). This causes contractile proteins in the working my-ocardial cells to separate (relax). The cell can be stimulated again if another electrical impulse arrives at the cell membrane. Repolarization proceeds from the epicardium to the endo-cardium. On the ECG, the ST-segment and T wave represent ventricular repolarization.

Phases of the Cardiac Action Potential

The action potential of a cardiac cell consists of five phases labeled 0 to 4. These phases reflect the rapid sequence of voltage changes that occur across the cell membrane during the electrical cardiac cycle. Phases 1, 2, and 3 have been referred to as *electrical systole*. Phase 4 has been referred to as *electrical diastole*. The configuration of the action potential varies depending on the location, size, and function of the cardiac cell. Figure 2-5 shows the action potential of a normal ventricular muscle cell.

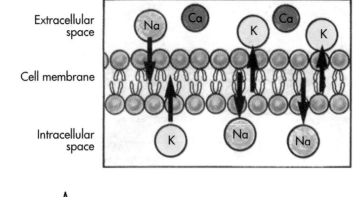

Figure 2-6
Phase 0 of the cardiac action potential represents depolarization. Na+ moves rapidly into the cell through Na+ channels. K+ leaves the cell and Ca++ moves slowly into the cell through Ca++ channels.

—— *ECG Pearl*

Phases of the Cardiac Action Potential
Phase 0—rapid depolarization
Phase 1—early rapid repolarization
Phase 2—plateau
Phase 3—final rapid repolarization
Phase 4—resting membrane potential

Phase 0—Depolarization

The rapid entry of Na+ into the cell is largely responsible for phase 0 of the cardiac action potential. Phase 0 represents depolarization (Figure 2-6) and is called the rapid depolarization phase. Phase 0 begins when the cell receives an impulse. Na+ moves rapidly into the cell through the Na+ channels. K+ leaves the cell, and Ca++ moves slowly into the cell through Ca++ channels. The cell depolarizes and cardiac contraction begins. Phase 0 is represented on the ECG by the QRS complex.

Phase 0 is also called the *upstroke*, *spike*, or *overshoot*.

The cells of the atria, ventricles, and the Purkinje fibers of the conduction system have many sodium channels. The SA and AV nodes of the heart have relatively few sodium channels. If the flow of sodium through the sodium channels is slowed or blocked:

* The heart rate slows.
* The cells become less excitable.
* The speed of conduction decreases.

Phase 0 of the cardiac action potential is followed immediately by repolarization. Repolarization is divided into three phases.

Phase 1—Early Repolarization

During phase 1 of the cardiac action potential, the Na+ channels partially close, slowing the flow of Na+ into the cell. At the same time, Cl− enters the cell and K+ leaves it through K+ channels. The result is a decrease in the number of positive electrical charges within the cell. This produces a small negative deflection in the action potential (see Figure 2-5).

Phase 0 is mainly determined by the flow of sodium into the heart's cells. Phases 1 through 3 are mainly related to the flow of potassium out of the cell.

Phase 2—Plateau Phase

Phase 2 is the plateau phase of the action potential (Figure 2-7). During this phase, Ca++ slowly enters the cell through Ca++ channels. The cells of the atria, ventricles, and the Purkinje fibers of the conduction system have many calcium channels. K+ continues to slowly leave the cell through K+ channels. The plateau phase allows cardiac muscle to sustain an increased period of contraction. The cells of the atria, ventricles, and Purkinje fibers spend less time in phase 2 if the flow of calcium through calcium channels is slowed or blocked. Medications such as calcium channel blockers slow the rate at which calcium passes through the cells (see Drug Pearl on the next page). Phase 2 is responsible for the ST-segment on the ECG. The ST-segment reflects the early part of repolarization of the right and left ventricles. Hypercalcemia and medications such as digitalis shorten the ST-segment.

Ca++ plays an important role in the process of contraction.

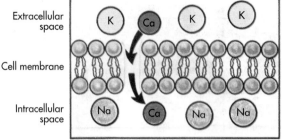

Figure 2-7
Phase 2 (plateau phase) of the cardiac action potential is caused by the slow inward movement of Ca++ and slow outward movement of K+ from the cell.

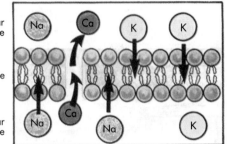

Figure 2-8
During phase 4, there is an excess of Na+ inside the cell and an excess of K+ outside the cell. The sodium-potassium pump is activated to move Na+ out of the cell and move K+ back into the cell.

Drug Pearl

Examples of Calcium Channel Blockers

Generic Name	Trade Name
diltiazem	Cardizem, Cardizem CD, Cardizem SR, Dilacor XR, Diltiazem XT, Tiazac
verapamil	Calan, Calan SR, Covera-HS, Isoptin, Isoptin SR, Verelan, Verelan PM
amlodipine	Norvasc
felodipine	Plendil
bepridil	Vascor
nisoldipine	Sular
nicardipine	Cardene, Cardene SR
nifedipine	Adalat, Adalat CC, Procardia, Procardia XL

Phase 3—Final Rapid Repolarization

Repolarization is complete by the end of phase 3.

Phase 3 begins with the downslope of the action potential (see Figure 2-5). The cell rapidly completes repolarization as K+ flows quickly out of the cell. Na+ and Ca++ channels close, stopping the entry of Na+ and Ca++. The rapid movement of K+ out of the cell causes the inside to become progressively more electrically negative. The cell gradually becomes more sensitive to external stimuli until its original sensitivity is restored. Phase 3 of the action potential corresponds with the T wave (ventricular repolarization) on the ECG. If potassium channels are blocked, the result is a longer action potential.

Phase 4—Resting Membrane Potential

Phase 4 of the cardiac action potential represents the fully polarized state of the resting cardiac cell.

Phase 4 is the resting membrane potential (return to resting state) (Figure 2-8). During phase 4, there is an excess of Na+ inside the cell and an excess of K+ outside the cell. The Na+-K+ pump is activated to move Na+ out of the cell and K+ back into the cell. The heart is "polarized" during this phase (ready for discharge). The cell will remain in this state until the cell membrane is reactivated by another stimulus.

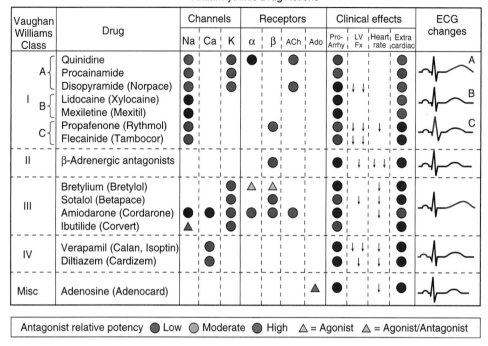

Figure 2-9
This figure is a modification of the Sicilian Gambit drug classification system and includes designation by the Vaughn-Williams system. The sodium channel blockers are subdivided into the A, B, and C subgroups based on their relative potency. The targets of antiarrhythmic drugs, listed across the columns, are the ion channels (sodium, calcium, and potassium) and the receptors (alpha-adrenergic, beta-adrenergic, cholinergic [ACH], and adenosinergic [ADO]). The next columns compare the drugs' clinical actions. These include proarrhythmic potential (Proarrhy), effect on left ventricular function (LV Fx), effects on heart rate (Heart Rate), and potential for extra cardiac side effects (Extra Cardiac). The ECG tracings indicate the changes (in color) that are caused by usual dosages of the drug (i.e., PR interval, QRS interval, and QT interval). The drugs are listed in rows with their brand names shown in parentheses. The symbols in the table indicate the drugs' relative potency as agonists or antagonists. The solid triangle indicates the biphasic effects of bretylium initially to release norepinephrine and act as an agonist and subsequently to block further release and act as an antagonist of adrenergic tone. The number of arrows and their direction indicate the magnitude and direction of effect of the drugs on heart rate and left ventricular function (i.e., inotropy).

Normally, the heart beats at a very regular rate and rhythm. If this pattern is interrupted, an abnormal heart rhythm can result. Healthcare professionals use the terms **arrhythmia** and **dysrhythmia** interchangeably to refer to an abnormal heart rhythm. Medications used to correct irregular heartbeats and slow down hearts that beat too fast are called antiarrhythmics. Antiarrhythmic medications are classified by their effects on the cardiac action potential (Figure 2-9).

PROPERTIES OF CARDIAC CELLS

When a nerve is stimulated, a chemical (neurotransmitter) is released. The chemical crosses the space between the end of the nerve and the muscle membrane (neuromuscular junction). The chemical binds to receptor sites on the muscle membrane and stimulates the receptors. An electrical impulse develops and travels along the muscle membrane, resulting in contraction. Thus, a skeletal muscle contracts only after it is stimulated by a nerve.

The heart is unique because it has pacemaker cells that can generate an electrical impulse without being stimulated by a nerve. The ability of cardiac pacemaker cells to create an electrical impulse without being stimulated from another source is called **automaticity**. Automaticity is a property of all cells of the heart. However, the heart's normal pacemaker

The SA node, atrioventricular (AV) junction, and Purkinje fibers are important parts of the heart's electrical conduction system.

usually prevents other areas of the heart from assuming this function. Normal concentrations of K+, Na+, and Ca++ are important in maintaining automaticity. Increased blood concentrations of these electrolytes decrease automaticity. Decreased concentrations of K+ and Ca++ in the blood increase automaticity.

Excitability (irritability) refers to the ability of cardiac muscle cells to respond to an outside stimulus. The stimulus may be from a chemical, mechanical, or electrical source.

Conductivity refers to the ability of a cardiac cell to receive an electrical impulse and conduct it to an adjoining cardiac cell. All cardiac cells possess this characteristic. The intercalated disks present in the membranes of cardiac cells are responsible for the property of conductivity. They allow an impulse in any part of the myocardium to spread throughout the heart. The speed with which the impulse is conducted can be altered by factors such as sympathetic and parasympathetic stimulation and medications.

Contractility refers to the ability of myocardial cells to shorten in response to an impulse. This results in contraction. Normally, the heart contracts in response to an impulse that begins in the SA node. The strength of the heart's contraction can be improved with certain medication, such as digitalis, dopamine, and epinephrine.

—— *ECG Pearl*

Properties of Cardiac Cells
Automaticity
Excitability (irritability)
Conductivity
Contractility

REFRACTORY PERIODS

Refractoriness is a term used to describe the period of recovery that cells need after being discharged before they are able to respond to a stimulus. In the heart, the refractory period is longer than the contraction itself.

Absolute Refractory Period

During the **absolute refractory period** (also known as the effective refractory period), the cell will not respond to further stimulation. This means that the myocardial working cells cannot contract and the cells of the electrical conduction system cannot conduct an electrical impulse—no matter how strong the stimulus. As a result, tetanic (sustained) contractions cannot be provoked in cardiac muscle.

On the ECG, the absolute refractory period corresponds with the onset of the QRS complex to the peak of the T wave. It includes phases 0, 1, 2, and part of phase 3 of the cardiac action potential (Figure 2-10).

Relative Refractory Period

During the **relative refractory period** (also known as the vulnerable period), some cardiac cells have repolarized to their threshold potential and can be stimulated to respond (depolarize) to a stronger than normal stimulus (Figure 2-10). This period corresponds with the downslope of the T wave on the ECG.

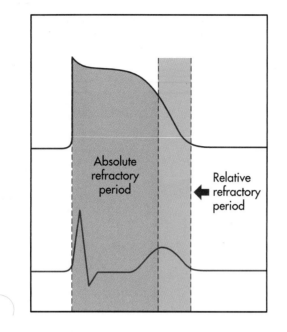

Figure 2-10
The absolute and relative refractory periods correlated with the action potential of a cardiac muscle cell and an ECG tracing.

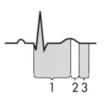

Figure 2-11
1) The absolute refractory period, 2) relative refractory period, and 3) the supernormal period.

Supernormal Period

After the relative refractory period is a **supernormal period**. A weaker than normal stimulus can cause cardiac cells to depolarize during this period. On the ECG, this corresponds with the end of the T wave. It is possible for dysrhythmias to develop during this period (see Figure 2-11).

The supernormal period extends from the end of phase 3 to the beginning of phase 4 of the cardiac action potential.

CONDUCTION SYSTEM

The specialized electrical (pacemaker) cells in the heart are arranged in a system of pathways called the **conduction system.** In the normal heart, the cells of the conduction system are interconnected. The conduction system makes sure that the chambers of the heart contract in a coordinated fashion. Normally, the pacemaker site with the fastest firing rate controls the heart.

Pacemaker cells may also be referred to as conducting cells.

Sinoatrial Node

The normal heartbeat is the result of an electrical impulse that begins in the sinoatrial (sinus or SA) node. In an adult, the SA node is about 10 to 20 mm long and 2 to 3 mm wide. Different types of cells are found in the SA node. Slightly less than half of the cells are thought to be pacemaker cells. The others are thought to be responsible for conducting the electrical impulse within the SA node and to its borders.

The SA node is the area of the heart that contains the greatest concentration of pacemaker cells.

The heart's pacemaker cells have a built-in (intrinsic) rate that becomes slower and slower from the SA node down to the end of the His-Purkinje system. The intrinsic rate of the SA

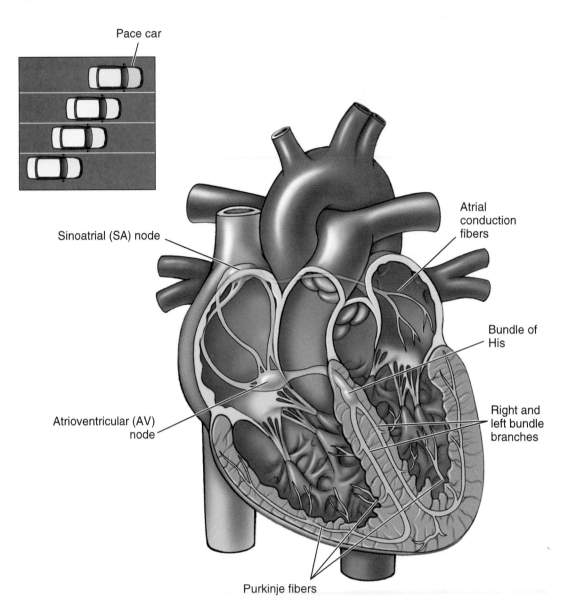

Figure 2-12
The conduction system.

node is 60 to 100 bpm. The SA node is normally the primary pacemaker of the heart because it has the fastest firing rate of all of the heart's normal pacemaker sites. Other areas of the heart can assume pacemaker responsibility if:

- The SA node fails to fire (generate an impulse).
- The SA node fires too slowly.
- The SA node fails to activate the surrounding atrial myocardium.

The SA node is located in the upper posterior part of the right atrium where the superior vena cava and the right atrium meet (Figure 2-12). It lies less than 1 mm from the epicardial surface and is richly supplied by sympathetic and parasympathetic nerve fibers. Stimulation of sympathetic nerves will result in an increase in heart rate. The heart rate normally increases during exercise or stress. Stimulation of the vagus nerve will result in a decrease in heart rate. The heart rate normally slows during rest or sleep. The SA node receives its blood supply from the SA node artery that runs lengthwise through the center of the node. The SA node artery originates from the right coronary artery in about 60% of people.

The fibers of the SA node connect directly with the fibers of the atria. As the impulse leaves the SA node, it is spread from cell to cell in wavelike form across the atrial muscle. As the

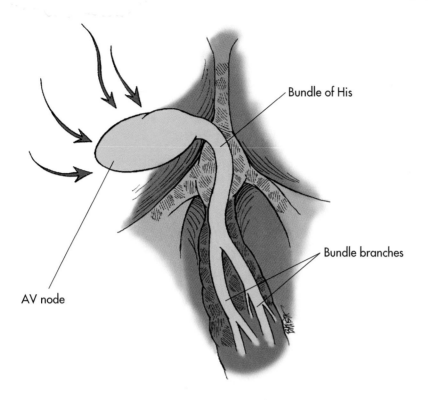

Bundle of His

Bundle branches

AV node

Figure 2-13
The AV junction consists of the AV node and the non-branching portion of the bundle of His.

impulse spreads, it stimulates the right atrium, the interatrial septum, and then the left atrium. This results in contraction of the right and left atria at almost the same time. Because a fibrous skeleton separates the atrial myocardium from the ventricular myocardium, the electrical stimulus affects only the atria.

Conduction through the AV node begins before atrial depolarization is completed. The impulse is spread to the AV node by means of three internodal pathways. They have been identified as the anterior, middle, and posterior internodal pathways. These pathways consist of a mixture of working myocardial cells and specialized conducting fibers. The anterior internodal pathway (tract) is called Bachmann's bundle, the middle Wenckebach's bundle, and the posterior Thorel's pathway. Bachmann's bundle conducts impulses to the left atrium.

It normally takes about 50 ms for an impulse to travel from the SA node, through the atrial muscle, and down to the AV node.

Atrioventricular Junction

The internodal pathways merge gradually with the cells of the AV node. Depolarization and repolarization are slow in the AV node, making this area vulnerable to blocks in conduction (AV blocks). The **AV junction** is the AV node and the nonbranching portion of the bundle of His (Figure 2-13). This area consists of specialized conduction tissue that provides the electrical links between the atria and ventricles. When the AV junction is bypassed by an abnormal pathway, the abnormal route is called an **accessory pathway**. An accessory pathway is an extra bundle of working myocardial tissue that forms a connection between the atria and ventricles outside the normal conduction system.

AV Node

The **AV node** is a group of cells located in the floor of the right atrium immediately behind the tricuspid valve and near the opening of the coronary sinus. In an adult, the AV node is about 22 mm long, 10 mm wide, and 3 mm thick. The AV node is supplied by the right coronary artery in 85% to 90% of people. In the remainder, the left circumflex artery provides the blood supply. The AV node is supplied by both sympathetic and parasympathetic nerve fibers.

As the impulse from the atria enters the AV node, there is a delay in conduction of the impulse to the ventricles. This delay occurs in part because the fibers in the AV junction are

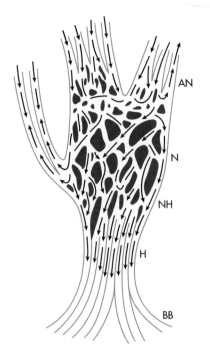

Figure 2-14
The AV junction. AN = atrionodal; N = nodal; NH = nodal-His; H = bundle of His; BB = bundle branches.

When atrial rates are very fast (e.g., atrial fibrillation), the AV node helps regulate the number of impulses reaching the ventricles to protect them from dangerously fast rates.

smaller than those of atrial muscle and have few gap junctions. If this delay did not occur, the atria and ventricles would contract at about the same time. The delay in conduction allows the atria to empty blood into the ventricles before the next ventricular contraction begins. This increases the amount of blood in the ventricles, increasing stroke volume.

The AV node has been divided into three functional regions according to their action potentials and responses to electrical and chemical stimulation (Figure 2-14):

- Atrionodal (AN) or upper junctional region (also called the transitional zone)
- Nodal (N) region, the midportion of the AV node
- Nodal-His (NH) or lower junctional region where the fibers of the AV node merge gradually with the bundle of His

The primary delay in the spread of the electrical impulse from the atria to the ventricles occurs in the AN and N areas of the AV node.

Bundle of His

The bundle of His is also called the common bundle or the atrioventricular bundle.

The speed of impulse conduction is fastest in the His-Purkinje system. It is slowest in the SA and AV nodes.

After passing through the AV node, the electrical impulse enters the **bundle of His**. It is located in the upper portion of the interventricular septum. The bundle of His has pacemaker cells capable of discharging at an intrinsic rate of 40 to 60 bpm. The bundle of His conducts the electrical impulse to the right and left bundle branches (Figure 2-15).

The bundle of His is normally the only electrical connection between the atria and the ventricles. It receives a dual blood supply from branches of the left anterior and posterior descending coronary arteries. Because of this dual blood supply, the bundle of His is less vulnerable to ischemia. The term **His-Purkinje system** or His-Purkinje network refers to the bundle of His, bundle branches, and Purkinje fibers.

Right and Left Bundle Branches

The right bundle branch innervates the right ventricle. The left bundle branch spreads the electrical impulse to the interventricular septum and left ventricle, which is thicker and more muscular than the right ventricle. The left bundle branch divides into three divisions called **fascicles**.

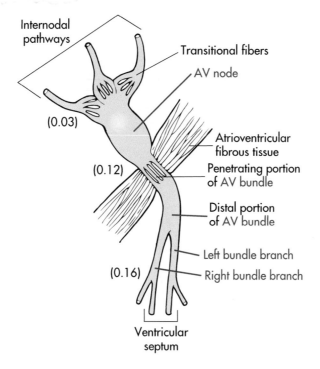

Internodal pathways

Transitional fibers

AV node

(0.03)

Atrioventricular fibrous tissue

(0.12)

Penetrating portion of AV bundle

Distal portion of AV bundle

Left bundle branch

(0.16)

Right bundle branch

Ventricular septum

Figure 2-15
The AV node, bundle of His (AV bundle), and bundle branches. The numbers represent the time from the origin of an impulse in the SA node.

Fascicles are small bundles of nerve fibers. The three fascicles are called the anterior fascicle, posterior fascicle, and the septal fascicle. The anterior fascicle spreads the electrical impulse to the anterior portions of the left ventricle. The posterior fascicle relays the impulse to the posterior portions of the left ventricle, and the septal fascicle relays the impulse to the midseptum.

Purkinje Fibers

The right and left bundle branches divide into smaller and smaller branches and then into a special network of fibers called the **Purkinje fibers**. These fibers spread from the interventricular septum into the papillary muscles. They continue downward to the apex of the heart, making up an elaborate web that penetrates about one third of the way into the ventricular muscle mass. The fibers then become continuous with the muscle cells of the right and left ventricles. The Purkinje fibers have pacemaker cells capable of firing at a rate of 20 to 40 bpm (see ECG Pearl below). The electrical impulse spreads rapidly through the right and left bundle branches and the Purkinje fibers to reach the ventricular muscle. The electrical impulse spreads from the endocardium to the myocardium, finally reaching the epicardial surface. The ventricular walls are stimulated to contract in a twisting motion that wrings blood out of the ventricular chambers and forces it into arteries.

—— *ECG Pearl*

Normal Pacemaker Sites

SA node (primary pacemaker)	60-100 bpm
AV junction	40-60 bpm
Purkinje fibers	20-40 bpm

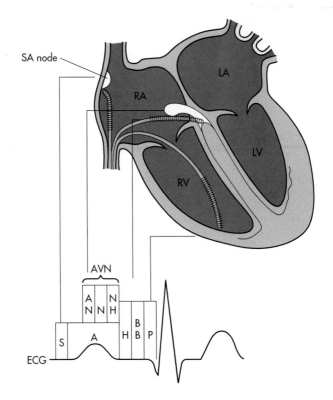

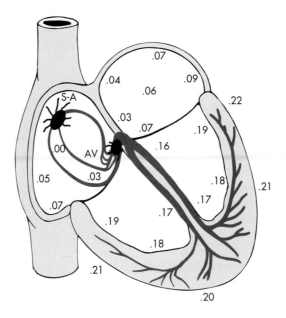

Figure 2-16 shows the sequence of activation through the conduction system. Remember that an electrical impulse precedes muscle contraction. As you can see in this figure, an impulse that begins in the SA node is not recorded on the ECG. However, the first upright waveform that you see (the P wave) shows the spread of that impulse throughout the atria (atrial depolarization). The AV node is stimulated at approximately the peak of the P wave. A summary of the conduction system is shown in Table 2-2. Figure 2-17 shows the time it takes for an impulse to reach different parts of the heart.

TABLE 2-2   Summary of the Conduction System

Structure	Location	Function	Intrinsic Pacemaker
SA node	Right atrial wall just inferior to opening of superior vena cava	Primary pacemaker; initiates impulse that is normally conducted throughout the left and right atria	60-100 bpm
AV node	Floor of the right atrium immediately behind the tricuspid valve and near the opening of the coronary sinus	Receives impulse from SA node and delays relay of the impulse to the bundle of His, allowing time for the atria to empty their contents into the ventricles before the onset of ventricular contraction.	
Bundle of His	Superior portion of interventricular septum	Receives impulse from AV node and relays it to right and left bundle branches	40-60 bpm
Right and left bundle branches	Interventricular septum	Receives impulse from bundle of His and relays it to Purkinje fibers	
Purkinje fibers	Ventricular myocardium	Receives impulse from bundle branches and relays it to ventricular myocardium	20-40 bpm

CAUSES OF DYSRHYTHMIAS

Abnormal heart rhythms (dysrhythmias) are usually due to one of three basic mechanisms:

- Enhanced automaticity
- Triggered activity
- Reentry

Enhanced Automaticity

Enhanced automaticity is an abnormal condition in which:

- Cardiac cells that are not normally associated with a pacemaker function begin to depolarize spontaneously; or
- A pacemaker site other than the SA node increases its firing rate beyond that which is considered normal.

Possible reasons for enhanced automaticity are shown in the ECG Pearl below. Examples of rhythms associated with enhanced automaticity include atrial flutter; atrial fibrillation; supraventricular tachycardia; premature atrial, junctional, or ventricular complexes; ventricular tachycardia or ventricular fibrillation; junctional tachycardia; accelerated idioventricular rhythm, and accelerated junctional rhythm.

—— *ECG Pearl*

Possible Causes of Enhanced Automaticity
Catecholamines, such as epinephrine
Administration of atropine sulfate
Digitalis toxicity
Acidosis
Alkalosis
Hypoxia
Myocardial ischemia or infarction
Electrolyte disturbances such as hypokalemia, hyperkalemia, or hypocalcemia

Triggered Activity

An escape pacemaker is a pacemaker site other than the SA node. For example, the AV junction is an escape pacemaker. If the SA node fails to fire, the escape pacemaker sites serve as a fail-safe mechanism to make sure another site steps in and assumes pacing responsibility.

Triggered activity results from abnormal electrical impulses that sometimes occur during repolarization, when cells are normally quiet. These abnormal electrical impulses are called afterdepolarizations. Triggered activity requires a stimulus to initiate depolarization. It occurs when pacemaker cells from a site other than the SA node and myocardial working cells depolarize more than once after being stimulated by a single impulse.

Causes of triggered activity are shown in the ECG Pearl below . Triggered activity can result in atrial or ventricular beats that occur alone, in pairs, in "runs" (three or more beats), or as a sustained ectopic rhythm.

—— *ECG Pearl*

Causes of Triggered Activity
Hypoxia
Increase in catecholamines
Hypomagnesemia
Myocardial ischemia or injury
Medications that prolong repolarization (e.g., quinidine)

Reentry

Normally, an impulse spreads through the heart only once after it is initiated by pacemaker cells.

Reentry is the spread of an impulse through tissue already stimulated by that same impulse. An electrical impulse is delayed or blocked (or both) in one or more areas of the conduction system while the impulse is conducted normally through the rest of the conduction system. This results in the delayed electrical impulse entering cardiac cells that have just been depolarized by the normally conducted impulse. Reentry requires three conditions (Figure 2-18):

- A potential conduction circuit or circular conduction pathway
- A block within part of the circuit
- Delayed conduction with the remainder of the circuit

Figure 2-18
Reentry requires 1) a potential conduction circuit or circular conduction pathway, 2) a block within part of the circuit, and 3) delayed conduction with the remainder of the circuit.

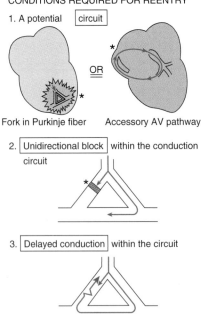

CONDITIONS REQUIRED FOR REENTRY

1. A potential circuit

OR

Fork in Purkinje fiber   Accessory AV pathway

2. Unidirectional block within the conduction circuit

3. Delayed conduction within the circuit

If the area the delayed impulse stimulates is relatively refractory, the impulse can cause depolarization of those cells, producing a single premature beat or repetitive electrical impulses. This can result in short periods of an abnormally fast heart rate. Common causes of reentry are shown in the ECG Pearl below. Examples of rhythms associated with reentry are paroxysmal supraventricular tachycardia (PSVT); ventricular tachycardia; and premature atrial, junctional, or ventricular complexes.

—— *ECG Pearl*

Common Causes of Reentry
Hyperkalemia
Myocardial ischemia
Some antiarrhythmic medications

Escape Beats or Rhythms

Escape is the term used when the SA node slows down or fails to initiate depolarization, and a lower site spontaneously produces electrical impulses, assuming responsibility for pacing the heart. Escape beats or rhythms are protective mechanisms to maintain cardiac output. They originate in the AV junction or the ventricles. Examples of escape beats or rhythms include junctional escape beats, junctional rhythm, idioventricular rhythm (also known as a ventricular escape rhythm), and ventricular escape beats.

Conduction Disturbances

Conduction disturbances may occur because of trauma, drug toxicity, electrolyte disturbances, myocardial ischemia, or infarction. Conduction may be too rapid or too slow. Examples of rhythms associated with disturbances in conduction include AV blocks.

ELECTROCARDIOGRAM

The electrocardiogram (ECG) records the electrical activity of a large mass of atrial and ventricular cells as specific waveforms and complexes. The electrical activity within the heart can be observed by means of electrodes connected by cables to an ECG machine. Think of the ECG as a voltmeter that records the electrical voltages (potentials) generated by depolarization of the heart's cells. The basic function of the ECG is to detect current flow as measured on the patient's skin.

ECG monitoring may be used to:

- Monitor a patient's heart rate
- Evaluate the effects of disease or injury on heart function
- Evaluate pacemaker function
- Evaluate the response to medications (e.g., antiarrhythmics)
- Obtain a baseline recording before, during, and after a medical procedure

The ECG *can* provide information about:

- The orientation of the heart in the chest
- Conduction disturbances
- Electrical effects of medications and electrolytes
- The mass of cardiac muscle
- The presence of ischemic damage

The first ECG was introduced by Willem Einthoven, a Dutch physiologist, in the early 1900s. No matter how sophisticated the cardiac monitor, no matter how many additional features the monitor may include, the ECG is simply a display of the electrical activity recorded on the body's surface.

The ECG does *not* provide information about the mechanical (contractile) condition of the myocardium. To evaluate the effectiveness of the heart's mechanical activity, you must assess the patient's pulse and blood pressure.

—— *ECG Pearl*

A standard ECG does not directly record the activity of the heart's electrical system. These structures are too small to produce detectable voltage on the body surface. What you see on the ECG is the activation and recovery of the working cells of the heart.[3] It *is* possible to record signals from the heart's electrical system. However, this requires the use of specialized equipment, signal-averaging techniques, or the use of recording electrodes placed in the heart.

Electrodes

To minimize distortion (artifact), be sure the conductive jelly in the center of the electrode is not dry, and avoid placing the electrodes directly over bony prominences.

Three types of electrodes used for surface (skin) electrocardiography are the metal disk, metal suction cup, and the disposable disk. Disposable disk electrodes consist of an adhesive ring with a conductive substance in the center. The conductive media of the electrode conducts skin surface voltage changes through wires to a cardiac monitor.

It is desirable to remove oil and dead cells from the patient's skin before applying electrodes. Skin oil and dead cells may be removed by a variety of techniques. For some time alcohol swabs were used for this purpose. The alcohol helped remove the oil, while a brisk rub with the swab eliminated some of the dead cells. However, while the alcohol works to remove the skin oil, it further dries out the skin. Therefore, most electrode manufacturers recommend NOT using alcohol. A brisk dry rub of the skin should be used instead. Many electrode manufacturers include an abrasive area on the disposable backing of the electrode for this purpose, but a gauze sponge works well too. Specific skin prep tools are also commercially available.

Do not rely on the color-coding of ECG cables. Colors are not standard and often vary.

It is important to define three terms as they apply in this text: electrode, lead, and cable.

- **Electrode** refers to the paper, plastic, or metal device that contains conductive media and is applied to the patient's skin. Electrodes are applied at specific locations on the patient's chest wall and extremities to view the heart's electrical activity from different angles and planes.
- **Cable** refers to the wire that attaches to the electrode and conducts current back to the cardiac monitor. One end of a monitoring cable is attached to the electrode and the other end to an ECG machine (Figure 2-19).
- **Lead** is used in two ways. The term lead refers to the actual tracing obtained and the position of the electrode. For example, the term "V_1 position" represents its proper location on the chest wall, while "lead V_1" refers to the tracing obtained from that position.

Leads

A lead is a record (tracing) of electrical activity between two electrodes. Each lead records the *average* current flow at a specific time in a portion of the heart. Leads allow viewing the heart's electrical activity in two different planes: frontal (coronal) and horizontal (transverse). Frontal plane leads view the heart from the front of the body. Horizontal plane leads view the heart as if the body were sliced in half horizontally. We'll discuss these leads in more detail a little later in this chapter. A 12-lead ECG provides views of the heart in both the frontal and horizontal planes and views the surfaces of the left ventricle from 12 different angles.

There are three types of leads: standard limb leads, augmented limb leads, and chest (precordial) leads. Each lead has a positive (+) electrode (pole). Think of the positive electrode as an eye looking in at the heart. The part of the heart that each lead "sees" is determined by two factors. The first factor is the dominance of the left ventricle on the ECG and the second is the position of the positive electrode on the body. Because the ECG does not directly measure the heart's electrical activity, it does not "see" all of the current flow-

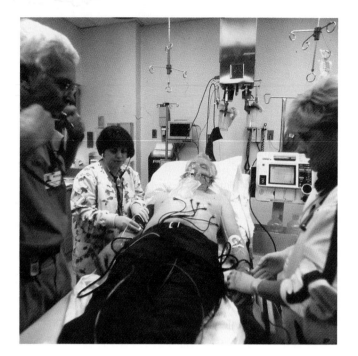

Figure **2-19**
Electrodes are applied at specific locations on the patient's chest wall and extremities to view the heart's electrical activity from different angles and planes.

Figure 2-20
The position of the positive electrode on the body determines the portion of the heart "seen" by each lead.

ing through the heart. What the ECG *does* see is the net result of countless individual currents competing in a tug-of-war. For example, the QRS complex, which represents ventricular depolarization, is not a display of all the electrical activity occurring in the right and left ventricles. It is the net result of a tug-of-war produced by the many individual currents in both the right and left ventricles. Since the left ventricle is much larger than the right, the left overpowers it. What is seen in the QRS complex is the remaining electrical activity of the left ventricle, i.e., the portion not used to cancel out the right ventricle. Therefore, in a normally conducted beat, the QRS complex represents the electrical activity occurring in the left ventricle.[4]

The second factor, position of the positive electrode on the body, determines which portion of the left ventricle is seen by each lead. You can commit the view of each lead to memory, or you can easily figure it out by remembering where the positive electrode is located (Figure 2-20).

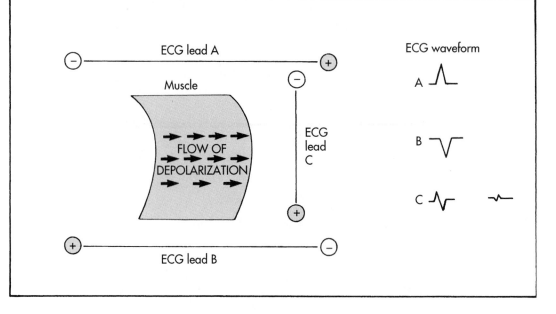

Figure 2-21
A) If the wave of depolarization moves toward the <u>positive</u> electrode, the waveform recorded on the ECG graph paper will be upright. B) If the wave of depolarization moves toward the <u>negative</u> electrode, the waveform produced will be inverted. C) A biphasic (partly positive, partly negative) waveform is recorded when the wave of depolarization moves perpendicularly to the positive electrode.

—— *ECG Pearl*

Types of Leads
Standard limb leads
Augmented limb leads
Chest (precordial or "V") leads

Each waveform that you see is related to a specific electrical event in the heart.

When electrical activity is not detected, a straight line is recorded. This line is called the **baseline** or **isoelectric line**. A **waveform** (deflection) is movement away from the baseline in a positive (upward) or negative (downward) direction. If the wave of depolarization (electrical impulse) moves toward the positive electrode, the waveform recorded on ECG graph paper will be upright (positive deflection). If the wave of depolarization moves toward the negative electrode, the waveform recorded will be inverted (downward or negative deflection). A **biphasic** (partly positive, partly negative) waveform or a straight line is recorded when the wave of depolarization moves perpendicularly to the positive electrode (Figure 2-21).

Frontal Plane Leads

Frontal plane leads view the heart from the front of the body as if it were flat (Figure 2-22). Directions in the frontal plane are superior, inferior, right, and left. Six leads view the heart in the frontal plane: three bipolar leads and three unipolar leads.

A **bipolar lead** is an ECG lead that has a positive and negative electrode. Each lead records the difference in electrical potential between two selected electrodes. Leads I, II, and III are called *standard limb leads* or *bipolar leads*.

A lead that consists of a single positive electrode and a reference point is called a **unipolar lead**. These leads are also called *unipolar limb leads* or *augmented limb leads*. The reference point (with zero electrical potential) lies in the center of the heart's electrical field (left of the interventricular septum and below the AV junction).

Leads aVR, aVL, and aVF are augmented limb leads. The electrical potential produced by the augmented leads is normally relatively small. The ECG machine augments (magnifies) the amplitude of the electrical potentials detected at each extremity by about 50% over those recorded at the bipolar leads.

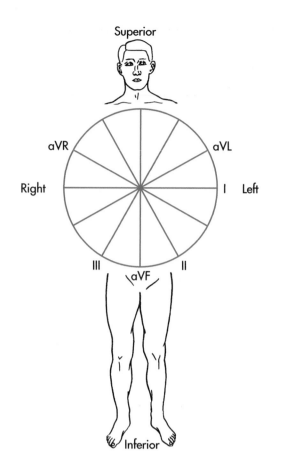

Figure **2-22**
Frontal plane leads.

Horizontal Plane Leads

Horizontal plane leads view the heart as if the body were sliced in half horizontally. Directions in the horizontal plane are anterior, posterior, right, and left. Six chest (precordial or "V") leads view the heart in the horizontal plane (Figure 2-23). This allows a view of the front and left side of the heart. The chest leads are identified as V_1, V_2, V_3, V_4, V_5, and V_6. Each electrode placed in a "V" position is a positive electrode. The negative electrode is found at the electrical center of the heart. Thus the chest leads are also unipolar leads.

The chest leads record differences in electrical potential through electrodes placed on the chest wall.

—— *ECG Pearl*

While it may not be immediately obvious, your patient's position can have an effect on the ECG. One reason for differences between tracings obtained in various positions is that while the electrode does not move when the patient changes position, the position of the heart does move relative to that electrode.[4]

Standard Limb Leads

Leads I, II, and III make up the standard limb leads. If an electrode is placed on the right arm, left arm, and left leg, three leads are formed. Since each of these three leads has a distinct negative pole and a distinct positive pole, they are considered bipolar. The positive electrode is located at the left wrist in lead I, while leads II and III both have their positive electrode located at the left foot. The difference in electrical potential between the positive pole and its corresponding negative pole is measured by each lead.

Leads I, II, and III were the first leads used when the electrocardiogram was developed.

An imaginary line joining the positive and negative electrodes of a lead is called the **axis** of the lead. The axes of these three limb leads form an equilateral triangle with the heart at the center (Einthoven's triangle) (Figure 2-24). Although placement of the left leg electrode may

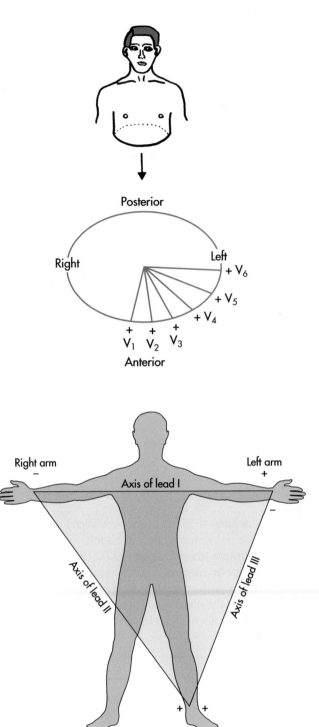

Figure 2-23
Horizontal plane leads.

Figure 2-24
Einthoven's triangle.

appear to make the triangle out of balance, it is nevertheless an equilateral triangle because all electrodes are about equidistant from the electrical field of the heart.[1] Einthoven's triangle is a way of showing that the two arms and the left leg form apices of a triangle surrounding the heart. The two apices at the upper part of the triangle represent the points at which the two arms connect electrically with the fluids around the heart. The lower apex is the point at which the left leg connects with the fluids.[2]

Over the years, electrode placement for leads I, II, and III has been altered and moved to the patient's chest. This has been done to allow for patient movement and to minimize distortion on the ECG tracing. However, proper electrode positioning for these leads includes placement on the patient's extremities. Where the electrodes are placed on the extremity does not matter as long as bony prominences are avoided.

—— *ECG Pearl*

Einthoven expressed the relationship between leads I, II, and III as the sum of any complex in leads I and III equals that of lead II. Thus, lead I + III = II. Stated another way, the voltage of a waveform in lead I plus the voltage of the same waveform in lead III equals the voltage of the same waveform in lead II. For example, when you look at leads I, II, and III, if the R wave in lead II does not appear to be the sum of the voltage of the R waves in leads I and III, the leads may have been incorrectly applied.

—— *ECG Pearl*

Leads I, II, III, aVR, aVL, and aVF are obtained from electrodes placed on the patient's arms and legs. The deltoid area is suitable for electrodes attached to the arms and is easily accessed. Either the thigh or lower leg is suitable for the leg electrodes. Use the more convenient site. Be sure that the patient's limbs are resting on a supportive surface. This decreases muscle tension in the patient's arms and legs and helps minimize distortion of the ECG tracing (artifact). Should circumstances require that the leads be placed on the torso, be certain to position them as close to the appropriate limb as possible.[4]

Lead I

Lead I records the difference in electrical potential between the left arm (+) and right arm (−) electrodes. The positive electrode is placed on the left arm and the negative electrode is placed on the right arm. The third electrode is a ground that minimizes electrical activity from other sources (Figure 2-25, *A*). Lead I views the lateral surface of the left ventricle. The QRS in lead I is normally predominantly positive because the direction of depolarization is toward the positive electrode.

Lead II

Lead II records the difference in electrical potential between the left leg (+) and right arm (−) electrodes. The positive electrode is placed on the left leg, and the negative electrode is placed on the right arm (Figure 2-25, *B*). Lead II views the inferior surface of the left ventricle. The QRS in lead II is normally positive because the direction of depolarization is predominantly toward the positive electrode. This lead is commonly used for cardiac monitoring because positioning of the positive and negative electrodes in this lead most closely resembles the normal pathway of current flow in the heart.

Lead III

Lead III records the difference in electrical potential between the left leg (+) and left arm (−) electrodes. In lead III the positive electrode is placed on the left leg and the negative electrode is placed on the left arm (Figure 2-25, *C*). Lead III views the inferior surface of the left ventricle. P waves seen in this lead may normally be positive, negative, or biphasic and are usually of lower amplitude than in lead II (Figure 2-26). The QRS in lead III is normally predominantly positive, although the R wave is not as tall as in lead II.

A summary of the standard limb leads can be found in Table 2-3.

Augmented Limb Leads

Leads aVR, aVL, and aVF are augmented limb leads. The electrical potential produced by the augmented leads is normally relatively small. The ECG machine augments (magnifies) the amplitude of the electrical potentials detected at each extremity by approximately 50% over those recorded at the bipolar leads. The "a" in aVR, aVL, and aVF refers to augmented. The

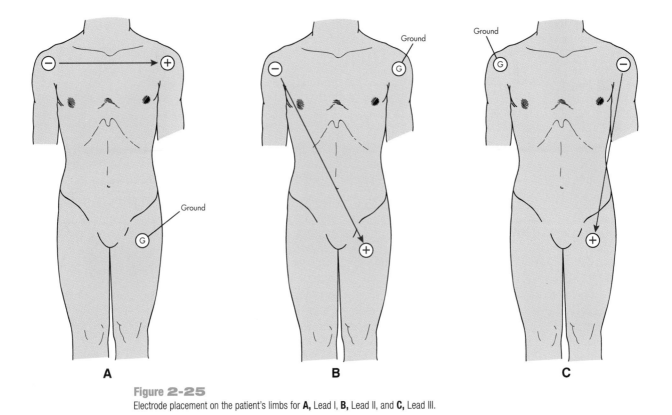

A　　　　　　**B**　　　　　　**C**

Figure 2-25

Electrode placement on the patient's limbs for **A,** Lead I, **B,** Lead II, and **C,** Lead III.

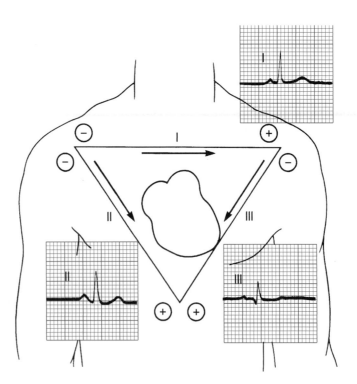

Figure 2-26

A comparison of the wave-
forms recorded in the
standard limb leads.

TABLE 2-3	Summary of Standard Limb Leads		
Lead	Positive Electrode	Negative Electrode	Heart Surface Viewed
I	Left arm	Right arm	Lateral
II	Left leg	Right arm	Inferior
III	Left leg	Left arm	Inferior

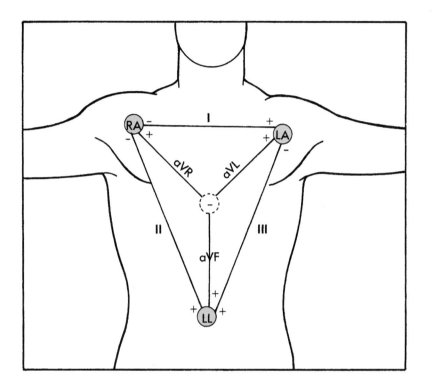

Figure 2-27
View of the standard limb leads and augmented leads.

"V" refers to voltage. The "R" refers to right arm, the "L" to left arm, and the "F" to left foot (leg). The position of the positive electrode corresponds to the last letter in each of these leads. The positive electrode in aVR is located on the right arm, aVL has a positive electrode at the left arm, and aVF has a positive electrode positioned on the left leg (Figure 2-27).

While leads aVR, aVL, and aVF have a distinct positive pole, they do not have a distinct negative pole. Since they have only one true pole, they are referred to as unipolar leads. In place of a single negative pole these leads have multiple negative poles, creating a negative field (central terminal), of which the heart is at the center. Theoretically, this makes the heart the negative electrode. The augmented voltage leads are not the only unipolar leads in the standard 12-lead ECG.[4] The chest leads, discussed in the next section, are also unipolar.

Lead aVR

Lead aVR views the heart from the right shoulder (the positive electrode) and views the base of the heart (primarily the atria and the great vessels). This lead does not view any wall of the heart. P waves and QRS complexes are normally negative in this lead because the direction of depolarization is away from the positive electrode.

Lead aVL

Lead aVL views the heart from the left shoulder (the positive electrode) and is oriented to the lateral wall of the left ventricle. The QRS in lead aVL is neither primarily positive nor negative because the direction of depolarization is essentially perpendicular to the positive and negative electrodes.

TABLE 2-4	Summary of Augmented Leads	
Lead	Positive Electrode	Heart Surface Viewed
aVR	Right arm	None
aVL	Left arm	Lateral
aVF	Left leg	Inferior

Lead aVF

Lead aVF views the heart from the left foot (leg) (positive electrode) and views the inferior surface of the left ventricle. The QRS in lead aVF is positive because the direction of depolarization is primarily toward the positive electrode.

A summary of augmented leads can be found in Table 2-4.

Chest Leads

Because their location varies, do not use the nipples as landmarks for chest electrode placement.

The six chest leads are unipolar leads that view the heart in the horizontal plane. The chest leads are identified as V_1, V_2, V_3, V_4, V_5, and V_6. Each electrode placed in a V position is a positive electrode. Because the chest leads are unipolar, the positive electrode for each lead is placed at a specific location on the chest. The heart is the theoretical negative electrode.

The wave of ventricular depolarization normally moves from right to left. In the right chest leads (V_1 and V_2), the QRS deflection is predominantly negative (moving away from the positive chest electrode). As the chest electrode is placed further left, the wave of depolarization (R wave progression) is moving toward the positive electrode. Thus the QRS deflection recorded as the electrode is moved to the left becomes progressively more positive.

—— ECG Pearl

All of the electrode positions refer to the location of the gel. For example, the gel of the V_1 electrode, not the entire adhesive patch, is positioned in the fourth intercostal space, just to the right of the sternum.[4]

Lead V_1

Lead V_1 is recorded with the positive electrode in the fourth intercostal space, just to the right of the sternum (Figure 2-28). The P waves in this lead may be positive, negative, or biphasic. The QRS in this lead is normally negative.

Lead V_2

Lead V_2 is recorded with the positive electrode in the fourth intercostal space, just to the left of the sternum. P waves in this lead may be positive, negative, or biphasic. The QRS is typically biphasic.

Lead V_3

Lead V_3 is recorded with the positive electrode on a line midway between V_2 and V_4. P waves in this lead should be upright. The QRS may be biphasic.

Lead V_4

Lead V_4 is recorded with the positive electrode in the left midclavicular line in the fifth intercostal space. P waves in this lead should be upright. The QRS may be biphasic. If a right ventricular MI is suspected, lead V_4 may be moved to the same anatomic location but on the right side of the chest. The lead is then called V_4R and is viewed for ECG changes consistent with acute MI.

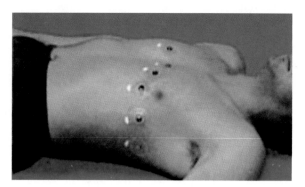

Figure 2-28
Anatomic placement of the chest leads.

TABLE 2-5	Summary of Chest Leads	
Lead	Positive Electrode Position	Heart Surface Viewed
V_1	Right side of sternum, 4th intercostal space	Septum
V_2	Left side of sternum, 4th intercostal space	Septum
V_3	Midway between V_2 and V_4	Anterior
V_4	Left midclavicular line, 5th intercostal space	Anterior
V_5	Left anterior axillary line at same level as V_4	Lateral
V_6	Left midaxillary line at same level as V_4	Lateral

Lead V_5

Lead V_5 is recorded with the positive electrode in the left anterior axillary line at the same level as V_4. P waves and QRS complexes should be upright in this lead.

Lead V_6

Lead V_6 is recorded with the positive electrode in the left midaxillary line at the same level as V_4. P waves and QRS complexes should be upright in this lead.

A summary of the chest leads can be found in Table 2-5.

Right Chest Leads

Other chest leads that are not part of a standard 12-lead ECG may be used to view specific surfaces of the heart. When a right ventricular myocardial infarction is suspected, right chest leads are used. Placement of right chest leads is identical to placement of the standard chest leads except it is done on the right side of the chest (Figure 2-29). If time does not permit obtaining all of the right chest leads, the lead of choice is V_4R. The right chest leads and their placement are:

Lead V_1R	Lead V_2
Lead V_2R	Lead V_1
Lead V_3R	Midway between V_2R and V_4R
Lead V_4R	Right midclavicular line, fifth intercostal space
Lead V_5R	Right anterior axillary line at same level as V_4R
Lead V_6R	Right midaxillary line at same level as V_4R

Posterior Chest Leads

On a standard 12-lead ECG, no leads look directly at the posterior surface of the heart. Additional chest leads may be used for this purpose. These leads are placed further left and toward the back. All of the leads are placed on the same horizontal line as V_4 to V_6. Lead V_7 is placed at the posterior axillary line. Lead V_8 is placed at the angle of the scapula (posterior scapular line), and lead V_9 is placed over the left border of the spine (Figure 2-30).

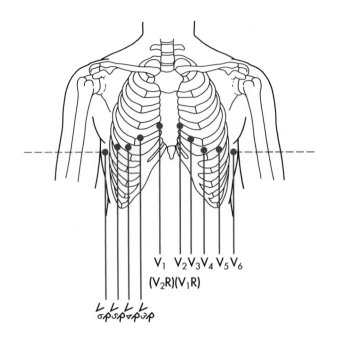

Figure 2-29
Anatomic placement of the left and right chest leads.

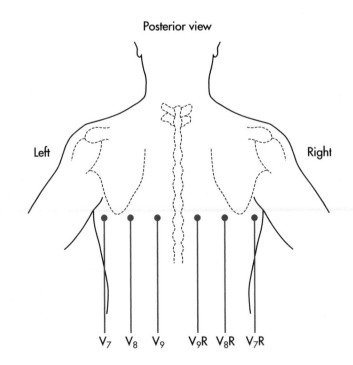

Figure 2-30
Posterior precordial lead placement.

Modified Chest Leads

Leads II, MCL₁, and MCL₆ are the most commonly used for continuous ECG monitoring.

The modified chest leads (MCL) are bipolar chest leads that are variations of the unipolar chest leads. Each modified chest lead consists of a positive and negative electrode applied to a specific location on the chest. Accurate placement of the positive electrode is important.

The modified chest leads are useful in detecting bundle branch blocks, differentiating right and left premature beats, and differentiating supraventricular tachycardia (SVT) from ventricular tachycardia (VT).

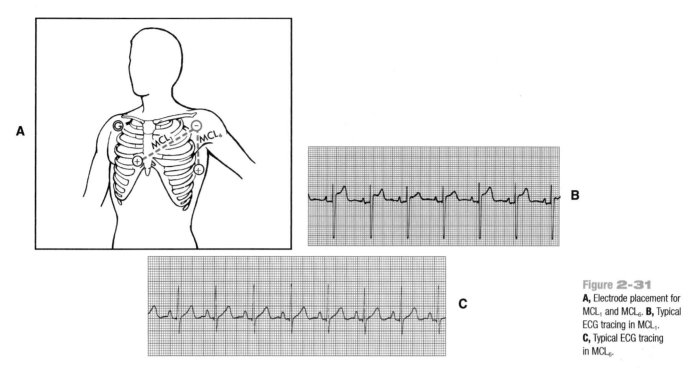

Figure 2-31
A, Electrode placement for MCL$_1$ and MCL$_6$. **B,** Typical ECG tracing in MCL$_1$. **C,** Typical ECG tracing in MCL$_6$.

Lead MCL$_1$

Lead MCL$_1$ is a variation of the chest lead V$_1$ and views the ventricular septum. The negative electrode is placed below the left clavicle toward the left shoulder, and the positive electrode is placed to the right of the sternum in the fourth intercostal space (Figure 2-31, *A*). In this lead the positive electrode is in a position to the right of the left ventricle. Because the primary wave of depolarization is directed toward the left ventricle, the QRS complex recorded in this lead will normally appear negative (Figure 2-31, *B*).

Lead MCL$_6$

Lead MCL$_6$ is a variation of the chest lead V$_6$ and views the low lateral wall of the left ventricle. The negative electrode is placed below the left clavicle toward the left shoulder and the positive electrode is placed at the fifth intercostal space, left midaxillary line. An example of a typical ECG tracing recorded in this lead is shown in Figure 2-31, *C*.

—— *ECG Pearl*

Leads MCL$_1$ and V$_1$ are similar but not identical. In V$_1$, the negative electrode is calculated by the ECG machine at the center of the heart. In MCL$_1$, the negative electrode is located just below the left clavicle.[4]

ECG PAPER

Remember that the ECG is a graphical representation of the heart's electrical activity. When you place electrodes on the patient's body and connect them to an ECG, the machine records the voltage (potential difference) between the electrodes. The needle (or pen) of the ECG moves a specific distance depending on the voltage measured. This recording is made on ECG paper.

ECG paper is graph paper made up of small and large boxes measured in millimeters. The smallest boxes are 1-mm wide and 1-mm high (Figure 2-32). The horizontal axis of the paper corresponds with *time*. Time is used to measure the interval between or duration of specific cardiac events. Time is stated in seconds.

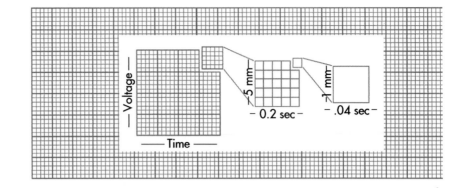

Figure 2-32
The horizontal axis represents time. The vertical axis represents amplitude or voltage.

Figure 2-33
When the ECG machine is properly calibrated, a 1-millivolt electrical signal will produce a deflection measuring exactly 10 millimeters tall.

Five large boxes, each consisting of five small boxes, represent 1 sec. Fifteen large boxes equal an interval of 3 sec. Thirty large boxes represent 6 sec.

The rate at which ECG paper goes through the printer is adjustable. Standard paper speed is 25 mm/sec. ECG paper normally records at a constant speed of 25 mm/sec. Thus each horizontal 1-mm box represents 0.04 sec (25 mm/sec x 0.04 sec = 1 mm). Look closely at the boxes in Figure 2-32. You can see that the lines after every five small boxes on the paper are heavier. The heavier lines indicate one large box. Because each large box is the width of five small boxes, a large box represents 0.20 sec.

—— *ECG Pearl*

The rate at which the paper goes through the printer is adjustable and is designated on the 12-lead. Standard paper speed is 25 mm/sec. A faster paper speed makes the rhythm appear slower and the QRS complex wider. Thus in cases of rapid heart rates, a faster paper speed makes it easier to see the waveforms and analyze the rhythm. A slower paper speed makes the rhythm appear faster and the QRS narrower.[4]

When the ECG machine is properly calibrated, 1 mV = 10 mm.

The vertical axis of the ECG paper measures the *voltage* or *amplitude* of a waveform. Voltage is measured in millivolts (mV). Voltage may be a positive or negative value. Amplitude is measured in millimeters (mm). The ECG machine's sensitivity must be calibrated so that a 1-mV electrical signal will produce a deflection measuring exactly 10-mm tall (Figure 2-33). When properly calibrated, a small box is 1-mm high (0.1 mV), and a large box (equal to five small boxes) is 5-mm high (0.5 mV). Clinically, the height of a waveform is usually stated in millimeters, not millivolts.

—— *ECG Pearl*

Possible Causes of Low Amplitude Waveforms
Normal variant
Obesity
Emphysema
Extensive myocardial infarction
Pericardial effusion
Pleural effusion
Hypothyroidism

TABLE 2-6	Terminology
Waveform	Movement away from the baseline in either a positive or negative direction
Segment	A line between waveforms; named by the waveform that precedes or follows it
Interval	A waveform and a segment
Complex	Several waveforms

WAVEFORMS

A waveform is movement away from the baseline in either a positive (upward) or negative (downward) direction (Table 2-6). Waveforms are named alphabetically, beginning with P, QRS, T, and U. A waveform that is partly positive and partly negative is biphasic. A waveform that rests on the baseline is isoelectric.

P Wave

Remember that an impulse that begins in the SA node is not recorded on the ECG. However, the spread of that impulse throughout the atria (atrial depolarization) is observed. The first waveform in the cardiac cycle is the *P wave*. The first half of the P wave is recorded when the electrical impulse that originated in the SA node stimulates the right atrium and reaches the AV node (Figure 2-34). The downslope of the P wave reflects stimulation of the left atrium. Thus the P wave represents atrial depolarization and the spread of the electrical impulse throughout the right and left atria.

Activation of the SA node occurs before the onset of the P wave and is not observed on the ECG.

The atria contract a fraction of a second after the P wave begins. The atria begin to repolarize at the same time as the ventricles depolarize. A waveform representing atrial repolarization is usually not seen on the ECG because it is small and buried in the QRS complex.

The beginning of the P wave is recognized as the first abrupt or gradual deviation from the baseline; its end is the point at which the waveform returns to the baseline (Figure 2-35).

Normal Characteristics of the P Wave

- Smooth and rounded
- No more than 2.5 mm in height
- No more than 0.11 sec in duration
- Positive in leads I, II, aVF, and V_2 through V_6

A P wave normally precedes each QRS complex.

Abnormal P Waves

Tall and pointed (peaked) or wide and notched P waves may be seen in conditions such as chronic obstructive pulmonary disease (COPD), congestive heart failure (CHF), or in valvular disease and may be indicative of atrial enlargement (Figure 2-36).

P waves that begin at a site other than the SA node (ectopic P waves) may be positive or negative in lead II. If the ectopic pacemaker is in the atria, the P wave will be upright. If the ectopic pacemaker is in the AV junction, the P wave will be negative (inverted) in lead II.

Enlargement of the right atrium produces an abnormally tall initial part of the P wave. The latter part of the P wave is prominent in left atrial enlargement.

QRS Complex

A **complex** consists of several waveforms. The QRS complex consists of the Q wave, R wave, and S wave. It represents the spread of the electrical impulse through the ventricles (ventricular depolarization). Normally, depolarization triggers contraction of ventricular tissue. Thus, shortly after the QRS complex begins, the ventricles contract (Figure 2-37). The QRS complex is significantly larger than the P wave because depolarization of the ventricles involves a

Atrial repolarization usually takes place during this time, but the QRS complex overshadows it on the ECG.

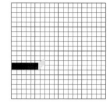

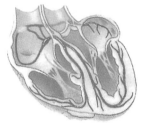

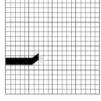

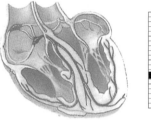

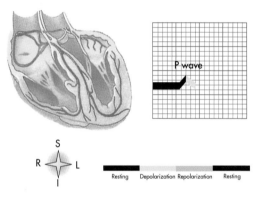

Figure 2-34

The first wave in the cardiac cycle is the P wave. The first half of the P wave reflects stimulation of the right atrium. The downslope of the P wave reflects stimulation of the left atrium.

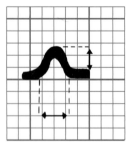

Figure 2-35

The beginning of the P wave is recognized as the first abrupt or gradual deviation from the baseline. Its end is the point at which the waveform returns to the baseline.

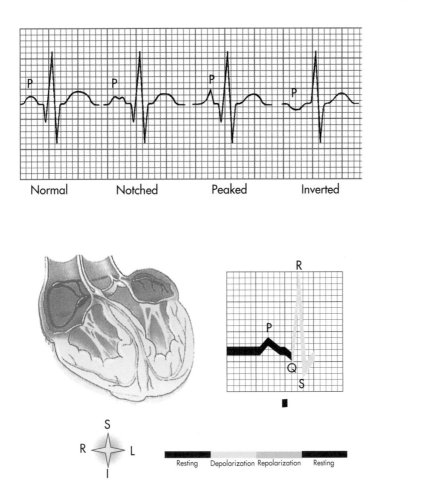

Figure 2-36
Abnormal P waves may be notched, tall and pointed (peaked), or inverted (negative).

Figure 2-37
The QRS complex represents ventricular depolarization.

considerably greater muscle mass than depolarization of the atria. A QRS complex normally follows each P wave. One or even two of the three waveforms that make up the QRS complex may not always be present.

Q Wave

The QRS complex begins as a downward deflection, the *Q wave*. A Q wave is **always** a negative waveform. The Q wave represents depolarization of the interventricular septum, which is activated from left to right. In lead II, the direction of the current flow is almost perpendicular to it, and more current is moving away from the positive electrode than is moving toward it.

In lead MCL$_1$, depolarization of the interventricular septum will appear as a small, upright R wave. In this lead, this is the first deflection of a normal QRS complex.

It is important to differentiate normal (physiologic) Q waves from pathologic Q waves. With the exception of leads III and aVR, a normal Q wave in the limb leads is less than 0.04 sec (one small box) in duration and less than one-third the height of the R wave in that lead. An abnormal (pathologic) Q wave is more than 0.04 sec in duration or more than one-third the height of the following R wave in that lead.

—— *ECG Pearl*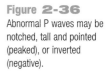

Myocardial infarction is one possible cause of abnormal Q waves. In the early hours of infarction, an abnormal Q wave may not have developed to its full width or amplitude. Therefore, a single ECG tracing may not identify an abnormal Q wave. In a patient with a suspected MI, be sure to look at Q waves closely. Even if the initial ECG tracings do not show Q waves that are more than 0.04 sec in duration or equal to or more than one-third the amplitude of the QRS complex, pathology must be considered if the Q waves become wider or deeper in each subsequent tracing.

R and S Waves

The QRS complex continues as a large, upright, triangular waveform known as the R wave. The R wave is the first positive (upright) waveform following the P wave. The S wave is the negative waveform following the R wave. The R and S waves represent simultaneous depolarization of the right and left ventricles. Because of its greater muscle mass, the QRS complex generally represents the electrical activity occurring in the left ventricle.

Variations of the QRS Complex

Although the term QRS complex is used, not every QRS complex contains a Q wave, R wave, and S wave. To review, when the first deflection of the QRS complex is negative (below the baseline), the waveform is called a *Q wave*. The *R wave* is the first positive deflection (above the baseline) in the QRS complex. A negative deflection following the R wave is called an *S wave*.

If the QRS complex consists entirely of a positive waveform, it is called an *R wave*. If the complex consists entirely of a negative waveform, it is called a *QS wave*. If there are two positive deflections in the same complex, the second is called *R prime* and is written *R′*. If there are two negative deflections following an R wave, the second is called *S prime* and is written *S′*. Capital (upper case) letters are used to designate waveforms of relatively large amplitude, and small (lower case) letters are used to label relatively small waveforms (Figure 2-38).

Measuring the Duration of the QRS Complex

The QRS duration is a measurement of the time required for ventricular depolarization. The width of a QRS complex is most accurately determined when it is viewed and measured in more than one lead. The measurement should be taken from the QRS complex with the longest duration and clearest onset and end. The beginning of the QRS complex is measured from the point where the first wave of the complex begins to deviate from the baseline. The point at which the last wave of the complex begins to level out or distinctly change direction at, above, or below the baseline marks the end of the QRS complex. In adults, the normal duration of the QRS complex varies between 0.06 and 0.10 sec. If an electrical impulse does not follow the normal ventricular conduction pathway, it will take longer to depolarize the myocardium. This delay in conduction through the ventricle produces a wider QRS complex.

Normal Characteristics of the QRS Complex

- Normal duration of the QRS complex in an adult varies between 0.06 and 0.10 sec.
- A normal Q wave is less than 0.04 sec in duration and less than one-third of the amplitude of the R wave in that lead.

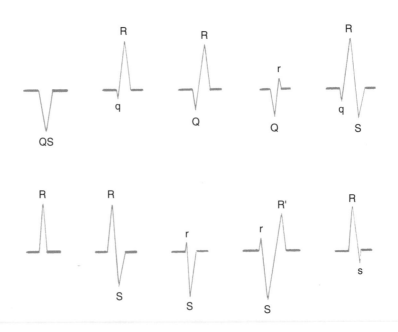

Abnormal QRS Complexes

- Duration of an abnormal QRS complex is greater than 0.10 sec.
- Duration of a QRS caused by an impulse originating in an ectopic pacemaker in the Purkinje network or ventricular myocardium is usually greater than 0.12 sec and often 0.16 sec or greater.
- If the impulse originates in a bundle branch, the duration of the QRS may be only slightly greater than 0.10 sec. For example, a QRS measuring 0.10 to 0.12 sec is called an incomplete bundle branch block. A QRS measuring more than 0.12 sec is called a complete bundle branch block. This is discussed in more detail in Chapter 9.

If the spread of the impulse through the ventricles is slowed, the duration of the QRS is prolonged. This may be seen in conditions such as bundle branch block.

T Wave

Ventricular repolarization is represented on the ECG by the T wave (Figure 2-39). The absolute refractory period is still present during the beginning of the T wave. At the peak of the T wave, the relative refractory period has begun. It is during the relative refractory period that a stronger than normal stimulus may produce ventricular dysrhythmias.

The normal T wave is slightly asymmetric: the peak of the waveform is closer to its end than to the beginning, and the first half has a more gradual slope than the second half. The beginning of the T wave is identified as the point where the slope of the ST-segment appears to become abruptly or gradually steeper. The T wave ends when it returns to the baseline. Examples of T waves are shown in Figure 2-40.

It may be difficult to clearly determine the onset and end of the T wave.

The direction of the T wave is normally the same as the QRS complex that precedes it. This is because depolarization begins at the endocardial surface and spreads to the epicardium. Repolarization begins at the epicardium and spreads to the endocardium.

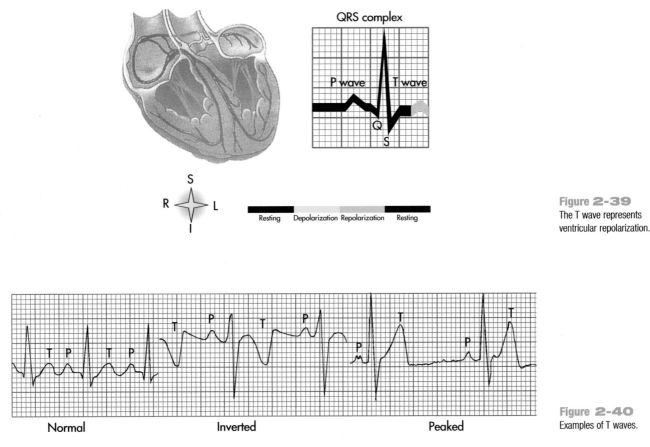

Figure 2-39
The T wave represents ventricular repolarization.

Figure 2-40
Examples of T waves.

Normal   Inverted   Peaked

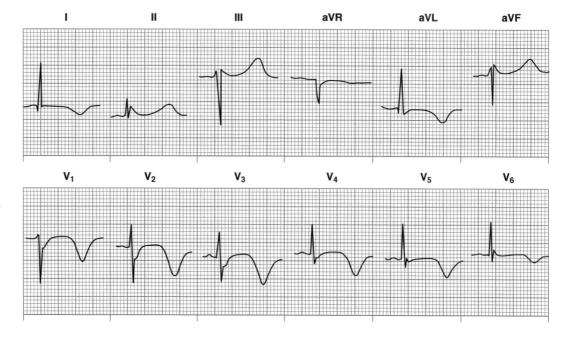

Figure 2-41
The ECG of a patient with acute subarachnoid hemorrhage shows giant T wave inversion. Subarachnoid hemorrhage may cause deeply inverted T waves, usually with markedly prolonged QT intervals, simulating the pattern seen in myocardial infarction.

In the limb leads, lead II most commonly reveals the tallest T wave.

Normal Characteristics of the T Wave

- Slightly asymmetric
- T waves are usually 5 mm or less in height in any limb lead or 10 mm in any chest lead; T waves are usually 0.5 mm or more in height in leads I and II.

Abnormal T Waves

- A T wave following an abnormal QRS complex is usually opposite in direction of the QRS. In other words, when the QRS complex points down, the T wave points up, and vice versa. This may be seen with ventricular beats/rhythms and in bundle branch block.
- Negative T waves suggest myocardial ischemia.
- Tall, pointed (peaked) T waves are commonly seen in hyperkalemia.
- Low-amplitude T waves may be seen in hypokalemia.
- Significant cerebral disease (e.g., subarachnoid hemorrhage) may be associated with deeply inverted T waves, often called cerebral T waves (Figure 2-41).

—— *ECG Pearl*

T wave inversion, which may occur simultaneously with ST-segment elevation, suggests the presence of myocardial ischemia. The development of pathologic Q waves provides evidence that tissue death has occurred. A pathologic Q wave indicates the presence of dead myocardial tissue and, subsequently, a loss of electrical activity.

U Wave

The amplitude of the normal U wave is usually proportional to the T wave in the same lead, ranging between 5% and 25% of the T wave's amplitude.

A U wave is a small waveform that, when seen, follows the T wave. The mechanism of the U wave is not definitely known. One theory suggests that it represents repolarization of the Purkinje fibers. Normal U waves are small, round, and less than 1.5 mm in amplitude. Some causes of tall U waves include:

- Electrolyte imbalance (e.g., hypokalemia)
- Medications (e.g., quinidine, procainamide, disopyramide, amiodarone, digitalis, phenothiazines)

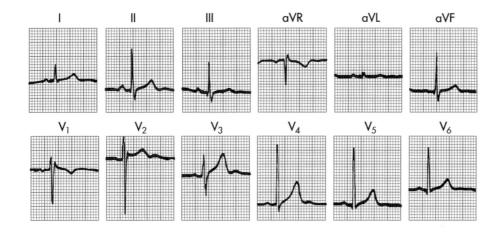

Figure **2-42**
Normal U waves (best
viewed in leads V_2 through
V_4) in a 22-year-old man.

- Hyperthyroidism
- Central nervous system disease
- Long QT syndrome

U waves are most easily seen when the heart rate is slow and are difficult to identify when the rate exceeds 90 bpm. When seen, they are normally tallest in leads V_2 and V_3 (Figure 2-42). U waves usually appear in the same direction as the T wave that precedes it. Negative U waves are strongly suggestive of organic heart disease and may be seen in patients with ischemic heart disease.

When the QT interval is prolonged, a U wave may appear to merge with the T wave.

Characteristics of the U Wave

- Rounded and symmetric
- Usually less than 1.5 mm in height and smaller than that of the preceding T wave
- In general, a U wave more than 1.5 mm in height in any lead is considered abnormal.

SEGMENTS

A **segment** is a line between waveforms. It is named by the waveform that precedes or follows it.

——— *ECG Pearl*

Important Segments
PR-segment
ST-segment
TP-segment

PR-segment

The PR-segment is the horizontal line between the end of the P wave and the beginning of the QRS complex (Figure 2-43). It represents activation of the AV node, the bundle of His, the bundle branches, and the Purkinje fibers. The PR-segment appears isoelectric because the potentials generated by these structures are too small to produce detectable voltage on the body surface.[3] Atrial repolarization also occurs during this period.

The PR-segment is part of the PR interval.

The duration of the PR-segment depends on duration of the P wave and impulse conduction through the AV junction. Most of the conduction delay during the PR-segment is a result of

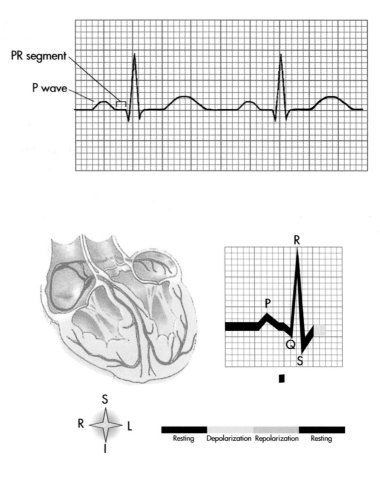

Figure 2-43
The PR segment.

Figure 2-44
The ST-segment represents the early part of repolarization of the right and left ventricles.

slow conduction within the AV node. The PR-segment may be depressed in patients with ventricular hypertrophy or chronic pulmonary disease.

ST-segment

The term ST-segment is used regardless of whether the final wave of the QRS complex is an R or an S wave.

The portion of the ECG tracing between the QRS complex and the T wave is the ST-segment (Figure 2-44). The ST-segment represents the early part of repolarization of the right and left ventricles. The normal ST-segment begins at the isoelectric line, extends from the end of the S wave, and curves gradually upward to the beginning of the T wave.

ST-segment elevation provides the strongest ECG evidence for the early recognition of myocardial infarction.

The point where the QRS complex and the ST-segment meet is called the *junction* or *J-point* (Figure 2-45). Various conditions may cause displacement of the ST-segment from the isoelectric line in either a positive or negative direction. Myocardial ischemia, injury, and infarction are among the causes of ST-segment deviation. When looking for ST-segment elevation or depression, we are particularly interested in the early portion of the ST-segment. Find a QRS complex on the ECG and follow that QRS complex to the end. Look to see where the end of the QRS complex makes a sudden sharp change in direction. That point identifies the J-point. It may be difficult to clearly determine the J-point in patients with rapid heart rates or hyperkalemia. The ST-segment is considered elevated if the segment is deviated above the baseline. It is considered depressed if the segment is deviated below it.

In a patient presenting with an acute coronary syndrome, ST-segment depression suggests ischemia. ST-segment elevation suggests myocardial injury. Other causes of ST-segment elevation may represent a normal variant, pericarditis, or ventricular aneurysm, among other causes. Pericarditis causes ST-segment elevation in all or virtually all leads.

ST-segment elevation in the shape of a "smiley" face (upward concavity) is usually benign, particularly when it occurs in an otherwise healthy, asymptomatic patient (Figure 2-46). The appearance of coved ("frowny face") ST-segment elevation is called an *acute injury pattern*. Other possible shapes of ST-segment elevation seen with acute myocardial infarction are shown in Figure 2-47.

—— *ECG Pearl*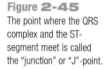

In a patient experiencing an acute coronary syndrome, keep in mind that myocardial injury refers to myocardial tissue that has been cut off from or experienced a severe reduction in its blood and oxygen supply. The tissue is not yet dead and may be salvageable if the blocked vessel can be quickly opened, restoring blood flow and oxygen to the injured area.

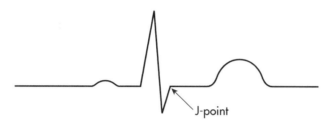

Figure 2-45
The point where the QRS complex and the ST-segment meet is called the "junction" or "J"-point.

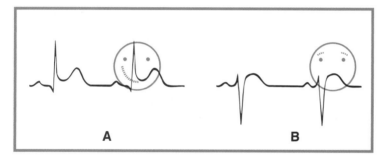

Figure 2-46
A, ST-segment elevation in the shape of a "smiley" face (upward concavity) is usually benign, particularly when it occurs in an otherwise healthy, asymptomatic patient. **B,** ST-segment elevation in the shape of a "frowny" face (downward concavity) is more often associated with an acute injury pattern.

Figure 2-47
Variable shapes of ST-segment elevations seen with acute myocardial infarctions.

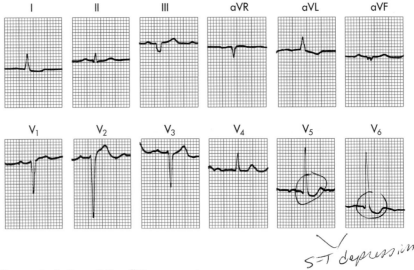

ST depression

Figure 2-48
Digitalis may produce a characteristic "scooping" of the ST-segment, as seen here in leads V_5 and V_6.

Normal Characteristics of the ST-segment
- Begins with the end of the QRS complex and ends with the onset of the T wave
- In the limb leads, the normal ST-segment is isoelectric (flat) but may normally be slightly elevated or depressed.
- In the chest leads, ST-segment deviation may vary from -0.5 to $+2$ mm.

Abnormal ST-segments
- ST-segment depression of more than $\frac{1}{2}$ mm is suggestive of myocardial ischemia.
- ST-segment elevation of more than 1 mm in the limb leads or 2 mm in the chest leads is suggestive of myocardial injury.
- A horizontal ST-segment (forming a sharp angle with the T wave) is suggestive of ischemia.
- Digitalis causes a depression (scoop) of the ST-segment sometimes referred to as a "dig dip" (Figure 2-48).

TP-segment

Proper machine calibration is critical when analyzing ST-segments. The ST-segment criteria described here applies *only* when the monitor is adjusted to standard calibration.[4]

The TP-segment is the portion of the ECG tracing between the end of the T wave and the beginning of the following P wave. When the heart rate is within normal limits, the TP-segment is usually isoelectric. With rapid heart rates, the TP-segment is often unrecognizable because the P wave encroaches on the preceding T wave.

When assessing for ST-segment displacement, first locate the J-point. Next use the TP-segment and the PR-segment to estimate the position of the isoelectric line. Then compare the level of the ST-segment to the isoelectric line (Figure 2-49). While some deviation of the ST-segment from the isoelectric line can be a normal finding, the following findings are considered significant if they are seen in two or more leads facing the same anatomic area of the heart (also known as contiguous leads):

- ST-segment depression of more than $\frac{1}{2}$ mm (suggests myocardial ischemia)
- ST-segment elevation (suggests myocardial injury)
  - More than 1 mm in the limb leads
  - More than 2 mm in the chest leads

—— *ECG Pearl*

There is some difference of opinion as to where ST-segment deviation should be measured. Some authorities simply measure deviation at the J-point while others look for deviation 0.04 sec after the J-point. Still others measure ST-segment deviation 0.06 sec after the J-point. Compare the ST-segment deviation to the isoelectric line. The TP-segment is best used for this comparison; however, some authorities prefer to use the PR-segment as the baseline.[4]

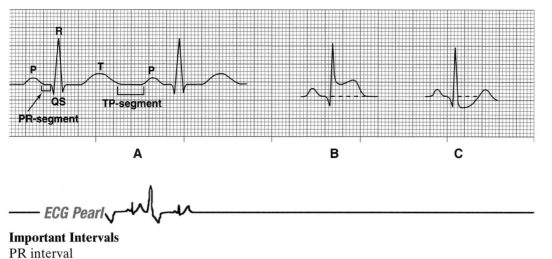

Figure 2-49
The TP-segment. **A,** The
PR- and TP-segments are
used as the baseline from
which to determine the
presence of ST-segment
elevation or depression.
B, ST-segment elevation.
C, ST-segment depression.

—— *ECG Pearl*

Important Intervals
PR interval
QT interval

INTERVALS

PR Interval

An **interval** is a waveform and a segment. The P wave plus the PR-segment equals the PR interval (PRI) (Figure 2-50). The PR interval is measured from the point where the P wave leaves the baseline to the beginning of the QRS complex. The term PQ interval is preferred by some because it is the period actually measured unless a Q wave is absent.

The P wave + the PR segment = the PR interval (PRI).

Remember that the P wave reflects depolarization of the right and left atria. The PR-segment represents the spread of the impulse through the AV node, bundle of His, right and left bundle branches, and the Purkinje fibers (Figure 2-51). The PRI changes with heart rate but normally measures 0.12 to 0.20 sec in adults. As the heart rate increases, the duration of the PR interval shortens. A conduction problem above the level of the bundle branches will largely affect the P wave and PR interval.

The PRI does not include the duration of conduction from the SA node to the right atrium.

Normal Characteristics of the PR Interval
- Normally measures 0.12 to 0.20 sec in adults; may be shorter in children and longer in older persons
- Normally shortens as heart rate increases
- Normally lengthens as heart rate decreases

Measuring how quickly or slowly an electrical impulse spreads through the heart provides important information about the condition of the heart's conduction system and the muscle itself.

Abnormal PR Intervals
A long PR interval (greater than 0.20 sec) indicates the impulse was delayed as it passed through the atria or AV node. Prolonged PR intervals may be seen in patients taking beta-blockers or calcium channel blockers, first-degree AV block, hypothyroidism, and digitalis toxicity, among other conditions. The P wave associated with a prolonged PR interval may be normal or abnormal.

A PR interval of less than 0.12 sec may be seen when the impulse originates in an ectopic pacemaker in the atria close to the AV node or in the AV junction. A shortened PR interval may also occur if the electrical impulse progresses from the atria to the ventricles through an abnormal conduction pathway that bypasses the AV node and depolarizes the ventricles earlier than usual. Wolff-Parkinson-White and Lown-Ganong-Levine syndromes are examples of conditions in which this may be seen.

QT Interval

The QT interval represents total ventricular activity—the time from ventricular depolarization (activation) to repolarization (recovery). The QT interval is measured from the begin-

The term *QT interval* is used regardless of whether the QRS complex begins with a Q or R wave.

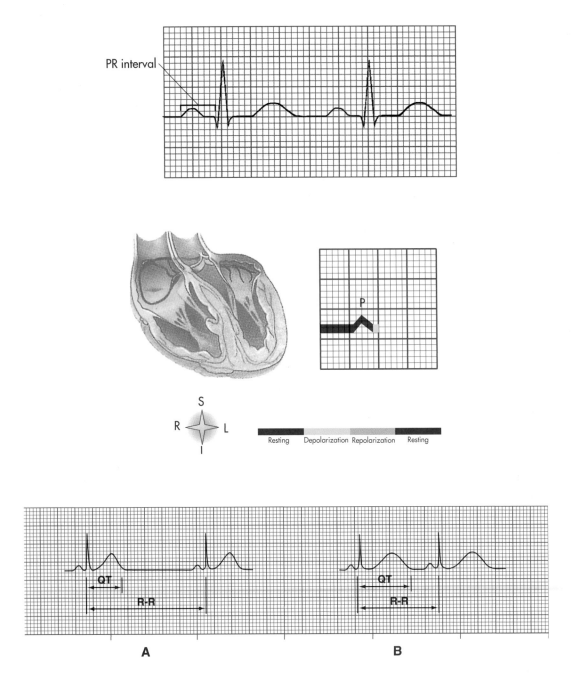

Figure 2-50
The PR interval.

Figure 2-51
The PR interval reflects depolarization of the right and left atria (P wave) and the spread of the impulse through the AV node, bundle of His, right and left bundle branches, and the Purkinje fibers (PR segment).

Figure 2-52
Measuring the QT interval. **A,** The QT interval is normal because it is much less than the R-R interval. **B,** The QT interval is prolonged because it is more than half the R-R interval.

ning of the QRS complex to the end of the T wave. In the absence of a Q wave, the QT interval is measured from the beginning of the R wave to the end of the T wave.

The duration of the QT interval varies according to age, gender, and heart rate. To quickly determine the QT interval, measure the interval between two consecutive R waves (R-R interval) and divide the number by two. Measure the QT interval. If the measured QT interval is less than half the R-R interval, it is probably normal (Figure 2-52). A QT interval that is approximately half the R-R interval is considered borderline. A QT interval that is more than half the R-R interval is considered prolonged.

Digitalis and hyper-calcemia **shorten** the QT interval.

Many conditions, such as electrolyte disorders, and medications, such as amiodarone, can prolong the QT interval. A prolonged QT interval indicates a lengthened relative refractory period (vulnerable period). This puts the ventricles at risk for life-threatening dysrhythmias, such as torsades de pointes (TdP). A prolonged QT interval may be congenital or acquired.

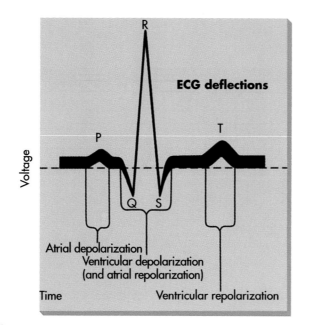

ECG deflections

Voltage

P

R

Q   S

T

Atrial depolarization

Ventricular depolarization
(and atrial repolarization)

Time　　　　　　Ventricular repolarization

Figure **2-53**
The ECG waveforms—
P, QRS, and T.

— *ECG Pearl*

The duration of the QT interval varies according to age, gender, and heart rate. As the heart rate increases, the QT interval shortens (decreases). As the heart rate decreases, the QT interval lengthens (increases). Because of the variability of the QT interval with the heart rate, it can be measured more accurately if it is corrected (adjusted) for the patient's heart rate. The corrected QT interval is noted as QTc. Many clinicians do not consider the QT interval abnormally long unless the QT interval corrected for the heart rate exceeds 0.44 sec.

R-R and P-P Intervals

The R-to-R (R-R) and P-to-P (P-P) intervals are used to determine the rate and regularity of a cardiac rhythm. To evaluate the regularity of the ventricular rhythm on a rhythm strip, the interval between two consecutive R-R waves is measured. The distance between succeeding R-R intervals is measured and compared. If the ventricular rhythm is regular, the R-R intervals will measure the same.

To evaluate the regularity of the atrial rhythm, the same procedure is used but the interval between two consecutive P-P waves is measured and compared to succeeding P-P intervals.

Figure 2-53 displays the ECG waveforms, and Figure 2-54 displays important ECG intervals discussed in this chapter.

ARTIFACT

Accurate ECG rhythm recognition requires a tracing in which the waveforms and intervals are free of distortion. Distortion of an ECG tracing by electrical activity that is noncardiac in origin is called **artifact**. Because artifact can mimic various cardiac dysrhythmias, including ventricular fibrillation, it is essential to evaluate the patient before initiating any medical intervention.

Artifact may be caused by loose electrodes, broken ECG cables or broken wires, muscle tremor, patient movement, external chest compressions, and 60-cycle interference. Proper

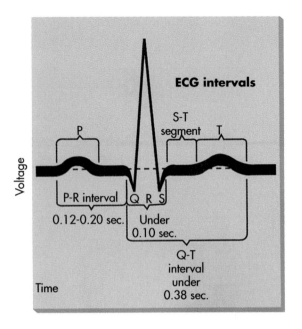

Figure 2-54
The ECG segments and intervals—PR interval, QRS duration, ST segment, QT interval.

preparation of the patient's skin and evaluation of the monitoring equipment (electrodes, wires) before use can minimize the problems associated with artifact.

—— *ECG Pearl*

Causes of Artifact
Loose electrodes
Broken ECG cables or broken wires
Muscle tremor
Patient movement
External chest compressions
60-cycle interference

Loose Electrodes

An irregular baseline may be identified by bizarre, irregular deflections of the baseline on the ECG paper. This may be the result of a broken lead wire, poor electrical contact, or a loose electrode (Figure 2-55). When hair is present in large quantities, it may interfere with electrode adhesion. When the gel is in contact with hair instead of skin, penetration will be hindered. A simple disposable razor may be used to remove hair before placing the electrodes, but many prefer to use electric clippers instead. Whatever device is used, it is important to remove the hair in the area where the electrodes will be applied.

Patient Movement/Muscle Activity

A wandering baseline may occur because of normal respiratory movement (particularly when electrodes have been applied directly over the ribs) or because of poor electrode contact with the patient's skin. Seizures, shivering, tense muscles, or Parkinson's disease may cause muscle tremor artifact (Figure 2-56). Consider clipping the ECG cable to the patient's clothing to minimize excessive movement.

60-Cycle (AC) Interference

A phenomenon known as 60-cycle interference may be caused by improperly grounded electrical equipment or other electrical interference (Figure 2-57). If 60-cycle interference is observed, check for crossing of cable wires with other electrical wires (e.g., bed control) or

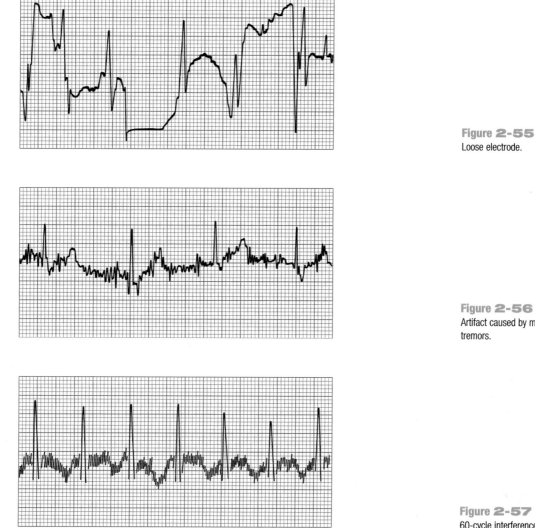

Figure 2-55
Loose electrode.

Figure 2-56
Artifact caused by muscle tremors.

Figure 2-57
60-cycle interference.

frayed and broken wires. Verify that all electrical equipment is properly grounded and that the cable electrode connections are clean.

ANALYZING A RHYTHM STRIP

It is essential to develop a systematic approach to rhythm analysis and consistently apply it when analyzing a rhythm strip. If you don't, you are more likely to miss something important. Begin analyzing the rhythm strip from left to right.

Assess the Rate

There are several methods used for calculating heart rate (Figure 2-58). A discussion of each method follows.

Method 1: Six-Second Method

Most ECG paper is printed with 1-sec or 3-sec markers on the top or bottom of the paper. To determine the ventricular rate, count the number of complete QRS complexes within a period of 6 seconds and multiply that number by 10 to find the number of complexes in 1 minute. This method may be used for regular and irregular rhythms. This is the simplest, quickest, and most commonly used method of rate measurement.

5 large boxes = 1 second, 15 large boxes = 3 seconds, 30 large boxes = 6 seconds.

Figure **2-58**
Calculating heart rate.
Method 1: Number of R-R
intervals in 6 seconds ×
10 (e.g., 8 × 10 =
80/min). Method 2:
Number of large boxes be-
tween QRS complexes di-
vided into 300 (e.g., 300
divided by 4 = 75/min).
Method 3: Number of
small boxes between QRS
complexes divided into
1500 (e.g., 1500 divided
by 18 = 84/min).

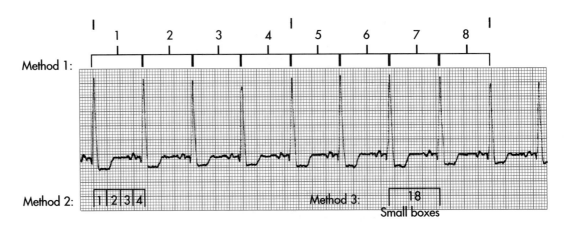

Method 2: Large Boxes

To determine the ventricular rate, count the number of large boxes between two consecutive R waves (R-R interval) and divide into 300. To determine the atrial rate, count the number of large boxes between two consecutive P waves (P-P interval) and divide into 300 (Table 2-7). This method is best used if the rhythm is regular; however, it may be used if the rhythm is irregular and a rate range (slowest and fastest rate) is given.

Method 3: Small Boxes

Each 1-mm box on the graph paper represents 0.04 sec. There are 1500 boxes in 1 minute (60 secs/min divided by 0.04 sec/box = 1500 boxes/min). To calculate the ventricular rate, count the number of small boxes between two consecutive R waves and divide into 1500. To determine the atrial rate, count the number of small boxes between two consecutive P waves and divide into 1500. This method is time-consuming but accurate. If the rhythm is irregular, a rate range should be given.

Method 4: Sequence Method

To determine ventricular rate, select an R wave that falls on a dark vertical line. Number the next 6 consecutive dark vertical lines as follows: 300, 150, 100, 75, 60, and 50 (Figure 2-59). Note where the next R wave falls in relation to the 6 dark vertical lines already marked. This is the heart rate.

Assess Rhythm/Regularity

The term rhythm is used to indicate the site of origin of an electrical impulse (e.g., sinus rhythm, junctional rhythm) and to describe the regularity or irregularity of waveforms.

For accuracy, the R-R or P-P intervals should be evaluated across an entire 6-second rhythm strip.

The waveforms on an ECG strip are evaluated for regularity by measuring the distance between the P waves and QRS complexes. If the rhythm is regular, the R-R intervals (or P-P intervals, if assessing atrial rhythm) are the same. Generally, a variation of plus or minus 10% is acceptable. For example, if there are 10 small boxes in an R-R interval, an R wave could be "off" by 1 small box and still be considered regular.

Rhythm/regularity may also be determined by counting the small squares between intervals and comparing the intervals with each other.

Ventricular Rhythm

To determine if the ventricular rhythm is regular or irregular, measure the distance between two consecutive R-R intervals. Place one point of a pair of calipers (or make a mark on a piece of paper) on the beginning of an R wave. Place the other point of the calipers (or make a second mark on the paper) on the beginning of the R wave of the next QRS complex. Without adjusting the calipers, evaluate each succeeding R-R interval. (If paper is used, lift the paper and move it across the rhythm strip). Compare the distance measured with the other R-R intervals. If the ventricular rhythm is regular, the R-R intervals will measure the same.

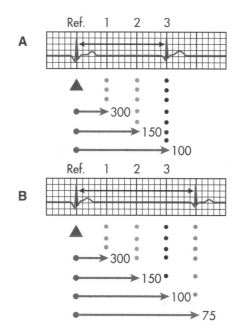

Figure 2-59
Determining heart rate—
sequence method. To mea-
sure the ventricular rate,
find a QRS complex that
falls on a heavy dark line.
Count 300, 150, 100, 75,
60, and 50 until a second
QRS complex occurs. This
will be the heart rate.
A, Heart rate = 100.
B, Heart rate = 75.

TABLE 2-7	Heart Rate Determination Based on the Number of Large Boxes		
Number of Large Boxes	**Heart Rate (bpm)**	**Number of Large Boxes**	**Heart Rate (bpm)**
1	300	6	50
2	150	7	43
3	100	8	38
4	75	9	33
5	60	10	30

Atrial Rhythm

To determine if the atrial rhythm is regular or irregular, follow the same procedure previously described for evaluation of ventricular rhythm but measure the distance between two consecutive P-P intervals (instead of R-R intervals) and compare that distance with the other P-P intervals. The P-P intervals will measure the same if the atrial rhythm is regular.

Terminology

Various terms may be used to describe an irregular rhythm. If the variation between the shortest and longest R-R intervals (or P-P intervals) is less than four small boxes (0.16 sec), the rhythm is termed *essentially regular*. For example, the underlying rhythm may be regular but the pattern may be periodically interrupted by ectopic beats that arise from a part of the heart other than the SA node.

An irregular rhythm may be normal, fast, or slow.

If the shortest and longest R-R intervals vary by more than 0.16 sec, the rhythm is considered *irregular*. A *regularly irregular rhythm* is one in which the R-R intervals are not the same, the shortest and longest R-R intervals vary by more than 0.16 sec, and there is a repeating pattern of irregularity. An *irregularly irregular rhythm* is one in which the R-R intervals are not the same, there is no repeating pattern of irregularity, and the shortest and longest R-R intervals vary by more than 0.16 sec.

A regularly irregular rhythm may be due to grouped beating (a repeating pattern of irregularity). An irregularly irregular rhythm may also be called a grossly or totally irregular rhythm.

—— *ECG Pearl*

Generally, a variation of plus or minus 10% is acceptable and the rhythm is still considered regular.

Identify and Examine P Waves

Some dysrhythmias may not have a P wave before the QRS complex such as atrial fibrillation, junctional rhythms, and ventricular rhythms.

To locate P waves, look to the left of each QRS complex. Normally, one P wave precedes each QRS complex, they occur regularly, and look similar in size, shape, and position. If no P wave is present, the rhythm originated in the AV junction or the ventricles.

If one P wave is present before each QRS and the QRS is **narrow**:

- Is the P wave positive? If so, the rhythm probably began in the SA node.
- Is the P wave negative or absent? If so, and the QRS complexes occur regularly, the rhythm probably started in the AV junction.

Assess Intervals (Evaluate Conduction)

PR Interval

Dysrhythmias such as AV blocks are associated with abnormal PR intervals.

Measure the PR interval. The PR interval is measured from the point where the P wave leaves the baseline to the beginning of the QRS complex. The normal PR interval is 0.12 to 0.20 sec. If the PR intervals are the same, they are said to be constant. If the PR intervals are different, is there a pattern? In some dysrhythmias, the duration of the PR interval will increase until a P wave appears with no QRS after it. This is referred to as "lengthening" of the PR interval. PR intervals that vary in duration and have no pattern are said to be "variable."

QRS Duration

A QRS complex of 0.10 second or less (narrow) is presumed to be supraventricular in origin.

Identify the QRS complexes and measure their duration. The beginning of the QRS is measured from the point where the first wave of the complex begins to deviate from the baseline. The point at which the last wave of the complex begins to level out at, above, or below the

TABLE 2-8	Summary of Normal Waveform Configuration			
Lead Type	Heart Surface Viewed	Lead	P Wave	Q Wave
Limb	Lateral	Lead I	Positive	Small
Limb	Inferior	Lead II	Positive	Small or none
Limb	Inferior	Lead III	Positive, negative, or biphasic	Small or none. If large, must also be present in aVF to be diagnostic.
Limb	None	aVR	Negative	Small, none, or large
Limb	Lateral	aVL	Positive, negative, or biphasic	Small, none, or large. If large, must also be present in lead I, V_5, or V_6 to be diagnostic.
Limb	Inferior	aVF	Positive	Small or none
Chest	Septum	V_1	Positive, negative, or biphasic	None; possible QS
Chest	Septum	V_2	Positive	None; possible QS
Chest	Anterior	V_3	Positive	Small or none
Chest	Anterior	V_4	Positive	Small or none
Chest	Lateral	V_5	Positive	Small
Chest	Lateral	V_6	Positive	Small

baseline marks the end of the QRS complex. The QRS is considered narrow (normal) if it measures 0.10 sec or less and wide if it measures more than 0.10 sec.

QT Interval

Measure the QT interval in the leads that show the largest amplitude T waves. The QT interval is measured from the beginning of the QRS complex to the end of the T wave. If there is no Q wave, measure the QT interval from the beginning of the R wave to the end of the T wave. If the measured QT interval is less than half the R-R interval, it is probably normal. This method of QT interval measurement works well as a general guideline until the ventricular rate exceeds 100 bpm.

Evaluate the Overall Appearance of the Rhythm

ST-segment

Determine the presence of ST-segment elevation or depression. The TP and PR-segments are used as the baseline from which to evaluate the degree of displacement of the ST-segment from the isoelectric line. The ST-segment is considered elevated if the segment is deviated above the baseline and is considered depressed if the segment deviates below it.

T Wave

Evaluate the T waves. Are the T waves upright and of normal height? The T wave following an abnormal QRS complex is usually opposite in direction of the QRS. Negative T waves suggest myocardial ischemia. Tall, pointed (peaked) T waves are commonly seen in hyperkalemia.

A summary of normal waveform configuration can be found in Table 2-8.

A prolonged QT interval indicates a lengthened relative refractory period (vulnerable period), which puts the ventricles at risk for life-threatening dysrhythmias such as TdP.

R Wave	S Wave	ST-segment	T Wave
Largest waveform	Small (< R) or none	May vary from +1 to −0.5 mm	Positive
Large	Small (< R) or none	May vary from +1 to −0.5 mm	Positive
None to large	None to large	May vary from +1 to −0.5 mm	Positive, negative, or biphasic
Small or none	Large (may be QS)	May vary from +1 to −0.5 mm	Negative
Small, none, or large	None to large	May vary from +1 to −0.5 mm	Positive, negative, or biphasic
Small, none, or large	None to large	May vary from +1 to −0.5 mm	Positive, negative, or biphasic
< S wave or none (QS)	Large (may be QS)	May vary from 0 to +3 mm	Positive, negative, or biphasic
< S wave or none (QS); progressively larger; small R' may be present	Large (may be QS)	May vary from 0 to +3 mm	Positive
R<S, R>S, or R = S; progressively larger	Large; S>R, S<R, or S=R	May vary from 0 to +3 mm	Positive
Progressively large waveform; R > S	Progressively smaller; S < R	Usually isoelectric; may vary from +1 to −0.5 mm	Positive
Progressively larger waveform; < 26 mm	Progressively smaller; < S wave in V₄	Usually isoelectric; may vary from +1 to −0.5 mm	Positive
Largest waveform; < 26 mm	Smallest; < S wave in V₅	Usually isoelectric; may vary from +1 to −0.5 mm	Positive

Interpret the Rhythm and Evaluate Its Clinical Significance

Interpret the rhythm, specifying the site of origin (pacemaker site) of the rhythm (sinus), the mechanism (bradycardia), and the ventricular rate. For example, "sinus bradycardia at 38 bpm." Evaluate the patient's clinical presentation to determine how he or she is tolerating the rate and rhythm.

REFERENCES

1. Conover MB: *The 12 electrocardiogram leads in understanding electrocardiography,* ed 7, St Louis, 1996, Mosby, pp 3-11.
2. Guyton AC, Hall JE: The normal electrocardiogram. *In textbook of medical physiology,* ed 9, Philadelphia, 1996, WB Saunders, pp 129-134.
3. Mirvis DM, Goldberger AL: Electrocardiography. In Braunwald E, editor: *Heart disease: a textbook of cardiovascular medicine,* ed 6, Philadelphia, 2001, WB Saunders, pp 82-128.
4. Phalen T, Aehlert B: *The 12-lead ECG in acute coronary syndromes.* 2006, Mosby.

S T O P & R E V I E W

Multiple Choice

Identify the letter of the choice that best completes the statement or answers the question.

_B_ 1. In an adult, the normal duration of the QRS complex is:
   a. 0.12-0.20 sec
   b. 0.06-0.10 sec
   c. 0.04-0.14 sec
   d. 0.20-0.38 sec

_D_ 2. The PR interval is considered prolonged if it is more than _____ seconds in duration.
   a. 0.06
   b. 0.12
   c. 0.18
   d. 0.20

_B_ 3. On the ECG, the time necessary for the spread of an electrical impulse through the AV node, bundle of His, right and left bundle branches, and the Purkinje fibers is reflected by the:
   a. TP-segment
   b. PR-segment
   c. QT interval
   d. QRS duration

Completion

Complete each sentence or statement.

4. The appearance of coved ("frowny face") ST-segment elevation is called a(n) ___Acute___ ___Injury___ ___Pattern___.

5. A line between waveforms is called a(n) ___Segment___.

6. _____ is the spread of an impulse through tissue already stimulated by that same impulse.

Short Answer

7. Indicate the inherent rates for each of the following pacemaker sites:

   Sinoatrial (SA) node: ___60-100___

   Atrioventricular (AV) junction: ___40-60___

   Ventricles: ___20-40___

8. List four (4) properties of cardiac cells.
   1.
   2.
   3.
   4.

9. List three (3) uses for ECG monitoring.
   1. heart rate
   2. Pacemaker function
   3. Evaluate effects of disease or injury of the heart function

10. Complete the following chart:

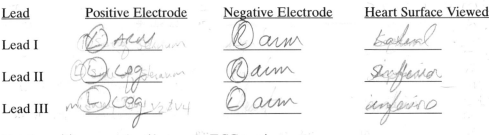

Lead	Positive Electrode	Negative Electrode	Heart Surface Viewed
Lead I	(+) Arm	(−) arm	lateral
Lead II	(+) Leg	(−) arm	inferior
Lead III	(+) Leg V₃ & V₄	(−) arm	inferior

11. List three (3) causes of artifact on an ECG tracing.
    1. loose electrodes
    2. Broken ECG wires/cables
    3. 60 cycle interference

12. List six (6) steps used in ECG rhythm analysis.
    1. Assess Rate
    2. Assess Rythem
    3. Identify & examine P waves
    4. Assess intervals
    5. Evaluate overall appearance of the rythem
    6. Interpret the Rythem & evaluate its clinical purpose

Matching

a. aVR, aVL, aVF

b. Specialized cells of the heart's electrical conduction system capable of spontaneously generating and conducting electrical impulses

c. Measured on the vertical axis of ECG paper

d. Corresponds with the onset of the QRS complex to the peak of the T wave

e. I, II, III

f. 20-40 bpm

g. Surface of the left ventricle viewed by leads II, III, and aVF

h. Working cells of the myocardium that contain contractile filaments

i. Distortion of an ECG tracing by electrical activity that is noncardiac in origin

j. Surface of the left ventricle viewed by leads I, aVL, V_5, and V_6

k. 40-60 bpm

l. Represents total ventricular activity—the time from ventricular depolarization to repolarization

m. Movement of ions across a cell membrane causing the inside of the cell to become more positive

n. 60-100 bpm

o. Corresponds with the downslope of the T wave

p. Measured on the horizontal axis of ECG paper

q. Movement of ions across a cell membrane in which the inside of the cell is restored to its negative charge

r. Portion of the ECG tracing used to determine the degree of ST-segment displacement

_I_ 13. Artifact

_Q_ 14. Repolarization

_N_ 15. Intrinsic rate of the SA node

_O_ 16. Relative refractory period

_J_ 17. Lateral

_E_ 18. Bipolar limb leads

_L_ 19. QT interval

_P_ 20. Time

_R_ 21. TP-segment

_G_ 22. Inferior

_A_ 23. Unipolar limb leads

_B_ 24. Pacemaker cells

_F_ 25. Intrinsic rate of ventricles

_M_ 26. Depolarization

_C_ 27. Voltage/amplitude

_D_ 28. Absolute refractory period

_K_ 29. Intrinsic rate of the AV junction

_H_ 30. Myocardial cells

ECG Crossword

Across

4. An important electrolyte that affects cardiac function
6. Depolarization is caused by the movement of __ into the cell.
7. The ability of cardiac muscle cells to respond to an outside stimulus
9. The spread of an impulse through tissue already stimulated by that same impulse
12. Amplitude of a waveform is measured in __. *millivolts*
14. The P wave represents __ depolarization.
16. A(n) __ pacemaker is a pacemaker site other than the SA node.
18. The __ interval represents total ventricular activity. *QT*
19. The QRS complex represents __ depolarization. *ventricular*
21. Several waveforms *complex*
22. During this period, a weaker than normal stimulus can cause depolarization of cardiac cells.
25. This medication will increase the heart rate and force of contraction.
27. The T wave represents ventricular __.
28. One of the directions in the horizontal plane *Anterior*
29. Element or compound that, when melted or dissolved in water or another solvent, breaks into ions *Electrolyte*

Down

1. A waveform and a segment
2. Each electrode placed in a "V" position is a __ electrode. *Positive*
3. On ECG paper, each __ 1-mm box represents 0.04 sec.
4. The ability of a membrane channel to conduct electrolytes once it is open
5. The difference in electrical charges across the cell membrane *membrane Potential*
8. The "a" in aVR, aVL, and aVF *Augmented*
10. Electrocardiogram
11. This condition causes ST-segment elevation in all or virtually all leads.
13. Phase 3 of the action potential corresponds with the __ __ on the ECG. *T-WAVE*
15. An ECG machine is a sophisticated __. *Voltmeter*
17. When the inside of a cell is more negative than the outside, it is said to be __.
19. The relative refractory period is also called the __ period.
20. The stimulus that alters the electrical charges across the cell membrane may be electrical, mechanical, or __. *chemical ?*
23. In leads I and II, the right arm is __. *Negative*
24. $\frac{1}{1000}$ of a volt *millivolt ?*
26. Electrically charged particle *Ion*

PRACTICE *Rhythm Strips*

Identification and Measurements

For each of the following rhythm strips determine the atrial and ventricular rates; label the P wave, QRS complex, and T wave; and measure the PR interval, QRS duration, and QT interval. Determine if the atrial and ventricular rhythm for each strip is regular or irregular. *Not all waveforms will be present in each of the following rhythm strips.*

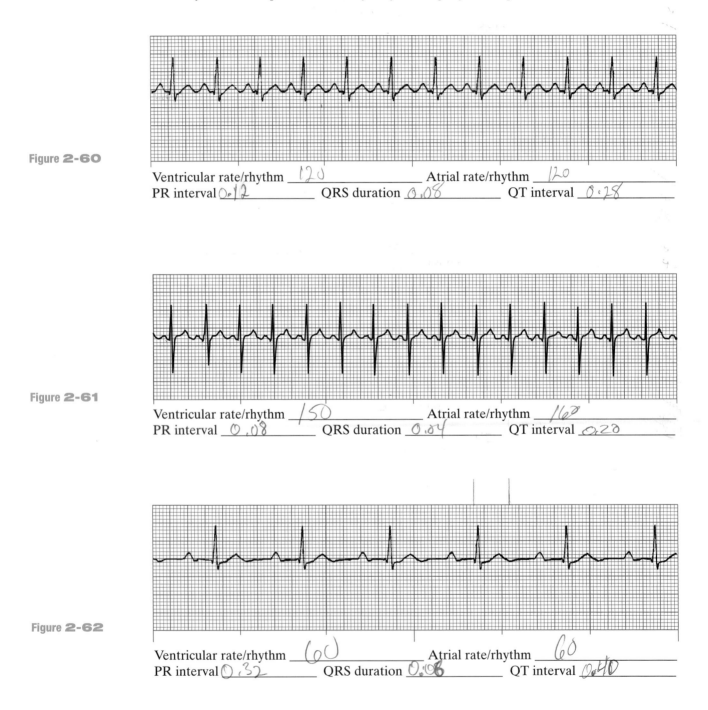

Figure **2-60**

Ventricular rate/rhythm __120__   Atrial rate/rhythm __120__
PR interval __0.12__   QRS duration __0.08__   QT interval __0.28__

Figure **2-61**

Ventricular rate/rhythm __150__   Atrial rate/rhythm __160__
PR interval __0.08__   QRS duration __0.04__   QT interval __0.20__

Figure **2-62**

Ventricular rate/rhythm __60__   Atrial rate/rhythm __60__
PR interval __0.32__   QRS duration __0.08__   QT interval __0.40__

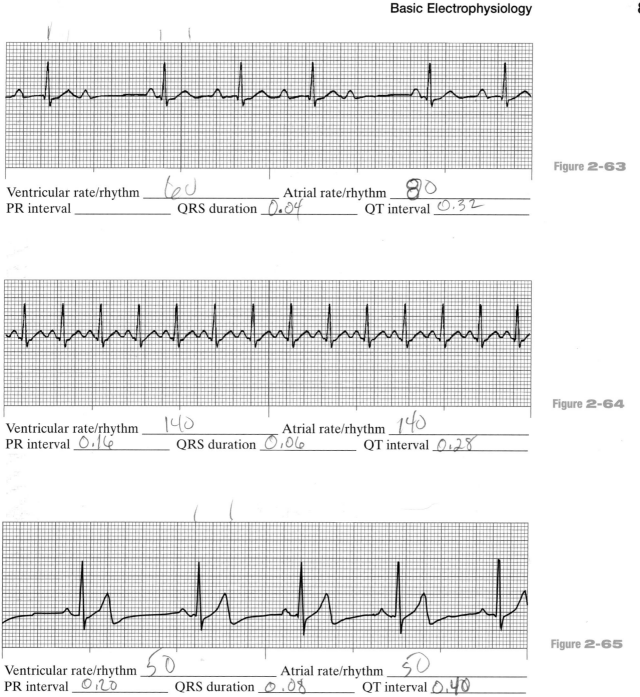

Figure 2-63

Ventricular rate/rhythm ___60___   Atrial rate/rhythm ___80___
PR interval _____   QRS duration _0.04_   QT interval _0.32_

Figure 2-64

Ventricular rate/rhythm ___140___   Atrial rate/rhythm ___140___
PR interval _0.16_   QRS duration _0.06_   QT interval _0.28_

Figure 2-65

Ventricular rate/rhythm ___50___   Atrial rate/rhythm ___50___
PR interval _0.20_   QRS duration _0.08_   QT interval _0.40_

Sinus Mechanisms

OBJECTIVES

On completion of this chapter, you should be able to:

1. Describe the ECG characteristics of a sinus rhythm.
2. Describe the ECG characteristics, possible causes, signs and symptoms, and emergency management of each of the following dysrhythmias that originate in the sinoatrial node:
   a. Sinus bradycardia
   b. Sinus tachycardia
   c. Sinus arrhythmia
   d. Sinoatrial block
   e. Sinus arrest

INTRODUCTION

The normal heartbeat is the result of an electrical impulse that starts in the sinoatrial (SA) node. Normally, pacemaker cells within the SA node spontaneously depolarize more rapidly than other cardiac cells. As a result the SA node usually dominates other areas that may be depolarizing at a slightly slower rate. The impulse is sent to cells at the outside edge of the SA node and then to the myocardial cells of the surrounding atrium.

A rhythm that begins in the SA node has the following characteristics:

- A positive (upright) P wave before each QRS complex
- P waves that look alike
- A constant PR interval
- A regular atrial and ventricular rhythm (usually)

An electrical impulse that begins in the SA node may be affected by the following:

- Medications
- Diseases or conditions that cause the heart rate to speed up, slow down, or beat irregularly
- Diseases or conditions that delay or block the impulse from leaving the SA node
- Diseases or conditions that prevent an impulse from being generated in the SA node

Most (but not all) rhythms that begin in the SA node are regular.

A **dysrhythmia** (also called an arrhythmia) is a sign of abnormal electrical activity.

SINUS RHYTHM

Sinus rhythm is the name given to a normal heart rhythm. Sinus rhythm reflects normal electrical activity—that is, the rhythm starts in the SA node and then heads down the normal conduction pathway through the atria, AV junction, bundle branches, and ventricles. This results in depolarization of the atria and ventricles. The SA node normally produces electrical impulses faster than any other part of the heart's conduction system. As a result, the SA node is normally the heart's primary pacemaker. A person's heart rate varies with age (Table 3-1). In adults and adolescents, the SA node normally fires at a regular rate of 60 to 100 bpm.

Sinus rhythm is sometimes called a regular sinus rhythm (RSR) or normal sinus rhythm (NSR).

—— *ECG Pearl* 〰〰〰〰〰〰〰〰〰〰〰〰〰〰〰〰〰〰〰〰〰〰〰〰〰〰

In this chapter you will begin learning the characteristics of specific ECG rhythms. Study these characteristics carefully and commit them to memory. Throughout this text, all ECG characteristics pertain to the adult patient unless otherwise noted.

How Do I Recognize It?

Figure 3-1 is an example of a sinus rhythm. Let's look at this rhythm strip closely. A sinus rhythm has a regular atrial and ventricular rhythm. Find the QRS complexes on the rhythm strip. Place one point of your calipers (or make a mark on a piece of paper) on the beginning

Remember, a variation of plus or minus 10% is acceptable and the rhythm is still considered regular.

TABLE 3-1 Normal Heart Rates by Age	
Age	Beats per Minute* (bpm)
Infant (1 to 12 months)	100-160
Toddler (1 to 3 years)	90-150
Preschooler (4 to 5 years)	80-140
School-age (6 to 12 years)	70-120
Adolescent (13 to 18 years)	60-100
Adult	60-100

*Pulse rates for a sleeping child may be 10% lower than the low rate listed in age group.

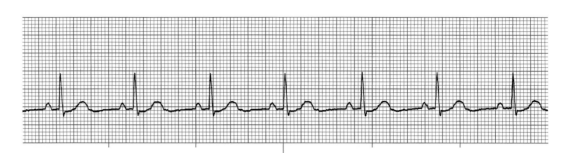

TABLE 3-2	**Characteristics of Sinus Rhythm**
Rate	60-100 bpm
Rhythm	P-P interval regular, R-R interval regular
P waves	Positive (upright) in lead II, one precedes each QRS complex, P waves look alike
PR interval	0.12-0.20 second and constant from beat to beat
QRS duration	0.10 second or less unless an intraventricular conduction delay exists

of an R wave. Place the other point of the calipers (or make a second mark on the paper) on the beginning of the R wave of the next QRS complex. Without adjusting the calipers, evaluate each succeeding R-R interval. (If you are using paper, lift the paper and move it across the rhythm strip.) The R-R intervals are regular. Since you have already identified the R waves, determine the ventricular rate. In this rhythm strip, the ventricular rate is 70 bpm. Remember, the built-in (intrinsic) rate for a rhythm that begins in the SA node is 60 to 100 bpm. Therefore the rate of the rhythm in our example fits within the criteria for a sinus rhythm.

Now look to the left of the QRS complexes to find the P waves on the rhythm strip. A rhythm that begins in the SA node should have a positive (upright) P wave (in lead II) before each QRS complex. When you look at this rhythm strip, you can see one upright P wave before each QRS complex. Every P wave looks alike. Measure the P-to-P interval to see if the P waves occur regularly. Then determine the atrial rate. You'll find that the P waves occur regularly at a rate of 70 bpm.

If there is a delay in conduction through the bundle branches, the QRS may be wide (>0.10 sec).

Now measure the PR interval and QRS duration. In a sinus rhythm, the PR interval measures 0.12 to 0.20 sec and is constant from beat to beat. In this example, the PR interval is 0.16 sec. The QRS complex normally measures 0.10 sec or less. In our example, the QRS measures 0.06 sec. Now interpret the rhythm, specifying the site of origin (pacemaker site) of the rhythm and the ventricular rate. Since the rhythm shown in Figure 3-1 fits the ECG criteria for a sinus rhythm, your identification should be, "Sinus rhythm at 70 bpm." A summary of the ECG characteristics of a sinus rhythm are shown in Table 3-2.

SINUS BRADYCARDIA

brady = slow

If the SA node fires at a rate slower than normal for the patient's age, the rhythm is called **sinus bradycardia**. The rhythm starts in the SA node and then travels the normal pathway of conduction through the atria, AV junction, bundle branches, and ventricles. This results in atrial and ventricular depolarization. In adults and adolescents, a sinus bradycardia has a heart rate of less than 60 bpm. The term *severe sinus bradycardia* is sometimes used to describe a sinus bradycardia with a rate of less than 40 bpm.

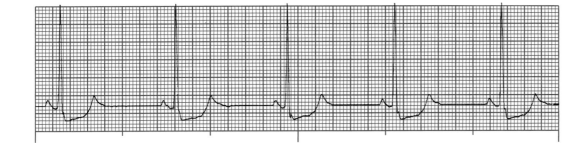

Figure 3-2
Sinus bradycardia at
48 bpm, ST-segment
depression.

TABLE 3-3	**Characteristics of Sinus Bradycardia**
Rate	Less than 60 bpm
Rhythm	P-P interval regular, R-R interval regular
P waves	Positive (upright) in lead II, one precedes each QRS complex, P waves look alike
PR interval	0.12-0.20 second and constant from beat to beat
QRS duration	0.10 second or less unless an intraventricular conduction delay exists

How Do I Recognize It?

Figure 3-2 is an example of sinus bradycardia. Table 3-3 lists the ECG characteristics of sinus bradycardia. You'll note they are the same as the characteristics of a sinus rhythm with one exception—the rate. The rate of a sinus rhythm is 60 to 100 bpm. The rate of a sinus bradycardia is less than 60 bpm. In our example, the atrial and ventricular rate is 48 bpm. ST-segment depression is also present. Correct identification of this rhythm would be, "Sinus bradycardia at 48 bpm with ST-segment depression."

The QT interval may be longer than normal because of the slower heart rate.

What Causes It?

Sinus bradycardia occurs in adults during sleep and in well-conditioned athletes. It is also present in up to 35% of people younger than 25 years of age while at rest. Sinus bradycardia is common in some myocardial infarctions. Stimulation of the vagus nerve can also result in slowing of the heart rate. For example, coughing, vomiting, straining to have a bowel movement, or sudden exposure of the face to cold water can result in slowing of the heart rate. Carotid sinus pressure can also slow the heart rate. In people who have a sensitive carotid sinus, slowing of the heart rate can occur when a tight collar is worn or with the impact of the stream of water on the neck while in the shower. Other causes of sinus bradycardia are shown in the ECG Pearl below.

Prolonged standing can also cause slowing of the heart rate.

Remember that cardiac output equals stroke volume times heart rate. Therefore a decrease in either stroke volume or heart rate may result in a decrease in cardiac output. A patient with an unusually slow heart may complain of weakness and/or dizziness. Fainting (syncope) can occur. Decreasing cardiac output will eventually produce hemodynamic compromise. Signs and symptoms of hemodynamic compromise are shown in the ECG Pearl on the following page.

— *ECG Pearl*

Causes of Sinus Bradycardia
- Inferior myocardial infarction
- Posterior myocardial infarction
- Disease of the SA node
- Vagal stimulation
- Hypoxia
- Hypothermia
- Increased intracranial pressure
- Hypothyroidism
- Hypokalemia
- Post heart transplant
- Hyperkalemia
- Obstructive sleep apnea
- Medications such as calcium channel blockers, digitalis, beta-blockers, amiodarone, and sotalol

ECG Pearl

Signs and Symptoms of Hemodynamic Compromise
- Changes in mental status (restlessness, confusion, possible loss of consciousness)
- Low blood pressure
- Chest pain
- Shortness of breath
- Signs of shock
- Congestive heart failure
- Pulmonary congestion
- Fall in urine output
- Cold, clammy skin

What Do I Do About It?

Many patients tolerate a heart rate of 50 to 60 bpm but become symptomatic when the rate drops below 50 bpm.

Assess how the patient tolerates the rhythm at rest and with activity. If the patient has no symptoms, no treatment is necessary. If the patient is symptomatic because of the slow rate, treatment may include oxygen, IV access, and administration of atropine and/or transcutaneous pacing. In the setting of a myocardial infarction, sinus bradycardia is often transient. A slow heart rate can be beneficial in the patient who has had an MI (and has no symptoms due to the slow rate). This is because the heart's demand for oxygen is less when the heart rate is slow.

Drug Pearl

Atropine is a vagolytic medication used to increase heart rate. *Vago* refers to the vagus nerves (right and left), which are main nerves of the parasympathetic division of the autonomic nervous system (ANS). *Lytic* refers to "lyse," which means to interfere with. Atropine works by blocking chemicals at the endings of the vagus nerves. This allows more activity from the sympathetic division of the ANS. As a result, the rate at which the SA node can fire is increased. Atropine also increases the rate at which an impulse is conducted through the AV node. It has little or no effect on the force of contraction.

SINUS TACHYCARDIA

tachy = fast

If the SA node fires at a rate faster than normal for the patient's age, the rhythm is called **sinus tachycardia.** Sinus tachycardia begins and ends gradually. The rhythm starts in the SA node and heads down the normal pathway of conduction through the atria, AV junction, bundle branches, and ventricles. This results in atrial and ventricular depolarization.

How Do I Recognize It?

At very fast rates, it may be hard to tell the difference between a P wave and T wave.

The QT interval normally shortens as heart rate increases.

Figure 3-3 is an example of sinus tachycardia. Table 3-4 lists the ECG characteristics of sinus tachycardia. When looking at the rhythm strip, you'll see that it looks much like a sinus rhythm except that it is faster. Keep in mind that normal heart rates vary with age. In adults, the rate associated with sinus tachycardia is usually between 101 and 180 bpm. Because an infant or child's heart rate can transiently increase during episodes of crying, pain, or in the presence of a fever, the term *tachycardia* is used to describe a significant and persistent increase in heart rate. In infants, a tachycardia is a heart rate of more than 200 bpm. In a child older than 5 years of age, a tachycardia is a heart rate of more than 160 bpm. In our example, the atrial and ventricular rate is 129 bpm. ST-segment depression is also present. If you were asked to say what Figure 3-3 shows, the correct response would be, "Sinus tachycardia at 129 bpm with ST-segment depression."

What Causes It?

Sinus tachycardia is a normal response to the body's demand for increased oxygen because of many conditions (see the ECG Pearl on the following page). The patient is often aware of an increase in heart rate. Some patients complain of palpitations, a racing heart, or "pounding" in their chest.

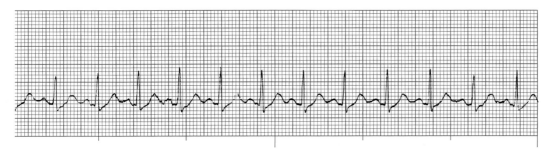

Figure 3-3
Sinus tachycardia at
129 bpm.

TABLE 3-4	Characteristics of Sinus Tachycardia
Rate	101-180 bpm
Rhythm	P-P interval regular, R-R interval regular
P waves	Positive (upright) in lead II, one precedes each QRS complex, P waves look alike
	At very fast rates it may be hard to tell the difference between a P wave and a T wave
PR interval	0.12-0.20 second (may shorten with faster rates) and constant from beat to beat
QRS duration	0.10 second or less unless an intraventricular conduction delay exists

In a patient with coronary artery disease, sinus tachycardia can cause problems. The heart's demand for oxygen increases as the heart rate increases. As the heart rate increases, there is less time for the ventricles to fill and less blood for the ventricles to pump out with each contraction. This can lead to decreased cardiac output. Since the coronary arteries fill when the ventricles are at rest, rapid heart rates decrease the time for coronary artery filling. This decreases the heart's blood supply. Chest discomfort can result if the supply of blood and oxygen to the heart is inadequate. Sinus tachycardia in a patient who is having an acute MI may be an early warning signal for heart failure, cardiogenic shock, and more serious dysrhythmias.

This rhythm is seen in some patients with acute MI, especially those with an anterior infarction.

ECG Pearl

Causes of Sinus Tachycardia
- Exercise
- Fever
- Pain
- Fear and anxiety
- Hypoxia
- Congestive heart failure
- Acute myocardial infarction
- Infection
- Sympathetic stimulation
- Shock
- Dehydration, hypovolemia
- Pulmonary embolism
- Hyperthyroidism
- Medications such as epinephrine, atropine, dopamine, and dobutamine
- Caffeine-containing beverages
- Nicotine
- Drugs such as cocaine, amphetamines, "ecstasy," cannabis

What Do I Do About It?

Treatment for sinus tachycardia is directed at correcting the underlying cause—for example, fluid replacement, relief of pain, removal of offending medications or substances, reducing fever, and/or relieving anxiety. Sinus tachycardia in a patient experiencing an acute MI may be treated with beta-blockers. Beta-blockers such as atenolol (Tenormin) or metoprolol (Lopressor) are given to slow the heart rate and decrease myocardial oxygen demand, provided there are no signs of heart failure or other contraindications to beta-blocker therapy.

Never shock a sinus tachycardia—treat the reason for the tachycardia.

— ECG Pearl

In a patient presenting with an acute coronary syndrome, common sites for chest discomfort include the upper part of chest; beneath the sternum radiating to the neck and jaw; beneath the sternum radiating down the left arm; epigastric; epigastric radiating to the neck, jaw, and arms; neck and jaw; left shoulder; and the intrascapular region.

SINUS ARRHYTHMIA

As you have seen so far, the SA node fires quite regularly most of the time. When it fires irregularly, the resulting rhythm is called **sinus arrhythmia**. Sinus arrhythmia begins in the SA node and follows the normal pathway of conduction through the atria, AV junction, bundle branches, and ventricles, resulting in atrial and ventricular depolarization. Sinus arrhythmia that is associated with the phases of respiration and changes in intrathoracic pressure is called *respiratory sinus arrhythmia*. Sinus arrhythmia that is not related to the respiratory cycle is called *nonrespiratory sinus arrhythmia*.

How Do I Recognize It?

A sinus arrhythmia usually occurs at a rate of 60 to 100 bpm. If sinus arrhythmia is associated with a slower than normal rate, it is called *sinus brady-arrhythmia*. If the rhythm is associated with a faster than normal rate, it is known as *sinus tachy-arrhythmia*.

Let's look at the rhythm strip in Figure 3-4. How does this rhythm differ from the others we have discussed so far? Without using calipers or a piece of paper, you can see that it is irregular. Recognizing that, the rhythm can't be a sinus rhythm (because a sinus rhythm is regular). Now, let's determine the atrial and ventricular rate. Since the rhythm is irregular, it is best to give a rate range. To do that we will need to find the slowest part of the rhythm and calculate that rate. We will then need to find the fastest part of the rhythm and calculate that rate. Looking from left to right, the slowest part of this rhythm strip appears to be between the fifth and sixth beats (they have the longest R-R and P-P interval). The rate between these beats is 54 bpm. The distance between the second and third beats and fourth and fifth beats appears to be the same. These beats are the fastest in this rhythm strip (they have the shortest R-R and P-P interval). The rate between these beats is 88 bpm. This rhythm strip was obtained from a healthy 26-year-old adult at rest. If we were able to see the patient and watch his respiratory rate and ECG at the same time, you would see a pattern. The patient's heart rate increases gradually during inspiration (R-R intervals shorten) and decreases with expiration (R-R intervals lengthen). Looking closely at the rest of the rhythm strip, you can see one upright P wave before each QRS complex. The PR interval and QRS duration are within normal limits. To identify this rhythm, we will call it a sinus arrhythmia at 54 to 88 bpm. Table 3-5 lists the characteristics of sinus arrhythmia.

What Causes It?

In respiratory sinus arrhythmia, the changes in rhythm disappear when the patient holds his breath.

Respiratory sinus arrhythmia is a normal phenomenon that occurs with changes in intrathoracic pressure. The heart rate increases with inspiration (R-R intervals shorten) and decreases with expiration (R-R intervals lengthen). Sinus arrhythmia is most commonly observed in children and adults younger than 30 years of age.

Nonrespiratory sinus arrhythmia can be seen in people with normal hearts but is more likely in older individuals and in those with heart disease. It is common after acute inferior wall MI and may be seen with increased intracranial pressure. Nonrespiratory sinus arrhythmia may be the result of effects of medications (such as digitalis and morphine) or carotid sinus pressure.

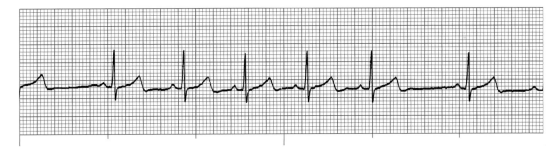

Figure 3-4
Sinus arrhythmia at 54 to
88 bpm.

TABLE 3-5	Characteristics of Sinus Arrhythmia
Rate	Usually 60-100 bpm, but may be slower or faster
Rhythm	Irregular, phasic with respiration; heart rate increases gradually during inspiration (R-R intervals shorten) and decreases with expiration (R-R intervals lengthen)
P waves	Positive (upright) in lead II, one precedes each QRS complex, P waves look alike
PR interval	0.12-0.20 second and constant from beat to beat
QRS duration	0.10 second or less unless an intraventricular conduction delay exists

What Do I Do About It?

Sinus arrhythmia usually does not require treatment unless it is accompanied by a slow heart rate that causes hemodynamic compromise. If hemodynamic compromise is present, IV atropine may be indicated.

SINOATRIAL BLOCK

In sinoatrial (SA) block, the pacemaker cells within the SA node initiate an impulse but it is blocked as it exits the SA node. This is thought to occur because of failure of the transitional cells in the SA node to conduct the impulse from the pacemaker cells to the surrounding atrium. Thus SA block is a disorder of conductivity.

Sinoatrial block is also called sinus exit block.

How Do I Recognize It?

The rhythm of the SA node is not affected by SA block because impulses are generated regularly. However, because an impulse is blocked as it exits the SA node, the atria are not activated. This appears on the ECG as a single missed beat (a P wave, QRS complex, and T wave are missing). The pause caused by the missed beat is the same as (or an exact multiple of) the distance between two P-P intervals of the underlying rhythm.

Look at the example of SA block in Figure 3-5. As you quickly scan the rhythm strip from left to right, the pause between the third and fourth beats should be obvious. The atrial and ventricular rhythm is irregular because of the pause. (It is also correct to say that the atrial and ventricular rhythms are regular except for the event; in this case, the pause is the event). Begin analyzing the rhythm strip by determining atrial and ventricular rate and regularity. Since there is a pause, it is best to give a rate range. In our example, the rate varies from 36 to 71 bpm. You can see a positive P wave in front of each QRS complex. The P waves look alike. The PR interval is normal and constant from beat to beat. The QRS complex is normal. Because the P waves are upright and each P wave is associated with a QRS complex, we know that the underlying rhythm came from the SA node. So far, we can identify this rhythm as a sinus rhythm with a ventricular rate of 36 to 71 bpm.

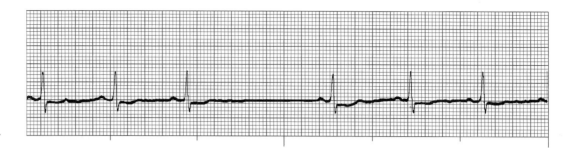

Figure 3-5
Sinus rhythm at a rate of
36 to 71 bpm with an
episode of sinoatrial block.

TABLE 3-6	**Characteristics of Sinoatrial Block**
Rate	Usually normal but varies because of the pause
Rhythm	Irregular due to the pause(s) caused by the SA block — the pause is the same as (or an exact multiple of) the distance between two other P-P intervals
P waves	Positive (upright) in lead II, P waves look alike. When present, one precedes each QRS complex.
PR interval	0.12-0.20 second and constant from beat to beat
QRS duration	0.10 second or less unless an intraventricular conduction delay exists

Now we need to figure out what caused the pause between beats 3 and 4. First, look to the left of the pause and examine the waveforms of the beat that comes before the pause. Compare these waveforms to the others in the rhythm strip. It is important to do this because sometimes waveforms "hide" on top of other waveforms and distort their shape. In our example, nothing seems to be amiss. Now use your calipers or paper and plot P waves and R waves from left to right across the strip. When you do this, make a mark on the rhythm strip where the next PQRST cycle should have occurred. You will find that exactly one PQRST cycle is missing. The P-P interval is an exact multiple of the distance between two P-P intervals of the underlying sinus rhythm. This occurred because impulses were generated regularly but failed to exit the SA node between beats 3 and 4. To complete our identification of this rhythm, we will explain the pause as an SA block. Putting it all together, we have a sinus rhythm at a rate of 36 to 71 bpm with an episode of SA block. Table 3-6 lists the ECG characteristics of SA block.

What Causes It?

SA block is rather uncommon. Causes of SA block are shown in the ECG Pearl below. If episodes of SA block are frequent and/or accompanied by a slow heart rate, the patient may show signs and symptoms of hemodynamic compromise.

—— *ECG Pearl*

Causes of SA Block
- Acute MI
- Medications such as digitalis, quinidine, procainamide, or salicylates
- Coronary artery disease
- Myocarditis
- Congestive heart failure
- Carotid sinus sensitivity
- Increased vagal tone

What Do I Do About It?

If the episodes of SA block are transient and there are no significant signs or symptoms, the patient is observed. If signs of hemodynamic compromise are present and are the result of medication toxicity, the offending agents should be withheld. If the episodes of SA block are frequent, IV atropine, temporary pacing, or insertion of a permanent pacemaker may be needed.

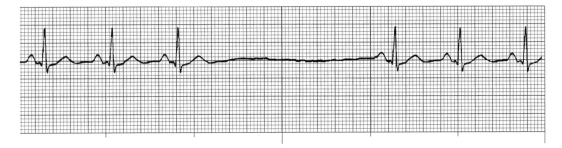

Figure 3-6
Sinus rhythm at a rate of
24 to 81 bpm with an
episode of sinus arrest.

TABLE 3-7	**Characteristics of Sinus Arrest**
Rate	Usually normal but varies because of the pause
Rhythm	Irregular—the pause is of undetermined length (more than one PQRST complex is missing) and is not the same distance as other P-P intervals
P waves	Positive (upright) in lead II, P waves look alike. When present, one precedes each QRS complex.
PR interval	0.12-0.20 second and constant from beat to beat
QRS duration	0.10 second or less unless an intraventricular conduction delay exists

SINUS ARREST

Sinus arrest is a disorder of the property of automaticity. In sinus arrest, the pacemaker cells of the SA node fail to initiate an electrical impulse for one or more beats. When the SA node fails to initiate an impulse, an escape pacemaker site (the AV junction or ventricles) should assume responsibility for pacing the heart. If they do not, you will see absent PQRST complexes on the ECG.

Sinus arrest is also called sinus pause or SA arrest.

How Do I Recognize It?

Figure 3-6 shows an example of sinus arrest. Looking at the rhythm strip from left to right, you can see a period of no electrical activity between the third and fourth beats. Begin analyzing the rhythm strip by determining atrial and ventricular rate and regularity. Because the rhythmicity of this dysrhythmia occurs as the result of a specific event and the remainder of the rhythm is regular, the regularity (rhythm) may be described as irregular or as regular except for the event. Since there is a pause, it is best to give a rate range. In our example, the rate varies from 24 to 81 bpm. You can see a positive P wave in front of each QRS complex. The P waves look alike. The PR interval is normal and constant from beat to beat. The QRS complex is normal. Because the P waves are upright and each P wave is associated with a QRS complex, we know that the underlying rhythm came from the SA node. Therefore the underlying rhythm is a sinus rhythm with a ventricular rate of 24 to 81 bpm.

Now let's try to explain what caused the pause between beats 3 and 4. Look to the left of the pause and examine the waveforms of the beat that comes before the pause. Compare these waveforms to the others in the rhythm strip. There does not appear to be any distortion of the waveforms. Using your calipers or paper, plot P waves and R waves from left to right across the strip. When you do this, make a mark on the rhythm strip where the next PQRST cycles should have occurred. You will find that more than one PQRST cycle is missing. Because the SA node periodically failed to produce impulses, the P-P intervals are not exact multiples of other P-P intervals. This is characteristic of a sinus arrest. To complete our identification of this rhythm strip, we must add this explanation for the pause we saw. Therefore our final identification is a sinus rhythm at a rate of 24 to 81 bpm with an episode of sinus arrest. Table 3-7 lists the ECG characteristics of sinus arrest.

What Causes It?

Causes of sinus arrest include hypoxia, myocardial ischemia or infarction, hyperkalemia, digitalis toxicity, reactions to medications such as beta-blockers and calcium channel blockers, carotid sinus sensitivity, or increased vagal tone. Signs of hemodynamic compromise such as weakness, lightheadedness, dizziness, or syncope may be associated with this dysrhythmia.

What Do I Do About It?

If the episodes of sinus arrest are transient and there are no significant signs or symptoms, observe the patient. If hemodynamic compromise is present, IV atropine may be indicated. If the episodes of sinus arrest are frequent and/or prolonged (more than 3 seconds), temporary pacing or insertion of a permanent pacemaker may be warranted.

Table 3-8 lists a summary of the characteristics of sinus mechanisms.

TABLE 3-8	Sinus Mechanisms—Summary of Characteristics		
	Sinus Rhythm	Sinus Bradycardia	Sinus Tachycardia
Rate	60-100	<60	101-180
Rhythm	Regular	Regular	Regular
P Waves (lead II)	Positive, one precedes each QRS	Positive, one precedes each QRS	Positive, one precedes each QRS
PR Interval	0.12-0.20 sec	0.12-0.20 sec	0.12-0.20 sec
QRS	0.10 sec or less unless abnormally conducted	0.10 sec or less unless abnormally conducted	0.10 sec or less unless abnormally conducted

Sinus Arrhythmia	SA Block	Sinus Arrest
Usually 60-100	Varies	Varies
Irregular, typically phasic with respiration	Regular except for the event; pause is the same (or an exact multiple of) as the distance between two P-P intervals of underlying rhythm	Regular except for the event; pause of undetermined length—Not a multiple of other P-P Intervals
Positive, one precedes each QRS	When present, positive, one precedes each QRS	When present, positive, one precedes each QRS
0.12-0.20 sec	When present, 0.12-0.20 sec	When present, 0.12-0.20 sec
0.10 sec or less unless abnormally conducted	0.10 sec or less unless abnormally conducted	0.10 sec or less unless abnormally conducted

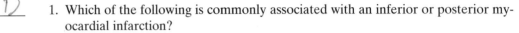

S T O P & **REVIEW**

Multiple Choice

Identify the letter of the choice that best completes the statement or answers the question.

_D_   1. Which of the following is commonly associated with an inferior or posterior myocardial infarction?
a. Sinus tachycardia
b. Sinus bradycardia
c. SA block
d. Sinus arrhythmia

_D_   2. Which of the following correctly reflects the ECG criteria for a sinus rhythm?
a. P waves that are uniform in appearance and inverted in lead II, one preceding
each QRS complex
b. PR interval exceeding 0.20 second
c. More P waves than QRS complexes
d. P waves that are uniform in appearance and upright in lead II, one preceding
each QRS complex

Matching

a. Beta-blockers
b. Sinus arrhythmia
c. Purkinje fibers/ventricles
d. 60-100 bpm
e. Atropine
f. Sinus arrest
g. Dysrhythmia
h. AV junction

i. Conductivity
j. 0.06-0.10 sec
k. Automaticity
l. SA block
m. Less than 60 bpm
n. Stroke volume times heart rate
o. Sinus tachycardia
p. Smooth, rounded, upright

_J_   3. Normal QRS duration in an adult
_K_   4. Sinus arrest is a disorder of __.
_L_   5. Dysrhythmia with a pause of unde-
termined length that is not the same
distance as other P-P intervals
_M_   6. Rate associated with a sinus bradycardia
_F/O_ 7. SA block is a disorder of __.
8. Dysrhythmia that originates from
the SA node and has a ventricular
rate of 101-180 bpm
_P_   9. Appearance of P waves that originate from the SA node
_N_ 10. Cardiac output
_C_ 11. Pacemaker with an intrinsic rate of
20-40 bpm
_D_ 12. Normal rate for a sinus rhythm
_E_ 13. This medication may be used to increase heart rate if the QRS is narrow and the patient is symptomatic
because the rate is slow

_F_ 14. Dysrhythmia with a pause that is
the same as (or an exact multiple
of) the distance between two
other P-P intervals
_A_ 15. Medications that may be administered to slow the heart rate and
decrease myocardial oxygen
demand
_B_ 16. Common dysrhythmia associated
with respiratory rate
_H_ 17. If the SA node fails to generate
an impulse, the next (escape)
pacemaker that should generate
an impulse
_G_ 18. Any disturbance or abnormality
in a normal rhythmic pattern

Short Answer

19. Without looking back in the chapter, see if you can answer the following questions about the characteristics of a sinus rhythm.

Rate: _60 – 100_

Rhythm: _Atrial & ventricular rythum   P–P & R–R are regular_

P waves: _Positive & upright_

PR interval (PRI): _0.12 – 0.20_

QRS duration: _0.10_

Keep the ECG characteristics of sinus rhythm in mind as you answer the following questions.

20. What is the most important difference between sinus rhythm and sinus bradycardia?

Rate is >60 BPM in Synus brady

21. What is the most important difference between sinus rhythm and sinus tachycardia?

Rate is >101 to 180 Bpm

22. What is the most important difference between sinus rhythm and sinus arrhythmia?

Rythem is irregular, phasic w/ Respirations

23. List five signs or symptoms of hemodynamic compromise.
   1. mental status change (Restlossness, Confusion)
   2. ↓ Blood Pressure
   3. chest pain
   4. SOB
   5. CHF

24. List five causes of sinus tachycardia.

   1. Exercise

   2. Fever

   3. Pain

   4. Fear/anxiety

   5. CHF

ECG Crossword

Across

2. Atropine is a __ medication.
6. This rhythm occurs when the pacemaker cells of the SA node fail to initiate an electrical impulse for one or more beats.
8. A medication that can cause a sinus tachycardia
11. One possible cause of sinus tachycardia
13. If episodes of SA block or sinus arrest occur frequently, a __ may be needed.
15. __ may be used to slow the rate of a sinus tachycardia in a patient having an acute MI.
16. P waves that come from the SA node are __ in lead II.
17. This medication may be used to treat a symptomatic bradycardia.
18. This type of sinus arrhythmia is associated with the breathing cycle.

Down

1. The QT interval normally __ as the heart rate increases.
3. If sinus tachycardia is caused by hypovolemia, treatment should include __ __.
4. When the SA node fires irregularly, a sinus __ results.
5. A common site for chest discomfort is beneath the __.
6. Sinus arrhythmia associated with a slower than normal rate is called sinus __.
9. Sinus arrest is a disorder of the property of __.
10. An example of a beta-blocker
12. Sinus __ is the name used to describe a rhythm that begins in the SA node but is slower than the normal rate for the patient's age.
13. In sinus arrest, more than one __ cycle is missing.
14. SA block is a disorder of the property of __.

PRACTICE *Rhythm Strips*

For each of the following rhythm strips, determine the atrial and ventricular rate and rhythm, measure the PR interval and QRS duration, and then identify the rhythm. All strips were recorded in lead II unless otherwise noted.

This rhythm strip is from a 33-year-old woman complaining of abdominal pain.

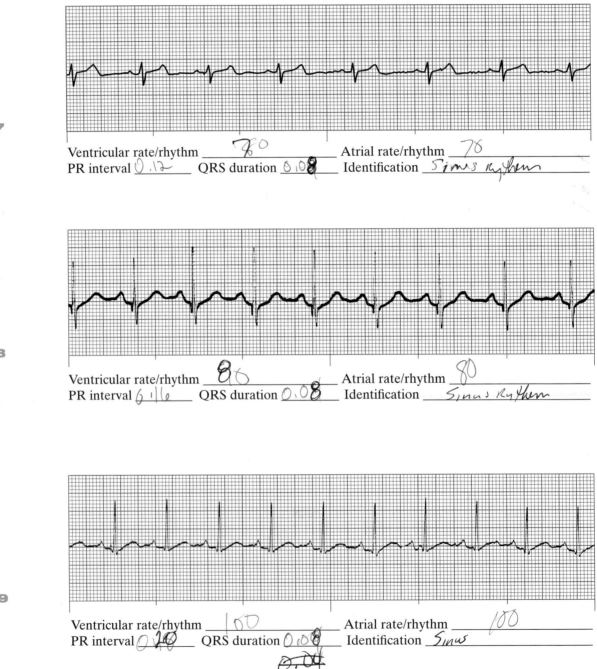

Figure 3-7

Ventricular rate/rhythm ___80___   Atrial rate/rhythm ___78___
PR interval _0.12_ QRS duration _0.08_ Identification _Sinus Rhythm_

Figure 3-8

Ventricular rate/rhythm ___80___   Atrial rate/rhythm ___80___
PR interval _0.16_ QRS duration _0.08_ Identification _Sinus Rhythm_

Figure 3-9

Ventricular rate/rhythm ___100___   Atrial rate/rhythm ___100___
PR interval _0.20_ QRS duration _0.08_ Identification _Sinus_
                              _0.04_

This rhythm strip is from a 73-year-old man complaining of chest pain. He has a history of hypertension and lung disease. Medications include aspirin, albuterol, and Lotensin.

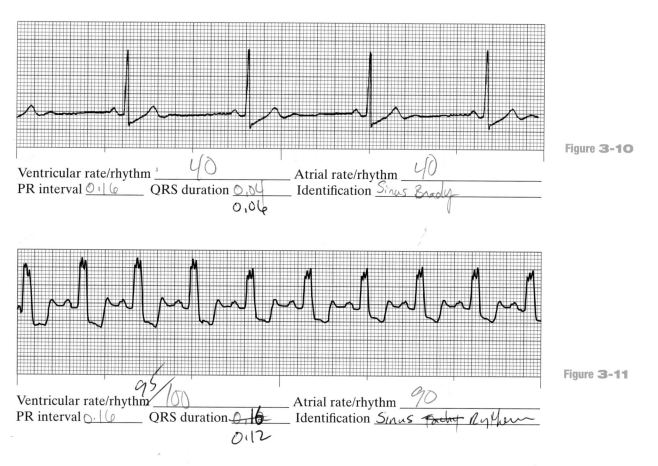

Figure 3-10

Ventricular rate/rhythm _40_ Atrial rate/rhythm _40_
PR interval _0.16_ QRS duration _0.04_ Identification _Sinus Brady_
_0.06_

Figure 3-11

Ventricular rate/rhythm _95/100_ Atrial rate/rhythm _90_
PR interval _0.16_ QRS duration _0.16_ Identification _Sinus Tachy Rythem_
_0.12_

This rhythm strip is from an 86-year-old woman complaining of chest pain that she rates a 4 on a 0 to 10 scale. BP 142/72.

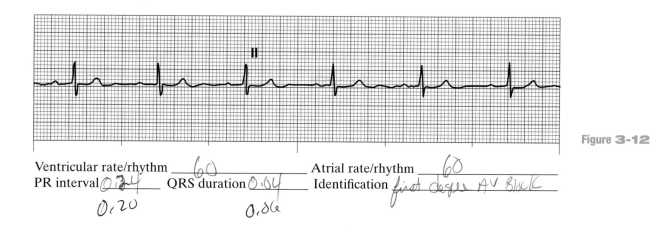

Figure 3-12

Ventricular rate/rhythm _60_ Atrial rate/rhythm _60_
PR interval _0.24_ QRS duration _0.04_ Identification _first degree AV Block_
_0.20_ _0.06_

This rhythm strip is from a 70-year-old man complaining of weakness.

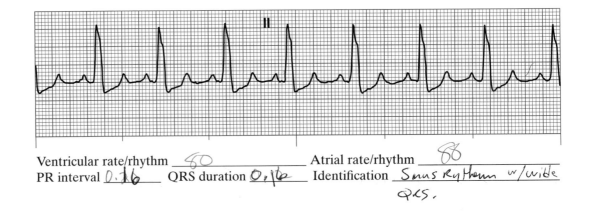

Figure **3-13**

Ventricular rate/rhythm ___80___   Atrial rate/rhythm ___88___
PR interval _0.16_   QRS duration _0.16_   Identification _Sinus Rythem w/wide_
QRS.

This rhythm strip is from a 35-year-old man complaining of a sudden onset of severe substernal chest pain. He has no significant past medical history and takes no medications. Initial BP 56/0.

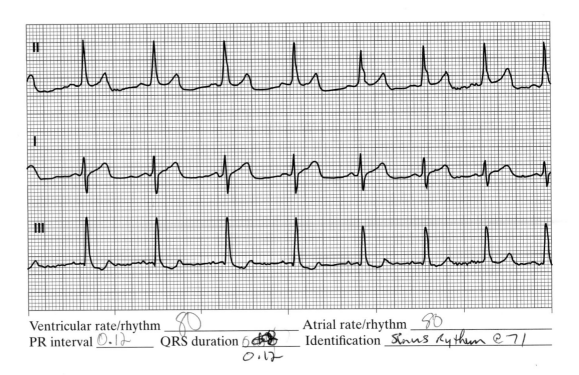

Figure **3-14**

Ventricular rate/rhythm ___80___   Atrial rate/rhythm ___80___
PR interval _0.12_   QRS duration _0.12_   Identification _Sinus Rythem @ 71_
_0.12_

This rhythm strip is from a 79-year-old woman with a nosebleed. BP 222/118.

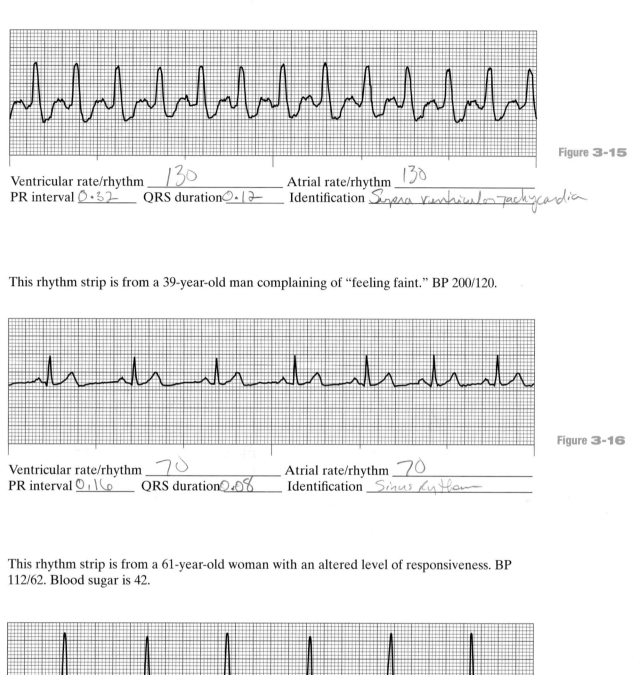

Figure 3-15

Ventricular rate/rhythm _130_ Atrial rate/rhythm _130_
PR interval _0.32_ QRS duration _0.12_ Identification _Supra ventricular Tachycardia_

This rhythm strip is from a 39-year-old man complaining of "feeling faint." BP 200/120.

Figure 3-16

Ventricular rate/rhythm _70_ Atrial rate/rhythm _70_
PR interval _0.16_ QRS duration _0.08_ Identification _Sinus Rythm_

This rhythm strip is from a 61-year-old woman with an altered level of responsiveness. BP 112/62. Blood sugar is 42.

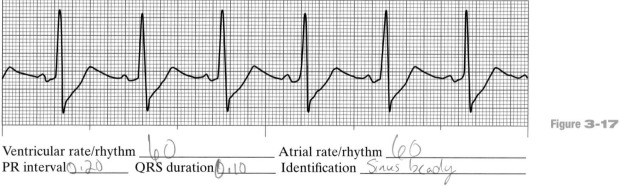

Figure 3-17

Ventricular rate/rhythm _60_ Atrial rate/rhythm _60_
PR interval _0.20_ QRS duration _0.10_ Identification _Sinus brady_

This rhythm strip is from a 26-year-old man after a seizure.

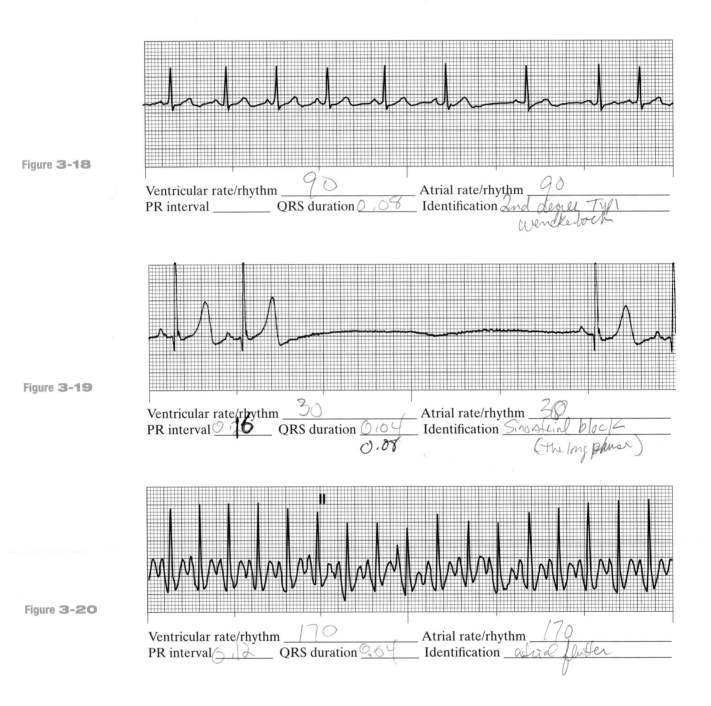

Figure 3-18

Ventricular rate/rhythm ___90___ Atrial rate/rhythm ___90___
PR interval _____ QRS duration _0.08_ Identification _2nd degree Type 1_
Wenckebach

Figure 3-19

Ventricular rate/rhythm ___30___ Atrial rate/rhythm ___30___
PR interval _0.16_ QRS duration _0.04_ Identification _Sinoatrial block_
_0.08_ _(The long pause)_

Figure 3-20

Ventricular rate/rhythm ___170___ Atrial rate/rhythm ___170___
PR interval _0.12_ QRS duration _0.04_ Identification _atrial flutter_

Atrial Rhythms

OBJECTIVES

On completion of this chapter, you should be able to:

1. Describe the ECG characteristics, possible causes, signs and symptoms, and initial emergency care for each of the following dysrhythmias:
   a. Premature atrial complexes (PACs)
   b. Wandering atrial pacemaker (multiformed atrial rhythm)
   c. Multifocal atrial tachycardia (MAT)
   d. Atrial tachycardia (AT)
   e. Atrioventricular nodal reentrant tachycardia (AVNRT)
   f. Atrioventricular reentrant tachycardia (AVRT)
   g. Atrial flutter
   h. Atrial fibrillation (AF)
2. Explain the concepts of altered automaticity, triggered activity, and reentry.
3. Explain the difference between a compensatory and noncompensatory pause.
4. Explain the terms *bigeminy*, *trigeminy*, *quadrigeminy*, and *run* when used to describe premature complexes.
5. Explain the terms *wandering atrial pacemaker* and *multifocal atrial tachycardia*.
6. Explain the term *paroxysmal supraventricular tachycardia* (PSVT).
7. List four examples of vagal maneuvers.
8. Discuss the indications and procedure for synchronized cardioversion.
9. Discuss preexcitation syndrome and name its three major forms.

INTRODUCTION

The atria are thin-walled, low-pressure chambers that receive blood from the systemic circulation and lungs. There is normally a continuous flow of blood from the superior and inferior vena cavae into the atria. Approximately 70% of this blood flows directly through the atria and into the ventricles before the atria contract. When the atria contract, an additional 30% is added to filling of the ventricles. This additional contribution of blood because of atrial contraction is called **atrial kick**.

P waves reflect atrial depolarization. A rhythm that begins in the SA node has one positive (upright) P wave before each QRS complex. A rhythm that begins in the atria will have a positive P wave that is shaped differently than P waves that begin in the SA node. This difference in P wave configuration occurs because the impulse begins in the atria and follows a different conduction pathway to the AV node.

Atrial Dysrhythmias: Mechanisms

Atrial dysrhythmias reflect abnormal electrical impulse formation and conduction in the atria. They result from altered automaticity, triggered activity, or reentry. Altered automaticity and triggered activity are disorders in impulse *formation*. Reentry is a disorder in impulse *conduction*. Dysrhythmias that result from disorders of impulse formation are often referred to as automatic. Dysrhythmias that result from a disorder in impulse conduction are referred to as reentrant.

Altered Automaticity

Altered automaticity occurs in normal pacemaker cells and in myocardial working cells that do not normally function as pacemaker sites. In altered automaticity, these cells fire and initiate impulses before a normal SA node impulse. If the rapid firing rate occurs for more than 50% of the day, it is said to be incessant. The rapid firing rate may also occur periodically. In these cases it is said to be episodic. Atrial dysrhythmias associated with altered automaticity include premature atrial complexes and atrial fibrillation.

—— *ECG Pearl*

Causes of Altered Automaticity
- Ischemia
- Drug toxicity
- Hypocalcemia
- Imbalance of electrolytes across the cardiac cell membrane

Triggered Activity

Triggered activity results from abnormal electrical impulses that sometimes occur during repolarization (afterdepolarizations), when cells are normally quiet. Triggered activity occurs when escape pacemaker and myocardial working cells fire more than once after stimulation by a single impulse. Triggered activity can result in atrial or ventricular beats that occur alone, in pairs, in "runs" (three or more beats), or as a sustained ectopic rhythm.

—— *ECG Pearl*

Causes of Triggered Activity
- Hypoxia
- Catecholamine increase
- Hypomagnesemia
- Myocardial ischemia and injury
- Medications that prolong repolarization (e.g., quinidine)

Reentry

Reentry (reactivation) is a condition in which an impulse returns to stimulate tissue that was previously depolarized. Reentry requires[1] (Figure 4-1) the following:

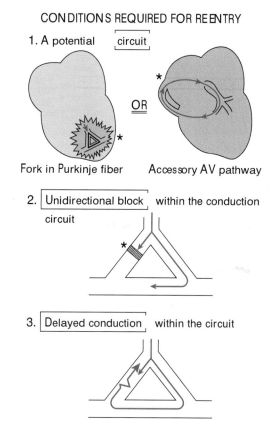

CONDITIONS REQUIRED FOR REENTRY

1. A potential [circuit]

OR

Fork in Purkinje fiber   Accessory AV pathway

2. [Unidirectional block] within the conduction circuit

3. [Delayed conduction] within the circuit

Figure 4-1
Reentry requires (1) a potential conduction circuit or circular conduction pathway, (2) a block within part of the circuit, and (3) delayed conduction with the remainder of the circuit.

- A potential conduction circuit or circular conduction pathway
- A block within part of the circuit
- Delayed conduction within the remainder of the circuit

Normally, an impulse spreads through the heart only once after it is initiated by pacemaker cells. In reentry, an electrical impulse is delayed or blocked (or both) in one or more areas of the conduction system while being conducted normally through the rest of the system. This results in the delayed electrical impulse entering cardiac cells that have just been depolarized by the normally conducted impulse. If the delayed impulse stimulates a relatively refractory area, the impulse can cause those cells to fire. This can produce a single early (premature) beat or repetitive electrical impulses, resulting in short periods of rapid rhythms (tachydysrhythmias).

Macroreentry circuits and microreentry circuits are two main types of reentry circuits. If the reentry circuit involves conduction through a large area of the heart, such as the entire right or left atrium, it is called a macroreentry circuit. A reentry circuit involving conduction within a small area is called a microreentry circuit. Atrial rhythms associated with reentry include atrial flutter, AV nodal reentrant tachycardia (AVNRT), and AV reentrant tachycardia (AVRT).

— ECG Pearl

Common Causes of Reentry
- Hyperkalemia
- Myocardial ischemia
- Some antiarrhythmic medications

Factors that influence heart rate include hormone levels (e.g., thyroxin, epinephrine, norepinephrine), medications, stress, anxiety, fear, and body temperature.

Most atrial dysrhythmias are not life-threatening, but some may be associated with extremely fast ventricular rates. Increases in heart rate shorten all phases of the cardiac cycle, but the most important is a decrease in the length of time spent in diastole. Remember that as the heart rate increases, there is less time for the ventricles to fill and less blood for the ventricles to pump out with each contraction. Thus an excessively fast heart rate can lead to decreased cardiac output.

PREMATURE ATRIAL COMPLEXES

How Do I Recognize It?

—— *ECG Pearl*

Premature beats appear early, that is, they occur before the next expected beat. Premature beats are identified by their site of origin:

- Premature atrial complexes (PACs)
- Premature junctional complexes (PJCs)
- Premature ventricular complexes (PVCs)

A **premature atrial complex** (PAC) occurs when an irritable site (focus) within the atria fires before the next SA node impulse is due to fire. This interrupts the sinus rhythm. If the irritable site is close to the SA node, the atrial P wave will look very similar to the P waves initiated by the SA node. The P wave of a PAC may be biphasic (partly positive, partly negative), flattened, notched, or pointed.

When compared with the P-P intervals of the underlying rhythm, a PAC is premature—occurring before the next expected sinus P wave. PACs are identified by the following:

- Early (premature) P waves
- Positive (upright) P waves (in lead II) that differ in shape from sinus P waves
- Early P waves that may or may not be followed by a QRS complex

Let's look closely at the rhythm strip in Figure 4-2. Remember that P waves that begin in the SA node are normally smooth and rounded. Atrial P waves will look different. Using a pen or pencil, mark an "S" (for SA node) above each normal looking P wave. Mark an "A" above those P waves that look different. When you are finished, you should have an "A" marked over the P waves in beats 2, 7, and 10. The rest of the P waves should be marked with an "S."

You'll notice that the waveforms marked with an "S" above them occur regularly except when they are interrupted by the three atrial beats. Using the sinus beats as your guide, determine the atrial and ventricular rates. The atrial and ventricular rates are 111 bpm. Based on the rate (more than 100 bpm) and an upright P wave before each QRS, we know that the underlying rhythm is a sinus tachycardia.

Using your calipers (or a piece of paper), find two sinus beats that appear next to each other (such as beats 4 and 5). Now move your calipers (or paper) to the right. If beat 6 occurred on time, it will line up with your calipers (or paper). It is on time. Now move your calipers to the right again. The right point of your calipers shows where the next sinus beat should have occurred. You can see that beat 7 occurred earlier than expected. This is a premature beat. When you continue this process you will find that beat 10 is also early. Working backward (and without adjusting your calipers), if you place the left point of your calipers on beat 1 in the rhythm strip, you'll see that beat 2 is also early. So far we can identify this rhythm as a sinus tachycardia at 111 bpm with three premature beats.

The term *complex* is used instead of *contraction* to correctly identify an early beat because the ECG depicts electrical activity, not mechanical function of the heart. Some areas of the country prefer the term "conduction" instead of complex.

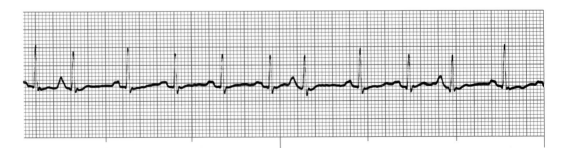

Figure 4-2
Sinus tachycardia with three PACs. From the left beats 2, 7, and 10 are PACs.

Since premature beats can start from more than one area of the heart, we must identify where the premature beat came from. To do this, we must examine the premature beats more closely. Look carefully at beats 2, 7, and 10. The QRS complexes look the same as those of the underlying rhythm. This is because the impulse is conducted normally through the AV junction, bundle branches, and ventricles. Now look to the left of the QRS complex in each of these early beats and look at the P waves. Each P wave is positive (upright) but looks different than the P waves of the sinus beats. This is an important finding and one that tells you that the P waves came from the atria. The early beats are premature atrial complexes. To complete our identification of this rhythm, we have a sinus tachycardia at 111 bpm with three premature atrial complexes. The ECG characteristics of PACs are shown in Table 4-1.

A PAC is not an entire rhythm—it is a single beat. Therefore you must identify the underlying rhythm and the ectopic beat(s).

—— ECG Pearl

A PAC has a positive P wave before the QRS complex. Sometimes the P waves are clearly seen and sometimes they are not. If the P wave of an early beat isn't obvious, look for it in the T wave of the preceding beat. The T wave of the preceding beat may be of higher amplitude than other T waves or have an extra "hump." This suggests the presence of a hidden P wave.

Noncompensatory Versus Compensatory Pause

A **noncompensatory (incomplete)** pause often follows a PAC. This represents the delay during which the SA node resets its rhythm for the next beat. A **compensatory (complete)** pause often follows premature ventricular complexes (PVCs). To find out whether or not the pause following a premature complex is compensatory or noncompensatory, measure the distance between three normal beats. Then compare that measurement to the distance between three beats, one of which includes the premature complex. The pause is *noncompensatory* if the normal beat following the premature complex occurs before it was expected (i.e., the period between the complex before and after the premature beat is less than two normal R-R intervals). The pause is *compensatory* if the normal beat following the premature complex occurs when expected (i.e., the period between the complex before and after the premature beat is the same as two normal R-R intervals).

Aberrantly Conducted PACs

If a PAC occurs very early, the right bundle branch can be slow to respond to the impulse (refractory). The impulse travels down the left bundle branch with no problem. Stimulation of the left bundle branch subsequently results in stimulation of the right bundle branch. The QRS will appear wide (greater than 0.10 sec) because of this delay in ventricular depolarization. PACs associated with a wide QRS complex are called **aberrantly conducted PACs**. This indicates that conduction through the ventricles is abnormal. Figure 4-3 shows a rhythm strip with two PACs. The first PAC *(arrow)* was conducted abnormally, producing a wide QRS complex. The second PAC *(arrow)* was conducted normally. Compare the T waves before each PAC with those of the underlying sinus bradycardia.

TABLE 4-1	Characteristics of Premature Atrial Complexes (PACs)
Rate	Usually within normal range, but depends on underlying rhythm
Rhythm	Regular with premature beats
P waves	Premature (occurring earlier than the next expected sinus P wave), positive (upright) in lead II, one before each QRS complex, often differ in shape from sinus P waves–may be flattened, notched, pointed, biphasic, or lost in the preceding T wave
PR interval	May be normal or prolonged depending on the prematurity of the beat
QRS duration	Usually 0.10 sec or less but may be wide (aberrant) or absent, depending on the prematurity of the beat; the QRS of the PAC is similar in shape to those of the underlying rhythm unless the PAC is abnormally conducted

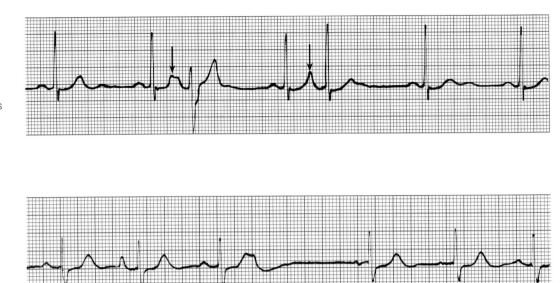

Figure 4-3
Premature atrial complexes with and without abnormal conduction (aberrancy).

Figure 4-4
Sinus rhythm with a non-conducted (blocked) PAC.

Nonconducted PACs

Sometimes, when a PAC occurs very early and close to the T wave of the preceding beat, only a P wave may be seen with no QRS after it (appearing as a pause) (Figure 4-4). This type of PAC is called a *nonconducted* or *blocked* PAC because the P wave occurred too early to be conducted. Nonconducted PACs occur because the AV junction is still refractory to stimulation and unable to conduct the impulse to the ventricles (thus no QRS complex). Look for the early P wave in the T wave of the preceding beat.

PACs: Patterns

When PACs occur in pairs, they are referred to as an atrial couplet.

PACs may occur in the following patterns:

- Pairs (coupled): Two PACs in a row
- "Runs" or "bursts": Three or more PACs in a row; often called paroxysmal (meaning "sudden") atrial tachycardia (PAT) or paroxysmal supraventricular tachycardia (PSVT)
- Atrial bigeminy (bigeminal PACs): Every other beat is a PAC
- Atrial trigeminy (trigeminal PACs): Every third beat is a PAC
- Atrial quadrigeminy (quadrigeminal PACs): Every fourth beat is a PAC

What Causes It?

PACs are very frequent in the elderly.

PACs may be due to altered automaticity or reentry. PACs are very common and can occur at any age. Their presence does not necessarily imply underlying cardiac disease. Causes of PACs include the following:

- Emotional stress
- Congestive heart failure
- Acute coronary syndromes
- Mental and physical fatigue
- Atrial enlargement
- Valvular heart disease
- Digitalis toxicity
- Electrolyte imbalance
- Hyperthyroidism
- Stimulants: caffeine, tobacco, cocaine

What Do I Do About It?

PACs usually do not require treatment if they are infrequent. The patient may complain of a "skipped beat" or occasional "palpitations" (if PACs are frequent) or may be unaware of their occurrence. In susceptible individuals, frequent PACs may set off episodes of atrial fibrillation, atrial flutter, or PSVT. Frequent PACs are treated by correcting the underlying cause:

Count the patient's pulse for a full minute.

- Reducing stress
- Reducing or eliminating stimulants
- Treating congestive heart failure
- Correcting electrolyte imbalances

If needed, frequent PACs may be treated with beta-blockers, calcium channel blockers, and/or antianxiety medications.

WANDERING ATRIAL PACEMAKER

How Do I Recognize It?

Multiformed atrial rhythm is an updated term for the rhythm formerly known as **wandering atrial pacemaker**. With this rhythm, the size, shape, and direction of the P waves vary, sometimes from beat to beat. The difference in the look of the P waves is a result of the gradual shifting of the dominant pacemaker between the SA node, the atria, and/or the AV junction (Figure 4-5). Wandering atrial pacemaker is associated with a normal or slow rate and irregular P-P, R-R, and PR intervals because of the different sites of impulse formation. The QRS duration is normally 0.10 sec or less than because conduction through the ventricles is usually normal. The ECG characteristics of wandering atrial pacemaker are shown in Table 4-2.

Lead II (continuous)

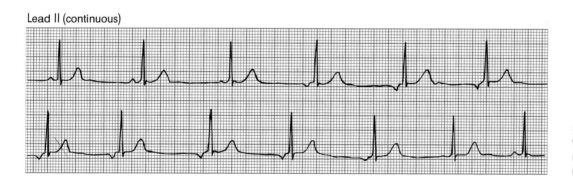

Figure 4-5
Wandering atrial pacemaker. Continuous strip (lead II).

TABLE 4-2	Characteristics of Wandering Atrial Pacemaker (Multiformed Atrial Rhythm)
Rate	Usually 60-100 bpm, but may be slow; if the rate is greater than 100 bpm, the rhythm is termed *multifocal* (or *chaotic*) *atrial tachycardia*
Rhythm	May be irregular as the pacemaker site shifts from the SA node to ectopic atrial locations and the AV junction
✱ P waves	Size, shape, and direction may change from beat to beat; at least three different P wave configurations (seen in the same lead) are required for a diagnosis of wandering atrial pacemaker or multifocal atrial tachycardia *must 3 different beats that are different*
PR interval	Variable
QRS duration	0.10 sec or less unless an intraventricular conduction delay exists

— *ECG Pearl*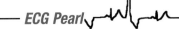

At least three different P wave configurations, seen in the same lead, are required for a diagnosis of wandering atrial pacemaker or multifocal atrial tachycardia.

What Causes It?

Wandering atrial pacemaker may be observed in normal, healthy hearts (particularly in athletes) and during sleep. It may also occur with some types of underlying heart disease and with digitalis toxicity. This dysrhythmia usually produces no signs and symptoms unless it is associated with a slow rate.

What Do I Do About It?

Wandering atrial pacemaker is usually a transient rhythm that resolves on its own when the firing rate of the SA node increases and the sinus resumes pacing responsibility. If the rhythm occurs because of digitalis toxicity, the drug should be withheld.

MULTIFOCAL ATRIAL TACHYCARDIA

How Do I Recognize It?

MAT is also called
chaotic atrial
tachycardia.

When the wandering atrial pacemaker is associated with a ventricular rate greater than 100 bpm, the rhythm is called **multifocal atrial tachycardia (MAT)** (Figure 4-6). In MAT, multiple ectopic sites stimulate the atria.

— *ECG Pearl*

Multifocal atrial tachycardia may be confused with atrial fibrillation because both rhythms are irregular; however, P waves (although varying in size, shape, and direction) are clearly visible in MAT.

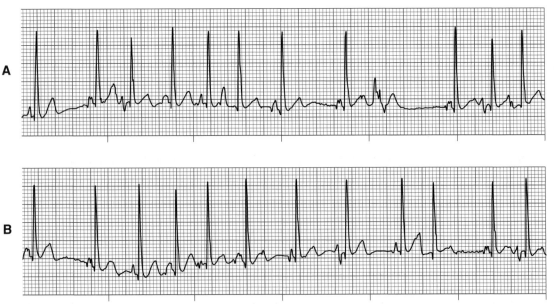

Figure 4-6
A, Multifocal atrial tachycardia (MAT), also known as chaotic atrial tachycardia. **B,** Premature atrial complexes (PACs) occur at varying cycle lengths and with differing shapes.

What Causes It?

Multifocal atrial tachycardia is most often seen in the following:

- Severe chronic obstructive pulmonary disease (COPD)
- Hypoxia
- Acute coronary syndromes
- Digoxin toxicity
- Rheumatic heart disease
- Theophylline toxicity
- Electrolyte imbalances

What Do I Do About It?

Treatment of MAT is directed at the underlying cause. If the patient is stable and symptomatic but you are uncertain if the rhythm is MAT, you can try a vagal maneuver (see the box below). If vagal maneuvers are ineffective, you can try adenosine IV. Remember that MAT is the result of random and chaotic firing of multiple sites in the atria. MAT does not involve reentry through the AV node. Therefore it is unlikely that vagal maneuvers or giving adenosine will terminate the rhythm. However, they may momentarily slow the rate enough so that you can look at the P waves and determine the specific type of tachycardia. By determining the type of tachycardia, treatment specific to that rhythm can be given.

If you know the rhythm is MAT and the patient is symptomatic, treatment may include medications such as calcium channel blockers. Beta-blockers are usually contraindicated because of the presence of severe underlying pulmonary disease.

Because the patient's pulse is irregular with this rhythm, count the patient's pulse for a full minute.

Vagal Maneuvers

Vagal maneuvers are methods used to stimulate baro-receptors located in the internal carotid arteries and the aortic arch. Stimulation of these receptors results in reflex stimulation of the vagus nerve and release of acetyl-choline. Acetylcholine slows conduction through the AV node, resulting in slowing of the heart rate. Although there is some overlap of the right and left vagus nerves, it is thought that the right vagus nerve has more fibers to the SA node and atrial muscle and the left vagus more fibers to the AV node and some ventricular muscle.

Examples of vagal maneuvers include:
- Coughing
- Squatting
- Breath-holding
- Carotid sinus pressure. This procedure is performed with the patient's neck extended. Firm pressure is applied just underneath the angle of the jaw for up to 5 seconds (Figure 4-7). Carotid pressure should be avoided in older patients and in patients with carotid artery bruits. Simultaneous, bilateral carotid pressure should *never* be performed.
- Application of a cold stimulus to the face (e.g., a wash-cloth soaked in iced water, cold pack, or crushed ice mixed with water in a plastic bag or glove) for up to 10 seconds. This technique is often effective in infants and young children. When using this method, do not obstruct the patient's mouth or nose or apply pressure to the eyes.

- Valsalva's maneuver. Instruct the patient to blow through an occluded straw or take a deep breath and bear down as if having a bowel movement for up to 10 seconds. This strains the abdominal muscles and increases intrathoracic pressure.
- Gagging. Use a tongue depressor or culturette swab to briefly touch the back of the throat.

When using vagal maneuvers, keep the following points in mind:
- Make sure oxygen, suction, a defibrillator, and emergency medications are available before attempting the procedure.
- A 12-lead ECG recording is desirable when a vagal maneuver is performed.
- Continuous monitoring of the patient's ECG is *essential*. Note the onset and end of the vagal maneuver on the ECG rhythm strip.
- In general, a vagal maneuver should not be continued for more than 10 seconds.
- Application of external ocular pressure may be dangerous and should not be used because of the risk of retinal detachment.
- Carotid massage is less effective in children than in adults and is not recommended.

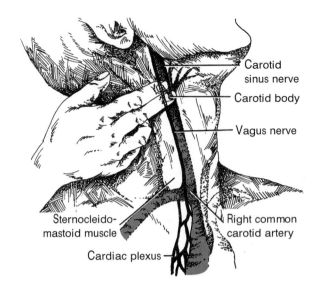

Figure 4-7
Carotid sinus pressure. The carotid sinus (carotid body) is located at the bifurcation of the carotid artery at the angle of the jaw.

Carotid sinus nerve
Carotid body
Vagus nerve
Sternocleido-mastoid muscle
Right common carotid artery
Cardiac plexus

Drug Pearl

- **Adenosine** is found naturally in all body cells and is rapidly metabolized in the blood vessels. Adenosine slows the rate of the SA node, slows conduction time through the AV node, can interrupt reentry pathways that involve the AV node, and can restore sinus rhythm in SVT.
- Reentry circuits are the underlying mechanism for many episodes of SVT. Adenosine acts at specific receptors to cause a temporary block of conduction through the AV node, interrupting these reentry circuits.
- Adenosine has an onset of action of 10 to 40 seconds and duration of 1 to 2 minutes. Because of its short half-life (10 seconds), and to boost delivery of the drug to its site of action in the heart, select the injection port on the IV tubing that is nearest the patient. Administer the drug using a two-syringe technique. Prepare one syringe with the drug, and the other with a normal saline flush. Insert both syringes into the injection port in the IV tubing. Administer the medication IV as rapidly as possible (i.e., over a period of seconds) and *immediately* follow with the saline flush. If the patient has a central line in place, the dosages of adenosine should be reduced to avoid prolonged bradycardia or severe side effects.
- Adenosine may cause facial flushing because the drug causes mild dilation of blood vessels in the skin. Coughing, dyspnea, and bronchospasm may occur because it is a mild bronchoconstrictor. Adenosine should be avoided in patients with severe asthma.
- A 12-lead ECG recording is desirable when adenosine is used.
- Adenosine should be used with caution in patients with severe coronary artery disease because vasodilation of normal coronary vessels may produce ischemia in vulnerable territory. It should be used only with full resuscitative equipment available.[2]

SUPRAVENTRICULAR TACHYCARDIA

AV nodal reentrant tachycardia is also called AV nodal reciprocating tachycardia. AV reentrant tachycardia is also called AV reciprocating tachycardia.

Supraventricular arrhythmias (SVA) begin above the bifurcation of the bundle of His. This means that supraventricular arrhythmias include rhythms that begin in the SA node, atrial tissue, or the AV junction. The term **supraventricular tachycardia** (SVT) includes three main types of fast rhythms, which are shown in Figure 4-8.

- *Atrial tachycardia (AT)*. In AT, an irritable site in the atria fires automatically at a rapid rate.
- *AV nodal reentrant tachycardia (AVNRT)*. In AVNRT, fast and slow pathways in the AV node form an electrical circuit or loop. The impulse spins around the AV nodal (junctional) area.
- *AV reentrant tachycardia (AVRT)*. In AVRT, the impulse begins above the ventricles but travels via a pathway other than the AV node and bundle of His.

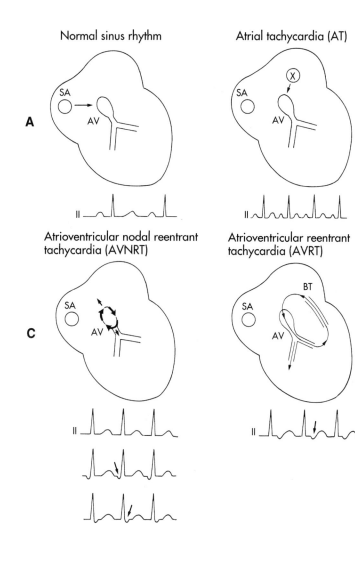

Normal sinus rhythm

Atrial tachycardia (AT)

A

B

Atrioventricular nodal reentrant tachycardia (AVNRT)

Atrioventricular reentrant tachycardia (AVRT)

C

D

Figure 4-8
Types of supraventricular tachycardias. **A,** Normal sinus rhythm is presented here as a reference.
B, Atrial tachycardia. **C,** AV nodal reentrant tachycardia (AVNRT). **D,** AV reentrant tachycardia (AVRT).

ATRIAL TACHYCARDIA

How Do I Recognize It?

Atrial tachycardia is usually the result of altered automaticity or triggered activity. It consists of a series of rapid beats from an irritable site in the atria. Atrial tachycardia is often precipitated by a PAC. This rapid atrial rate overrides the SA node and becomes the pacemaker. Conduction of the atrial impulse to the ventricles is often 1:1. This means that every atrial impulse is conducted to the ventricles. Atrial tachycardia looks similar to sinus tachycardia, but atrial P waves differ in shape from sinus P waves. An example of this rhythm is shown in Figure 4-9.

The term **paroxysmal** is used to describe a rhythm that starts or ends suddenly. Some physicians use this term to describe the sudden onset or end of a patient's symptoms. Atrial tachycardia that starts or ends suddenly is called **paroxysmal atrial tachycardia** (**PAT**). With very rapid atrial rates, the AV node begins to filter some of the impulses coming to it. By doing so it protects the ventricles from excessively rapid rates. When the AV node selectively filters conduction of some of these impulses, the rhythm is called **paroxysmal atrial tachycardia with block**. PAT with block is often associated with disease of the AV node, medications that slow conduction through the AV node, or digitalis toxicity. When PAT with block exists, more than one P wave is present before each QRS. When the AV node blocks every other atrial impulse from traveling to the ventricles the rhythm is called PAT with 2:1 block (Figure 4-10).

When three or more PACs occur in a row at a rate of more than 100 bpm, atrial tachycardia is present.

PAT may last for minutes, hours, or days.

Figure 4-9
Atrial tachycardia (a type of supraventricular tachycardia) that ends spontaneously with the abrupt resumption of sinus rhythm. The P waves of the tachycardia (rate: about 150 bpm) are superimposed on the preceding T waves.

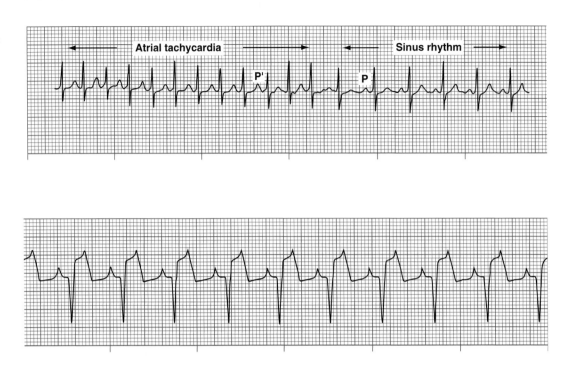

Figure 4-10
Atrial tachycardia with 2:1 block. P waves are clearly seen before the QRS complexes. Others are hidden in the T waves. Atrial rate is 180 bpm. Ventricular rate is 90 bpm.

TABLE 4-3	Characteristics of Atrial Tachycardia
Rate	100-250 bpm
Rhythm	Regular
P waves	One positive P wave precedes each QRS complex in lead II; P waves differ in shape from sinus P waves; an isoelectric baseline is usually present between P waves
PR interval	May be shorter or longer than normal
QRS duration	0.10 second or less unless an intraventricular conduction delay exists

There is more than one type of atrial tachycardia. Multifocal atrial tachycardia has already been discussed.

- Atrial tachycardia that begins in a small area (focus) within the heart is called focal atrial tachycardia. There are several types of focal atrial tachycardia. Focal atrial tachycardia may be due to an automatic, triggered, or reentrant mechanism. A patient with focal atrial tachycardia often presents with paroxysmal atrial tachycardia. The atrial rate is usually between 100 and 250 bpm and rarely 300 bpm.
- Automatic atrial tachycardia (also called ectopic atrial tachycardia) is another type of AT in which a small cluster of cells with altered automaticity fire. The impulse is spread from the cluster of cells to the surrounding atrium and then to the ventricles via the AV node. This type of AT often has a "warm up" period. This means there is a progressive shortening of the P-P interval for the first few beats of the arrhythmia. Automatic AT gradually slows down as it ends. This has been called a "cool down" period. The atrial rate is usually between 100 and 250 bpm. P waves look different from sinus P waves but are still related to the QRS complex. Vagal maneuvers do not usually stop the tachycardia, but they may slow the ventricular rate.

The ECG characteristics of atrial tachycardia are shown in Table 4-3.

—— *ECG Pearl*

It is important to look closely for P waves in all dysrhythmias, but it is very important when trying to figure out the origin of a tachycardia. If P waves are not visible in one lead, try looking in another before finalizing your rhythm diagnosis.

What Causes It?

Atrial tachycardia can occur in persons with normal hearts or in patients with organic heart disease. Atrial tachycardia associated with automaticity or triggered activity is often related to an acute event including:

- Stimulant use (such as caffeine, albuterol, theophylline, cocaine)
- Infection
- Electrolyte imbalance
- Acute illness with excessive catecholamine release
- Myocardial infarction

What Do I Do About It?

Signs and symptoms associated with atrial tachycardia vary widely and may include the following:

- Asymptomatic
- Palpitations
- Fluttering sensation in the chest
- Chest pressure
- Dyspnea
- Fatigue
- Dizziness or lightheadedness
- Syncope or near-syncope

When taking the patient's history, try to find out how often the episodes occur, how long they last, and possible triggers.

It is important to find out if the patient's palpitations are regular or irregular. Palpitations that occur regularly with a sudden onset and end are usually caused by AVNRT or AVRT. Irregular palpitations may be a result of premature complexes, atrial fibrillation, or multifocal atrial tachycardia.[2] Tachycardias may cause syncope because the rapid ventricular rate decreases cardiac output and blood flow to the brain. Syncope is most likely to occur just after the onset of a rapid atrial tachycardia or when the rhythm stops abruptly. Predisposed persons may experience angina or congestive heart failure.

—— *ECG Pearl*

The signs and symptoms experienced by a patient with a tachycardia depend on the following:

- Ventricular rate
- How long the tachycardia lasts
- General health, presence of underlying heart disease

The faster the heart rate, the more likely the patient is to have signs and symptoms resulting from the rapid rate.

If episodes of atrial tachycardia are short, the patient may be asymptomatic. If atrial tachycardia is sustained and the patient is symptomatic because of the rapid rate, treatment usually includes oxygen, intravenous (IV) access, and vagal maneuvers. Although AT will rarely stop with vagal maneuvers, they are used to try to stop the rhythm or slow conduction through the AV node. If this fails, antiarrhythmic medications should be tried. Adenosine is the drug of choice, except for patients with severe asthma. A significant percentage of ATs will terminate with administration of adenosine.[2] If needed, calcium channel blockers or beta-blockers may be used to slow the ventricular rate. Cardioversion seldom stops automatic ATs but may be successful for ATs caused by reentry or triggered automaticity. Synchronized cardioversion should be considered for patients with drug-resistant arrhythmia.[2]

A rhythm that lasts from three beats up to 30 seconds is a nonsustained rhythm. A sustained rhythm is one that lasts more than 30 seconds.

Atrial tachycardia with AV block often occurs because of excess digitalis. In these cases, the patient's ventricular rate is not excessively fast. The drug should be withheld and serum digoxin levels obtained. Long-term medication therapy may include the use of calcium channel blockers or beta-blockers. When atrial tachycardia is difficult to control and causes serious signs and symptoms, radiofrequency catheter ablation may be necessary. When catheter ablation is performed, electrophysiologic studies are done to locate the abnormal pathways and reentry circuits in the heart. Once localized, a special ablation catheter is placed at the site of the abnormal pathway. Low-energy, high-frequency current is delivered through this catheter. With each burst of energy from the catheter, an area of tissue is destroyed (ablated). The energy is applied in various areas until the unwanted pathway is no longer functional and the circuit is broken.

Drug Pearl

- **Amiodarone** directly depresses the automaticity of the SA and AV nodes, slows conduction through the AV node and in the accessory pathway of patients with Wolff-Parkinson-White syndrome, inhibits alpha- and beta-adrenergic receptors, and possesses both vagolytic and calcium-channel blocking properties. Because of these properties, amiodarone is used for a wide range of both atrial and ventricular dysrhythmias in adults and children.
- Amiodarone prolongs the PR, QRS, and QT intervals and has an additive effect with other medications that prolong the QT interval (e.g., procainamide, phenothiazines, some tricyclic antidepressants, thiazide diuretics, sotalol). Although prolongation of the QRS duration and QT interval may be beneficial in some patients, it may also increase the risk for Torsades de Pointes (a type of polymorphic VT associated with a long QT interval).
- Hypotension, bradycardia, and AV block are side effects of amiodarone administration. Slow the infusion rate or discontinue if seen.

Synchronized Cardioversion

Synchronized cardioversion is the delivery of a shock to the heart to terminate a rapid dysrhythmia. A synchronized shock means the shock is timed to avoid the vulnerable period during the cardiac cycle. On the ECG, this period occurs during the peak of the T wave to approximately the end of the T wave. When the "sync" control is pressed, the machine searches for the highest (R wave deflection) or deepest (QS deflection) part of the QRS complex. When a QRS complex is detected, the monitor places a "flag" or "sync marker" on the complex that may appear as an oval, square, line, or highlighted triangle on the ECG display, depending on the monitor used. When the shock controls are pressed while the defibrillator is charged in "sync" mode, the machine will discharge energy only if both discharge buttons are pushed and the monitor tells the defibrillator that a QRS complex has been detected.

Indications (Unstable Patient)
- All tachycardias (except sinus tachycardia) with a ventricular rate >150 bpm and serious signs and symptoms related to the tachycardia

Procedure
- If the patient is awake and time permits, administer sedation unless contraindicated.
- Turn the monitor/defibrillator on. Attach ECG electrodes to monitor the patient's ECG. NOTE: Some devices allow monitoring and cardioversion via disposable self-adhesive monitoring/defibrillation pads. In this case, additional ECG electrodes are not necessary. If self-adhesive pads are to be used, place them in proper position on the patient's bare chest.

- Select a lead with an optimum QRS complex amplitude (positive or negative) and no artifact, or if monitoring through disposable defibrillation electrodes, select the "paddles" lead. Run an ECG strip to document the patient's rhythm.
- Press the "sync" control on the defibrillator. Make sure the machine is "marking" or "flagging" each QRS complex. If sync markers do not appear or appear elsewhere on the ECG display, adjust the gain (ECG size) until the markers occur within each QRS complex. If adjusting the gain does not result in sync markers within each QRS complex, select another lead or reposition the ECG electrodes.
- If hand-held paddles are used, apply conductive gel to the paddles or place disposable pre-gelled defibrillator pads on the patient's bare chest. Place the defibrillator paddles on the patient's chest and apply firm pressure.
- Make sure the machine is in "sync" mode, select the appropriate energy level on the defibrillator, charge the defibrillator, and recheck the ECG rhythm. If the rhythm is unchanged, call "clear!" and look around you. Make sure everyone is clear of the patient, bed, and any equipment connected to the patient. Make sure oxygen is not flowing over the patient's chest.
- If the area is clear, press and hold both discharge buttons at the same time until the shock is delivered. There may be a slight delay while the machine detects the next QRS complex. Release the shock controls after the shock has been delivered.
- Reassess the rhythm. If the tachycardia persists, make sure the machine is in sync mode before delivering another shock.

AV NODAL REENTRANT TACHYCARDIA (AVNRT)

AVNRT is the most common type of SVT. It is caused by reentry in the area of the AV node. In the normal AV node, there is only one pathway through which an electrical impulse is conducted from the SA node to the ventricles. Patients with AVNRT have two conduction pathways within the AV node that conduct impulses at different speeds and recover at different rates. The fast pathway conducts impulses rapidly but has a long refractory period (slow recovery time). The slow pathway conducts impulses slowly but has a short refractory period (fast recovery time) (Figure 4-11). Under the right conditions, the fast and slow pathways can form an electrical circuit or loop. As one side of the loop is recovering, the other is firing.

AVNRT is usually caused by a PAC that is spread by the electrical circuit. This allows the impulse to spin around in a circle indefinitely, reentering the normal electrical pathway with each pass around the circuit. The result is a very rapid and regular rhythm that ranges from 150 to 250 bpm.

Look at the example of AVNRT in Figure 4-12. You can see narrow-QRS complexes that occur at a regular rate of 168 bpm. P waves are not clearly seen. Because AVNRT begins in the area of the AV node, the impulse spreads to the atria and ventricles at almost the same time. This results in P waves that are usually hidden in the QRS complex. If the ventricles are stimulated first and then the atria, a negative (inverted) P wave will appear after the QRS in leads II, III, and aVF. When the atria are depolarized after the ventricles, the P wave typically distorts the end of the QRS complex. Since P waves are not seen before the QRS complex, the PR interval is not measurable. In our example of AVNRT, you can see ST-segment depression. ST-segment changes (usually depression) are common in patients with supraventricular tachycardias. In most patients, these ST-segment changes are thought to be the result of repolarization changes. However, in elderly patients and those with a high likelihood of ischemic heart disease, ST-segment changes may represent ECG changes consistent with an acute coronary syndrome. The patient should be watched closely. Appropriate laboratory

Although AVNRT begins in the area of the AV node and could be discussed in the junctional rhythms chapter, it is discussed here because it was once thought to be a type of paroxysmal atrial tachycardia.

Premature complexes may be triggered by stress, caffeine, nicotine, or medications that increase heart rate.

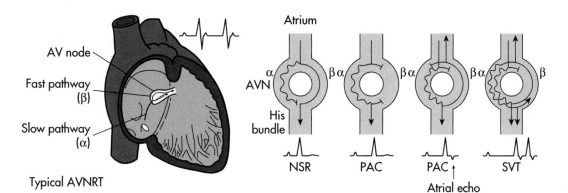

Figure 4-11
Schematic for SVT due to AV nodal reentry. *AV,* AV node, *NSR,* normal sinus rhythm, *PAC,* premature atrial complex, *SVT,* supraventricular tachycardia.

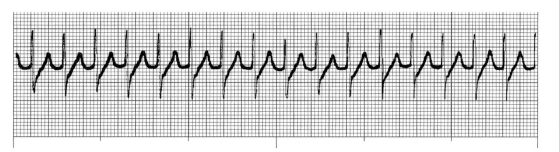

Figure 4-12
AV nodal reentrant tachycardia (AVNRT).

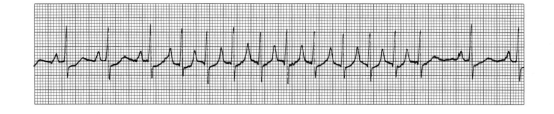

Figure 4-13
Paroxysmal supraventricular tachycardia (PSVT).

TABLE 4-4	Characteristics of AV Nodal Reentrant Tachycardia (AVNRT)
Rate	150-250 bpm
Rhythm	Ventricular rhythm is usually very regular
P waves	P waves are often hidden in the QRS complex. If the ventricles are stimulated first and then the atria, a negative (inverted) P wave will appear after the QRS in leads II, III, and aVF. When the atria are depolarized after the ventricles, the P wave typically distorts the end of the QRS complex.
PR interval	P waves are not seen before the QRS complex; therefore the PR interval is not measurable
QRS duration	0.10 second or less unless an intraventricular conduction delay exists

tests and a 12-lead ECG should be obtained to rule out infarction as needed. The ECG characteristics of AVNRT are summarized in Table 4-4.

PSVT is discussed here since most supraventricular tachycardias are due to AVNRT.

A regular, narrow-QRS tachycardia that starts or ends suddenly is called **paroxysmal supraventricular tachycardia** (PSVT) (Figure 4-13). P waves are seldom seen because they are hidden in T waves of preceding beats. The QRS is narrow unless there is a problem with conduction of the impulse through the ventricles, as in a bundle branch block.

What Causes It?

AVNRT can occur at any age.

Whether a person is born with a tendency to have AVNRT or whether it develops later in life for an unknown reason has not been clearly determined. AVNRT is common in young, healthy persons with no structural heart disease. It occurs more often in women than in men. AVNRT also occurs in persons with COPD, coronary artery disease, valvular heart disease, congestive heart failure, and digitalis toxicity. AVNRT can cause angina or myocardial infarction in patients with coronary artery disease.

—— *ECG Pearl*

Possible triggers of AVNRT
- Hypoxia
- Stress
- Overexertion
- Anxiety

- Caffeine
- Smoking
- Sleep deprivation
- Medications

What Do I Do About It?

Recurrent episodes vary in frequency, duration, and severity from several times a day to every 2 to 3 years.

Treatment depends on the severity of the patient's signs and symptoms. Signs and symptoms that may be associated with rapid ventricular rates include the following:

- Palpitations (common)
- Lightheadedness
- Neck vein pulsations
- Syncope or near-syncope
- Dyspnea
- Weakness

- Nausea
- Nervousness, anxiety
- Chest pain or pressure
- Signs of shock
- Congestive heart failure

If the patient is stable but symptomatic (and symptoms are due to the rapid heart rate), treatment usually includes oxygen, IV access, and vagal maneuvers. If vagal maneuvers do not slow the rate or cause conversion of the tachycardia to a sinus rhythm, the first medication given is usually adenosine. If the patient is unstable, treatment usually includes oxygen, IV access, and sedation (if the patient is awake and time permits), followed by synchronized cardioversion.

AVNRT is usually responsive to vagal maneuvers.

Recurrent AVNRT may require treatment with a long-acting calcium channel blocker or beta-blocker. Patients who are resistant to drug therapy or who do not wish to remain on life-long medications for the dysrhythmia are candidates for radiofrequency catheter ablation. Catheter ablation has become the treatment of choice in the management of patients with symptomatic recurrent episodes of AVNRT. It is successful in permanently interrupting the circuit and curing the dysrhythmia in most cases.

AV REENTRANT TACHYCARDIA (AVRT)

The next most common type of SVT is AV reentrant tachycardia (AVRT).

What Causes It?

AVRT involves a pathway of impulse conduction outside the AV node and bundle of His. **Preexcitation** is a term used to describe rhythms that originate from above the ventricles but in which the impulse travels via a pathway other than the AV node and bundle of His. As a result, the supraventricular impulse excites the ventricles earlier than would be expected if the impulse traveled by way of the normal conduction system. Patients with preexcitation syndromes are prone to AVRT.

Remember, normally the AV node is the only electrical connection between the atria and ventricles.

During fetal development, strands of myocardial tissue form connections between the atria and ventricles, outside the normal conduction system. These strands normally become nonfunctional shortly after birth. In patients with preexcitation syndrome, these connections persist as congenital malformations of working myocardial tissue. Because these connections bypass part or all of the normal conduction system, they are called **accessory pathways**. The term **bypass tract** is used when one end of an accessory pathway is attached to normal conductive tissue. This pathway may connect the right atrial and ventricular walls, the left atrial and ventricular walls, or connect the atrial and ventricular septa on either the right or the left side.

There are three major forms of preexcitation syndrome. Each is differentiated by its accessory pathway or bypass tract[1] (Figure 4-14).

Some people have more than one accessory pathway.

1. In **Wolff-Parkinson-White (WPW) syndrome**, the accessory pathway is called the Kent bundle. This bundle connects the atria directly to the ventricles, completely bypassing the normal conduction system.
2. In **Lown-Ganong-Levine (LGL) syndrome**, the accessory pathway is called the James bundle. This bundle connects the atria directly to the lower portion of the AV node, thus partially bypassing the AV node. In LGL syndrome, one end of the James bundle is attached to normal conductive tissue. This congenital pathway may be called a *bypass tract*.
3. Another unnamed preexcitation syndrome involves the *Mahaim fibers*. These fibers do not bypass the AV node but originate below the AV node and insert into the ventricular wall, bypassing part or all of the ventricular conduction system.

Because WPW is the most common type of preexcitation syndrome, it will be the focus of our discussion regarding AVRT. The incidence of WPW in Western countries is 1.5 to 3.1 per 1000 persons.[4] It is more common in men than women. Sixty to 70% of people with WPW have no associated heart disease. WPW is one of the most common causes of tachydysrhythmias in infants and children. Although the accessory pathway in WPW is believed to be con-

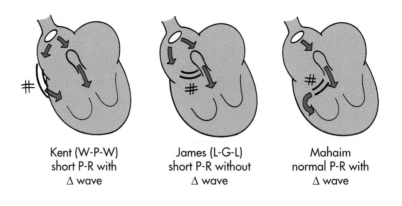

Kent (W-P-W)
short P-R with
Δ wave

James (L-G-L)
short P-R without
Δ wave

Mahaim
normal P-R with
Δ wave

genital in origin, symptoms associated with preexcitation often do not appear until young adulthood. Among patients with WPW syndrome, about 3% have first-degree relatives with a preexcitation syndrome.[5]

ECG Pearl

In a 2003 study of 317 pediatric patients with WPW syndrome, 28 patients (9%) had multiple accessory pathways—21 patients had 2 pathways, 6 had 3 pathways, and 1 patient had 4 pathways.[3]

How Do I Recognize It?

The ECG characteristics of WPW described here are usually seen when the patient is not having a tachycardia.

WPW syndrome usually goes undetected until it manifests in a patient as a tachycardia. In WPW associated with a sinus rhythm, the P wave looks normal. Remember that the AV node normally delays the impulse it receives from the SA node. If this delay did not occur, the atria and ventricles would contract at about the same time. The delay in conduction allows the atria to empty blood into the ventricles before the next ventricular contraction begins. The PR interval is short (less than 0.12 sec) because the impulse travels very quickly across the accessory pathway, bypassing the normal delay in the AV node (Figure 4-15).

Delta waves are the result of initial activation of the ventricles by conduction over the accessory pathway.

As the impulse crosses the insertion point of the accessory pathway in the ventricular muscle, that part of the ventricle is stimulated earlier (preexcited) than if the impulse had followed the normal conduction pathway through the bundle of His and Purkinje fibers. On the ECG, preexcitation of the ventricles can be seen as a **delta wave** in some leads. A delta wave is an initial slurring of the QRS complex (Figure 4-16).

The ST-segment and T wave changes seen in WPW can mimic myocardial ischemia or injury.

Normally, conduction through the Purkinje fibers is very fast. In WPW, the spread of the impulse is slow because it must spread from working cell to working cell in the ventricular muscle. This is because the accessory pathway bypasses the specialized cells of the heart's conduction system. Because the impulse spreads slowly through the working cells, the delay in conduction results in a QRS that is usually more than 0.12 sec in duration. The QRS complex seen in WPW is actually a combination of the impulse that preexcites the ventricles through the accessory pathway and the impulse that follows the normal conduction pathway through the AV node. As a result, the end (terminal) portion of the QRS usually looks normal. However, since the ventricles are activated abnormally, they repolarize abnormally. This is seen on the ECG as ST-segment and T wave changes. The direction of the ST-segment and T wave changes are usually opposite the direction of the delta wave and QRS complex. An example of WPW is shown in Figure 4-17. The ECG characteristics of WPW are summarized in Table 4-5.

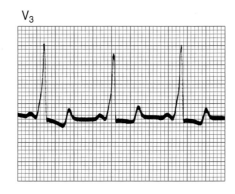

V₃

Figure 4-15
Lead V₃. Typical WPW pattern showing the short PR interval, delta wave, wide QRS complex, and secondary ST and T-wave changes.

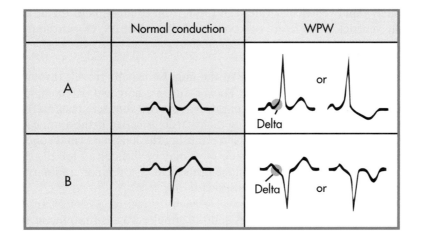

	Normal conduction	WPW
A		Delta or
B		Delta or

Figure 4-16
Delta waves may be positive or negative. **A,** The usual appearance of WPW in leads where the QRS complex is mainly upright. **B,** The usual appearance of WPW when the QRS is predominantly negative. Negative delta waves may simulate pathologic Q waves—mimicking myocardial infarction.

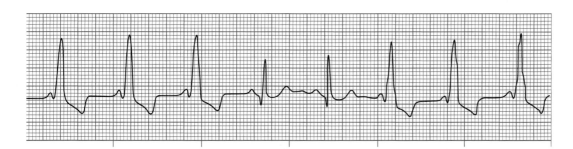

Figure 4-17
This rhythm strip shows an example of intermittent preexcitation. The first three beats show preexcitation. This is followed by abrupt normalization of the QRS complex in the next two beats. The preexcitation pattern returns for the final three beats.

TABLE 4-5	**Characteristics of Wolff-Parkinson-White (WPW) Syndrome**
Rate	Usually 60-100 bpm, if the underlying rhythm is sinus in origin
Rhythm	Regular, unless associated with atrial fibrillation
P waves	Normal and positive in lead II unless WPW is associated with atrial fibrillation
PR interval	If P waves are observed, less than 0.12 second
QRS duration	Usually greater than 0.12 second. Slurred upstroke of the QRS complex (delta wave) may be seen in one or more leads.

ECG Pearl

Recognizing WPW
- Short PR interval
- Delta wave
- Widening of the QRS

Persons with preexcitation syndromes are predisposed to tachydysrhythmias. This is because the accessory pathway:

- Bypasses the protective blocking mechanism provided by the AV node
- Provides a mechanism for reentry

There are three main types of tachydysrhythmias that occur in WPW syndrome. The most common is AVRT, followed by atrial fibrillation and atrial flutter. Atrial fibrillation and atrial flutter that occur in the presence of an accessory pathway are particularly dangerous. This is because extremely rapid ventricular rates can result from conduction of the atrial impulses directly into the ventricles. There are two types (subclasses) of AVRT—orthodromic AVRT and antidromic AVRT.

Orthodromic AVRT has a narrow QRS complex unless there is a conduction delay within the ventricles.

When a PAC occurs in a patient with WPW, the impulse usually travels through the AV node and bundle of His to the ventricles. This results in a narrow QRS complex. The impulse then travels through the accessory pathway from the ventricle back to the atrium. This sets up a reentry circuit. The resulting tachycardia is called orthodromic AVRT. In orthodromic AVRT, the ventricles are depolarized using the heart's normal conduction pathway. The accessory pathway is used for reentry. It may be difficult to tell the difference between orthodromic AVRT and AVNRT since both have fast, regular, and narrow QRS complexes (Figure 4-18).

Antidromic AVRT has a wide QRS complex.

In some patients with WPW, a PAC occurs and the impulse travels from the atrium to the ventricle using the accessory pathway. This results in a wide QRS complex. The impulse then travels through the AV node (or a second accessory pathway). The resulting tachycardia is called antidromic AVRT. In antidromic AVRT, the ventricles are depolarized using the accessory pathway. The pathway for reentry is via the AV node. Antidromic AVRT is less common than orthodromic AVRT, occurring in only 5% to 10% of patients with WPW syndrome.[2] Because antidromic AVRT and ventricular tachycardia are fast rhythms with wide QRS complexes, it is difficult to tell the difference between them.

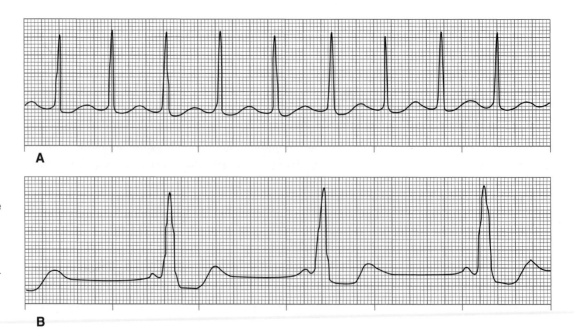

Figure 4-18
A, Supraventricular tachycardia in a child with Wolff-Parkinson-White (WPW) syndrome. Note the normal QRS complexes during the tachycardia. **B,** Later, the typical features of WPW syndrome are visible (short P-R interval, delta wave, and wide QRS).

A

B

What Do I Do About It?

Common signs and symptoms associated with WPW and a rapid ventricular rate include the following:

- Palpitations
- Lightheadedness
- Shortness of breath
- Anxiety
- Weakness
- Dizziness
- Chest discomfort
- Signs of shock

If the patient is symptomatic because of the rapid ventricular rate, treatment will depend on how unstable the patient is, the width of the QRS complex (wide or narrow), and the regularity of the ventricular rhythm. Consultation with a cardiologist is recommended. A stable but symptomatic patient with orthodromic (narrow QRS) AVRT is usually treated with oxygen, IV access, and attempts to slow or convert the rhythm with vagal maneuvers. If vagal maneuvers fail, IV medications such as amiodarone may be used. Don't give drugs that slow or block conduction through the AV node, such as adenosine, digoxin, diltiazem, or verapamil. They may speed up conduction through the accessory pathway. This can result in a further increase in heart rate.

A stable but symptomatic patient with antidromic (wide QRS) AVRT is usually treated with oxygen, IV access, and IV procainamide or amiodarone.[2] If the patient has signs of heart failure, amiodarone is preferred over procainamide because it depresses contractility less than amiodarone. If the patient is unstable, preparations should be made for synchronized cardioversion.

> Some people with WPW never have symptoms.

ATRIAL FLUTTER

Atrial flutter is an ectopic atrial rhythm in which an irritable site fires regularly at a very rapid rate.

How Do I Recognize It?

Atrial flutter has been classified into two types.

- Type I atrial flutter is caused by reentry. In this type of atrial flutter, an impulse circles around a large area of tissue, such as the entire right atrium. Type I atrial flutter is also called typical or classical atrial flutter. In type I atrial flutter, the atrial rate ranges from 250 to 350 bpm.
- Type II atrial flutter is called atypical or very rapid atrial flutter. The precise mechanism of type II atrial flutter has not been defined. Patients with this type of atrial flutter often develop atrial fibrillation. In type II atrial flutter, the atrial rate ranges from 350 to 450 bpm.

In atrial flutter, an irritable focus within the atrium typically fires at a rate of about 300 bpm. Because of this extremely rapid stimulation, waveforms are produced that resemble the teeth of a saw, or a picket fence, called "flutter" waves. Flutter waves are best observed in leads II, III, aVF, and V_1. If each impulse were sent to the ventricles, the ventricular rate would equal 300 bpm. The healthy AV node protects the ventricles from these extremely fast atrial rates. Normally, the AV node cannot conduct faster than approximately 180 impulses/min. Thus, at an atrial rate of 300 bpm, every other impulse arrives at the AV node while it is still refractory. The resulting ventricular response of 150 bpm is called 2:1 conduction. (The ratio of the atrial rate [300 bpm] to the ventricular rate [150 bpm] is 2:1) (Figure 4-19). Conduction ratios in atrial flutter are usually even (2:1, 4:1, 6:1) but can vary. In persons with an accessory path-

> Atrial flutter with an atrial rate of 300 bpm and a ventricular rate of 75 bpm equals 4:1 conduction; 50 bpm equals 6:1 conduction, etc.

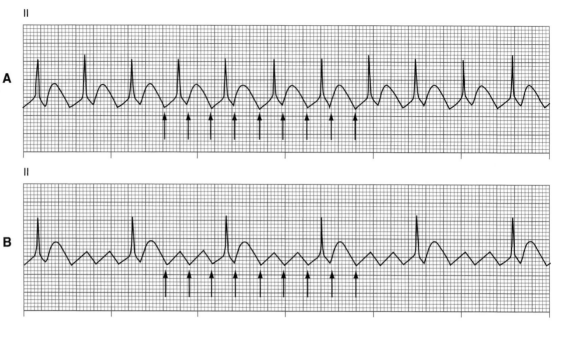

Figure 4-19 **A,** Atrial flutter. **A,** Atrial flutter with 2:1 conduction (atrial rate = 300 bpm, ventricular rate = 150 bpm). Flutter activity *(arrows)* appears as negative deflections that precede and immediately follow each QRS complex. **B,** Atrial flutter with 4:1 conduction (atrial rate = 300 bpm, ventricular rate = 75 bpm). As you can see, it is much easier to identify the sawtooth pattern of the flutter waves *(arrows)* with the slower ventricular rate.

way, atrial flutter may be associated with 1:1 conduction (because the AV node is bypassed), producing extremely rapid ventricular rates.

Conduction ratios in atrial flutter are often even (2:1, 4:1, 6:1), but variable conduction can also occur, producing an irregular ventricular rhythm.

Because P waves are not observed atrial flutter, the PR interval is not measurable. The QRS complex is usually 0.10 sec or less because atrial flutter is a supraventricular rhythm, and the impulse is conducted normally through the AV junction and ventricles. However, if flutter waves are buried in the QRS complex or if an intraventricular conduction delay exists, the QRS will appear wide (greater than 0.10 sec). If the AV node blocks the impulses coming to it at a regular rate, the resulting ventricular rhythm will be regular. If the AV node blocks the impulses at an irregular rate, the resulting ventricular rhythm will be irregular.

—— *ECG Pearl*

Atrial flutter or atrial fibrillation that has a ventricular rate of more than 100 bpm is described as "uncontrolled." The ventricular rate is considered "rapid" when it is 150 bpm or more. New-onset atrial flutter or fibrillation is often associated with a rapid ventricular rate. Atrial flutter or atrial fibrillation with a rapid ventricular response is commonly called "Afib with RVR" or "Aflutter with RVR."

Atrial flutter or atrial fibrillation that has a ventricular rate of less than 100 bpm is described as "controlled." A controlled ventricular rate may be the result of the following:
- A healthy AV node protecting the ventricles from very fast atrial impulses
- Medications used to control (block) conduction through the AV node, decreasing the number of impulses reaching the ventricles

When vagal maneuvers are used in atrial flutter, the response is usually sudden slowing and then a return to the former rate. Vagal maneuvers will not usually convert atrial flutter because the reentry circuit is located in the atria, not the AV node.

When atrial flutter is present with 2:1 conduction, it may be difficult to tell the difference between atrial flutter and sinus tachycardia, atrial tachycardia, AVNRT, AVRT, or PSVT. Vagal maneuvers may help identify the rhythm by temporarily slowing AV conduction and revealing the underlying flutter waves. An example of atrial flutter is shown in Figure 4-20. The ECG characteristics of atrial flutter are shown in Table 4-6.

What Causes It?

Atrial flutter is usually caused by a reentry circuit in which an impulse circles around a large area of tissue, such as the entire right atrium. It is usually a paroxysmal rhythm that is precip-

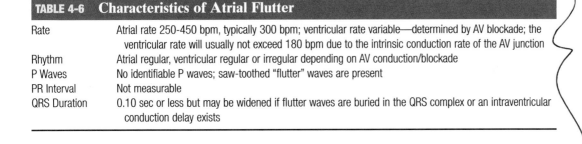

Figure **4-20**
Atrial flutter at 75 bpm.

TABLE 4-6	Characteristics of Atrial Flutter
Rate	Atrial rate 250-450 bpm, typically 300 bpm; ventricular rate variable—determined by AV blockade; the ventricular rate will usually not exceed 180 bpm due to the intrinsic conduction rate of the AV junction
Rhythm	Atrial regular, ventricular regular or irregular depending on AV conduction/blockade
P Waves	No identifiable P waves; saw-toothed "flutter" waves are present
PR Interval	Not measurable
QRS Duration	0.10 sec or less but may be widened if flutter waves are buried in the QRS complex or an intraventricular conduction delay exists

itated by a PAC. It may last for seconds to hours and occasionally 24 hours or more. Chronic atrial flutter is unusual. This is because the rhythm usually converts to sinus rhythm or atrial fibrillation, either on its own or with treatment.

—— *ECG Pearl*

Conditions Associated with Atrial Flutter
- Hypoxia
- Pulmonary embolism
- Chronic lung disease
- Mitral or tricuspid valve stenosis or regurgitation
- Pneumonia
- Ischemic heart disease

- Complication of myocardial infarction
- Cardiomyopathy
- Hyperthyroidism
- Digitalis or quinidine toxicity
- Cardiac surgery
- Pericarditis/myocarditis

What Do I Do About It?

The severity of signs and symptoms associated with atrial flutter vary, depending on the ventricular rate, how long the rhythm has been present, and the patient's cardiovascular status. The patient may be asymptomatic and not require treatment or may experience serious signs and symptoms. Patients with atrial flutter commonly present with complaints of palpitations, difficulty breathing, fatigue, or chest discomfort.

The faster the ventricular rate, the more likely the patient is to be symptomatic with this rhythm.

Synchronized cardioversion should be considered for any patient in atrial flutter who has serious signs and symptoms because of the rapid ventricular rate (such as low blood pressure, signs of shock, or heart failure). If atrial flutter is associated with a rapid ventricular rate and the patient is stable but symptomatic, treatment may be directed toward controlling the ventricular rate or converting the rhythm to a sinus rhythm. In the prehospital and Emergency Department setting, treatment is usually aimed at controlling the ventricular rate. If heart failure is not present, medications such as calcium channel blockers or beta-blockers are often used. If signs of heart failure are present, medications such as digoxin, diltiazem, or amiodarone may be used.

If the decision is made to convert the rhythm, it is important to first consider how long atrial flutter has been present. If the rhythm has been present for 48 hours or longer, anticoagulation is recommended before attempting to convert the rhythm with medications, synchronized cardioversion, or catheter ablation.[2] A widely accepted practice is to begin prophylactic anticoagulation 2 to 3 weeks before conversion and to continue therapy for about 4 weeks after conversion. Ibutilide (Corvert) is an antiarrhythmic used to chemically convert atrial fibrillation or atrial flutter to a sinus rhythm. For patients who respond to ibutilide, the average time to conversion is about 30 minutes. If synchronized cardioversion is performed, atrial flutter can be successfully converted to a sinus rhythm using low energy levels.

ATRIAL FIBRILLATION

AF is the most common dysrhythmia encountered in clinical practice.[6]

Atrial fibrillation (AF) occurs because of altered automaticity in one or several rapidly firing sites in the atria or reentry involving one or more circuits in the atria. Irritable sites in the atria fire at a rate of 400 to 600 times/min. These rapid impulses cause the muscles of the atria to quiver (fibrillate). This results in ineffectual atrial contraction, decreased stroke volume, a subsequent decrease in cardiac output, and loss of atrial kick.

How Do I Recognize It?

In atrial fibrillation, the AV node attempts to protect the ventricles from the hundreds of impulses bombarding it per minute. It does this by blocking many of the impulses generated by the irritable sites in the atria. The ventricular rate and rhythm are determined by the degree of blocking by the AV node of these rapid impulses.

Look at the example of atrial fibrillation in Figure 4-21. One of the first things you notice is that the ventricular rhythm is irregular. In AF, atrial depolarization occurs very irregularly. This results in an irregular ventricular rhythm. The ventricular rhythm associated with AF is described as irregularly irregular. Since the ventricular rhythm is irregular, we should give a ventricular rate range when describing the rhythm. In our example, the ventricular rate ranges from 67 to 120 bpm.

Because of the atrial muscle quivering and because there is no uniform wave of atrial depolarization in AF, there is no P wave. Instead, you see a baseline that looks erratic (wavy). This corresponds with the rapid atrial rate. These wavy deflections are called "fibrillatory waves." Since there is no P wave, we cannot measure a PR interval. The QRS complex is narrow because the impulse started above the bifurcation of the bundle of His and was conducted normally through the AV junction and ventricles.

Suspect toxicity resulting from digitalis, beta-blockers, or calcium channel blockers if AF occurs with a slow, regular ventricular rate. This can occur when a patient who has AF is prescribed medications to slow the ventricular rate. Excess medication can cause complete AV block (Figure 4-22).

Table 4-7 shows the ECG characteristics of AF.

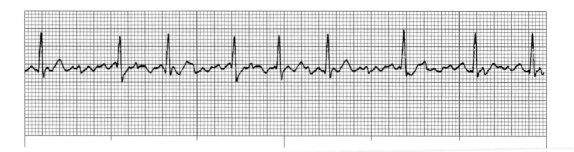

Figure 4-21
Atrial fibrillation with a ventricular response of 67 to 120 bpm.

What Causes It?

Atrial fibrillation can occur in patients with or without detectable heart disease or related symptoms. When AF occurs in young persons (younger than 60 years of age) without clinical or echocardiographic evidence of cardiopulmonary disease it is called lone atrial fibrillation.[6]

Patients who experience AF are at increased risk of having a stroke. Because the atria do not contract effectively and expel all of the blood within them, blood may pool within them and form clots. A stroke can result if a clot moves from the atria and lodges in an artery in the brain.

A clot may dislodge on its own or because of conversion to a sinus rhythm.

—— *ECG Pearl*

Conditions Associated with Atrial Fibrillation

- Idiopathic (no clear cause)
- Hypertension
- Ischemic heart disease
- Advanced age
- Rheumatic heart disease (especially mitral valve disease)
- Cardiomyopathy
- Congestive heart failure
- Congenital heart disease
- Sick sinus syndrome/degenerative conduction system disease
- Wolff-Parkinson-White syndrome
- Pericarditis

- Pulmonary embolism
- Chronic lung disease
- After surgery
- Diabetes
- Stress
- Sympathomimetics
- Excessive caffeine
- Hypoxia
- Hypokalemia
- Hypoglycemia
- Systemic infection
- Hyperthyroidism
- Electrocution

What Do I Do About It?

Atrial fibrillation may occur as a self-limiting episode, come and go, or exist as a sustained rhythm. The severity of signs and symptoms associated with AF varies. Treatment decisions are based on the ventricular rate, the duration of the rhythm, the patient's general health, and how the patient is tolerating the rhythm. AF with a rapid ventricular response may produce signs and symptoms that include lightheadedness, palpitations, dyspnea, chest discomfort, and low blood pressure.

TABLE 4-7	Characteristics of Atrial Fibrillation
Rate	Atrial rate usually 400-600 bpm; ventricular rate variable
Rhythm	Ventricular rhythm usually irregularly irregular
P waves	No identifiable P waves, fibrillatory waves present; erratic, wavy baseline
PR interval	Not measurable
QRS duration	0.10 sec or less but may be widened if an intraventricular conduction delay exists

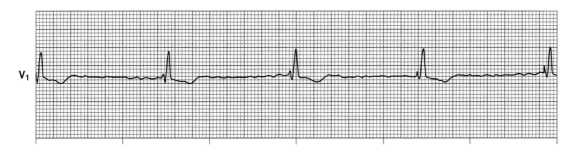

V₁

Figure 4-22
Atrial fibrillation with complete AV block. The ventricular rate is slow and regular because of the block.

If AF is associated with a rapid ventricular rate and the patient has serious signs and symptoms resulting from the rapid rate, synchronized cardioversion should be performed. If AF is associated with a rapid ventricular rate and the patient is stable but symptomatic, prehospital and Emergency Department treatment is usually aimed at controlling the ventricular rate. If heart failure is not present, medications such as calcium channel blockers, magnesium, or beta-blockers are often used. If signs of heart failure are present, medications such as digoxin, diltiazem, or amiodarone may be used. Anticoagulation is recommended before attempting to convert AF to a sinus rhythm if AF has been present for 48 hours or longer.

Catheter ablation is recommended for selected patients with AF, such as those who have AF with WPW syndrome and a history of syncope due to the rapid heart rate.

Table 4-8 contains a summary of atrial rhythm characteristics.

TABLE 4-8   Atrial Rhythms—Summary of Characteristics

	PACs	Wandering Atrial Pacemaker	Atrial Tachycardia
Rate	Usually within normal range, but depends on underlying rhythm	Usually 60-100 bpm; if rate greater than 100 bpm, rhythm is called multifocal atrial tachycardia	100-250 bpm
Rhythm	Regular with premature beats	May be irregular as pacemaker site shifts from SA node to ectopic atrial locations and AV junction	Regular
P Waves (lead II)	Premature, positive in lead II, one precedes each QRS, differ from sinus P waves, may be lost in preceding T wave	Size, shape, and direction may change from beat to beat	Atrial P waves differ from sinus P waves; isoelectric baseline usually present between P waves
PR Interval	May be normal or prolonged	Varies	May be shorter or longer than normal
QRS	0.10 sec or less unless abnormally conducted	0.10 sec or less unless abnormally conducted	0.10 sec or less unless abnormally conducted

REFERENCES

1. Crawford MV, Spence MI: Electrical complications in coronary artery disease: arrhythmias. In: *Common sense approach to coronary care,* ed 6, St Louis, 1995, Mosby, pp 208-274.
2. Blomström-Lundqvist C and others: ACC/AHA/ESC guidelines for the management of patients with supraventricular arrhythmias—executive summary: a report of the American College of Cardiology/American Heart Association Task Force on Practice Guidelines, and the European Society of Cardiology Committee for Practice Guidelines (Writing Committee to Develop Guidelines for the Management of Patients with Supraventricular Arrhythmias), *J Am Coll Cardiol* 42:1493-1531, 2003.
3. Weng KP, Wolff GS, Young ML: Multiple accessory pathways in pediatric patients with Wolff-Parkinson-White syndrome, *Am J Cardiol* 1178-1183, 2003.
4. Gollob MH, Green MS, Tang AS, Gollob T, Karibe A, Ali Hassan AS, Ahmad F, Lozado R, Shah G, Fananapazir L, Bachinski LL, Roberts R, Hassan AS: Identification of a gene responsible for familial Wolff-Parkinson-White syndrome, *N Engl J Med* 344:1823-1831, 2001. Erratum in: *N Engl J Med*;345:552, 2001; Hassan AS (corrected to Ali Hassan AS): *N Engl J Med* 346:300, January 2002.
5. Massumi RA: Familial Wolff-Parkinson-White syndrome with cardiomyopathy, *Am J Med* 43:931, 1967.
6. Fuster V and others: American College of Cardiology/American Heart Association/European Society of Cardiology Board: ACC/AHA/ESC guidelines for the management of patients with atrial fibrillation: executive summary. A Report of the American College of Cardiology/American Heart Association Task Force on Practice Guidelines and the European Society of Cardiology Committee for Practice Guidelines and Policy Conferences (Committee to Develop Guidelines for the Management of Patients With Atrial Fibrillation): developed in Collaboration with the North American Society of Pacing and Electrophysiology, *J Am Coll Cardiol* 38:1231-1266, October 2001.

AVNRT	Atrial Flutter	Atrial Fibrillation (AF)	WPW
150-250 bpm	Atrial rate 250-450 bpm, typically 300 bpm; ventricular rate variable—determined by AV blockade	Atrial rate 400-600 bpm; ventricular rate variable	60-100 bpm, if the underlying rhythm is sinus in origin
Ventricular rhythm is usually very regular	Atrial regular, ventricular regular or irregular	Ventricular rhythm usually irregularly irregular	Regular, unless associated with atrial fibrillation
P waves often hidden in QRS complex	No identifiable P waves; sawtoothed "flutter" waves present	No identifiable P waves; fibrillatory waves present; erratic, wavy baseline	Normal and positive in lead II unless WPW is associated with AF
If P waves are seen, the PRI will usually measure 0.12-0.20 sec	Not measurable	Not measurable	If P waves are seen, less than 0.12 sec
0.10 sec or less unless abnormally conducted	0.10 sec or less unless abnormally conducted	0.10 sec or less unless abnormally conducted	Usually greater than 0.12 second. Delta wave may be seen in one or more leads.

S T O P & REVIEW

True/False

Indicate whether the sentence or statement is true or false.

T   1. Atrial tachycardia is a form of supraventricular tachycardia.

F   2. A macroreentrant circuit is one that involves a small area of heart tissue, usually a few centimeters or less.

F   3. Most patients with type I atrial flutter develop atrial fibrillation.

           type II

Matching

a. Palpitations
b. Antidromic
c. Early P wave with no QRS following it
d. Premature atrial complex
e. 250-350 bpm
f. Anticoagulant
g. Atrial flutter
h. Orthodromic

i. Paroxysmal
j. Wolff-Parkinson-White syndrome
k. Decreased stroke volume
l. 400-600 bpm
m. Atrial fibrillation
n. Multiformed atrial rhythm
o. Adenosine

G   4. Waveforms resemble the teeth of a saw or picket fence before the QRS

L   5. Atrial rate associated with atrial fibrillation

O   6. Drug of choice for AVNRT

F   7. Before elective cardioversion, prophylactic treatment with a(n) __ is recommended for the patient in atrial flutter or fibrillation.

m   8. Irregularly irregular ventricular rhythm, no identifiable P waves

J   9. The most common preexcitation syndrome

N   10. Updated term for wandering atrial pacemaker

H   11. In this type of AVRT, the ventricles are depolarized using the heart's normal conduction pathway. The accessory pathway is used for reentry.

A   12. Common complaint in a patient with a rapid heart rate

E   13. Atrial rate associated with type I atrial flutter

K   14. Consequence of decreased ventricular filling time

D   15. Early beat initiated by an irritable atrial site

I   16. Sudden onset or cessation of a dysrhythmia

B   17. In this type of AVRT, the ventricles are depolarized using the accessory pathway. The pathway for reentry is via the AV node.

C   18. Nonconducted PAC

Short Answer

19. Why do some patients experience syncope with a tachycardia?

decrease in cardiac output causing decreased blood flow to brain

20. What is the most common type of supraventricular tachycardia (SVT)?

AV nodal Reentrant Tachycardia (AVNRT)

21. Paroxysmal atrial tachycardia is visible on a patient's cardiac monitor. What does "paroxysmal" mean?

a rythem that starts or stops suddenly

22. List the three main ECG findings associated with Wolff-Parkinson-White (WPW) syndrome.
    1. QRS usually > 0.12
    2. Rythem is regular unless associated with artrial fibrillation
    3. P waves normal & positive unless associated w/ artrial fibrillation
       Short PR interval

23. List the three dysrhythmias that most commonly occur in WPW syndrome.
    1. AVRT
    2. arterial fibrillation
    3. arterial flutter

24. Name the two types (subclasses) of AVRT.
    1. orthodromic
    2. Antidromic

25. Explain why patients who experience atrial fibrillation are at increased risk of having a stroke.

The atria do not contract fully, this causes the blood to pool which allows clots to form

ECG Crossword

Across

4. Common cause of reentry
7. Early __
9. Ventricular rhythm in atrial fibrillation
10. Another name for reentry
11. Cardiac glycoside
12. Premature atrial complex
13. __ syndrome is a type of preexcitation syndrome.
14. Every fourth beat comes from somewhere other than the SA node __.
17. WPW is associated with a __ PR interval.
18. Updated term for the rhythm formerly known as wandering atrial pacemaker
19. The delay following a PAC during which the SA node resets its rhythm for the next beat.

Down

1. Every third beat comes from somewhere other than the SA node.
2. Every other beat comes from somewhere other than the SA node.
3. This rhythm is an example of altered automaticity in normal pacemaker cells.
5. PACs associated with a wide QRS complex are called __ __ PACs.
6. Multifocal atrial tachycardia is also called __ atrial tachycardia.
8. A __ __ causes initial slurring of the QRS complex in WPW.
12. Common symptom during an episode of SVT
15. Baseline appearance in atrial fibrillation
16. A common cause of PACs

PRACTICE *Rhythm Strips*

For each of the following rhythm strips, determine the atrial and ventricular rate and rhythm, measure the PR interval and QRS duration, and then identify the rhythm. All strips were recorded in lead II unless otherwise noted. NOTE: These rhythm strips include sinus and atrial rhythms.

This rhythm strip is from a 35-year-old woman complaining of chest pain and palpitations.

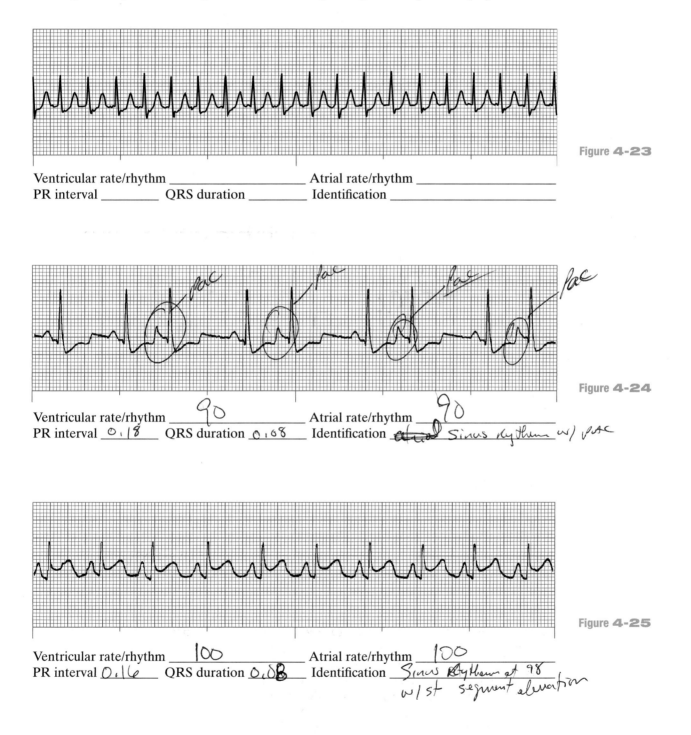

Figure **4-23**

Ventricular rate/rhythm _____ Atrial rate/rhythm _____
PR interval _____ QRS duration _____ Identification _____

Figure **4-24**

Ventricular rate/rhythm ___90___ Atrial rate/rhythm ___90___
PR interval _0.18_ QRS duration _0.08_ Identification ~~atrial~~ Sinus Rythem w/ PAC

Figure **4-25**

Ventricular rate/rhythm ___100___ Atrial rate/rhythm ___100___
PR interval _0.16_ QRS duration _0.08_ Identification Sinus Rythem at 98 w/ st segment elevation

This rhythm strip is from a 96-year-old man complaining of chest pain and palpitations. Medications include Lanoxin and Coumadin.

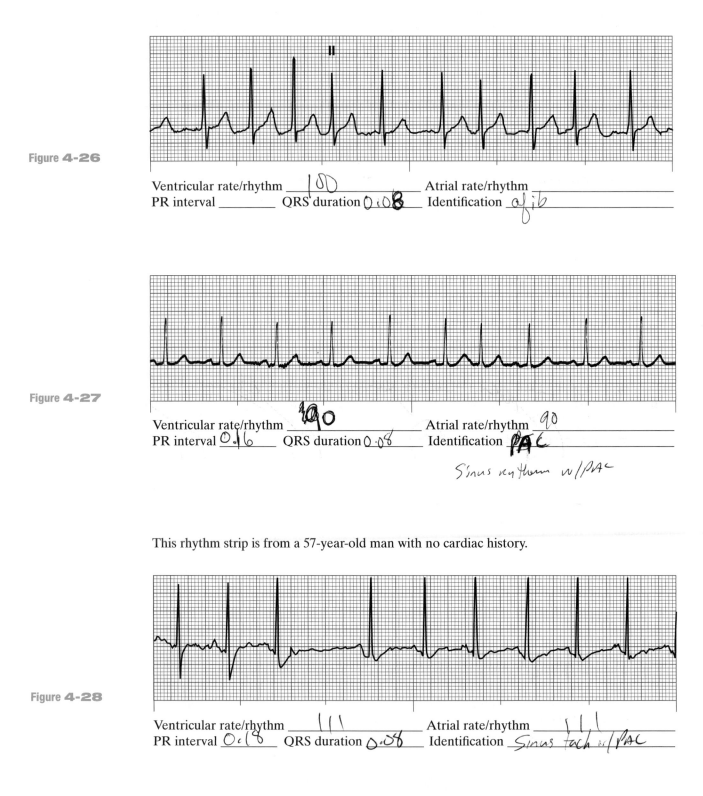

Figure **4-26**

Ventricular rate/rhythm _____100_____   Atrial rate/rhythm _____
PR interval _____ QRS duration 0.08___ Identification _afib_____

Figure **4-27**

Ventricular rate/rhythm _____90_____   Atrial rate/rhythm ___90_____
PR interval 0.16___ QRS duration 0.08___ Identification _PAC_____

Sinus rythum w/PAC

This rhythm strip is from a 57-year-old man with no cardiac history.

Figure **4-28**

Ventricular rate/rhythm _____111_____   Atrial rate/rhythm ___111_____
PR interval 0.18___ QRS duration 0.08___ Identification _Sinus tach w/PAC___

This rhythm strip is from a 74-year-old woman with difficulty breathing.

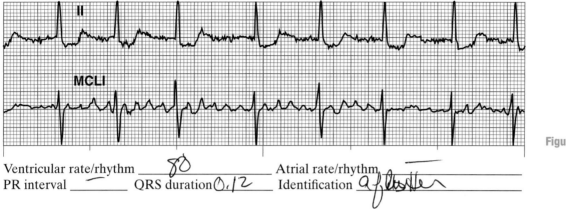

Figure **4-29**

Ventricular rate/rhythm ___80___ Atrial rate/rhythm _____
PR interval ___—___ QRS duration 0.12 Identification _a flutter_

This rhythm strip is from a 71-year-old man complaining of shoulder pain that has been present for 3 weeks.

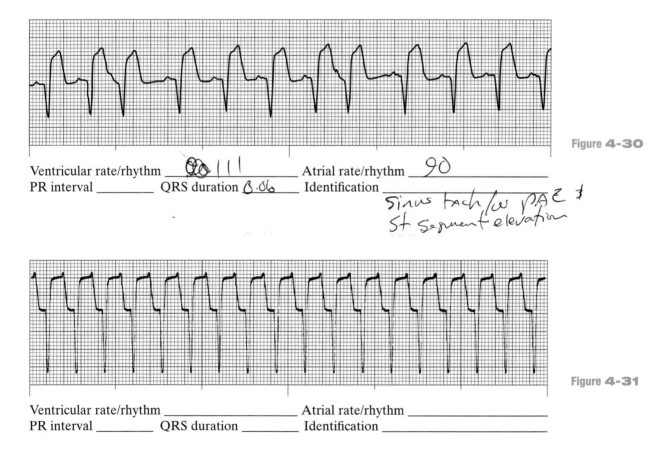

Figure **4-30**

Ventricular rate/rhythm ___111___ Atrial rate/rhythm ___90___
PR interval _____ QRS duration 0.06 Identification ___
Sinus tach /w PAC's &
ST Segment elevation_

Figure **4-31**

Ventricular rate/rhythm _____ Atrial rate/rhythm _____
PR interval _____ QRS duration _____ Identification _____

This rhythm strip is from an 82-year-old man complaining of back pain. Top = lead II, bottom = MCL₁.

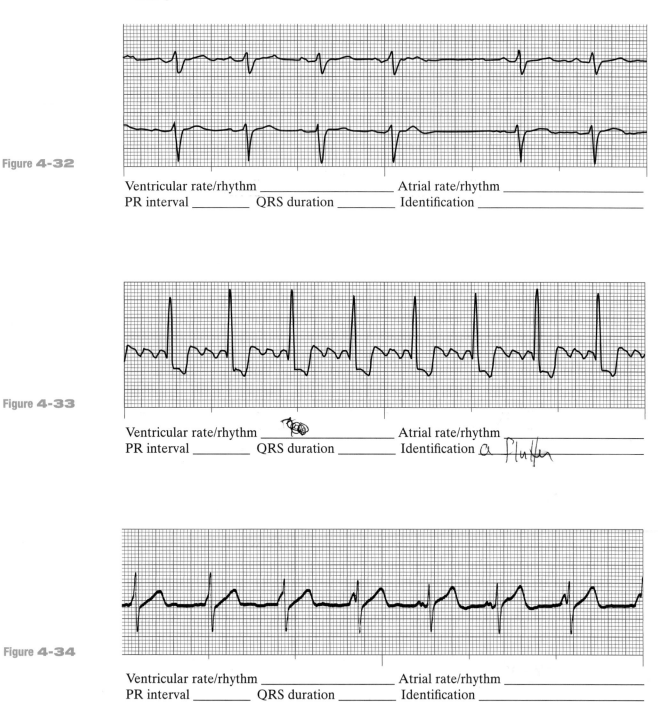

Figure **4-32**

Ventricular rate/rhythm _____ Atrial rate/rhythm _____
PR interval _____ QRS duration _____ Identification _____

Figure **4-33**

Ventricular rate/rhythm _____ Atrial rate/rhythm _____
PR interval _____ QRS duration _____ Identification *a flutter*

Figure **4-34**

Ventricular rate/rhythm _____ Atrial rate/rhythm _____
PR interval _____ QRS duration _____ Identification _____

These rhythm strips are from a 78-year-old man complaining of shortness of breath. He has a history of COPD, coronary artery disease, and hypertension.

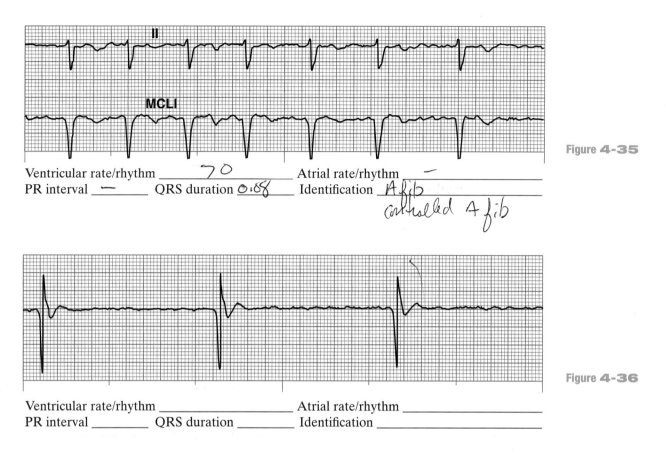

Figure **4-35**

Ventricular rate/rhythm _____*70*_____ Atrial rate/rhythm ____—____
PR interval __—__ QRS duration *0.08* Identification *A fib*
controlled A fib

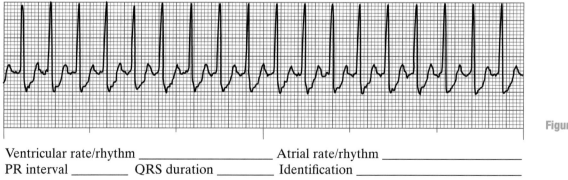

Figure **4-36**

Ventricular rate/rhythm _____ Atrial rate/rhythm _____
PR interval _____ QRS duration _____ Identification _____

This rhythm strip is from a 67-year-old woman complaining of dizziness and a "funny feeling" in her chest. She denies chest pain and is not short of breath.

Figure **4-37**

Ventricular rate/rhythm _____ Atrial rate/rhythm _____
PR interval _____ QRS duration _____ Identification _____

Figure **4-38**

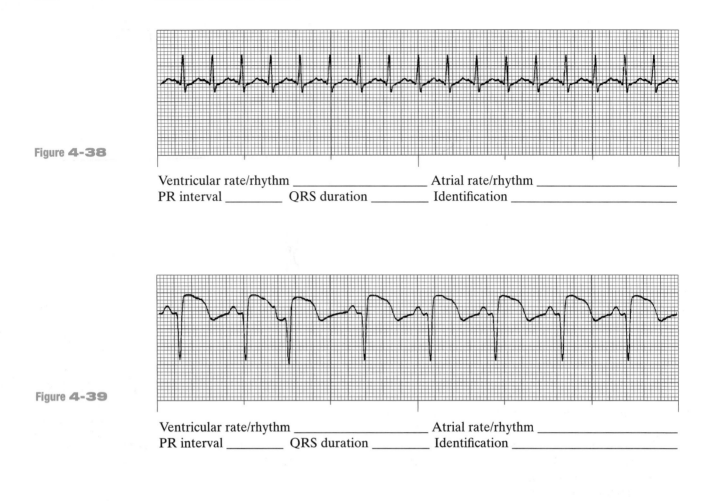

Ventricular rate/rhythm _____ Atrial rate/rhythm _____

PR interval _____ QRS duration _____ Identification _____

Figure **4-39**

Ventricular rate/rhythm _____ Atrial rate/rhythm _____

PR interval _____ QRS duration _____ Identification _____

Junctional Rhythms

OBJECTIVES

On completion of this chapter, you should be able to:

1. Describe the ECG characteristics, possible causes, signs and symptoms, and emergency management for the following dysrhythmias that begin in the AV junction:
   a. Premature junctional complexes
   b. Junctional escape beats
   c. Junctional escape rhythm
   d. Accelerated junctional rhythm
   e. Junctional tachycardia
2. Explain the difference between premature junctional complexes and junctional escape beats.

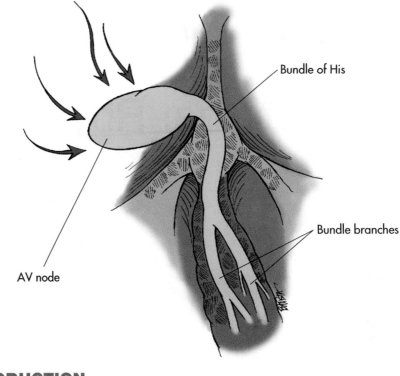

Figure 5-1
The AV junction.

INTRODUCTION

The AV node is a group of specialized cells located in the lower part of the right atrium, above the base of the tricuspid valve. The AV node's main job is to delay an electrical impulse. This allows the atria to contract and complete filling of the ventricles with blood before the next ventricular contraction.

After passing through the AV node, the electrical impulse enters the **bundle of His**. The bundle of His is located in the upper part of the interventricular septum. It connects the AV node with the two bundle branches. The bundle of His has pacemaker cells that are capable of discharging at a rhythmic rate of 40 to 60 bpm. The AV node and the nonbranching portion of the bundle of His are called the **AV junction** (Figure 5-1). The bundle of His conducts the electrical impulse to the right and left bundle branches.

Remember that the SA node is normally the heart's pacemaker. The AV junction may assume responsibility for pacing the heart if:

- The SA node fails to discharge (such as sinus arrest)
- An impulse from the SA node is generated but blocked as it exits the SA node (such as SA block)
- The rate of discharge of the SA node is slower than that of the AV junction (such as a sinus bradycardia or the slower phase of a sinus arrhythmia)
- An impulse from the SA node is generated and is conducted through the atria but is not conducted to the ventricles (such as an AV block)

Rhythms that begin in the AV junction used to be called nodal rhythms until electrophysiologic studies proved the AV node does not contain pacemaker cells. The cells nearest the bundle of His are actually responsible for secondary pacing function. Rhythms originating from the AV junction are now called **junctional dysrhythmias**.

When the atria are depolarized after the ventricles, the P wave typically distorts the end of the QRS complex.

If the AV junction paces the heart, the electrical impulse must travel in a backward (**retrograde**) direction to activate the atria. If a P wave is seen, it will be inverted in leads II, III, and aVF because the impulse is traveling away from the positive electrode (Figure 5-2). If the atria depolarize before the ventricles, an inverted P wave will be seen *before* the QRS complex (Figure 5-3) and the PR interval will usually measure 0.12 sec or less. The PR interval is shorter than usual

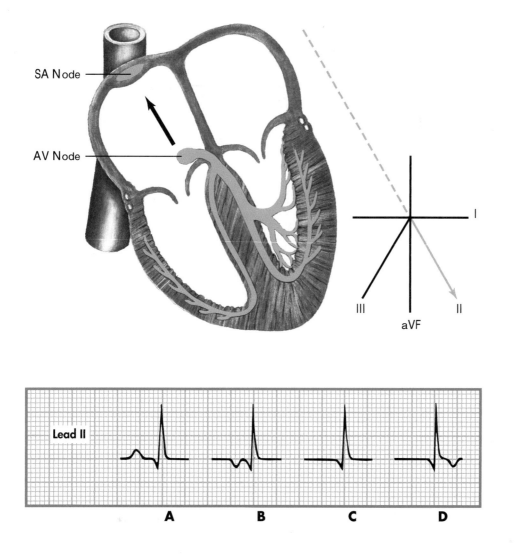

Figure 5-2
If the AV junction paces the
heart, the electrical im-
pulse must travel in a
backward (retrograde) di-
rection to activate the
atria. If a P wave is seen, it
will be inverted in leads II,
III, and aVF because the
impulse is traveling away
from the positive electrode.

Figure 5-3
A, With a sinus rhythm, the
P wave is positive (upright)
in lead II because the wave
of depolarization is moving
toward the positive elec-
trode. The P wave associ-
ated with a junctional beat
(in lead II) may be inverted
(retrograde) **(B)** and appear before the QRS, be
hidden by the QRS **(C)**, or
appear after the QRS **(D)**.

because an impulse that begins in the AV junction does not have to travel as far to stimulate the
ventricles. If the atria and ventricles depolarize at the same time, a P wave will not be visible because it will be hidden in the QRS complex. If the atria depolarize after the ventricles, an inverted P wave will appear *after* the QRS complex.

—— *ECG Pearl*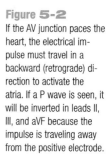

P waves are usually positive (upright) in leads aVR and I. Inverted P waves may be seen in
some, all, or none of the chest leads.

PREMATURE JUNCTIONAL COMPLEXES

How Do I Recognize It?

A **premature junctional complex** (PJC) occurs when an irritable site (focus) within the
AV junction fires before the next SA node impulse is due to fire. This interrupts the sinus
rhythm. Because the impulse is conducted through the ventricles in the usual manner, the
QRS complex will usually measure 0.10 sec or less. A noncompensatory (incomplete) pause
often follows a PJC. This pause represents the delay during which the SA node resets its
rhythm for the next beat.

PJCs are sometimes
called premature junc-
tional extrasystoles.

— ECG Pearl

You can usually tell the difference between a PAC and a PJC by the P wave. A PAC typically has an upright P wave before the QRS complex in leads II, III, and aVF. A P wave may or may not be present with a PJC. If a P wave is present, it is inverted (retrograde) and may precede or follow the QRS. PJCs can be misdiagnosed when the P wave of a PAC is buried in the preceding T wave.

Junctional complexes may come early (before the next expected sinus beat) or late (after the next expected sinus beat). If the complex is *early* it is called a premature junctional complex. If the complex is *late* it is called a junctional escape beat. To determine if a complex is early or late, we need to see at least two sinus beats in a row to establish the regularity of the underlying rhythm.

PJCs may occur in patterns—couplets, bigeminy, trigeminy, and quadrigeminy

Let's look at Figure 5-4. Looking at the overall rhythm, it appears to be irregular. All QRS complexes appear to be narrow, so we assume that all impulses started from above the ventricles. Using a pen or pencil, mark an "S" (for SA node) above each normal looking P wave. Mark a "J" (for junctional) above those P waves that are inverted or absent. When you are finished, you should have a "J" marked over the P waves in beats 2, 5, 8, and 11. The rest of the P waves should be marked with an "S." Now take your calipers or a piece of paper and mark the third and fourth complexes in Figure 5-4. We already determined that these complexes came from the SA node. These beats reflect the underlying rhythm. Calculate the atrial and ventricular rate between these beats. It is 136 bpm (1500 ÷ 11 small boxes). We now know that the underlying rhythm is a sinus tachycardia at 136 bpm. Now move your calipers or paper to the right. If beat 5 occurred on time (when the next sinus beat was expected), it will line up with your calipers (or paper). The fifth complex is early. It occurred *before* the next expected sinus beat. Therefore this complex is a PJC. The other beats that have an inverted P wave before the QRS are also PJCs.

A PJC is not an entire rhythm—it is a single beat. When identifying a rhythm, be sure to specify the underlying rhythm and the origin of the ectopic beat(s). In this rhythm strip we found that the underlying rhythm was a sinus tachycardia at 136 bpm. All of the ectopic beats were early and came from the AV junction. Therefore we would identify this rhythm strip as "sinus tachycardia at 136 bpm with frequent PJCs." Table 5-1 lists the ECG characteristics of PJCs.

TABLE 5-1	**Characteristics of Premature Junctional Complexes**
Rate	Usually within normal range, but depends on underlying rhythm
Rhythm	Regular with premature beats
P waves	May occur before, during, or after the QRS; if visible, the P wave is inverted in leads II, III, and aVF
PR interval	If a P wave occurs before the QRS, the PR interval will usually be ≤0.12 sec; if no P wave occurs before the QRS, there will be no PR interval
QRS duration	Usually 0.10 sec or less unless it is aberrantly conducted or an intraventricular conduction delay exists

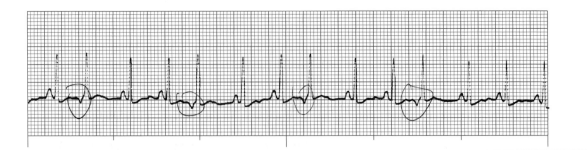

Figure 5-4
Sinus tachycardia at 136 bpm with frequent PJCs.

What Causes It?

PJCs are less common than either PACs or PVCs. Causes of PJCs include the following:

- Congestive heart failure
- Acute coronary syndromes
- Mental and physical fatigue
- Valvular heart disease
- Digitalis toxicity
- Electrolyte imbalance
- Rheumatic heart disease
- Stimulants: caffeine, tobacco

What Do I Do About It?

PJCs do not normally require treatment because most individuals who have PJCs are asymptomatic. However, PJCs may lead to symptoms of palpitations or the feeling of skipped beats. Lightheadedness, dizziness, and other signs of decreased cardiac output can occur if PJCs are frequent. If PJCs occur because of ingestion of stimulants or digitalis toxicity, these substances should be withheld.

—— *ECG Pearl*

Keep in mind that inverted P waves are normal in lead V_1. To determine if a beat or rhythm came from the AV junction using this lead, look for a short PR interval. Use lead II, III, or aVF to confirm your findings.

JUNCTIONAL ESCAPE BEATS/RHYTHM

How Do I Recognize It?

A junctional escape beat begins in the AV junction and appears *late* (after the next expected sinus beat). Junctional escape beats frequently occur during episodes of sinus arrest or follow pauses of nonconducted PACs. Take a look at Figure 5-5. Looking at the rhythm strip, you can see two normal looking beats on the left and two more on the far right. In the center of the strip is an odd-looking beat that appears in the middle of a very long pause between beats 2 and 4. Looking more closely at beats 1, 2, 4, and 5 you can see an upright P wave before each QRS complex. These beats came from the SA node. When you calculate the atrial and ventricular rates between these beats you will find that it is 71 bpm (1500 ÷ 21 small boxes). With this information we know that the underlying rhythm is a sinus rhythm. Using your calipers or a piece of paper, mark the first and second complexes. When you move the calipers or paper to the right, you can see that beat 3 came *late* (after the next expected sinus beat).

Now let's try to figure out where beat 3 came from and why. If you put your finger over beat 3, can you explain what happened? The long pause between beats 2 and 4 is an episode of sinus arrest. Remember that if the SA node fails to initiate an impulse, an escape pacemaker site (the AV junction or ventricles) should assume responsibility for pacing the heart. Look closely at beat 3. The QRS complex is narrow, the ST-segment is depressed, and there is no P wave before the QRS complex. If you compare the ST-segment of beat 3 with the others in the rhythm strip, you can see that the ST-segment in beat 3 is shaped differently. It appears that there is an inverted P wave in the ST-segment of this beat. The narrow-QRS complex and absence of a positive P wave before the QRS complex tells us the beat came from the AV junction. Because the beat is *late*, it is a junctional escape beat. (If beat 3 had been *early*, we would call it a PJC). So what happened here? The SA node fired in beats 1 and 2. When the sinus did not fire again when it should have, the AV junction kicked in and fired. Thus a

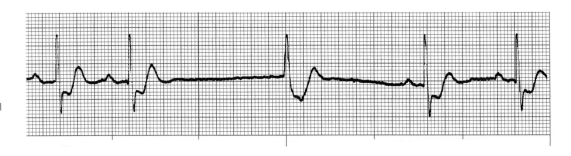

Figure 5-5
Sinus rhythm at 71 bpm
with a prolonged PR interval (0.24 sec), an episode
of sinus arrest, a junctional
escape beat, and ST-
segment depression.

TABLE 5-2	Characteristics of Junctional Escape Beats
Rate	Usually within normal range, but depends on underlying rhythm
Rhythm	Regular with **LATE** beats
P waves	May occur before, during, or after the QRS; if visible, the P wave is inverted in leads II, III, and aVF
PR interval	If a P wave occurs before the QRS, the PR interval will usually be ≤0.12 sec; if no P wave occurs before the QRS, there will be no PR interval
QRS duration	Usually 0.10 sec or less unless it is aberrantly conducted or an intraventricular conduction delay exists

junctional escape beat is *protective*—preventing cardiac standstill. There is a noncompensatory pause after the junctional escape beat during which the SA node resets. This is followed by two sinus beats.

The ST-segments of the beats in this rhythm strip are depressed. The PR interval of the sinus beats is prolonged; measuring 0.24 sec. Complete identification of the events that occurred in this rhythm strip would include the following description, "Sinus rhythm at 71 bpm with a prolonged PR interval (0.24 sec), an episode of sinus arrest, a junctional escape beat, and ST-segment depression." Table 5-2 shows the ECG characteristics of junctional escape beats.

—— *ECG Pearl*

Junctional escape beats and rhythms occur when the SA node fails to pace the heart or AV conduction fails.

The terms *junctional rhythm* and *junctional escape rhythm* are used interchangeably.

A junctional *rhythm* is several sequential junctional escape *beats*. Remember that the intrinsic rate of the AV junction is 40 to 60 bpm. Because a junctional rhythm starts from above the ventricles, the QRS complex is usually narrow and its rhythm is very regular. If the AV junction paces the heart at a rate slower than 40 bpm, the resulting rhythm is called a **junctional bradycardia**. This may seem confusing because the AV junction's normal pacing rate (40 to 60 bpm) *is* bradycardic. However, the term *junctional bradycardia* refers to a rate slower than normal for the AV junction. Figure 5-6 is a continuous rhythm strip. In Figure 5-6, *A,* you can see inverted (retrograde) P waves before the QRS complexes. In Figure 5-6, *B,* note the change in the location of the P waves. In the first beat, the retrograde P wave is seen before the QRS. In the second beat, no P wave is seen. In the remaining beats, the P wave is seen after the QRS complexes. Table 5-3 lists the ECG characteristics of a junctional rhythm.

What Causes It?

Junctional escape beats frequently occur during episodes of sinus arrest or following pauses of nonconducted PACs. Junctional escape beats may also be observed in healthy individuals during sinus bradycardia. Causes of a junctional rhythm include:

- Acute coronary syndromes (particularly inferior wall MI)
- Hypoxia
- Rheumatic heart disease

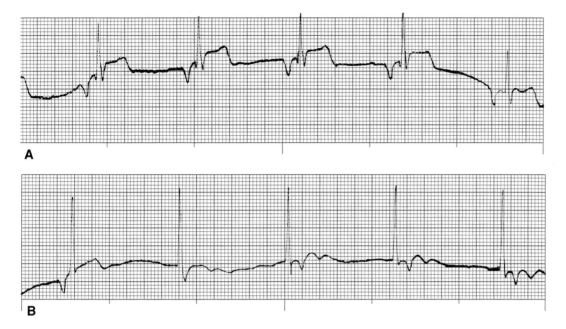

Figure 5-6
Junctional escape rhythm. Continuous strips. **A,** Note the inverted (retrograde) P waves before the QRS complexes. **B,** Note the change in the location of the P waves. In the first beat, the retrograde P wave is seen before the QRS. In the second beat, no P wave is seen. In the remaining beats, the P wave is seen after the QRS complexes.

TABLE 5-3	Characteristics of Junctional Escape Rhythm
Rate	40-60 bpm
Rhythm	Very regular
P waves	May occur before, during, or after the QRS; if visible, the P wave is inverted in leads II, III, and aVF
PR interval	If a P wave occurs before the QRS, the PR interval will usually be ≤0.12 sec; if no P wave occurs before the QRS, there will be no PR interval
QRS duration	Usually 0.10 sec or less unless it is aberrantly conducted or an intraventricular conduction delay exists

- Valvular disease
- SA node disease
- Increased parasympathetic tone
- Immediately after cardiac surgery
- Effects of medications including digitalis, quinidine, beta-blockers, and calcium channel blockers

What Do I Do About It?

The patient may be asymptomatic with a junctional escape rhythm or may experience signs and symptoms that may be associated with the slow heart rate and decreased cardiac output. Treatment depends on the cause of the dysrhythmia and the patient's presenting signs and symptoms. If the dysrhythmia is caused by digitalis toxicity, this medication should be withheld. If the patient's signs and symptoms are related to the slow heart rate, atropine and/or transcutaneous pacing should be considered. Other medications that may be used in the treatment of symptomatic bradycardia include dopamine and epinephrine intravenous infusions.

ACCELERATED JUNCTIONAL RHYTHM

How Do I Recognize It?

If the AV junction speeds up and fires at a rate of 61 to 100 bpm, the resulting rhythm is called an **accelerated junctional rhythm**. This rhythm is caused by enhanced automaticity of the bundle of His. The only ECG difference between a junctional rhythm and an accelerated

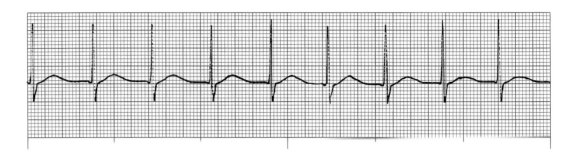

TABLE 5-4	**Characteristics of Accelerated Junctional Rhythm**
Rate	61-100 bpm
Rhythm	Very regular
P waves	May occur before, during, or after the QRS; if visible, the P wave is inverted in leads II, III, and aVF
PR interval	If a P wave occurs before the QRS, the PR interval will usually be ≤0.12 sec; if no P wave occurs before the QRS, there will be no PR interval
QRS duration	Usually 0.10 sec or less unless it is aberrantly conducted or an intraventricular conduction delay exists

junctional rhythm is the increase in the ventricular rate. Figure 5-7 is an example of an accelerated junctional rhythm. Table 5-4 shows the ECG characteristics of this rhythm.

What Causes It?

Causes of this dysrhythmia include digitalis toxicity, acute myocardial infarction, cardiac surgery, rheumatic fever, COPD, and hypokalemia.

What Do I Do About It?

The patient is usually asymptomatic because the ventricular rate is 61 to 100 bpm; however, the patient should be monitored closely. If the rhythm is caused by digitalis toxicity, this medication should be withheld.

—— *ECG Pearl*

Junctional Dysrhythmias at a Glance
- Junctional rhythm—40-60 bpm
- Accelerated junctional rhythm—61-100 bpm
- Junctional tachycardia—101-180 bpm

JUNCTIONAL TACHYCARDIA

How Do I Recognize It?

When the ventricular rate is greater than 150 bpm, it is difficult to distinguish junctional tachycardia from AV nodal reentrant tachycardia and AV reentrant tachycardia.

Junctional tachycardia is an ectopic rhythm that begins in the pacemaker cells found in the bundle of His. When three or more sequential PJCs occur at a rate of more than 100 bpm, a junctional tachycardia exists. Nonparoxysmal (gradual onset) junctional tachycardia usually starts as an accelerated junctional rhythm, but the heart rate gradually increases to more than 100 bpm. The usual ventricular rate for nonparoxysmal junctional tachycardia is 101 to 140 bpm. Paroxysmal junctional tachycardia starts and ends suddenly and is often precipitated by a PJC. The ventricular rate for paroxysmal junctional tachycardia is generally faster, 140 bpm or more. Figure 5-8 is an example of junctional tachycardia. Table 5-5 shows the ECG characteristics of this rhythm.

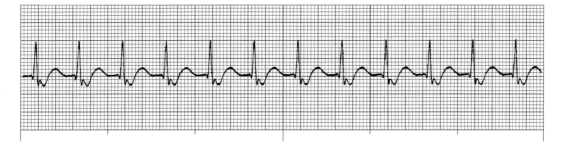

Figure 5-8
Junctional tachycardia at
120 bpm.

TABLE 5-5	**Characteristics of Junctional Tachycardia**
Rate	101-180 bpm
Rhythm	Very regular
P waves	May occur before, during, or after the QRS; if visible, the P wave is inverted in leads II, III, and aVF
PR interval	If a P wave occurs before the QRS, the PR interval will usually be ≤0.12 sec; if no P wave occurs before the QRS, there will be no PR interval
QRS duration	Usually 0.10 sec or less unless it is aberrantly conducted or an intraventricular conduction delay exists

What Causes It?

Junctional tachycardia is believed to be caused by enhanced automaticity. It may occur because of an acute coronary syndrome, congestive heart failure, theophylline administration, or digitalis toxicity.

What Do I Do About It?

With sustained ventricular rates of 150 bpm or more, the patient may complain of a "racing heart" and severe anxiety. Because of the fast ventricular rate, the ventricles may be unable to fill completely, resulting in decreased cardiac output. Junctional tachycardia associated with an acute coronary syndrome may:

- Increase myocardial ischemia
- Increase the frequency and severity of chest pain
- Extend the size of a myocardial infarction
- Cause congestive heart failure, hypotension, or cardiogenic shock
- Predispose the patient to ventricular dysrhythmias

The more rapid the rate, the greater the incidence of symptoms due to increased myocardial oxygen demand.

Treatment depends on the severity of the patient's signs and symptoms. If the patient tolerates the rhythm, observation is often all that is needed. If the patient is symptomatic as a result of the rapid rate, initial treatment should include oxygen and IV access. Since it is often difficult to distinguish junctional tachycardia from other narrow-QRS tachycardias, vagal maneuvers and, if necessary, IV adenosine may be used to help determine the origin of the rhythm. A beta-blocker or calcium channel blocker may be ordered (if no contraindications exist). If the rhythm is the result of digitalis toxicity, the drug should be withheld. If the rhythm is the result of theophylline administration, the infusion should be slowed or stopped. A summary of junctional rhythm characteristics can be found in Table 5-6.

In adults, junctional tachycardia is often a symptom of digitalis toxicity.

TABLE 5-6   Junctional Rhythms—Summary of Characteristics

	PJCs	Junctional Escape Beat	Junctional Escape Rhythm	Accelerated Junctional Rhythm	Junctional Tachycardia
Rate	Usually within normal range, but depends on underlying rhythm	Usually within normal range, but depends on underlying rhythm	40-60 bpm	61-100 bpm	101-180 bpm
Rhythm	Regular with premature beats	Regular with late beats	Regular	Regular	Regular
P Waves (leads II, III, aVF)	May occur before, during, or after the QRS; if visible, the P wave is inverted in leads II, III, and aVF	May occur before, during, or after the QRS; if visible, the P wave is inverted in leads II, III, and aVF	May occur before, during, or after the QRS; if visible, the P wave is inverted in leads II, III, and aVF	May occur before, during, or after the QRS; if visible, the P wave is inverted in leads II, III, and aVF	May occur before, during, or after the QRS; if visible, the P wave is inverted in leads II, III, and aVF
PR Interval	If a P wave occurs before the QRS, the PR interval will usually be ≤0.12 sec; if no P wave occurs before the QRS, there will be no PR interval	If a P wave occurs before the QRS, the PR interval will usually be ≤0.12 sec; if no P wave occurs before the QRS, there will be no PR interval	If a P wave occurs before the QRS, the PR interval will usually be ≤0.12 sec; if no P wave occurs before the QRS, there will be no PR interval	If a P wave occurs before the QRS, the PR interval will usually be ≤0.12 sec; if no P wave occurs before the QRS, there will be no PR interval	If a P wave occurs before the QRS, the PR interval will usually be ≤0.12 sec; if no P wave occurs before the QRS, there will be no PR interval
QRS	Usually 0.10 sec or less unless it is aberrantly conducted or an intraventricular conduction delay exists	Usually 0.10 sec or less unless it is aberrantly conducted or an intraventricular conduction delay exists	Usually 0.10 sec or less unless it is aberrantly conducted or an intraventricular conduction delay exists	Usually 0.10 sec or less unless it is aberrantly conducted or an intraventricular conduction delay exists	Usually 0.10 sec or less unless it is aberrantly conducted or an intraventricular conduction delay exists

S T O P & REVIEW

True/False

Indicate whether the sentence or statement is true or false.

_____ 1. PJCs are more common than PACs or PVCs.

_____ 2. A PJC produces a positive (upright) P wave in leads II, III, and aVF that comes before, during, or after the QRS complex.

_____ 3. Amiodarone is the drug of choice when treating a symptomatic patient with a junctional rhythm at a rate of 40 bpm.

Completion

Complete each sentence or statement.

4. If the AV junction paces the heart, the electrical impulse must travel in a backward direction to activate the atria. This is called _____ conduction.

5. A beat originating from the AV junction that appears later than the next expected sinus beat is called a _____ _____ _____.

Matching

a. Digitalis
b. Atropine
c. Inverted P wave occurs after the QRS complex in leads II, III, and aVF
d. P wave
e. Hidden within the QRS complex (not visible)

f. Accelerated junctional rhythm
g. 40-60 bpm
h. Inverted P wave appears before the QRS complex in leads II, III, and aVF
i. Ectopic
j. Premature junctional complex

_____ 6. Location of the P wave on the ECG if atrial depolarization precedes ventricular depolarization
_____ 7. A beat originating from the AV junction that appears earlier than the next expected sinus beat
_____ 8. Normal rate for the AV junction
_____ 9. Primary waveform used to differentiate PJCs from PACs
_____ 10. Medication used to increase heart rate
_____ 11. Location of the P wave on the ECG if atrial and ventricular depolarization occur simultaneously
_____ 12. Toxicity/excess of this medication is a common cause of junctional dysrhythmias.
_____ 13. Name given to a dysrhythmia that originates in the AV junction with a ventricular rate between 61-100 bpm
_____ 14. Impulse originating from a source other than the SA node
_____ 15. Location of the P wave on the ECG if atrial depolarization occurs after ventricular depolarization

16. Indicate the ventricular rates for each of the following junctional dysrhythmias.

    1. Junctional bradycardia _____

    2. Junctional tachycardia _____

    3. Accelerated junctional rhythm _____

    4. Junctional rhythm _____

17. List four reasons why the AV junction may assume responsibility for pacing the heart.
    1.

    2.

    3.

    4.

ECG Crossword

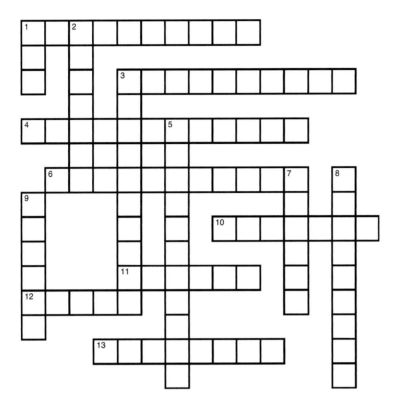

Across

1. This type of junctional tachycardia begins and ends suddenly.
3. AV node + bundle of His
4. Common complaint in a patient with a rapid heart rate
6. If the AV junction paces the heart at a rate slower than 40 bpm, the resulting rhythm is called a junctional __.
10. The PR interval associated with a junctional beat is usually __ than normal.
11. The QRS of a junctional beat or rhythm is usually __.
12. Helps differentiate PJCs and PACs
13. P waves in lead V_1 are normally __.

Down

1. Premature junctional complex
2. The ventricular rhythm in a rhythm that begins in the AV junction is normally very __.
3. Medication used to treat a number of dysrhythmias in adults and children
5. If the AV junction paces the heart at a rate of 61-100 bpm, the resulting rhythm is called a(n)__ junctional rhythm.
7. Junctional escape beats frequently occur during episodes of sinus __.
8. A __ junctional complex comes early.
9. A(n) __ beat comes late.

PRACTICE Rhythm Strips

For each of the following rhythm strips, determine the atrial and ventricular rate and rhythm, measure the PR interval and QRS duration, and then identify the rhythm. All strips were recorded in lead II unless otherwise noted.

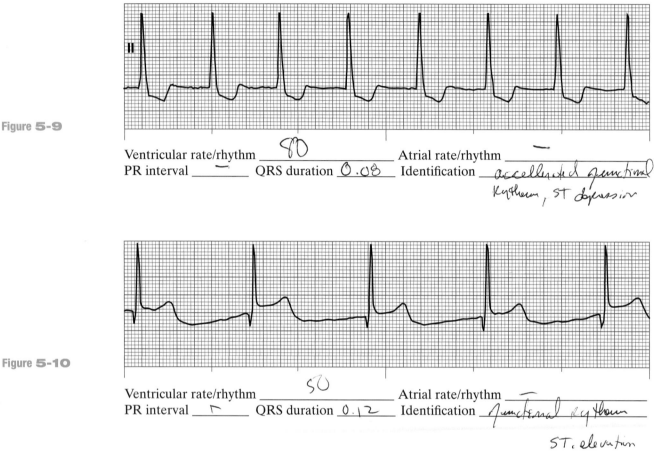

Figure 5-9

Ventricular rate/rhythm _____80_____ Atrial rate/rhythm _____—_____
PR interval _____—_____ QRS duration 0.08 Identification _accellerated junctional_
Rythem, ST depression

Figure 5-10

Ventricular rate/rhythm _____50_____ Atrial rate/rhythm _____—_____
PR interval ____⌐____ QRS duration 0.12 Identification _Junctional Rythem_
ST. elevation

This rhythm strip is from an 88-year-old woman who experienced a syncopal episode. Blood sugar is 96. Medications include verapamil. History includes myocardial infarction 9 years ago, stroke 5 years ago, hypertension, and diabetes.

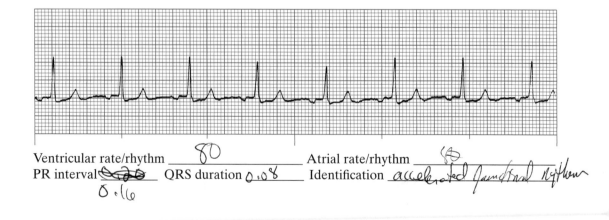

Figure 5-11

Ventricular rate/rhythm _____80_____ Atrial rate/rhythm _____80_____
PR interval _0.20_ QRS duration 0.08 Identification _accelerated junctional rythem_
_0.16_

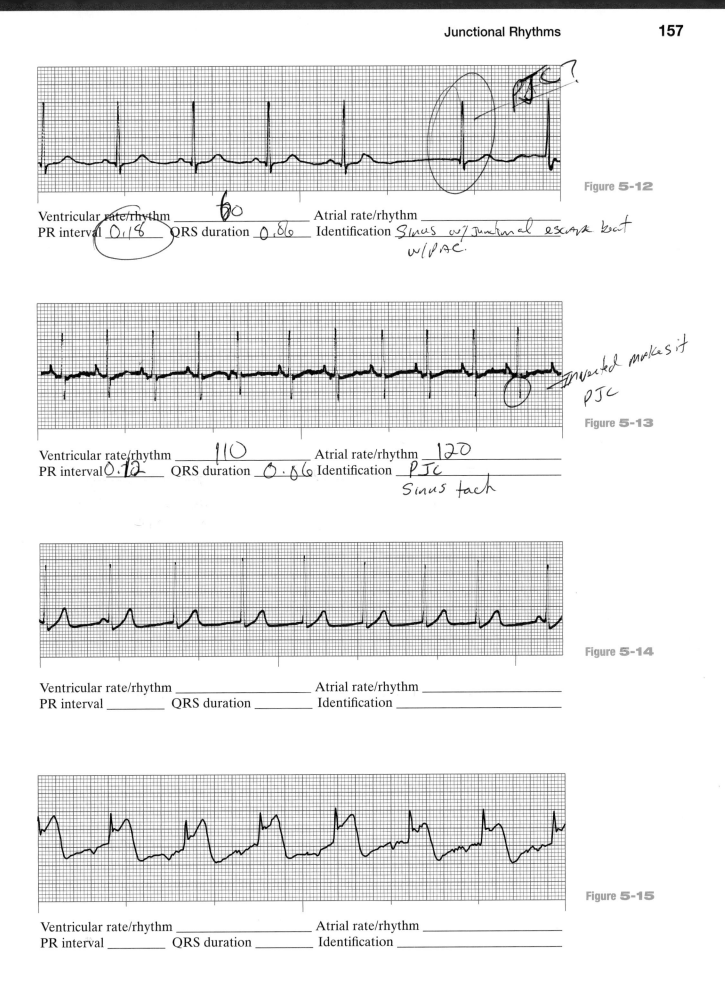

Figure **5-12**

Ventricular rate/rhythm _____ 60 _____   Atrial rate/rhythm _____
PR interval 0.18   QRS duration 0.86   Identification Sinus w/ Junctional escape beat
w/PAC.

PJC ?

Figure **5-13**

Inverted makes it PJC

Ventricular rate/rhythm _____ 110 _____   Atrial rate/rhythm _____ 120 _____
PR interval 0.12   QRS duration 0.86   Identification PJC
Sinus tach

Figure **5-14**

Ventricular rate/rhythm _____   Atrial rate/rhythm _____
PR interval _____ QRS duration _____ Identification _____

Figure **5-15**

Ventricular rate/rhythm _____   Atrial rate/rhythm _____
PR interval _____ QRS duration _____ Identification _____

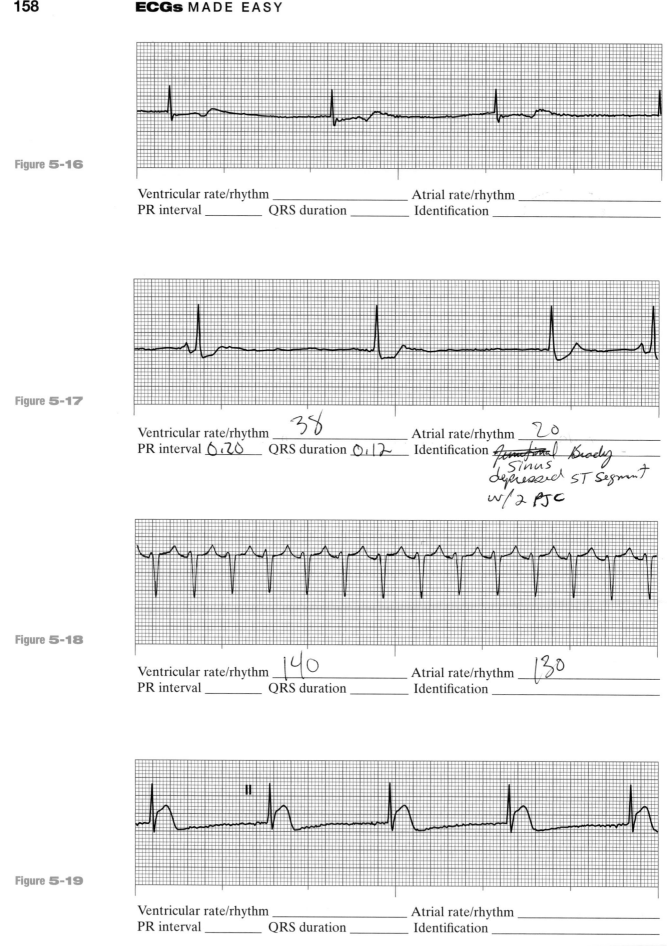

Figure 5-16

Ventricular rate/rhythm _____ Atrial rate/rhythm _____

PR interval _____ QRS duration _____ Identification _____

Figure 5-17

Ventricular rate/rhythm ____38____ Atrial rate/rhythm ____20____

PR interval _0.20_ QRS duration _0.12_ Identification ~~Junctional~~ Brady-
Sinus
depressed ST Segment
w/ 2 PJC

Figure 5-18

Ventricular rate/rhythm ___140___ Atrial rate/rhythm ___130___

PR interval _____ QRS duration _____ Identification _____

Figure 5-19

Ventricular rate/rhythm _____ Atrial rate/rhythm _____

PR interval _____ QRS duration _____ Identification _____

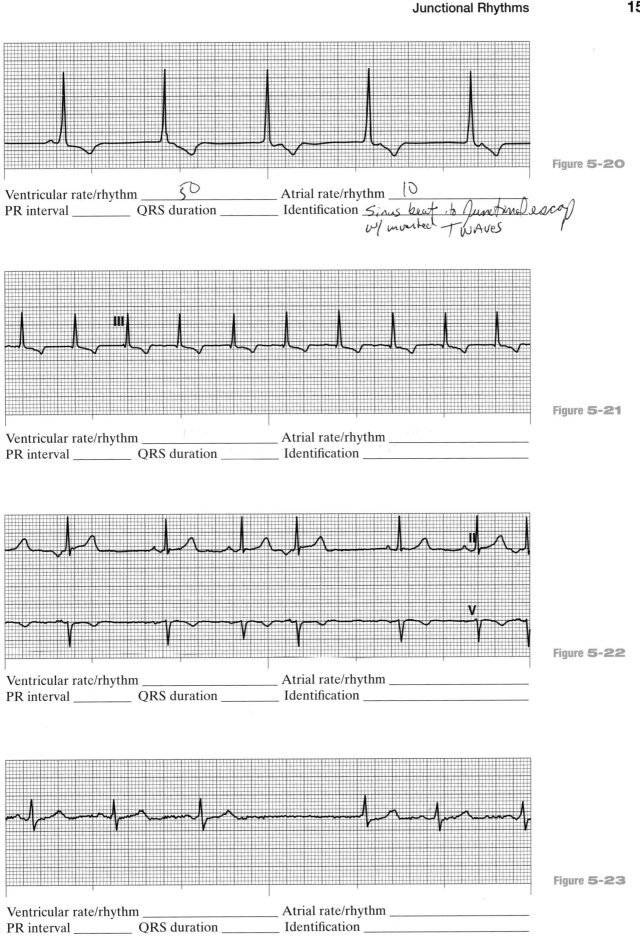

Figure 5-20

Ventricular rate/rhythm _____ 50 _____ Atrial rate/rhythm _____ 10 _____
PR interval _____ QRS duration _____ Identification _Sinus beat to Junctional escap_
w/ inverted T waves

Figure 5-21

Ventricular rate/rhythm _____ Atrial rate/rhythm _____
PR interval _____ QRS duration _____ Identification _____

Figure 5-22

Ventricular rate/rhythm _____ Atrial rate/rhythm _____
PR interval _____ QRS duration _____ Identification _____

Figure 5-23

Ventricular rate/rhythm _____ Atrial rate/rhythm _____
PR interval _____ QRS duration _____ Identification _____

CHAPTER 6

Ventricular Rhythms

OBJECTIVES

On completion of this chapter, you should be able to:

1. Describe the ECG characteristics, possible causes, signs and symptoms, and emergency management for the following dysrhythmias that originate in the ventricles:
   a. Premature ventricular complexes (PVCs)
   b. Ventricular escape beats
   c. Ventricular escape (idioventricular) rhythm (IVR)
   d. Accelerated idioventricular rhythm (AIVR)
   e. Ventricular tachycardia (VT)
   f. Polymorphic VT
   g. Torsades de pointes (TdP)
   h. Ventricular fibrillation (VF)
   i. Asystole
2. Explain the terms *bigeminy*, *trigeminy*, *quadrigeminy*, and *run* when used to describe premature complexes.
3. Explain the difference between premature ventricular complexes and ventricular escape beats.
4. Explain the terms *monomorphic* and *polymorphic ventricular tachycardia*.
5. Discuss long QT syndrome (LQTS).
6. State the purpose and procedure for defibrillation.
7. List the indications for defibrillation.
8. Explain the term *P-wave asystole*.
9. Explain the term *pulseless electrical activity*.

INTRODUCTION

The ventricles are the heart's least efficient pacemaker. If the ventricles function as the heart's pacemaker, they normally generate impulses at a rate of 20 to 40 bpm. The ventricles may assume responsibility for pacing the heart if:

- SA node fails to discharge
- Impulse from the SA node is generated but blocked as it exits the SA node
- Rate of discharge of the SA node is slower than that of the ventricles
- Irritable site in either ventricle produces an early beat or rapid rhythm

Normally an electrical impulse that begins in the SA node, atria, or AV junction results in depolarization of the right and left ventricles at about the same time. The resulting QRS complex is usually narrow, measuring less than 0.10 sec in duration.

> The shape of the QRS complex is influenced by the site of origin of the electrical impulse.

If an area of either ventricle becomes ischemic or injured, it can become irritable. This irritability affects the manner in which impulses are conducted. Ventricular beats and rhythms can start in any part of the ventricles and may occur as a result of reentry, enhanced automaticity, or triggered activity. When an ectopic site within a ventricle assumes responsibility for pacing the heart, the electrical impulse bypasses the normal intraventricular conduction pathway. This results in stimulation of the ventricles at slightly different times. As a result, ventricular beats and rhythms usually have QRS complexes that are abnormally shaped and longer than normal (greater than 0.12 sec).

> If the atria are depolarized after the ventricles, retrograde P waves may be seen.

Because ventricular depolarization is abnormal, ventricular repolarization is also abnormal. This results in changes in ST-segments and T waves. T waves are usually in a direction opposite that of the QRS complex. In other words, if the major QRS deflection is negative, the ST-segment is usually elevated and the T wave positive (upright). If the major QRS deflection is positive, the ST-segment is usually depressed and the T wave is usually negative (inverted). P waves are usually not seen with ventricular dysrhythmias, but if they are visible, they have no consistent relationship to the QRS complex (AV dissociation).

PREMATURE VENTRICULAR COMPLEXES

How Do I Recognize It?

A premature ventricular complex (PVC) arises from an irritable site within either ventricle. PVCs may be caused by enhanced automaticity or reentry. By definition, a PVC is *premature*, occurring earlier than the next expected sinus beat. The QRS of a PVC is typically equal to or greater than 0.12 sec because the PVC causes the ventricles to fire prematurely and in an abnormal manner (Figure 6-1). The T wave is usually in the opposite direction of the QRS complex. A full **compensatory pause** often follows a PVC (Figure 6-2). This occurs because the SA node is not affected by the PVC. It discharges at its regular rate and rhythm, including the period during and after the PVC.

> PVCs are also called premature ventricular extrasystoles or ventricular premature beats.

—— ECG Pearl

To determine whether or not the pause following a premature complex is compensatory or noncompensatory, measure the distance between three normal beats. Compare the distance between three beats, one of which includes the premature complex. The pause is compensatory (also called full or complete) if the normal beat following the premature complex occurs when expected (i.e., when the distance is the same).

—— ECG Pearl

"A full compensatory pause does not reliably differentiate ventricular ectopy from atrial ectopy because atrial ectopy may produce a similar compensatory pattern if it does not reset the SA node. In addition, when PVCs are retrogradely conducted to the atria, as in slow sinus rates, they can reset the SA node and a full compensatory pause may not be present."[1]

Figure 6-1
Premature beats. **A,** Sinus rhythm with premature atrial complexes. The fourth and sixth beats are preceded by premature P waves that look different from the normally conducted sinus beats. Note that the QRS complex that follows each of these PACs is narrow and identical in appearance to that of the sinus-conducted beats. **B,** Sinus rhythm with premature junctional complexes. The fourth and sixth beats are PJCs. Beat 4 is preceded by an inverted P wave with a short PR interval. There is no identifiable atrial activity associated with beat 6. **C,** Sinus rhythm with premature ventricular complexes. The fourth and sixth beats are very different in appearance from the normally conducted sinus beats. Beats 4 and 6 are PVCs. They are not preceded by P waves.

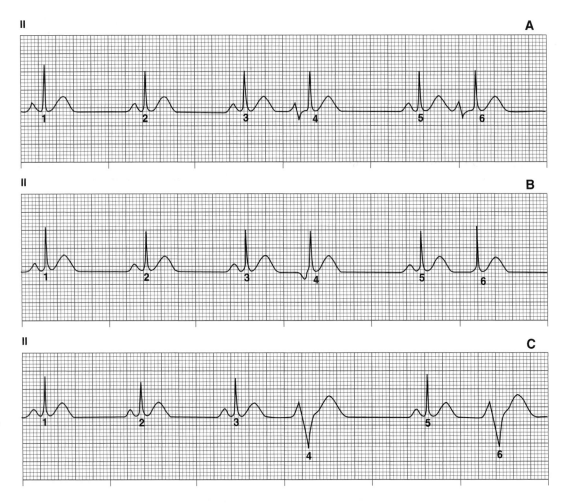

Figure 6-2
A, A premature ventricular complex (PVC) is often followed by a full compensatory pause. **B,** A premature atrial complex (PAC) is often followed by a noncompensatory (incomplete) pause.

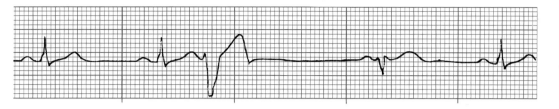

Figure 6-3
Sinus bradycardia with a PVC (third complex from the left) and a fusion beat (fourth complex from the left).

A **fusion beat** (Figure 6-3) is a result of an electrical impulse from a supraventricular site (such as the SA node) discharging at the same time as an ectopic site in the ventricles. Because fusion beats are a result of both supraventricular and ventricular depolarization, these beats do not resemble normally conducted beats, nor do they resemble true ventricular beats.

A PVC is not an entire rhythm—it is a single beat. Therefore it is important to identify the underlying rhythm and the ectopic beat(s), that is, "sinus tachycardia at 138 bpm with frequent PVCs."

Types of PVCs

PVCs may occur in the following patterns:

Three or more PVCs in a row at a rate of more than 100 bpm is a run of ventricular tachycardia.

- Pairs (couplets): Two sequential PVCs
- "Runs" or "bursts": Three or more PVCs in a row
- Bigeminal PVCs (ventricular bigeminy): Every other beat is a PVC
- Trigeminal PVCs (ventricular trigeminy): Every third beat is a PVC
- Quadrigeminal PVCs (ventricular quadrigeminy): Every fourth beat is a PVC

Uniform and Multiformed PVCs

Premature ventricular beats that look the same in the same lead and begin from the same anatomic site (focus) are called **uniform** PVCs (Figure 6-4). PVCs that look different from one another in the same lead are called **multiform** PVCs (Figure 6-5). The terms *unifocal* and *multifocal* are sometimes used to describe PVCs that are similar or different in appearance. Uniform PVCs are unifocal, but multiform PVCs are not necessarily multifocal.[2]

Multiform PVCs often, but do not always, arise from different anatomic sites.

Interpolated PVCs

A PVC may occur without interfering with the normal cardiac cycle. An **interpolated** PVC (Figure 6-6) does not have a full compensatory pause. It is "squeezed" between two regular complexes and does not disturb the underlying rhythm. The PR interval of the cardiac cycle following the PVC may be longer than normal.

If an interpolated PVC produces a palpable pulse, frequent interpolated PVCs may cause signs and symptoms because of an increased heart rate.

R-on-T PVCs

R-on-T PVCs occur when the R wave of a PVC falls on the T wave of the preceding beat (Figure 6-7). Because the T wave is vulnerable (relative refractory period) to any electrical stimulation, it is possible that a PVC occurring during this period of the cardiac cycle will precipitate VT or VF; however, VT and VF most commonly occur without a preceding R-on-T PVC, and most R-on-T PVCs do not precipitate a sustained ventricular tachydysrhythmia.[2]

Paired PVCs (Couplets)

Two PVCs in a row are called a **couplet** or **paired PVCs** (Figure 6-8). The appearance of couplets indicates the ventricular ectopic site is very irritable. Three or more PVCs in a row at a rate of more than 100 bpm is considered a "salvo," "run," or "burst" of ventricular tachycardia. The general characteristics of PVCs are shown in Table 6-1.

Couplets are also referred to as *two in a row* or *back-to-back* PVCs.

What Causes It?

PVCs are the most common dysrhythmia in healthy individuals and in those with organic heart disease. PVCs can occur in healthy persons with apparently normal hearts and for no

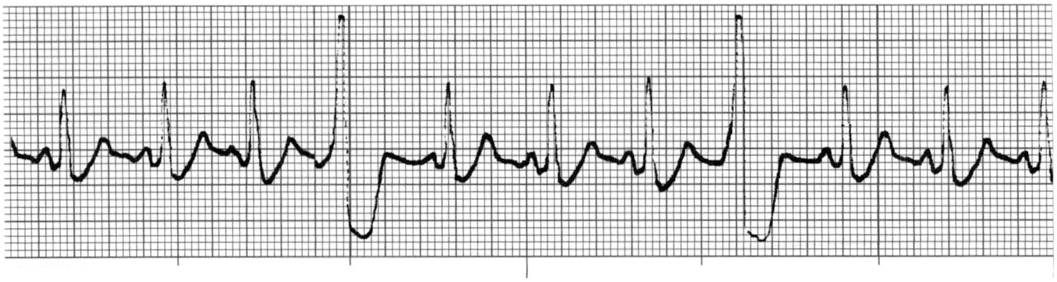

Figure 6-4
Sinus tachycardia with frequent uniform PVCs.

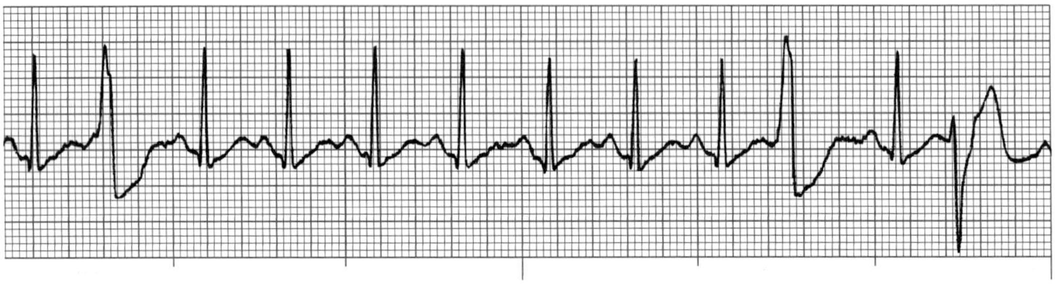

Figure 6-5
Sinus tachycardia with multiform PVCs.

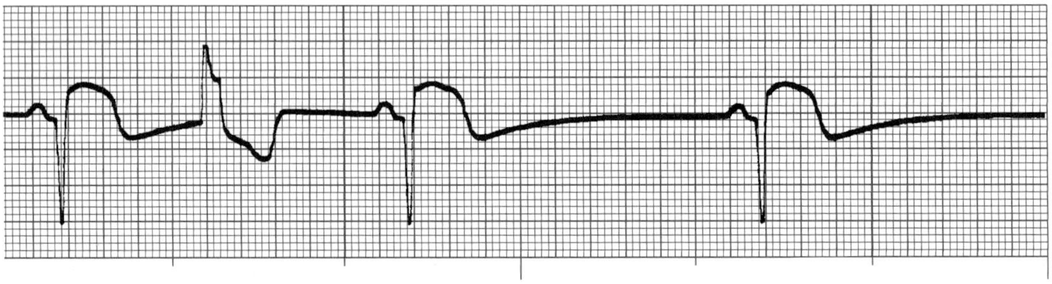

Figure 6-6
Sinus bradycardia with an interpolated PVC and ST-segment elevation.

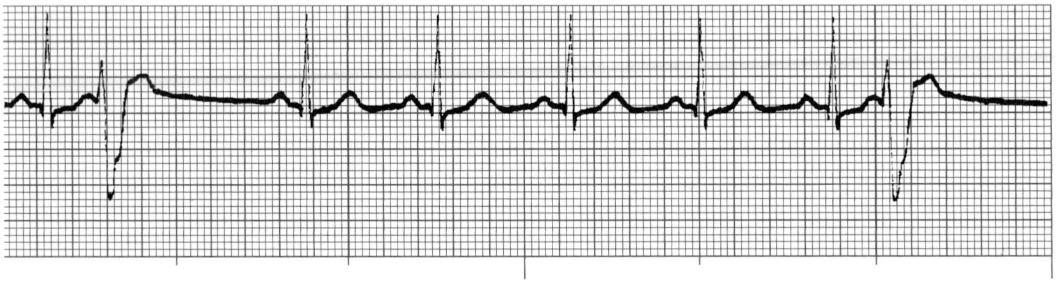

Figure 6-7
Sinus rhythm with two R-on-T PVCs.

Figure 6-8
Sinus rhythm with a run of VT and one episode of couplets.

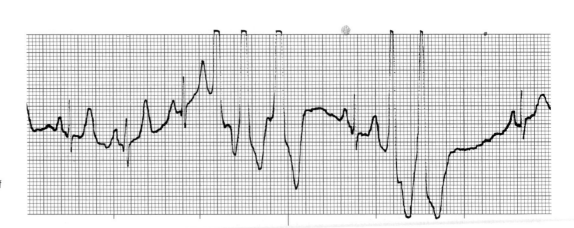

TABLE 6-1	Characteristics of Premature Ventricular Complexes
Rate	Usually within normal range, but depends on underlying rhythm
Rhythm	Essentially regular with premature beats; if the PVC is an interpolated PVC, the rhythm will be regular
P waves	Usually absent or, with retrograde conduction to the atria, may appear after the QRS (usually upright in the ST-segment or T wave)
PR interval	None with the PVC because the ectopic originates in the ventricles
QRS duration	Greater than 0.12 sec, wide and bizarre; T wave usually in opposite direction of the QRS complex

Common Causes of PVCs

- Normal variant
- Hypoxia
- Stress, anxiety
- Exercise
- Digitalis toxicity
- Acid-base imbalance
- Myocardial ischemia

- Electrolyte imbalance
- Congestive heart failure
- Increased sympathetic tone
- Acute coronary syndromes
- Stimulants (caffeine, tobacco)
- Medications (sympathomimetics, cyclic antidepressants, phenothiazines)

apparent cause. The frequency with which PVCs occur increases with age. PVCs can occur at rest or may be associated with exercise. Common causes of PVCs are shown in Box 6-1.

What Do I Do About It?

PVCs may or may not produce palpable pulses. Patients experiencing PVCs may be asymptomatic or complain of palpitations, a "racing heart," skipped beats, or chest or neck discomfort. These symptoms may be caused by the greater than normal contractile force of the postectopic beats or the feeling that the heart has stopped during the long pause after the premature complexes.[3] If the PVCs are frequent, signs of decreased cardiac output may be present.

Patients often describe premature beats as "flip-flops."

—— *ECG Pearl*

As with all cardiac dysrhythmias, it is important to treat the patient, not the monitor.

Treatment of PVCs depends on the cause, the patient's signs and symptoms, and on the clinical situation. Most patients experiencing PVCs do not require treatment with antiarrhythmic medications. Treatment of PVCs focuses on treatment of the underlying cause. In the setting of an acute coronary syndrome, treatment is directed at:

Routine use of medications to treat PVCs is no longer recommended.

- Ensuring adequate oxygenation
- Relieving pain
- Rapidly identifying and correcting hypoxia, heart failure, and electrolyte or acid-base abnormalities

VENTRICULAR ESCAPE BEATS/RHYTHM

How Do I Recognize It?

Remember that premature beats are *early* and escape beats are *late*. In order to determine if a complex is early or late, we need to see at least two sinus beats in a row to establish the regularity of the underlying rhythm. Although ventricular escape beats share some of the same physical characteristics as PVCs (wide QRS complexes, T waves deflected in a direction opposite the QRS), they differ in some very important areas.

- A PVC appears *early*, before the next expected sinus beat. PVCs often reflect irritability in some area of the ventricles. When PVCs cause serious symptoms, medications are sometimes used to reduce the frequency with which they occur or eliminate them completely.
- A **ventricular escape beat** occurs after a pause in which a supraventricular pacemaker failed to fire. Thus the escape beat is *late*, appearing after the next expected sinus beat. A ventricular escape beat is a *protective* mechanism. It protects the heart from more extreme slowing or even asystole. Because it is protective, you would not want to administer any medication that would "wipe out" the escape beat.

Take a look at Figure 6-9. When looking at this rhythm strip, one of the first things you notice is the beat with wide QRS complex. Although it looks interesting, let's first examine the rhythm systemically. The rhythm is essentially regular except for the single wide-QRS beat. There are upright P waves before beats 1, 2, 3, 5, and 6. When you calculate the atrial and ventricular rate, you find that the rate is 63 bpm. Now we know that the underlying rhythm is a sinus rhythm at 63 bpm. Next, let's examine the wide-QRS beat more closely and see what happened here. Look to the left of the wide-QRS beat and see if anything looks amiss. When you look closely at the T wave of beat 3, it has an extra "hump." If you take a moment to plot P waves across the strip, you'll find that this extra hump is actually an early P wave that was not conducted. This is a nonconducted PAC. When plotting the P waves, you should have noticed that the wide-QRS beat occurred *late*—after the next expected sinus beat. This is an escape beat. Because the QRS associated with it is *wide*, it is a *ventricular* escape beat. (A *junctional* escape beat is also late—but it usually has a *narrow* QRS). Notice that the T wave of this beat is deflected in a direction opposite its QRS complex. When you look at the PR intervals and ST-segments, you'll find that the PR interval is longer than normal (about 0.24 sec). For now, we will simply say that it is prolonged. We will explore the reasons for this and give it a name in the next chapter. ST-segment depression is also present. Our identification of this rhythm would include a description like,

TABLE 6-2	**Characteristics of Ventricular Escape Beats**
Rate	Usually within normal range, but depends on underlying rhythm
Rhythm	Essentially regular with late beats; the ventricular escape beat occurs *after* the next expected sinus beat
P waves	Usually absent or, with retrograde conduction to the atria, may appear after the QRS (usually upright in the ST-segment or T wave)
PR interval	None with the ventricular escape beat because the ectopic beat originates in the ventricles
QRS duration	Greater than 0.12 sec, wide and bizarre, T wave frequently in opposite direction of the QRS complex

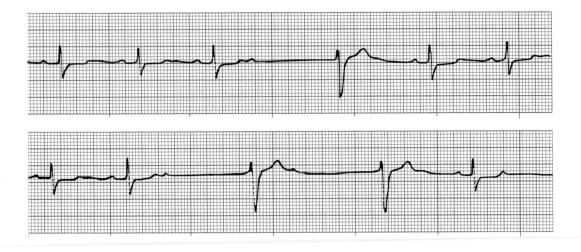

Figure 6-9
Sinus rhythm with a prolonged PR interval, ST-segment depression. Note the ventricular escape beats following nonconducted premature atrial complexes.

"Sinus rhythm at 63 bpm with a prolonged PR interval, nonconducted PAC, ventricular escape beat, and ST-segment depression." My goodness! That was one complicated rhythm strip! Table 6-2 lists the ECG characteristics of ventricular escape beats.

A ventricular escape or **idioventricular rhythm (IVR)** exists when three or more ventricular escape beats occur in a row at a rate of 20 to 40 bpm. This rate is the intrinsic firing rate of the ventricles. The QRS complexes seen in IVR are wide and bizarre because the impulses begin in the ventricles, bypassing the normal conduction pathway. When the ventricular rate slows to a rate of less than 20 bpm, some refer to the rhythm as an *agonal rhythm* or "dying heart." Figure 6-10 is an example of IVR. Table 6-3 describes the characteristics of this rhythm.

What Causes It?

IVR may occur when:

- The SA node and the AV junction fail to initiate an electrical impulse
- The rate of discharge of the SA node or AV junction becomes less than the intrinsic rate of the ventricles
- Impulses generated by a supraventricular pacemaker site are blocked

IVR may also occur because of myocardial infarction, digitalis toxicity, or metabolic imbalances.

What Do I Do About It?

Because the ventricular rate associated with IVR is slow (20 to 40 bpm) with a loss of atrial kick, the patient may experience serious signs and symptoms because of decreased cardiac output. If the patient has a pulse and is symptomatic because of the slow rate, transcutaneous pacing may be attempted. If the patient is not breathing and has no pulse despite the appearance of organized electrical activity on the cardiac monitor, a clinical situation called **pulseless electrical activity** (PEA) exists. Management of PEA should include CPR, giving oxygen, possible placement of an advanced airway, starting an IV, and an aggressive search for the underlying cause of the situation.

Medications such as lidocaine should be avoided in the management of this rhythm because lidocaine may abolish ventricular activity, possibly causing asystole in a patient with IVR.

TABLE 6-3	Characteristics of Idioventricular Rhythm (IVR)
Rate	20-40 bpm
Rhythm	Essentially regular
P waves	Usually absent or, with retrograde conduction to the atria, may appear after the QRS (usually upright in the ST-segment or T wave)
PR interval	None
QRS duration	Greater than 0.12 sec, T wave frequently in opposite direction of the QRS complex

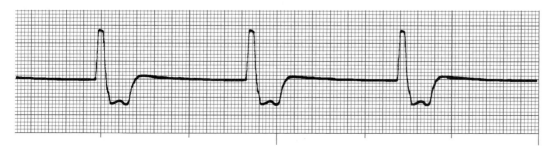

Figure 6-10
Idioventricular rhythm (IVR) at 35 bpm.

— *ECG Pearl*

Pulseless Electrical Activity

Pulseless electrical activity (PEA) is a clinical situation, not a specific dysrhythmia. PEA exists when organized electrical activity (other than VT) is observed on the cardiac monitor, but the patient is unresponsive, apneic, and a pulse cannot be felt. Many conditions may cause PEA. PATCH-4-MD can be used as an aid in memorizing some of the possible causes of PEA.

- **P**ulmonary embolism
- **A**cidosis
- **T**ension pneumothorax
- **C**ardiac tamponade
- **H**ypovolemia (most common cause of PEA)

- **H**ypoxia
- **H**eat/cold (hypothermia/hyperthermia)
- **H**ypokalemia/hyperkalemia (and other electrolytes)
- **M**yocardial infarction
- **D**rug overdose/accidents

PEA has a poor prognosis unless the underlying cause can be rapidly identified and appropriately managed. Treatment includes CPR, oxygen, possible placement of an advanced airway, IV access, an aggressive search for possible causes of the situation, and medications per current resuscitation guidelines.

ACCELERATED IDIOVENTRICULAR RHYTHM

How Do I Recognize It?

Some cardiologists consider the ventricular rate range of AIVR to be 41 to 120 bpm.

An **accelerated idioventricular rhythm (AIVR)** exists when three or more ventricular escape beats occur in a row at a rate of 41 to 100 bpm (Figure 6-11). AIVR is usually considered a benign escape rhythm that appears when the sinus rate slows and disappears when the sinus rate speeds up. Episodes of AIVR usually last a few seconds to a minute. Because AIVR usually begins and ends gradually, it is also called *nonparoxysmal VT*. Fusion beats are often seen at the onset and end of the rhythm. Table 6-4 shows the ECG characteristics of AIVR.

What Causes It?

AIVR occurs most often in the setting of acute MI.

AIVR is usually considered a benign escape rhythm. It is often seen during the first 12 hours of myocardial infarction. It is particularly common after successful reperfusion therapy. AIVR has been observed in patients with:

TABLE 6-4	**Characteristics of Accelerated Idioventricular Rhythm (AIVR)**
Rate	41-100 bpm
Rhythm	Essentially regular
P waves	Usually absent or, with retrograde conduction to the atria, may appear after the QRS (usually upright in the ST-segment or T wave)
PR interval	None
QRS duration	Greater than 0.12 sec, T wave frequently in opposite direction of the QRS complex

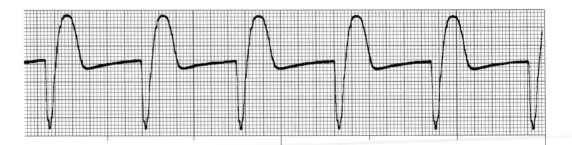

Figure 6-11
Accelerated idioventricular rhythm (AIVR) at 56 bpm.

- Digitalis toxicity
- Cocaine toxicity
- Subarachnoid hemorrhage
- Acute myocarditis
- Hypertensive heart disease
- Dilated cardiomyopathy

What Do I Do About It?

AIVR generally requires no treatment because the rhythm is protective and often transient, spontaneously resolving on its own. However, possible dizziness, lightheadedness, or other signs of hemodynamic compromise may occur because of the loss of atrial kick. Atropine may be ordered in an attempt to block the vagus nerve and stimulate the SA node to over-drive the ventricular rhythm. *Atrial* (not ventricular) pacing may be attempted to suppress AIVR.

— *ECG Pearl*

Electrical shocks are delivered to the heart of a patient in ventricular fibrillation (VF) or pulseless ventricular tachycardia (VT). What should you do if a shock terminates VF or pulseless VT and AIVR is now present on the monitor? A quick assessment reveals the patient has a pulse and is breathing on his own about 4 to 6 times/min. As you direct a coworker to assist the patient's respirations, the patient's pulse and blood pressure are assessed. The patient's BP is 94/53. The monitor shows AIVR at a rate of 100 bpm. Should anything be done about the patient's rhythm?

Confusion about what treatment should be instituted is common because the patient was pre-viously pulseless and now has a pulse, although the rhythm on the monitor is ventricular in origin. AIVR can be mistaken for VT if the ventricular rate is not counted and the patient assessed. Keep in mind that most patients do not develop serious signs and symptoms related to a tachycardia until the rate exceeds 150 bpm. Although medications are often used to sup-press VT that causes serious signs and symptoms, they are not generally used to suppress AIVR. In our patient scenario, a patient who was pulseless now has a pulse and is attempting to breathe on his own. These are positive signs. In a case such as this, "watchful waiting" is a reasonable course of action. Remember, AIVR is usually a transient rhythm. Close monitor-ing of the patient's vital signs and cardiac rhythm is essential.

VENTRICULAR TACHYCARDIA

How Do I Recognize It?

Ventricular tachycardia (VT) exists when three or more PVCs occur in a row at a rate greater than 100 bpm. If VT occurs as a short run lasting less than 30 seconds, it is called *nonsus-tained VT* (Figure 6-12). When VT persists for more than 30 seconds it is called *sustained VT* (Figure 6-13).

Monomorphic VT

VT, like PVCs, may originate from an ectopic focus in either ventricle. When the QRS com-plexes of VT are of the same shape and amplitude, the rhythm is called **monomorphic VT** (Figure 6-14). Monomorphic VT with a ventricular rate greater than 200 bpm is called ventric-ular flutter by some cardiologists. Table 6-5 lists the ECG characteristics of monomorphic VT.

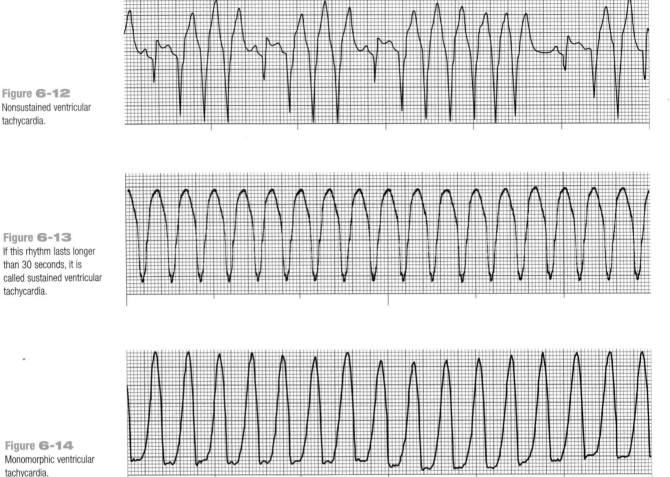

Figure 6-12
Nonsustained ventricular tachycardia.

Figure 6-13
If this rhythm lasts longer than 30 seconds, it is called sustained ventricular tachycardia.

Figure 6-14
Monomorphic ventricular tachycardia.

TABLE 6-5	Characteristics of Monomorphic Ventricular Tachycardia
Rate	101-250 bpm
Rhythm	Essentially regular
P waves	May be present or absent; if present, they have no set relationship to the QRS complexes appearing between the QRS's at a rate different from that of the VT
PR interval	None
QRS duration	Greater than 0.12 sec; often difficult to differentiate between the QRS and T wave

Polymorphic VT

When the QRS complexes of VT vary in shape and amplitude from beat to beat, the rhythm is called **polymorphic VT** (Figure 6-15). In polymorphic VT, the QRS complexes appear to twist from upright to negative or negative to upright and back.

Polymorphic VT is divided into two classifications based on its association with a normal or prolonged QT interval:

1. Normal QT
2. Long QT syndrome (LQTS)
   a. Acquired (iatrogenic)
   b. Congenital (idiopathic)

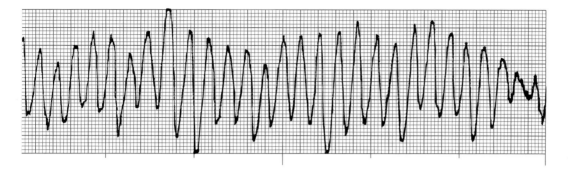

Figure 6-15
Polymorphic ventricular tachycardia. This rhythm strip is from a 77-year-old man 3 days post myocardial infarction (MI). His chief complaint at the onset of this episode was chest pain. He had a past medical history of a previous MI and an abdominal aortic aneurysm repair. The patient was given lidocaine and defibrillated several times without success. Laboratory work revealed a serum potassium (K+) level of 2.0. IV K+ was administered and the patient converted to a sinus rhythm with the next defibrillation.

Polymorphic VT that occurs in the presence of a long QT interval is called **Torsades de Pointes (TdP)**. *Torsades de pointes* is French for "twisting of the points," which describes the QRS that changes in shape, amplitude, and width and appears to "twist" around the isoelectric line, resembling a spindle. Polymorphic VT that occurs in the presence of a normal QT interval is simply referred to as *polymorphic VT* or *polymorphic VT resembling torsades de pointes*. Table 6-6 lists the ECG characteristics of polymorphic VT.

Long QT syndrome (LQTS) is an abnormality of the heart's electrical system. The mechanical function of the heart is entirely normal. The electrical problem is caused by defects in sodium and potassium channels that affect repolarization. These electrical defects prolong the QT interval, predisposing affected persons to TdP.

The usual fatal dysrhythmias are TdP and ventricular fibrillation.

LQTS may be acquired or inherited.

- The acquired form of LQTS is more common and usually caused by medications that prolong the QT interval (Table 6-7). Inherited LQTS is caused by mutations of genes that encode the sodium and potassium channels.
- Symptoms most commonly begin in preteen to teenage years but may present from a few days of age to middle age.
- The average age of persons who die of LQTS is 32 years.[4]
- QT interval prolongation and Torsades are more common in women, probably because of differences in ion channels between genders.[5]
- About one third of individuals who have LQTS never exhibit symptoms. A lack of symptoms does not exclude an individual or family from having LQTS.
- The usual symptoms of LQTS include syncope or sudden death. These events usually occur during physical activity or emotional stress, but they can also occur during sleep. The syncopal episodes are often misdiagnosed as the common faint (vasovagal event) or a seizure. Actual seizures are uncommon in LQTS, but epilepsy is one of the common errors in diagnosis.

Cases in which LQTS should be considered include the following:

- Recurrent syncope during physical exertion or emotional stress
- Sudden and unexplained loss of consciousness during childhood and teenage years
- Family history of unexplained syncope
- Family history of sudden, unexpected death
- Any young person who has an unexplained cardiac arrest
- Epilepsy in children

Common triggers of LQTS include swimming, running, being startled (an alarm clock, a loud horn, a ringing phone), anger, crying, test taking, and other stressful situations. The diagnosis of LQTS is commonly suspected or made from the ECG. Children and young adults should have an ECG as part of their evaluation for an unexplained loss of consciousness episode. Beta blockers, potassium supplements, and implantable defibrillators have been used for treatment of LQTS.

TABLE 6-6	**Characteristics of Polymorphic Ventricular Tachycardia**
Rate	150-300 bpm, typically 200-250 bpm
Rhythm	May be regular or irregular
P waves	None
PR interval	None
QRS duration	Greater than 0.12 sec; gradual alteration in amplitude and direction of the QRS complexes; a typical cycle consists of 5 to 20 QRS complexes

TABLE 6-7	**Causes of Acquired Long QT Syndrome**	
Medications	Antibiotics	Erythromycin
		Trimethoprim and sulfamethoxazole
		Pentamidine
	Antifungal medications	Ketoconazole
		Fluconazole
		Itraconazole
	Antihistamines	Terfenidine
		Astemizole
		Diphenhydramine
	Cardiac medications	Quinidine
		Procainamide
		Disopyramide
		Amiodarone
		Sotalol
		Bepridil
	Diuretics	Indapamide
	Gastrointestinal medications	Cisapride
	Psychotropic medications	Amitriptyline
		Desipramine
		Phenothiazines and derivatives
		Haloperidol
		Risperidone
Liquid-protein diets		
Hypothyroidism		
Central nervous system disease—subarachnoid hemorrhage		
Organophosphate insecticides		
Electrolyte abnormalities—hypokalemia, hypomagnesemia, hypocalcemia		
Myocarditis		

What Causes It?

Sustained monomorphic VT is often associated with underlying heart disease, particularly myocardial ischemia. It rarely occurs in patients without underlying heart disease. Common causes of VT include the following:

- Acute coronary syndromes
- Cardiomyopathy
- Tricyclic antidepressant overdose
- Digitalis toxicity
- Valvular heart disease
- Cocaine abuse
- Mitral valve prolapse
- Acid-base imbalance
- Trauma (e.g., myocardial contusion, invasive cardiac procedures)
- Electrolyte imbalance (e.g., hypokalemia, hyperkalemia, hypomagnesemia)

What Do I Do About It?

Signs and symptoms associated with VT vary. VT may occur with or without pulses. The patient who has sustained monomorphic VT may be stable for long periods of time. However, when the ventricular rate is very fast, or when myocardial ischemia is present, monomorphic VT can degenerate to polymorphic VT or ventricular fibrillation.

Syncope or near-syncope may occur because of an abrupt onset of VT. The patient's only warning symptom may be a brief period of lightheadedness. In victims of sudden cardiac death, VT deteriorating to VF was the rhythm observed in most cases.[6-9]

Sustained VT does not always produce signs of hemodynamic instability.

—— *ECG Pearl*

Signs and symptoms of hemodynamic instability related to VT
- Altered mental status
- Shock
- Chest pain
- Hypotension
- Shortness of breath
- Pulmonary congestion

Treatment is based on the patient's signs and symptoms and the type of VT. If the rhythm is monomorphic VT (and the patient's symptoms are due to the tachycardia):

- Stable but symptomatic patients are treated with oxygen, IV access, and ventricular antiarrhythmics (such as amiodarone) to suppress the rhythm.
- Unstable patients (usually a sustained heart rate of 150 bpm or more) are treated with oxygen, IV access, and sedation (if awake and time permits) followed by synchronized cardioversion.
- CPR and defibrillation are used to treat the pulseless patient in VT followed by defibrillation.
- In all cases, an aggressive search must be made for the cause of the VT.

If the rhythm is polymorphic VT, it is important to determine if the patient's QT interval just before the tachycardia is normal or prolonged.

- If the QT interval is normal and the patient is symptomatic due to the tachycardia:
  ◦ Treat ischemia if present.
  ◦ Correct electrolyte abnormalities.
  ◦ Proceed with electrical therapy or antiarrhythmic medications if necessary.
- If the QT interval is prolonged and the patient is symptomatic due to the tachycardia:
  ◦ Discontinue any medications the patient may be taking that prolong the QT interval.
  ◦ Correct electrolyte abnormalities.
  ◦ Proceed with electrical therapy or antiarrhythmic medications if necessary.

During VT, the severity of the patient's symptoms depend on how rapid the ventricular rate is, how long the tachycardia has been present, and the presence and extent of underlying heart disease.

—— *ECG Pearl*

A supraventricular tachycardia with an intraventricular conduction delay may be difficult to distinguish from VT. Keep in mind that VT is considered a potentially life-threatening dysrhythmia. If you are unsure whether a regular, wide-QRS tachycardia is VT or SVT with an intraventricular conduction delay, treat the rhythm as VT until proven otherwise. Obtaining a 12-lead ECG may help differentiate VT from SVT, but do not delay treatment if the patient is symptomatic.

VENTRICULAR FIBRILLATION

How Do I Recognize It?

Ventricular fibrillation (VF) is a chaotic rhythm that begins in the ventricles. In VF, there is no organized depolarization of the ventricles. The ventricular muscle quivers. As a result, there is no effective myocardial contraction <u>and no pulse.</u> The resulting rhythm looks chaotic with deflections that vary in shape and amplitude. No normal-looking waveforms are visible.

The patient in VF is unresponsive, apneic, and pulseless.

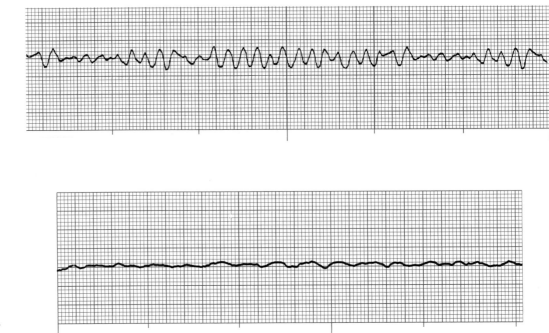

Figure 6-16
Coarse ventricular
fibrillation.

Figure 6-17
Fine ventricular fibrillation.

TABLE 6-8	**Characteristics of Ventricular Fibrillation**
Rate	Cannot be determined because there are no discernible waves or complexes to measure
Rhythm	Rapid and chaotic with no pattern or regularity
P waves	Not discernible
PR interval	Not discernible
QRS duration	Not discernible

VF with waves that are 3 or more mm high is called "coarse" VF (Figure 6-16). VF with low amplitude waves (less than 3 mm) is called "fine" VF (Figure 6-17). Table 6-8 lists the ECG characteristics of VF. Figure 6-18 illustrates a comparison of ventricular dysrhythmias.

—— *ECG Pearl*

Because artifact can mimic VF, ***always*** check the patient's pulse before beginning treatment for VF.

What Causes It?

Factors that increase the susceptibility of the myocardium to fibrillate include the following:

- Increased sympathetic nervous system activity
- Vagal stimulation
- Electrolyte imbalance
- Antiarrhythmics and other medications
- Environmental factors (e.g., electrocution)
- Hypertrophy
- Acute coronary syndromes
- Heart failure
- Arrhythmias

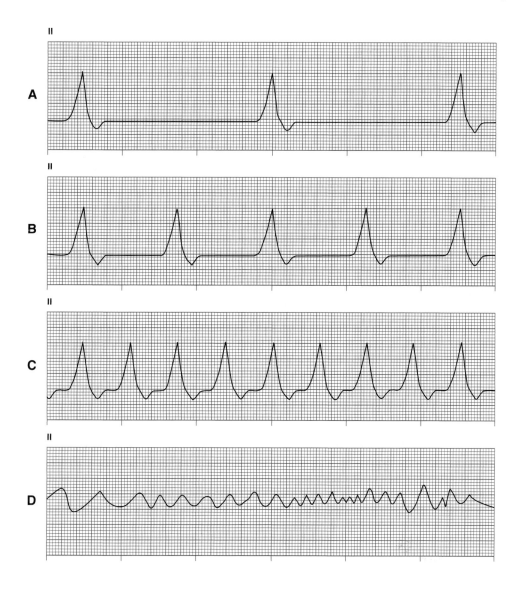

Figure 6-18
Comparison of ventricular dysrhythmias. **A,** Idioventricular rhythm at 38 bpm. **B,** Accelerated idioventricular rhythm at 75 bpm. **C,** Monomorphic ventricular tachycardia at 150 bpm. **D,** Coarse ventricular fibrillation.

What Do I Do About It?

"In patients who are known to have ischemic heart disease and whose ECGs are continuously monitored, cardiac arrest is most often a result of VT. In the setting of progressive myocardial ischemia, VT typically deteriorates into VF within an interval of 3 minutes. For this reason, first responders detect VF as the predominant rhythm after they arrive on the scene."[10]

Since no drugs used in cardiac arrest have been shown to improve survival to hospital discharge, the priorities of care in cardiac arrest due to pulseless VT or VF are CPR and defibrillation. For each minute of untreated VF, the success of defibrillation decreases by approximately 10%.[11] CPR and defibrillation may be followed by medications per current resuscitation guidelines.

— *ECG Pearl*

Cardiac Arrest Rhythms
- Ventricular fibrillation
- (Pulseless) ventricular tachycardia
- Asystole
- Pulseless electrical activity

— *ECG Pearl*

Electrical Therapy: Defibrillation
Description and Purpose
Defibrillation is the therapeutic delivery of an unsynchronized electrical current (the delivery of energy has no relationship to the cardiac cycle) through the myocardium over a very brief period to terminate a cardiac dysrhythmia. The shock attempts to deliver a uniform electrical current of sufficient intensity to simultaneously depolarize ventricular cells, including fibrillating cells, causing momentary asystole. This provides an opportunity for the heart's natural pacemakers to resume normal activity. The pacemaker with the highest degree of automaticity should then assume responsibility for pacing the heart.

Indications
- Pulseless VT
- Ventricular fibrillation

Procedure
- Turn on the power to the monitor/defibrillator.
- If you are using hand-held paddles, apply conductive gel to the paddles or place disposable pre-gelled defibrillator pads to the patient's bare chest. Place the defibrillator paddles on the patient's chest and apply firm pressure. If you are using self-adhesive monitoring/defibrillation pads, place them in proper position on the patient's bare chest.
- Verify the presence of VT or VF on the monitor.
- Select the appropriate energy level for the rhythm, charge the defibrillator, and recheck the ECG rhythm.
- If the rhythm is unchanged, call "Clear!" and look (360 degrees) around; make sure everyone is clear of the patient, bed, and any equipment connected to the patient; make sure oxygen is not flowing over the patient's chest (oxygen flow over the patient's chest during electrical therapy increases the risk of spark/fire).
- If the area is clear, depress both discharge buttons simultaneously to deliver the shock; after the shock has been delivered, release the buttons.
- Reassess the rhythm.

ASYSTOLE (CARDIAC STANDSTILL)

How Do I Recognize It?

Asystole is a total absence of ventricular electrical activity (Figure 6-19). There is no ventricular rate or rhythm, no pulse, and no cardiac output. Some atrial electrical activity may be evident. If atrial electrical activity is present, the rhythm is called "P-wave" asystole or ventricular standstill (Figure 6-20). Table 6-9 lists the ECG characteristics of asystole.

What Causes It?

The causes of asystole are the same as those for pulseless electrical activity. In addition, ventricular asystole may occur temporarily following termination of a tachycardia with medications, defibrillation, or synchronized cardioversion (Figure 6-21).

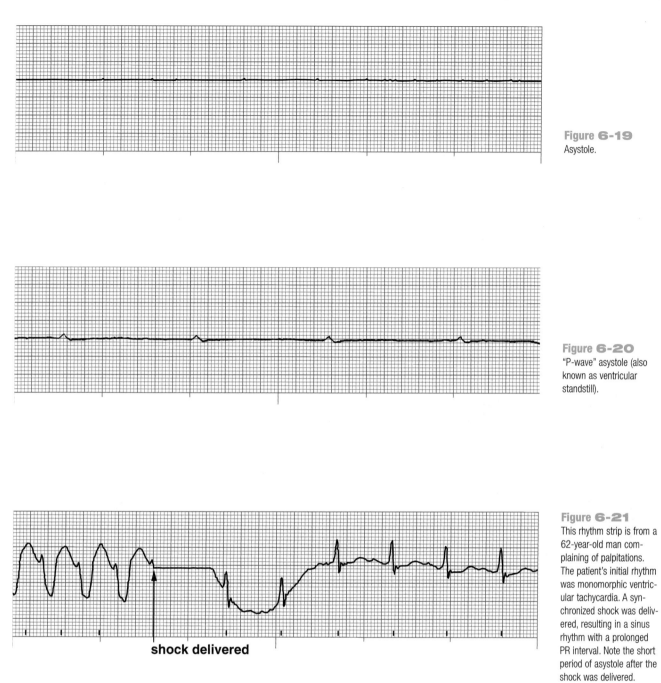

Figure 6-19
Asystole.

Figure 6-20
"P-wave" asystole (also known as ventricular standstill).

shock delivered

Figure 6-21
This rhythm strip is from a 62-year-old man complaining of palpitations. The patient's initial rhythm was monomorphic ventricular tachycardia. A synchronized shock was delivered, resulting in a sinus rhythm with a prolonged PR interval. Note the short period of asystole after the shock was delivered.

TABLE 6-9	**Characteristics of Asystole**
Rate	Ventricular usually not discernible but atrial activity may be seen ("P-wave" asystole)
Rhythm	Ventricular not discernible, atrial may be discernible
P waves	Usually not discernible
PR interval	Not measurable
QRS duration	Absent

ECG Pearl

When a "flat line" is observed on an ECG:

- Make sure the power to the monitor is on.
- Check the lead/cable connections.
- Make sure the correct lead is selected.
- Turn up the gain (ECG size) on the monitor.

If the rhythm appears to be asystole, confirm the rhythm in second lead because it is possible (although rare) that coarse VF may be present in some leads.

What Do I Do About It?

Treatment of asystole includes the following:

- Confirmation of the absence of a pulse
- Immediate CPR
- Confirmation of the rhythm in two leads
- Possible insertion of an advanced airway
- IV access
- Consideration of the possible causes of the rhythm
- Medications per current resuscitation guidelines
- Consider termination of efforts

Table 6-10 lists a summary of all ventricular rhythm characteristics.

REFERENCES

1. Crawford MV, Spence MI: *Electrical complications in coronary artery disease: arrhythmias in common sense approach to coronary care,* ed 6, St Louis, 1995, Mosby, p 220.
2. Goldberger AL: *Clinical electrocardiography: a simplified approach,* ed 6, St Louis, 1999, Mosby, pp 165-177.
3. Kinney MR, Packa DR, editors: *Andreoli's comprehensive cardiac care,* ed 8, St Louis, 1996, Mosby.
4. Meyer JS, Mehdirad A, Salem BI, Kulikowska A, Kulikowski P: Sudden arrhythmia death syndrome: importance of the long QT syndrome, *Am Fam Physician* 68(3):483-438, August 2003.
5. Peters RW, Gold MR: The influence of gender on arrhythmias, *Cardiol Rev* 12(2):97-105, March-April 2004. PMID: 14766024.
6. Panidis IP, Morganroth J: Holter monitoring and sudden cardiac death, *Cardiovasc Rev Rep* 5(3):283; 287-290; 297-299; 303-304, 1984.
7. Olshausen KV, Witt T, Pop T, Treese N, Bethge KP, Meyer J: Sudden cardiac death while wearing a Holter monitor, *Am J Cardiol* 67(5):381-386, 1991.
8. Milner PG, Platia EV, Reid PR, Griffith LS: Ambulatory electrocardiographic recordings at the time of fatal cardiac arrest, *Am J Cardiol* 56(10):588-592, 1985.
9. Panidis IP, Morganroth J: Sudden death in hospitalized patients: cardiac rhythm disturbances detected by ambulatory electrocardiographic monitoring, *J Am Coll Cardiol* 2(5):798-805, 1983.
10. Weil MH, Tang W, editors: *CPR: resuscitation of the arrested heart,* Philadelphia, 1999, Saunders.
11. Eisenberg MS, Horwood BT, Cummins RO, et al: Cardiac arrest and resuscitation. A tale of 29 cities, *Ann Emerg Med* 19:179-186, 1990.

| TABLE 6-10 | Ventricular Rhythms–Summary of Characteristics | | | |

	PVCs	Ventricular Escape Beat	Idioventricular Rhythm (IVR)	Accelerated Idioventricular Rhythm (AIVR)
Rate	Usually within normal range, but depends on underlying rhythm	Usually within normal range, but depends on underlying rhythm	20-40 bpm	41-100 bpm (some experts consider the rate 41-120 bpm)
Rhythm	Regular with *early* beats	Regular with *late* beats	Essentially regular	Essentially regular
P Waves (lead II)	Usually absent or, with retrograde conduction to the atria, may appear after the QRS (usually upright in ST-segment or T wave)	Usually absent or, with retrograde conduction to the atria, may appear after the QRS (usually upright in ST-segment or T wave	Usually absent or, with retrograde conduction to the atria, may appear after the QRS (usually upright in ST-segment or T wave)	Usually absent or, with retrograde conduction to the atria, may appear after the QRS (usually upright in ST-segment or T wave)
PR Interval	None	None	None	None
QRS	>0.12 sec	>0.12 sec	>0.12 sec	>0.12 sec

	Monomorphic Ventricular Tachycardia	Polymorphic VT	Ventricular Fibrillation	Asystole
Rate	101-250 bpm	150-300 bpm	Not discernible	None
Rhythm	Usually regular	Irregular	Chaotic	None
P Waves (lead II)	May be present or absent. If present, they have no set relationship to the QRS complexes appearing between the QRS's at a rate different from that of the VT.	Independent or none	Absent	Atrial activity may be observed ("P-wave" asystole)
PR Interval	None	None	None	None
QRS	>0.12 sec	>0.12 sec	Not discernible	Absent

STOP & REVIEW

Matching

a. Accelerated idioventricular rhythm
b. Procainamide
c. R-on-T phenomenon
d. Pair or couplet
e. Pulseless electrical activity

f. Idioventricular rhythm
g. Asystole
h. Ventricular fibrillation
i. Bigeminy
j. Fusion beat

_____ 1. Absence of electrical activity on the cardiac monitor
_____ 2. The result of an electrical impulse from a supraventricular site discharging at the same time as an ectopic site in the ventricles
_____ 3. Two sequential PVCs
_____ 4. Medication associated with prolongation of the QT interval
_____ 5. Chaotic rhythm associated with no breathing or pulse
_____ 6. Pattern in which every other beat is an ectopic beat
_____ 7. Essentially regular ventricular rhythm with a ventricular rate of 20-40 bpm
_____ 8. Name given a PVC falling on the T wave of the preceding beat
_____ 9. Clinical situation in which organized electrical activity (other than VT) is observed on the cardiac monitor, but there is an absence of mechanical contraction of the myocardial fibers
_____ 10. Essentially regular ventricular rhythm with a ventricular rate of 41-100 bpm

Short Answer

11. Explain the difference between a PVC and a ventricular escape beat.

12. List four common causes of premature ventricular complexes.
    1.

    2.

    3.

    4.

13. How do coarse and fine ventricular fibrillation differ?

14. What is the name given to polymorphic VT that occurs in the presence of a long QT interval?

15. List three reasons why the ventricles may assume responsibility for pacing the heart.
    1.

    2.

    3.

16. List five possible causes of asystole or pulseless electrical activity.
    1.

    2.

    3.

    4.

    5.

ECG Crossword

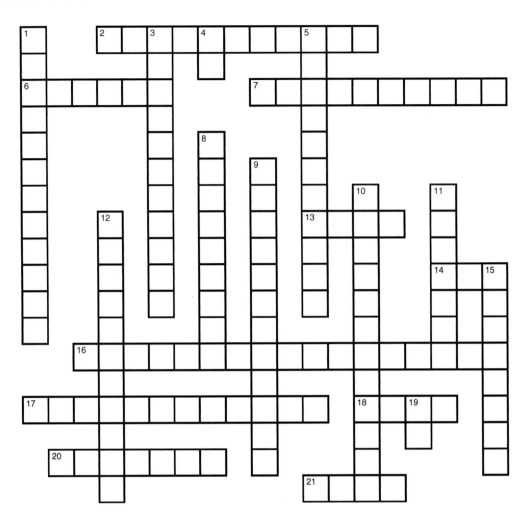

Across

2. Most common cause of pulseless electrical activity
6. A ventricular rhythm with a rate of less than 20 bpm is sometimes called an __ rhythm.
7. PVCs that originate from more than one site
13. This type of PVC occurs when the R wave of a PVC falls on the T wave of the preceding beat.
14. Abbreviation for pulseless electrical activity
16. A type of polymorphic VT that occurs in the presence of a long QT interval
17. A __ pause often follows a PVC.
18. Abbreviation for accelerated idioventricular rhythm
20. PVCs that look alike in the same lead
21. Ventricular beats are usually associated with a __ QRS complex.

Down

1. Ventricular __: every fourth beat is a PVC.
3. This type of VT has QRS complexes that vary in shape and amplitude from beat to beat.
4. Abbreviation for ventricular tachycardia
5. PVCs that look different from one another in the same lead
8. VT lasting for more than 30 sec is called __ VT.
9. A PVC is also called a premature ventricular __.
10. A PVC that is squeezed between two normal beats
11. Another name for a pair of PVCs
12. This type of VT has QRS complexes of the same shape and amplitude.
15. A ventricular escape beat helps protect the heart from __.
19. Abbreviation for ventricular fibrillation.

PRACTICE *Rhythm Strips*

For each of the following rhythm strips, determine the atrial and ventricular rate and rhythm, measure the PR interval and QRS duration, and then identify the rhythm. All strips were recorded in lead II unless otherwise noted.

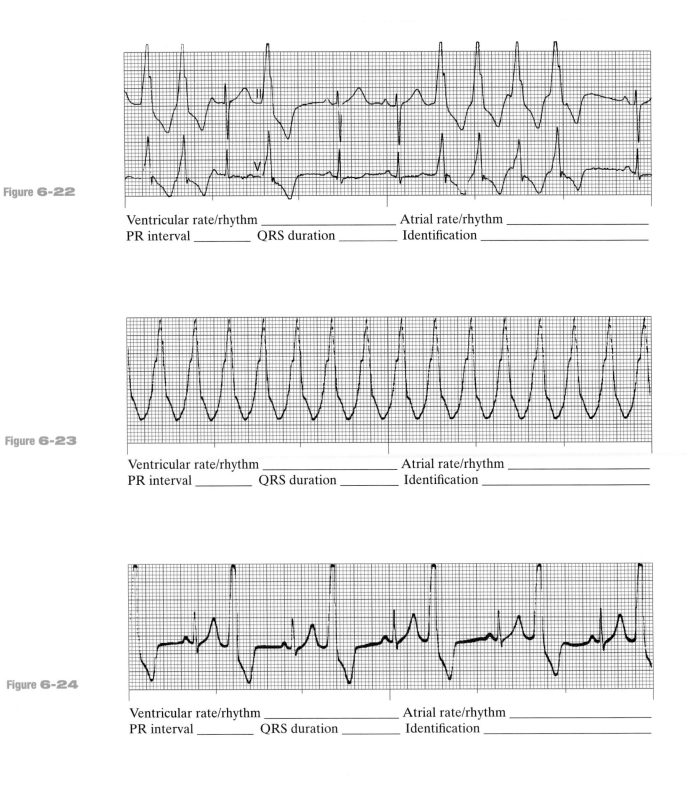

Figure 6-22

Ventricular rate/rhythm _____ Atrial rate/rhythm _____
PR interval _____ QRS duration _____ Identification _____

Figure 6-23

Ventricular rate/rhythm _____ Atrial rate/rhythm _____
PR interval _____ QRS duration _____ Identification _____

Figure 6-24

Ventricular rate/rhythm _____ Atrial rate/rhythm _____
PR interval _____ QRS duration _____ Identification _____

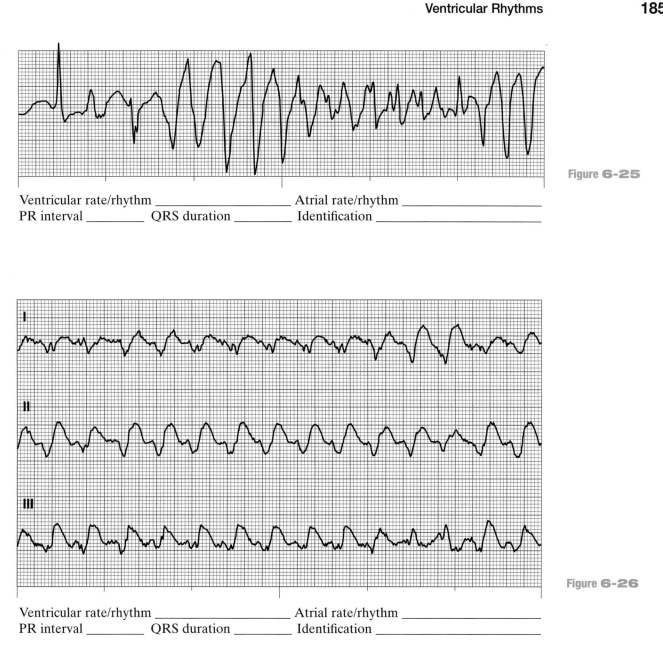

Figure **6-25**

Ventricular rate/rhythm _____ Atrial rate/rhythm _____
PR interval _____ QRS duration _____ Identification _____

Figure **6-26**

Ventricular rate/rhythm _____ Atrial rate/rhythm _____
PR interval _____ QRS duration _____ Identification _____

This rhythm strip is from a 61-year-old woman complaining of shortness of breath.
BP 176/110.

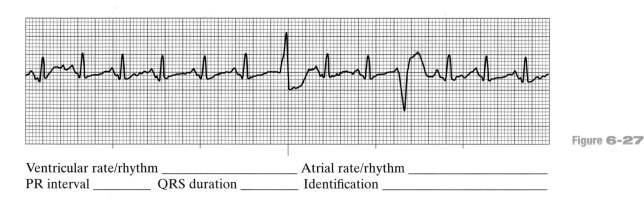

Figure **6-27**

Ventricular rate/rhythm _____ Atrial rate/rhythm _____
PR interval _____ QRS duration _____ Identification _____

This rhythm strip is from a 19-year-old male who walked into the emergency department after ingesting a number of unknown medications (per patient) in a suicide attempt. He became unresponsive 5 minutes after his arrival. Initial rhythms before the onset of this dysrhythmia were monomorphic VT and then complete AV block. After a brief episode of the above rhythm, the patient again converted to a complete AV block. Drug screen was negative. A transvenous pacemaker was inserted and the patient admitted to CCU.

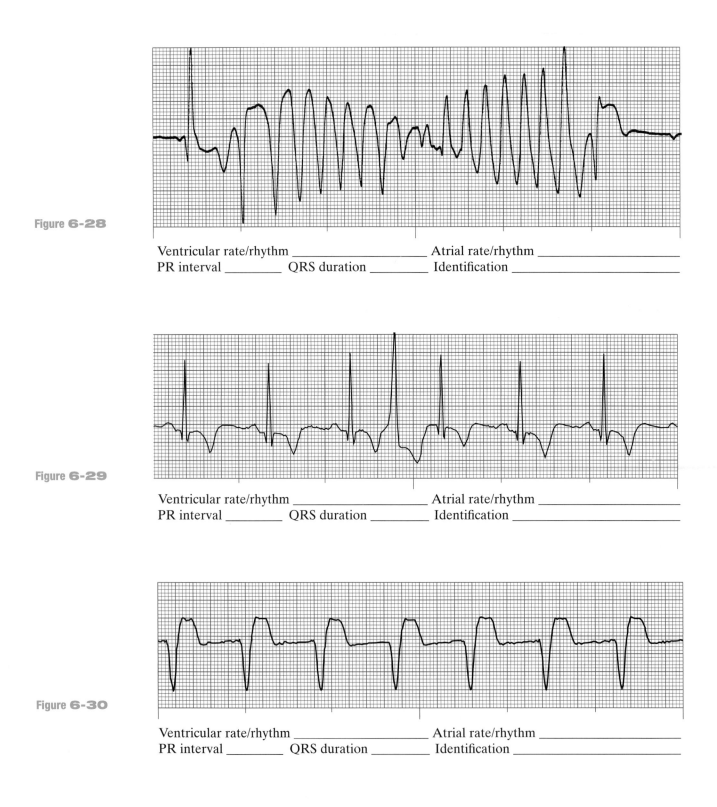

Figure 6-28

Ventricular rate/rhythm _____ Atrial rate/rhythm _____
PR interval _____ QRS duration _____ Identification _____

Figure 6-29

Ventricular rate/rhythm _____ Atrial rate/rhythm _____
PR interval _____ QRS duration _____ Identification _____

Figure 6-30

Ventricular rate/rhythm _____ Atrial rate/rhythm _____
PR interval _____ QRS duration _____ Identification _____

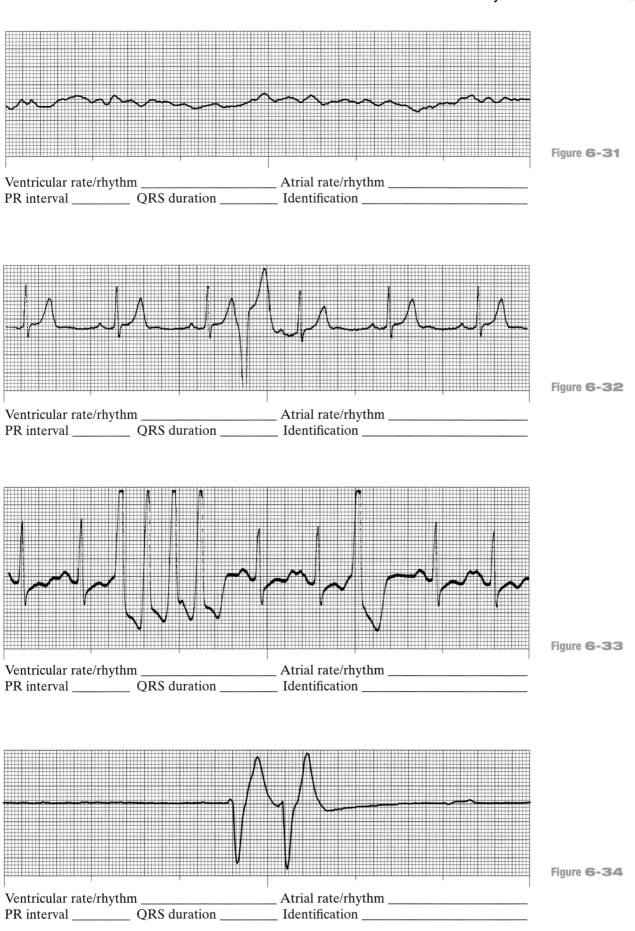

Figure **6-31**

Ventricular rate/rhythm _____ Atrial rate/rhythm _____
PR interval _____ QRS duration _____ Identification _____

Figure **6-32**

Ventricular rate/rhythm _____ Atrial rate/rhythm _____
PR interval _____ QRS duration _____ Identification _____

Figure **6-33**

Ventricular rate/rhythm _____ Atrial rate/rhythm _____
PR interval _____ QRS duration _____ Identification _____

Figure **6-34**

Ventricular rate/rhythm _____ Atrial rate/rhythm _____
PR interval _____ QRS duration _____ Identification _____

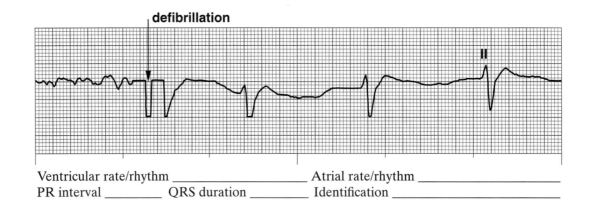

Figure 6-35

Ventricular rate/rhythm _____ Atrial rate/rhythm _____
PR interval _____ QRS duration _____ Identification _____

This rhythm strip is from a 37-year-old man who presented to the emergency department with seizures. He had a history of a 3-day methamphetamine binge. The rhythm converted with diltiazem (Cardizem).

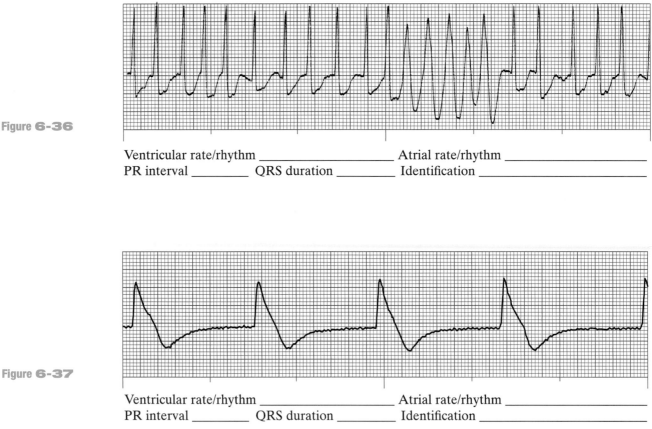

Figure 6-36

Ventricular rate/rhythm _____ Atrial rate/rhythm _____
PR interval _____ QRS duration _____ Identification _____

Figure 6-37

Ventricular rate/rhythm _____ Atrial rate/rhythm _____
PR interval _____ QRS duration _____ Identification _____

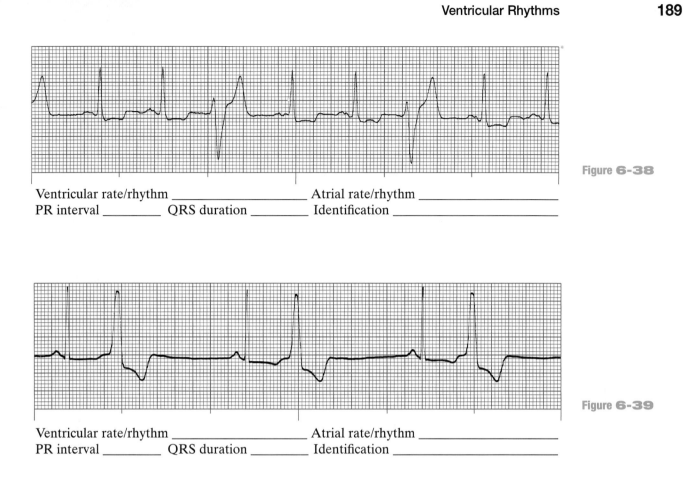

Figure 6-38

Ventricular rate/rhythm _____ Atrial rate/rhythm _____

PR interval _____ QRS duration _____ Identification _____

Figure 6-39

Ventricular rate/rhythm _____ Atrial rate/rhythm _____

PR interval _____ QRS duration _____ Identification _____

Atrioventricular (AV) Blocks

OBJECTIVES

On completion of this chapter, you should be able to:

Describe the ECG characteristics, possible causes, signs and symptoms, and emergency management for the following dysrhythmias:
- First-degree atrioventricular (AV) block
- Second-degree AV block, type I
- Second-degree AV block, type II
- Second-degree AV block, 2:1 conduction
- Third-degree AV block

INTRODUCTION

The **AV junction** is an area of specialized conduction tissue that provides the electrical links between the atrium and ventricle. If a delay or interruption in impulse conduction occurs within the AV node, bundle of His, or His-Purkinje system, the resulting dysrhythmia is called an AV block. AV blocks have been traditionally classified in two ways—according to the degree of block and/or according to the site of the block.

Remember that the PR interval reflects depolarization of the right and left atria (P wave) and the spread of the impulse through the AV node, bundle of His, right and left bundle branches, and the Purkinje fibers. The PR interval is the key to differentiating the *type* of AV block. The key to differentiating the *level* (location) of the block is the width of the QRS complex and, in second- and third-degree AV blocks, the rate of the escape rhythm.

—— *ECG Pearl*

Depolarization and repolarization are slow in the AV node making this area vulnerable to blocks in conduction (AV blocks).

In first-degree AV block, impulses from the sinoatrial (SA) node to the ventricles are *delayed* (not blocked). First-degree AV block usually occurs at the AV node (Figure 7-1). With second-degree AV blocks, there is an *intermittent* disturbance in conduction of impulses between the atria and ventricles. The site of block in second-degree AV block type I is typically at the AV node. The site of block in second-degree AV block type II is the bundle of His or, more commonly, the bundle branches. In third-degree AV block, there is a *complete* block in conduction of impulses between the atria and ventricles. The site of block in a third-degree AV block may be the AV node or, more commonly, the bundle of His or bundle branches (Table 7-1).

Second- and third-degree AV blocks may become serious enough to require the use of a natural escape pacemaker. Should such a pacemaker become a necessity, AV blocks that occur at the level of the AV node have a tremendous advantage. If required, there is usually a reliable junctional pacemaker available that can fire at 40 to 60 bpm. However, when the loca-

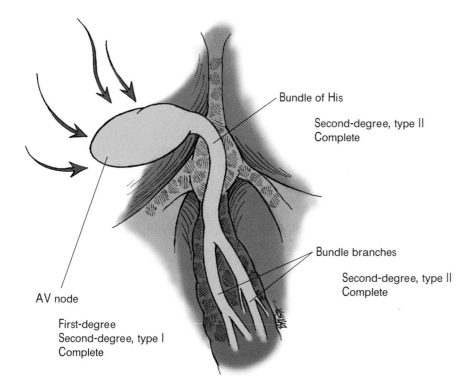

Bundle of His

Second-degree, type II
Complete

Bundle branches

Second-degree, type II
Complete

AV node

First-degree
Second-degree, type I
Complete

Figure 7-1
Locations of AV block.

TABLE 7-1 Classifications of AV Block	
Classification by Degree	
Name of Block	**Type of Block**
First-degree AV block	Incomplete
Second-degree AV block type I	Incomplete
Second-degree AV block type II	Incomplete
Third-degree AV block	Complete
Classification by Site/Location	
Site	**Name of Block**
AV node	First-degree AV block
	Second-degree AV block type I
	Third-degree AV block
Infranodal (subnodal)	
Bundle of His	Second-degree AV block type II (uncommon)
	Third-degree AV block
Bundle branches	Second-degree AV block type II (more common)
	Third-degree AV block

AV, atrioventricular.

tion of an AV block is below the AV junction, the only available pacemaker may be a slow ventricular one, firing at 20 to 40 bpm. Not only are ventricular pacemakers slow, they are prone to long pauses, making them less than reliable. Therefore, AV blocks at the level of the AV node usually have a more effective and reliable escape pacemaker than do AV blocks at the bundle of His or below.

—— *ECG Pearl*

The clinical significance of an AV block depends on the following:
- The degree (severity) of the block
- The rate of the escape pacemaker (junctional vs. ventricular)
- The patient's response to that ventricular rate

FIRST-DEGREE AV BLOCK

How Do I Recognize It?

The PR interval is usually between 0.21 and 0.48 seconds. Occasionally, a PR interval greater than 0.8 seconds may be seen.[1] However, PR intervals as long as 1 second or more have been reported.[2]

A PR interval of normal duration (0.12 to 0.20 seconds) indicates the electrical impulse was conducted normally through the atria, AV node, bundle of His, bundle branches, and Purkinje fibers. In first-degree AV block, all components of the ECG tracing are usually within normal limits except the PR interval. This is because electrical impulses travel normally from the SA node through the atria, but there is a delay in impulse conduction, usually at the level of the AV node. Despite its name, in first-degree AV block, the sinus impulse is not blocked (all sinus beats are conducted)—impulses are *delayed* for the same period before they are conducted to the ventricles. This delay in AV conduction results in a PR interval that is longer than normal (more than 0.20 seconds in duration) and constant.

In first-degree AV block, each P wave is followed by a QRS complex (1:1 relationship).

Let's look at the rhythm shown in Figure 7-2. The ventricular rhythm is regular at a rate of 60 bpm. Each QRS complex is preceded by an upright P wave. The atrial rhythm is also regular at a rate of 60 bpm. We now know that the underlying rhythm is a sinus rhythm at 60 bpm. The QRS duration is within normal limits. However the PR segment is longer than normal measuring 0.32 seconds, but constant before each QRS. The 1:1 relationship of

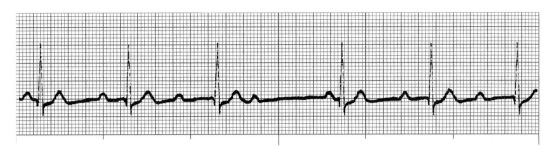

Figure 7-3
Second-degree AV block
type I at 43 to 60 bpm.

TABLE 7-3	**Characteristics of Second-Degree AV Block Type I**
Rate	Atrial rate is greater than the ventricular rate
Rhythm	Atrial regular (P's plot through time); ventricular irregular
P waves	Normal in size and shape; some P waves are not followed by a QRS complex (more P's than QRSs)
PR interval	Lengthens with each cycle (although lengthening may be very slight), until a P wave appears without a QRS complex; the PRI *after* the nonconducted beat is shorter than the interval preceding the nonconducted beat
QRS duration	Usually 0.10 sec or less but is periodically dropped

AV, atrioventricular.

more p's than QRS

and longer to conduct through the AV node. This appears on the ECG as lengthening PR intervals. In order to determine if the PR intervals remain the same or lengthen, we need to see two PQRST cycles in a row that do not contain extra waveforms. Beats 1, 2, and 3 allow us to do this because there is one P wave before each QRS. When you compare the PR intervals of these beats, the PR interval of beat 1 is short. The PRI of beat 2 is longer than beat 1, and the PRI of beat 3 is longer than the first two beats. Thus we can see that the PR intervals are getting progressively longer. The lengthening PR intervals eventually result in a P wave that falls during the refractory period of the ventricles. Because the ventricles are refractory, the sinus impulse is blocked. The blocked sinus impulse appears on the ECG as a P wave with no QRS after it (dropped beat). Thus the atria are depolarized (represented by the P wave), but the AV junction fails to conduct the impulse from the atria to the ventricles (reflected on the ECG by the absence of a QRS complex). Because QRS complexes are periodically dropped, the ventricular rhythm is irregular. The cycle then begins again. The repetition of this cyclic pattern is called "grouped beating." Our identification of this rhythm strip is, "Second-degree AV block type I at 43 to 60 bpm." ECG characteristics of second-degree AV block type I are shown in Table 7-3.

In second-degree AV block type I, any P-to-QRS ratio may be seen. For example, three P waves to two QRS complexes (3:2), 4:3, 5:4, and so forth.

What Causes It?

Second-degree AV block type I is usually caused by a conduction delay within the AV node. Remember that the right coronary artery supplies the AV node in 90% of the population. Thus, right coronary artery occlusions are associated with AV block occurring in the AV node.

If the right coronary artery is blocked, ischemia may develop in the AV node. As a result of this ischemia, there can be a disturbance in the balance between the parasympathetic and sympathetic divisions of the autonomic nervous system, resulting in an increase in parasympathetic tone. Once parasympathetic tone increases, conduction through the AV node is slowed. This slowing may manifest itself as a prolonged PR interval or dropped beats.

An increase in parasympathetic tone is the cause of most AV blocks complicating right coronary artery occlusions (inferior wall infarctions and right ventricular infarction).

What Do I Do About It?

The patient with this type of AV block is usually asymptomatic because the ventricular rate often remains nearly normal, and cardiac output is not significantly affected. If the patient is symptomatic and the rhythm is a result of medications, these substances should be withheld. If the heart rate is slow and serious signs and symptoms occur because of the slow rate, atropine and/or temporary pacing should be considered. When associated with an acute inferior wall MI, this dysrhythmia is usually transient. It usually resolves within 48 to 72 hours as the effects of parasympathetic stimulation disappear. When this rhythm occurs in conjunction with acute MI, the patient should be observed for increasing AV block.

Second-Degree AV Block, Type II (Mobitz Type II)

How Do I Recognize It?

Second-degree AV block type II is also called Mobitz type II AV block.

The conduction delay in second-degree AV block type II occurs below the AV node, either at the bundle of His or, more commonly, at the level of the bundle branches. This type of block is more serious than second-degree AV block type I and frequently progresses to third-degree AV block.

Look at Figure 7-4. You can see right away that the ventricular rhythm is irregular. Calculate the ventricular rate. Be sure to provide a rate range (slowest to fastest) since the ventricular rhythm is irregular. The ventricular rate ranges from about 20 to 60 bpm. You can quickly see that there are more P waves than QRS complexes in this rhythm strip. Use your calipers or paper to plot the P waves and see whether or not they occur on time. They do indeed occur regularly—although not every P wave is followed by a QRS complex. Now calculate the atrial rate. It is about 60 bpm. In second-degree AV block type II, each P wave occurs at a regular interval across the rhythm strip (all P waves will plot through on time) because the SA node is generating impulses in a normal manner. Impulses generated by the SA node are conducted to the ventricles at the same rate (appearing on the ECG as a constant PR interval) until an impulse is suddenly blocked—appearing on the ECG as a P wave with no QRS after it (dropped beat). Because QRS complexes are periodically dropped, the ventricular rhythm is irregular.

Look at the QRS complexes in Figure 7-4. They are wider than normal, measuring about 0.16 seconds. Remember that in second-degree AV block type I, the QRS is usually narrow because the block occurs at the level of the AV node. In second-degree AV block type II, the site of the block is lower in the conduction system—in the bundle of His (uncommon) or bundle branches (more common). If the block occurs in the bundle of His, the QRS will remain narrow. If the block occurs below the bundle of His, the QRS will be wide (more than 0.10 seconds in duration).

When AV block occurs in the setting of a left coronary artery occlusion (septal and anterior infarctions), the block is usually located in the bundle branches and most likely due to serious tissue injury or tissue death.

Now look closely at the PR intervals in the first two PQRST cycles in Figure 7-4 and compare them. Are they the same or different? Remember that in second-degree AV block type I, we found that the PR intervals lengthened until a P wave appeared with no QRS after it. In this rhythm strip, the PR intervals are the same and then a P wave suddenly appears with no QRS after it. When the PR intervals measure the same, we say that the PR interval is *constant*. This is an important difference between second-degree AV block type I and second-degree AV block type II. In second-degree AV block type II, the PR interval is usually within normal limits or slightly prolonged—but it is constant for the conducted beats. Examination of the ST-segments in this rhythm strip reveals ST-segment elevation. Our identification of the rhythm in Figure 7-4 is, "Second-degree AV block type II at a rate of 20 to 60 bpm with ST-segment elevation." The ECG characteristics of second-degree AV block type II are shown in Table 7-4.

What Causes It?

The bundle branches receive their primary blood supply from the left coronary artery. Thus disease of the left coronary artery or an anterior MI is usually associated with blocks that occur within the bundle branches. Second-degree AV block type II may also occur because of acute myocarditis or other types of organic heart disease.

What Do I Do About It?

Second-degree AV block type II may rapidly progress to third-degree AV block without warning.

The patient's response to this rhythm is usually related to the ventricular rate. If the ventricular rate is within normal limits, the patient may be asymptomatic. More commonly, the ventricular rate is significantly slowed and serious signs and symptoms result because of the slow rate and decreased cardiac output.

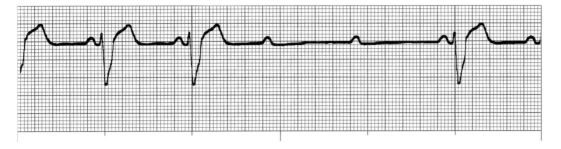

Figure **7-4**
Second-degree AV block
type II at 20 to 60 bpm,
ST-segment elevation.

TABLE 7-4	**Characteristics of Second-Degree AV Block Type II**
Rate	Atrial rate is greater than the ventricular rate; ventricular rate is often slow
Rhythm	Atrial regular (Ps plot through time), ventricular irregular
P waves	Normal in size and shape; some P waves are not followed by a QRS complex (more Ps than QRSs)
PR interval	Within normal limits or slightly prolonged but constant for the conducted beats; there may be some shortening of the PR interval that follows a nonconducted P wave
QRS duration	Usually 0.10 sec or greater, periodically absent after P waves

AV, atrioventricular.

Preparations should be made for pacing when this rhythm is recognized. The use of atropine should be avoided. In this situation, atropine will usually not improve the block but will increase the rate of discharge of the SA node. This may trigger a situation in which even fewer impulses are conducted through to the ventricles and the ventricular rate is further slowed.

Second-degree AV block type II is usually an indication for a permanent pacemaker.

—— *ECG Pearl* ⸺⁓⋀⋏⌐⁓↴⁓

Locating the probable site of an AV block plays a critical part in developing an effective treatment plan for AV block. Remember, when AV block is associated with an inferior wall MI and produces a narrow QRS complex, it is probably located in the AV node. However, when an anterior wall MI produces AV block it usually occurs in the bundle branches (infranodal) and displays a wide QRS complex. Infranodal AV blocks may quickly progress to a near-asystole state. Therefore, standby pacing is indicated when infranodal AV block complicates anterior wall MI. The rationale behind this strategy is this: If an AV block is known to be unstable and unlikely to respond to atropine, then applying the pacemaker on standby—even when the AV block is presently stable—is the best defense.[7]

Second-Degree AV Block, 2:1 Conduction (2:1 AV Block)

How Do I Recognize It?

Before we discuss 2:1 AV block, let's review a couple of very important points regarding second-degree AV blocks. So far you've learned how important it is to plot P waves to make sure they occur on time. You have also learned that there are differences in the PR interval patterns in second-degree AV block type I and type II. In order to see compare PR intervals, we must see two PQRST cycles in a row. If there are more P waves than QRSs and the P waves occur on time, you now know that you have some type of AV block. If you then look at the PR intervals, you can begin to differentiate what type of AV block it is.

For example, if the PR intervals get progressively longer and then a P wave appears with no QRS after it, you know that the rhythm is a second-degree AV block type I. If the PR intervals remain the same (constant) before the conducted beats, you know that the rhythm is a second-degree AV block type II. The QRS complex in a second-degree AV block type I is usually narrow. It is usually wide in a second-degree AV block type II.

When two conducted P waves occur in a row, the PR intervals of the consecutive beats should be compared to identify either type I or type II second-degree AV block.

Second-degree AV block with 2:1 conduction may be due to block within the AV node (type I) or more distal block within the His-Purkinje system (type II).[5]

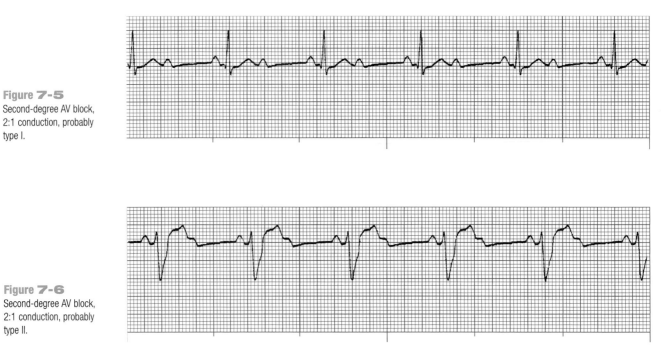

Figure 7-5
Second-degree AV block, 2:1 conduction, probably type I.

Figure 7-6
Second-degree AV block, 2:1 conduction, probably type II.

In 2:1 AV block, two P waves occur for every one QRS complex (2:1 conduction). Since there are no two PQRST cycles in a row from which to compare PR intervals, the decision as to what to term the rhythm is based on the width of the QRS complex. A 2:1 AV block associated with a narrow QRS complex (0.10 second or less) usually represents a form of second-degree AV block, type I (Figure 7-5). A 2:1 AV block associated with wide QRS complexes (greater than 0.10 seconds) is usually associated with a delay in conduction below the bundle of His—thus it is usually a type II block (Figure 7-6).

The terms *high-grade* or *advanced* second-degree AV block may be used to describe two or more consecutive P waves that are not conducted. For example, in 3:1 block, every third P wave is conducted; in 4:1 block, every fourth P wave is conducted. In cases of advanced AV block, it may be difficult to determine the type of second-degree block because the block may involve either a type I or type II mechanism. If the PR interval varies and its length is inversely related to the interval between the P wave and its preceding R wave, the rhythm is most likely a second-degree block type I.[6] If the PR interval is constant for all conducted beats, the rhythm is most likely a second-degree AV block type II.

A comparison of the types of second-degree AV blocks is shown in Figure 7-7. The ECG characteristics of 2:1 AV block are summarized in Table 7-5.

What Causes It? What Do I Do About It?
The causes and management of second-degree AV block with 2:1 conduction are those of type I or type II block previously described.

—— *ECG Pearl*

A Quick Look at P Waves and AV Blocks

AV Block	P Wave Conduction
First degree	All P waves conducted but delayed
Second degree	Some P waves conducted, others blocked
Third degree	No P waves conducted

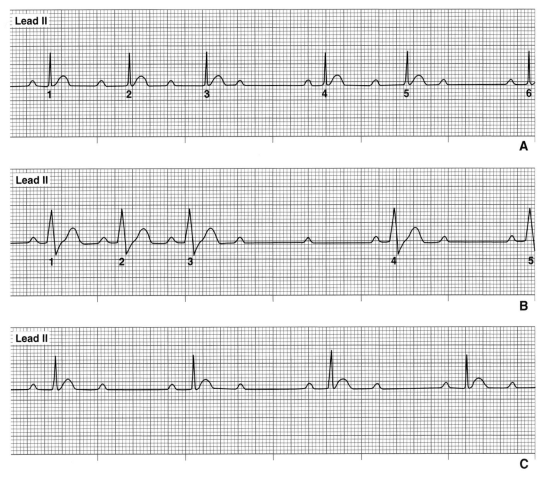

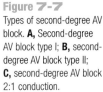

Figure 7-7
Types of second-degree AV
block. **A,** Second-degree
AV block type I; **B,** second-
degree AV block type II;
C, second-degree AV block
2:1 conduction.

TABLE 7-5	Characteristics of Second-Degree AV Block 2:1 Conduction (2:1 AV Block)
Rate	Atrial rate is twice the ventricular rate
Rhythm	Atrial regular (P's plot through time), ventricular regular
P waves	Normal in size and shape; every other P wave is followed by a QRS complex (more Ps than QRSs)
PR interval	Constant
QRS duration	Within normal limits, if the block occurs above the bundle of His (probably type I); wide if the block occurs below the bundle of His (probably type II); absent after every other P wave

AV, atrioventricular.

THIRD-DEGREE AV BLOCK

How Do I Recognize It?

Second-degree AV blocks are types of *incomplete* blocks because the AV junction conducts at least some impulses to the ventricles. In third-degree AV block, impulses generated by the SA node are blocked before reaching the ventricles, so no P waves are conducted. The atria and ventricles beat independently of each other. Thus third-degree AV block is also called *complete* AV block. The block may occur at the AV node, bundle of His, or bundle branches. A secondary pacemaker (either junctional or ventricular) stimulates the ventricles; therefore, the QRS may be narrow or wide, depending on the location of the escape pacemaker and the condition of the intraventricular conduction system.

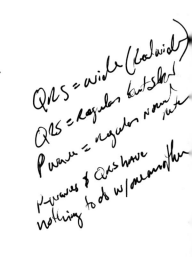

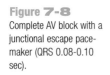

Figure **7-8**
Complete AV block with a junctional escape pacemaker (QRS 0.08-0.10 sec).

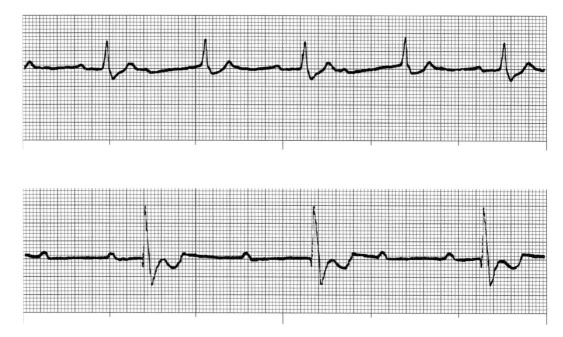

Figure **7-9**
Complete AV block with a ventricular escape pacemaker (QRS 0.12-0.14 sec).

TABLE 7-6	**Characteristics of Third-Degree AV Block**
Rate	Atrial rate is greater than the ventricular rate; ventricular rate determined by origin of the escape rhythm
Rhythm	Atrial regular (P's plot through time), ventricular regular; there is no relationship between the atrial and ventricular rhythms
P waves	Normal in size and shape
PR interval	None: The atria and ventricles beat independently of each other, thus there is no true PR interval
QRS duration	Narrow or wide depending on the location of the escape pacemaker and the condition of the intraventricular conduction system; narrow = junctional pacemaker, wide = ventricular pacemaker

AV, atrioventricular.

Third-degree AV block associated with an inferior MI is thought to be the result of a block above the bundle of His. It often occurs after progression from first-degree AV block or second-degree AV block type I. The resulting rhythm is usually stable because the escape pacemaker is usually junctional (narrow QRS complexes) with a ventricular rate of more than 40 bpm (Figure 7-8).

Third-degree AV block associated with an anterior MI is usually preceded by second-degree AV block type II or an intraventricular conduction delay (right or left bundle branch block). The resulting rhythm is usually unstable because the escape pacemaker is usually ventricular (wide QRS complexes) with a ventricular rate of less than 40 bpm (Figure 7-9). The ECG characteristics of third-degree AV block are shown in Table 7-6.

What Causes It?

When associated with an inferior MI, third-degree AV block often resolves on its own within a week. Third-degree AV block associated with an anterior MI may develop suddenly and without warning, usually 12 to 24 hours after the onset of acute ischemia.

What Do I Do About It?

Third-degree AV block that occurs with an acute anterior MI is often an indication for insertion of a permanent pacemaker.

The patient's signs and symptoms will depend on the origin of the escape pacemaker (junctional vs. ventricular) and the patient's response to a slower ventricular rate. If the QRS is narrow and the patient is symptomatic due to the slow rate, initial management consists of

TABLE 7-7	AV Blocks: Summary	
	Second-Degree AV Block Type I	**Second-Degree AV Block Type II**
Ventricular rhythm	Irregular	Irregular
PR interval	Progressively lengthening	Constant
QRS width	Usually narrow	Usually wide
	Second-Degree AV Block 2:1 Conduction	**Third-Degree (Complete) AV Block**
Ventricular rhythm	Regular	Regular
PR interval	Constant	None—No relationship between P waves and QRS complexes
QRS width	May be narrow or wide	May be narrow or wide

AV, atrioventricular.

TABLE 7-8	AV Blocks: Summary of Characteristics				
	First-Degree	**Second-Degree Type I**	**Second-Degree Type II**	**Second-Degree 2:1 Conduction**	**Third-Degree (Complete)**
Rate	Usually within normal range, but depends on underlying rhythm	Atrial rate > ventricular rate; both often within normal limits	Atrial rate > ventricular rate; ventricular rate often slow	Atrial rate > ventricular rate	Atrial rate > ventricular rate; ventricular rate determined by origin of escape rhythm
Rhythm	Atrial regular, ventricular regular	Atrial regular, ventricular irregular	Atrial regular, ventricular irregular	Atrial regular, ventricular regular	Atrial regular, ventricular regular
P waves (lead II)	Normal, one P wave precedes each QRS	Normal in size and shape; some P waves are not followed by a QRS complex (more Ps than QRSs)	Normal in size and shape; some P waves are not followed by a QRS complex (more Ps than QRSs)	Normal in size and shape; every other P wave is not followed by a QRS complex (more Ps than QRSs)	Normal in size and shape; some P waves are not followed by a QRS complex (more Ps than QRSs)
PR interval	> 0.20 sec and constant	Lengthens with each cycle until a P wave appears without a QRS	Normal or slightly prolonged but constant for conducted beats	Constant	None—The atria and ventricles beat independently of each other; thus there is no true PR interval
QRS	Usually 0.10 sec or less unless an intraventricular conduction delay exists	Usually 0.10 sec or less unless an intraventricular conduction delay exists	Usually > 0.10 sec, periodically absent after P waves	Within normal limits if block above bundle of His (probably type I); wide if block below bundle of His (probably type II); absent after every other P wave	Narrow or wide depending on location of escape pacemaker and condition of intraventricular conduction system

AV, atrioventricular.

atropine and/or transcutaneous pacing. If the QRS is wide and the patient is symptomatic due to the slow rate, transcutaneous pacing should be instituted while preparations are made for insertion of a transvenous pacemaker.

Table 7-7 will help you learn to recognize the differences between second- and third-degree AV blocks. First, determine if the ventricular rhythm is regular or irregular. Next, look at the PR intervals. Based on this information, you should be able to identify the rhythm strips in this chapter. A summary of AV block characteristics can be found in Table 7-8.

REFERENCES

1. Kahn MG: *Rapid ECG interpretation*, Philadelphia, 1997, WB Saunders.
2. Rusterholz AP, Marriott HJL: How long can the P-R interval be? *Am J Noninvasive Cardiol* 8:11-13, 1994.
3. Murphy JG: *Mayo clinical cardiology review*, ed 2, Philadelphia, 2001, Lippincott, Williams & Wilkins.
4. Barold SS: Indications for permanent cardiac pacing in first-degree AV block: class I, II, or III? *PACE* 19:747-751, 1996.
5. Padrid PJ, Kowey PR, editors: *Cardiac arrhythmias: mechanisms, diagnosis, and management*, Baltimore, 1995, Williams & Wilkins.
6. Chou T, Knilans TK: *Electrocardiography in clinical practice: adult and pediatric*, Philadelphia, 1996, WB Saunders.
7. Phalen T, Aehlert B: *The 12-lead ECG in acute coronary syndromes*, 2006, Mosby.

STOP & REVIEW

True/False

Indicate whether the sentence or statement is true or false.

____   1. Second-degree AV block type II occurs above the bundle of His.

____   2. The ventricular rhythm is regular in second-degree AV block type I.

Matching

a. 0.12-0.20 sec
b. Regular
c. Bundle of His or bundle branches
d. Progressive lengthening
e. AV node
f. First-degree AV block
g. Ventricular
h. AV node, bundle of His, bundle branches

i. Inferior wall
j. Third-degree AV block
k. Junctional
l. Anterior wall
m. Irregular
n. Constant
o. Second-degree AV block type II

____   3. A ___ escape rhythm may occur with a third-degree AV block, ventricular rate is usually 40 bpm or less.
____   4. Second-degree AV block type II is most commonly associated with an ___ myocardial infarction.
____   5. AV block that often progresses to a third-degree AV block without warning
____   6. AV block characterized by regular P-P intervals, regular R-R intervals, and a PR interval with no consistent value or pattern
____   7. PR interval pattern in second-degree AV block type II
____   8. Second-degree AV block type I is most commonly associated with a(n) ___ myocardial infarction.
____   9. PR interval pattern in second-degree AV block type I
____   10. Ventricular rhythm pattern in second-degree AV block types I and II
____   11. Normal duration of the PR interval
____   12. AV block characterized by a PR interval greater than 0.20 seconds and one P wave for each QRS complex
____   13. Location of the block in a third-degree AV block
____   14. Ventricular rhythm pattern in second-degree AV block 2:1 conduction and third-degree AV block
____   15. Location of the block in a second-degree AV block type II
____   16. Common location of the block in a second-degree AV block type I
____   17. A(n) ___ escape rhythm may occur with a third-degree AV block; usually has a narrow QRS and a ventricular rate of 40-60 bpm.

Short Answer

18. Indicate the ECG criteria for the following dysrhythmias.

	Second-Degree AV Block Type I	Third-Degree AV Block
Ventricular rhythm	_____	_____
PR interval	_____	_____
QRS width	_____	_____

19. Complete the following ECG criteria for second-degree AV block type I.

    Rate _____

    Rhythm _____

    P waves _____

    PR interval _____

    QRS duration _____

20. Which type of AV block has the greatest potential to deteriorate to sudden, third-degree AV block?

ECG Crossword

Across

2. This medication may be used to treat a symptomatic narrow-QRS bradycardia.
5. In 2:1 AV block, a QRS is __ after every other P wave.
7. One site for second-degree AV block type II and third-degree AV blocks
8. If P waves are not plotted, an AV block may be confused with a __ __.
12. The PR interval of a first-degree AV block is __ than 0.20 seconds.
13. Third-degree AV block associated with a(n) __ MI is thought to be due to a block above the bundle of His.
14. Second- or third-degree AV block that occurs with an acute anterior MI is often an indication for insertion of a __ pacemaker.

Down

1. The QRS complex of a second-degree type II AV block is usually __.
3. Ventricular rhythm pattern in second-degree AV block types I and II
4. This type of AV block usually produces no symptoms.
5. Usual site of block in a first-degree AV block
6. An older name for second-degree AV block type I
7. Uncommon site of block for a second-degree type II AV block
9. The QRS complex of an AV block in the area of the AV node is usually __.
10. A medication that may cause a prolonged PR interval
11. In second-degree AV block type I, the PR intervals __.

PRACTICE *Rhythm Strips*

For each of the following rhythm strips, determine the atrial and ventricular rates and rhythms, measure the PR interval and QRS duration, and identify the rhythm. All strips were recorded in lead II unless otherwise noted.

Figure **7-10**

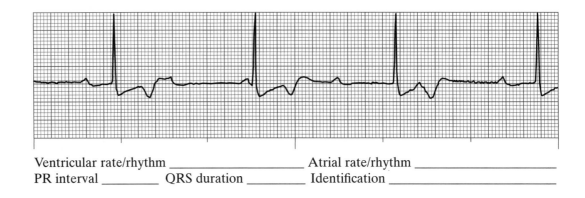

Ventricular rate/rhythm _____ Atrial rate/rhythm _____
PR interval _____ QRS duration _____ Identification _____

This rhythm strip is from an 83-year-old woman with syncope.

Figure **7-11**

Ventricular rate/rhythm _____ Atrial rate/rhythm _____
PR interval _____ QRS duration _____ Identification _____

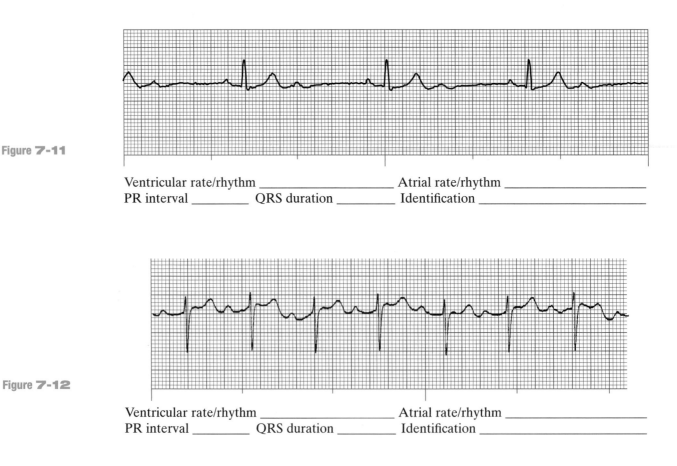

Figure **7-12**

Ventricular rate/rhythm _____ Atrial rate/rhythm _____
PR interval _____ QRS duration _____ Identification _____

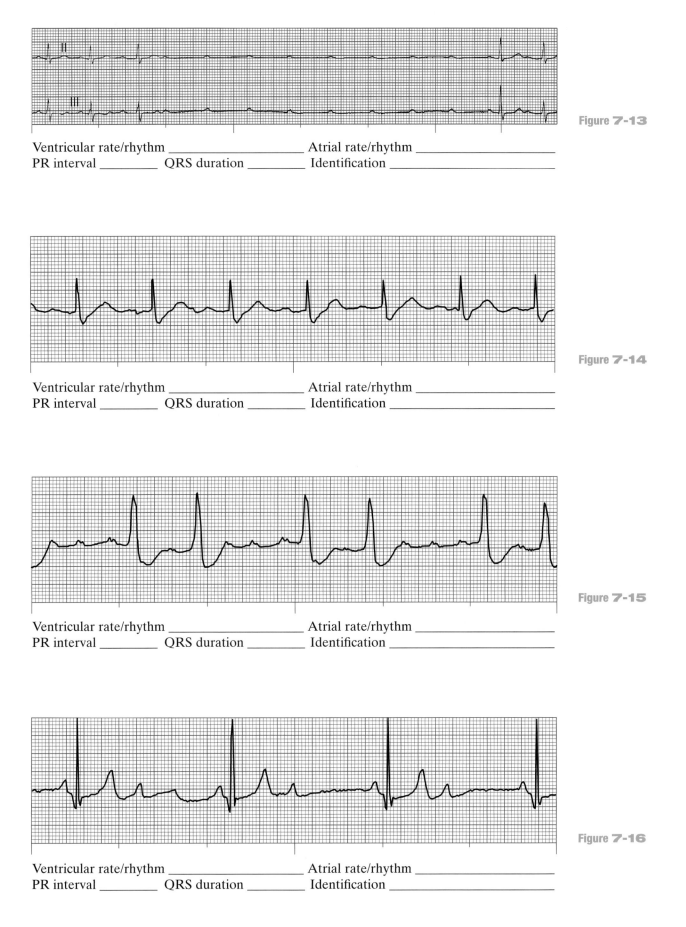

Figure 7-13

Ventricular rate/rhythm _____ Atrial rate/rhythm _____
PR interval _____ QRS duration _____ Identification _____

Figure 7-14

Ventricular rate/rhythm _____ Atrial rate/rhythm _____
PR interval _____ QRS duration _____ Identification _____

Figure 7-15

Ventricular rate/rhythm _____ Atrial rate/rhythm _____
PR interval _____ QRS duration _____ Identification _____

Figure 7-16

Ventricular rate/rhythm _____ Atrial rate/rhythm _____
PR interval _____ QRS duration _____ Identification _____

Figure **7-17**

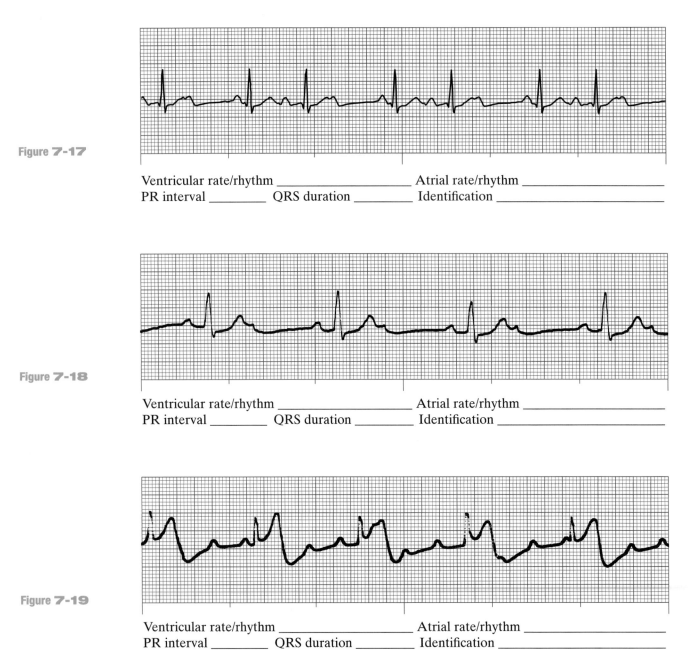

Ventricular rate/rhythm _____ Atrial rate/rhythm _____
PR interval _____ QRS duration _____ Identification _____

Figure **7-18**

Ventricular rate/rhythm _____ Atrial rate/rhythm _____
PR interval _____ QRS duration _____ Identification _____

Figure **7-19**

Ventricular rate/rhythm _____ Atrial rate/rhythm _____
PR interval _____ QRS duration _____ Identification _____

This rhythm strip is from a 77-year-old woman who stated she felt fine. She stopped at a blood pressure machine in Wal-Mart, and the machine would not read her pulse rate. She later went to her physician's office and then to the emergency department.

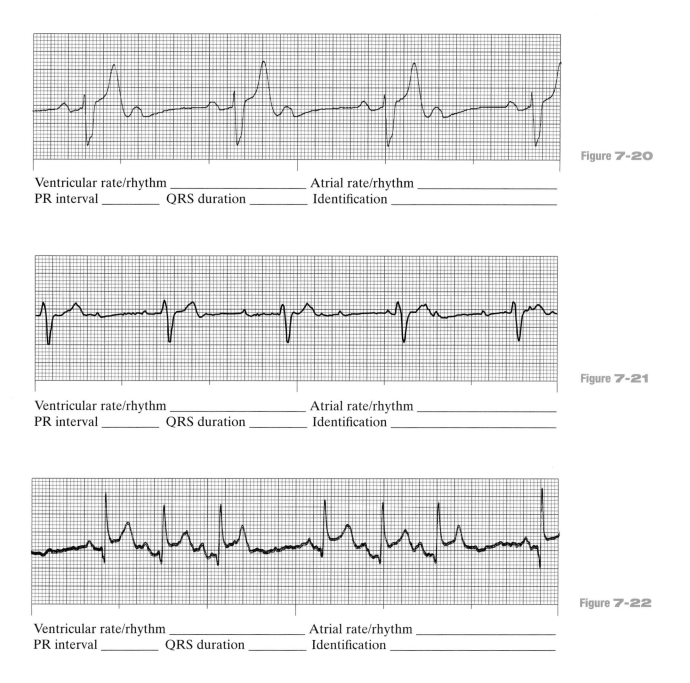

Figure 7-20

Ventricular rate/rhythm _____ Atrial rate/rhythm _____
PR interval _____ QRS duration _____ Identification _____

Figure 7-21

Ventricular rate/rhythm _____ Atrial rate/rhythm _____
PR interval _____ QRS duration _____ Identification _____

Figure 7-22

Ventricular rate/rhythm _____ Atrial rate/rhythm _____
PR interval _____ QRS duration _____ Identification _____

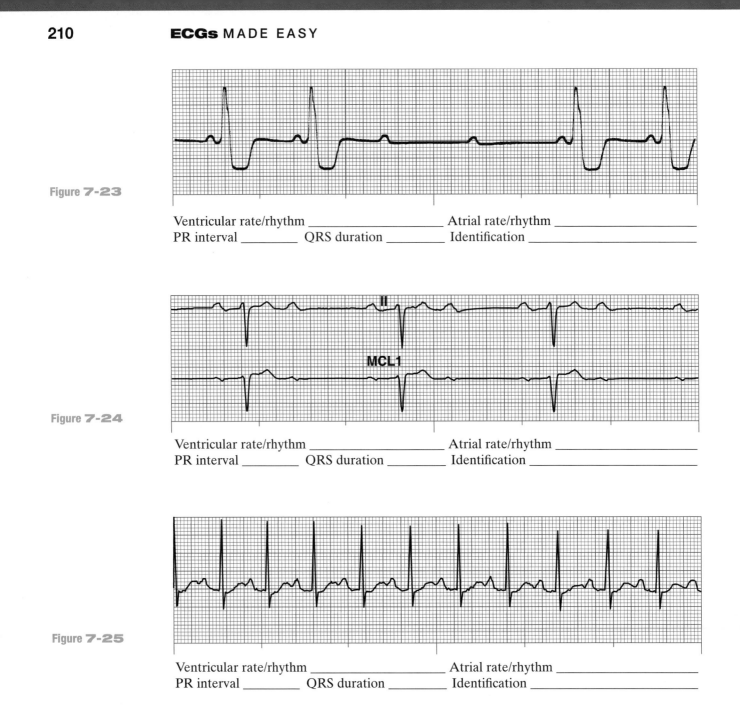

Figure **7-23**

Ventricular rate/rhythm _____ Atrial rate/rhythm _____
PR interval _____ QRS duration _____ Identification _____

Figure **7-24**

Ventricular rate/rhythm _____ Atrial rate/rhythm _____
PR interval _____ QRS duration _____ Identification _____

Figure **7-25**

Ventricular rate/rhythm _____ Atrial rate/rhythm _____
PR interval _____ QRS duration _____ Identification _____

CHAPTER 8

Pacemaker Rhythms

OBJECTIVES

On completion of this chapter, you should be able to:

1. Define the following terms: *sensitivity, capture, asynchronous, synchronous, threshold.*
2. Identify the components of a pacemaker system.
3. Describe a unipolar and bipolar pacing electrode.
4. Explain the differences between fixed-rate and demand pacemakers.
5. Describe the primary pacing modes.
6. Identify the cardiac chamber(s) stimulated by different pacing methods.
7. Describe the appearance of a typical pacemaker spike on the ECG.
8. Describe the appearance of the waveform on the ECG produced as a result of:
   a. Atrial pacing
   b. Ventricular pacing
9. Describe the benefits of atrioventricular (AV) sequential pacing.
10. Identify the primary indications for pacemaker therapy.
11. List three contraindications for transcutaneous pacing.
12. Identify the complications of pacing.
13. List three types of pacemaker malfunction.

PACEMAKER TERMINOLOGY

A wave: Atrial paced event; the atrial stimulus or the point in the intrinsic atrial depolarization (P wave) at which atrial sensing occurs; analogous to the P wave of intrinsic waveforms.

A-A interval: Interval between two consecutive atrial stimuli, with or without an interceding ventricular event; analogous to the P-P interval of intrinsic waveforms.

Asynchronous pacemaker: (Fixed rate) pacemaker that continuously discharges at a preset rate regardless of the patient's intrinsic activity.

Atrial pacing: Pacing system with a lead attached to the right atrium designed to correct abnormalities in the sinoatrial (SA) node (sick sinus syndrome).

Automatic interval: Period, expressed in milliseconds, between two consecutive paced events in the same cardiac chamber without an intervening sensed event (e.g., A-A interval, V-V interval); also known as the demand interval, basic interval, or pacing interval.

AV interval: In dual-chamber pacing, the length of time between an atrial-sensed or atrial-paced event and the delivery of a ventricular pacing stimulus; analogous to the P-R interval of intrinsic waveforms; also called the artificial or electronic P-R interval.

AV sequential pacemaker: Pacemaker that stimulates first the atrium, then the ventricle, mimicking normal cardiac physiology; a type of dual-chamber pacemaker.

Base rate: Rate at which the pulse generator paces when no intrinsic activity is detected; expressed in pulses per minute (ppm).

Bipolar lead: Pacing lead with two electrical poles that are external from the pulse generator; the negative pole is located at the extreme distal tip of the pacing lead; the positive pole is located several millimeters proximal to the negative electrode; the stimulating pulse is delivered through the negative electrode.

Capture: Ability of a pacing stimulus to successfully depolarize the cardiac chamber that is being paced; with one-to-one capture, each pacing stimulus results in depolarization of the appropriate chamber.

Demand (synchronous) pacemaker: Pacemaker that discharges only when the patient's heart rate drops below the preset rate for the pacemaker.

Dual-chamber pacemaker: Pacemaker that stimulates the atrium and ventricle; dual-chamber pacing is also called physiologic pacing.

Escape interval: Time measured between a sensed cardiac event and the next pacemaker output.

Fusion beat: In pacing, the ECG waveform that results when an intrinsic depolarization and a pacing stimulus occur simultaneously, and both contribute to depolarization of that cardiac chamber.

Hysteresis: Programmable feature in some demand pacemakers that allows programming of a longer escape interval between the intrinsic complex and the first paced event; the longer escape interval allows intrinsic beats an opportunity to inhibit the pacemaker.

Inhibition: Pacemaker response in which the output pulse is suppressed (inhibited) when an intrinsic event is sensed.

Interval: Period, measured in milliseconds, between any two designated cardiac events; in pacing, intervals are more useful than rate because pacemaker timing is based on intervals.

Intrinsic: Inherent; naturally occurring.

Milliampere (mA): Unit of measure of electrical current needed to elicit depolarization of the myocardium.

Output: Electrical stimulus delivered by the pulse generator, usually defined in terms of pulse amplitude (volts) and pulse width (milliseconds).

Pacemaker: Artificial pulse generator that delivers an electrical current to the heart to stimulate depolarization.

Pacemaker spike: Vertical line on the ECG that indicates the pacemaker has discharged.

Pacemaker syndrome: Adverse clinical signs and symptoms that limit a patient's everyday functioning and occur in the setting of an electrically normal pacing system; common signs and symptoms include weakness, fatigue, dizziness, near or full syncope, cough, chest pain, hypotension, dyspnea, and congestive heart failure; pacemaker syndrome is most commonly associated with a loss of AV synchrony (e.g., VVI pacing) but may also occur because of an inappropriate AV interval or inappropriate rate modulation.

Pacing interval: Period, expressed in milliseconds, between two consecutive paced events in the same cardiac chamber without an intervening sensed event (e.g., AA interval, VV interval); also known as the demand interval, basic interval, or automatic interval.

Pacing system analyzer (PSA): External testing and measuring device capable of pacing the heart during pacemaker implantation; used to determine appropriate pulse generator settings for the individual patient (e.g., pacing threshold, lead impedance, pulse amplitude).

Parameter: Value that can be measured and sometimes changed, either indirectly or directly; in pacing, parameter refers to a value that influences the function of the pacemaker (e.g., sensitivity, amplitude, mode).

Pulse generator: Power source that houses the battery and controls for regulating a pacemaker.

Rate modulation: Ability of a pacemaker to increase the pacing rate in response to physical activity or metabolic demand; some type of physiologic sensor is used by the pacemaker to determine the need for an increased pacing rate; also called rate adaptation or rate response.

R wave: In pacing, R wave refers to the entire QRS complex denoting an intrinsic ventricular event.

RV interval: Period from the intrinsic ventricular event and the ventricular-paced event that follows; the pacemaker's escape interval.

Sensing: Ability of a pacemaker to recognize and respond to intrinsic electrical activity; the pacemaker's response to sensed activity depends on its programmed mode and parameters.

Threshold: Minimum level of electrical current needed to consistently depolarize the myocardium.

Unipolar lead: Pacing lead with a single electrical pole at the distal tip of the pacing lead (negative pole) through which the stimulating pulse is delivered; in a permanent pacemaker with a unipolar lead, the positive pole is the pulse generator case.

V-A interval: In dual-chamber pacing, the interval between a sensed or ventricular-paced event and the next atrial-paced event.

V-V interval: Interval between two ventricular-paced events.

V wave: Ventricular-paced event; the ventricular stimulus or the point in the intrinsic ventricular depolarization (R wave) during which ventricular sensing occurs.

Ventricular pacing: Pacing system with a lead attached in the right ventricle.

PACEMAKER SYSTEMS

A **pacemaker** is an artificial pulse generator that delivers an electrical current to the heart to stimulate depolarization. Pacemaker systems are usually named according to where the electrodes are located and the route the electrical current takes to the heart. A pacemaker system (Figure 8-1) consists of a **pulse generator** (power source) and pacing lead(s). The pulse generator houses a battery and electronic circuitry to sense and analyze the patient's **intrinsic** rhythm and the timing circuitry for pacing stimulus output.[1] The circuitry works like a computer, converting energy from the battery into electrical pulses. A pacing lead is an insulated wire used to carry an electrical impulse from the pacemaker to the patient's heart. It also carries information about the heart's electrical activity back to the pacemaker. The exposed portion of the pacing lead is called an *electrode*, which is placed in direct contact with the heart.

Permanent Pacemakers

A permanent pacemaker is implanted in the body, usually under local anesthesia. Pacemaker wires are surrounded by plastic catheters. The pacemaker's circuitry is housed in a hermetically sealed case made of titanium that is airtight and impermeable to fluid.

The electrode of a permanent pacemaker may be unipolar or bipolar. It is placed transvenously or surgically. Once the electrode is in place, the pulse generator is usually implanted

A connector block on top of the pacemaker's metal container joins the pacing lead with the pacemaker.

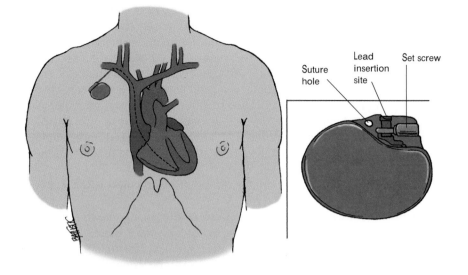

Figure 8-1
Permanent pacemaker.

into the subcutaneous tissue of the anterior chest just below the right or left clavicle. The electrode is then connected to the pulse generator. The patient's handedness, occupation, and hobbies determine whether the pacemaker is implanted on the right or left side. The non-dominant side is usually chosen to minimize interference with the patient's daily activities.[1]

Lithium batteries are almost exclusively used in modern pacemakers. Battery life depends on the following:

- How much energy is required for capture
- The percentage of time the device paces
- The number of cardiac chambers paced

When the battery gets low, the entire pacemaker is replaced because the battery is sealed inside the pacemaker.

Indications

Current indications for insertion of a permanent pacemaker include the following[2]:

- Third-degree AV block
- Symptomatic type II second-degree block
- Second-degree AV block with episodic ventricular arrhythmias
- Sick sinus syndrome
- Symptomatic bradycardias with syncope or presyncope
- Hypersensitive carotid artery syndrome
- Type I block with infra-His bundle block
- Specific subgroups of patients with triphasic and biphasic blocks at risk of developing sudden high-degree block

Temporary Pacemakers

The pulse generator of a temporary pacemaker is located externally.

Temporary pacing can be accomplished through transvenous, epicardial, or transcutaneous means.

- Transvenous pacemakers stimulate the endocardium of the right atrium or ventricle (or both) by means of an electrode introduced into a central vein, such as the subclavian or cephalic vein.

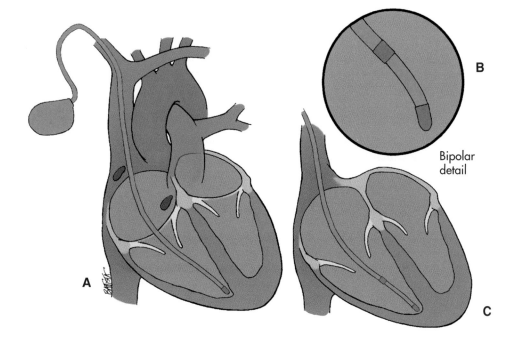

Figure 8-2
A, Unipolar and
B, C bipolar pacemaker
electrodes.

- Epicardial pacing is the placement of pacing leads directly onto or through the epicardium under direct visualization. Epicardial leads may be used when a patient is undergoing surgery and the outer surface of the heart is easy to reach. They are frequently used in neonates, children, and adolescents because of cardiac anatomy, small body size, and/or difficulty accessing the superior vena cava.
- Transcutaneous pacing (TCP) delivers pacing impulses to the heart using electrodes placed on the patient's thorax. TCP is also called *temporary external pacing* or *noninvasive pacing* and is covered later in this chapter.

Indications
Indications for emergent temporary pacing include:

- Hemodynamically significant bradycardia (blood pressure < 80 mm Hg systolic, change in mental status, pulmonary edema, angina)
- Bradycardia with escape rhythms unresponsive to drug therapy
- **Overdrive pacing** of tachycardia—supraventricular or ventricular—refractory to pharmacologic therapy or electrical countershock
- Bradyasystolic cardiac arrest

During overdrive pacing, the heart is paced briefly (seconds) at a rate faster than the rate of the tachycardia. The pacemaker is then stopped to allow return of the heart's intrinsic pacemaker.

Pacemaker Electrodes

Unipolar Electrodes
There are two types of pacemaker electrodes—unipolar and bipolar. A unipolar electrode (Figure 8-2) has one pacing electrode that is located at its distal tip. The negative electrode is in contact with the heart, and the pulse generator (located outside the heart) functions as the positive electrode. The **pacemaker spikes** produced by a unipolar electrode are often large because of the distance between the positive and negative electrodes.

Bipolar Electrodes
A bipolar pacemaker electrode contains a positive and negative electrode at the distal tip of the pacing lead wire. Most temporary transvenous pacemakers have bipolar electrodes. A permanent pacemaker may have either a bipolar or a unipolar electrode. The spike produced by a bipolar electrode is often small and difficult to see.

Pacemaker Modes

Fixed-Rate (Asynchronous) Pacemakers

A **fixed-rate pacemaker** continuously discharges at a preset rate (usually 70 to 80/min) regardless of the patient's heart rate. An advantage of the fixed-rate pacemaker is its simple circuitry, reducing the risk of pacemaker failure. However, this type of pacemaker does not sense the patient's own cardiac rhythm. This may result in competition between the patient's cardiac rhythm and that of the pacemaker. Ventricular tachycardia (VT) or ventricular fibrillation (VF) may be induced if the pacemaker were to fire during the T wave (vulnerable period) of a preceding patient beat. Fixed-rate pacemakers are not often used today.

Demand (Synchronous, Noncompetitive) Pacemakers

A **demand pacemaker** discharges only when the patient's heart rate drops below the pacemaker's preset (base) rate. For example, if the demand pacemaker was preset at a rate of 70 impulses per minute, it would sense the patient's heart rate and allow electrical impulses to flow from the pacemaker through the pacing lead to stimulate the heart only when the rate fell below 70 bpm. Demand pacemakers can be programmable or nonprogrammable. The voltage level and impulse rate are preset at the time of manufacture in nonprogrammable pacemakers.

It has been estimated that 7.4% to 15% of pacemakers fail in the first year.[3]

Pacemaker Identification Codes

Typically, only the first three letters are used to describe a pacemaker. The letter "R" in the fourth position is sometimes used because it indicates that the pacemaker is a rate-responsive device.

Pacemaker identification codes are used to assist in identifying a pacemaker's preprogrammed pacing, sensing, and response functions (Table 8-1). The first three letters are used for antibradycardia functions. The *first letter* of the code identifies the heart chamber (or chambers) paced (stimulated). The options available are as follows:

O, none
A, atrium
V, ventricle
D, dual (both atrium and ventricle)

A pacemaker used to pace only a single chamber is represented by either A (atrial) or V (ventricular). A pacemaker capable of pacing in both chambers is represented by D (dual).

The *second letter* identifies the chamber of the heart where patient-initiated (intrinsic) electrical activity is sensed by the pacemaker. The letter designations for the second letter are the same as the designations for the first.

Commonly encountered pacing modes are VVI, DVI, DDD, and DDDR.

The *third letter* indicates how the pacemaker will respond when it senses patient-initiated electrical activity:

O, no sensing
T, a pacemaker stimulus is triggered in response to a sensed event
I, sensing of intrinsic impulses inhibits the pacemaker from producing a stimulus
D, dual (a combination of triggered pacing and inhibition)

Most, if not all, pacemakers currently manufactured have communicating ability.

A pacemaker's rate responsiveness may also be referred to as rate modulation or rate adaptation.

The *fourth letter* is most often used in permanent pacing and identifies the availability of rate responsiveness and the number of reprogrammable functions available:

O, the pacemaker is not programmable or rate responsive (most commonly found on devices manufactured before mid-1970s)
P, simple programmability where the pacemaker is limited to one or two programmable parameters (e.g., rate or output)
M, multiprogrammability (i.e., more than two variables can be altered)
C, capability of transmitting and/or receiving data for informational or programming purposes
R, rate responsiveness, denoting the pacemaker's ability to automatically adjust its rate to meet the body's needs caused by increased physical activity

TABLE 8-1	**Pacemaker Codes**			
Chamber Paced (first letter)	Chamber Sensed (second letter)	Response to Sensing (third letter)	Programmable Functions (fourth letter)	Anti-tachycardia Functions (fifth letter)
O = None A = Atrium V = Ventricle D = Dual chamber atrium and ventricle)	O = None (fixed-rate pacemaker) A = Atrium V = Ventricle D = Dual chamber (atrium and ventricle)	O = None (fixed-rate pacemaker) T = Triggers pacing I = Inhibits pacing D = Dual (triggers and inhibits pacing)	O = None P = Simple programmability (rate and/or output) M = Multiprogrammable C = Communication R = Rate responsive	O = None P = Pacing (antitachycardia) S = Shock D = Dual (pacing and shock)

The *fifth letter* indicates the presence of one or more active antitachycardia functions and indicates how the pacemaker will respond to tachydysrhythmias:

O, the device has no antitachycardia functions
P, the device is capable of antitachycardia pacing
S, the device is capable of delivering synchronized and unsynchronized countershocks
D, the device is capable of antitachycardia pacing and synchronized and unsynchronized countershocks

> Implantable cardioverter defibrillators (ICDs) use the features designated by the fifth letter in the management of tachydysrhythmias.

When the SA node is diseased, the body loses its ability to physiologically adjust the heart rate in response to physical or emotional stressors. Rate-responsive pacemakers contain an artificial sensor (or more than one sensor) that detects physiologic changes and adjusts the heart rate accordingly. When the patient's activity increases, the sensor becomes the regulator of the patient's heart rate. The sensor detects a signal indicating a need for a rate faster than the pacemaker's base rate and instructs the pacemaker to provide electrical stimuli (output) at the sensor-indicated rate. The patient's physician determines the pacemaker's base rate and the upper sensor-driven rate of the device.

> Single-chamber or dual-chamber pacemakers can be rate responsive.

Metabolic parameters and nonmetabolic markers can be used to assess the body's physiologic demands. For example, vibration sensors detect body movement, impedance sensors detect respiratory rate and minute ventilation, and special sensors on the pacing electrode can detect central venous temperature, right atrial pressure, pH, and catecholamine levels, among other parameters.

> Two common types of sensors are an activity sensor and a minute ventilation sensor.

Single-Chamber Pacemakers

A pacemaker that paces a single heart chamber (either the atrium or ventricle) has one lead placed in the heart. Atrial pacing is achieved by placing the pacing electrode in the right atrium. Stimulation of the atria produces a pacemaker spike on the ECG, followed by a P wave (Figure 8-3). Atrial pacing may be used when the SA node is diseased or damaged, but conduction through the AV junction and ventricles is normal. This type of pacemaker is ineffective if an AV block develops because it cannot pace the ventricles.

Ventricular pacing is accomplished by placing the pacing electrode in the right ventricle. Stimulation of the ventricles produces a pacemaker spike on the ECG followed by a wide QRS, resembling a ventricular ectopic beat (Figure 8-4). The QRS complex is wide because a paced impulse does not follow the normal conduction pathway in the heart.

A single-chamber ventricular pacemaker can pace the ventricles but cannot coordinate pacing with the patient's intrinsic atrial rate. This results in asynchronous contraction of the atrium and ventricle (AV asynchrony). Because of this loss of AV synchrony, a ventricular-demand pacemaker is rarely used in a patient with an intact SA node. Conversely, a ventricular-demand pacemaker may be used for the patient with chronic atrial fibrillation.

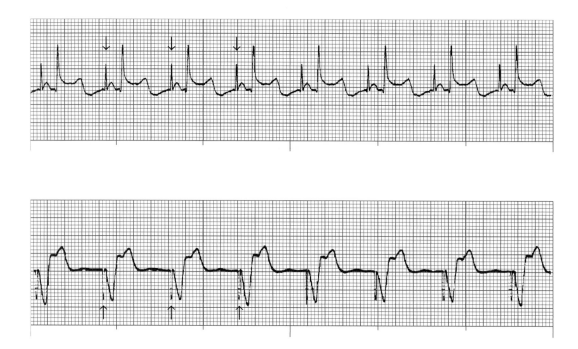

Figure 8-3
Atrial pacing. (*Arrows,*
pacer spikes)

Figure 8-4
Ventricular pacing.
(*Arrows,* pacer spikes)

The **ventricular-demand (VVI) pacemaker** is a common type of pacemaker. With this device, the pacemaker electrode is placed in the right ventricle (V); the ventricle is sensed (V) and the pacemaker is inhibited (I) when spontaneous ventricular depolarization occurs within a preset interval. When spontaneous ventricular depolarization does not occur within this preset interval, the pacemaker fires and stimulates ventricular depolarization at a preset rate.

Because a VVI pacemaker does not sense or pace atrial activity, P waves can appear anywhere in the cardiac cycle, with no relation to the QRS complexes. A disadvantage of VVI pacing is its fixed rate, regardless of the patient's level of physical activity.

Dual-Chamber Pacemakers

Dual-chamber pacing is also called physiologic pacing. Battery life for a dual-chamber pacemaker is about 5 to 9 years.

A pacemaker that paces both the atrium and ventricle has a two-lead system placed in the heart—one lead is placed in the right atrium, the other in the right ventricle. This type of pacemaker is called a dual-chamber pacemaker (Figure 8-5). An **AV sequential pacemaker** is an example of a dual-chamber pacemaker. The AV sequential pacemaker stimulates the right atrium and right ventricle sequentially (stimulating first the atrium, then the ventricle), mimicking normal cardiac physiology and thus preserving the atrial contribution to ventricular filling (atrial kick) (Figure 8-6).

The dual-chamber pacemaker may also be called a DDD pacemaker, indicating that both the atrium and ventricle are paced (D), both chambers are sensed (D), and the pacemaker has both a triggered and inhibited mode of response (D). When spontaneous atrial depolarization does not occur within a preset interval, the atrial pulse generator fires and stimulates atrial depolarization at a preset rate. The pacemaker is programmed to wait—simulating the normal delay in conduction through the AV node (the PR interval). The "artificial" or "electronic" PR interval is referred to as an **AV interval**. If spontaneous ventricular depolarization does not occur within a preset interval, the pacemaker fires and stimulates ventricular depolarization at a preset rate.

The presence of a dual-chamber pacemaker does not necessarily mean that the pacemaker is in DDD mode. Dual-chamber pacemakers can be programmed to VVI mode, depending on patient need (e.g., the development of chronic atrial fibrillation).

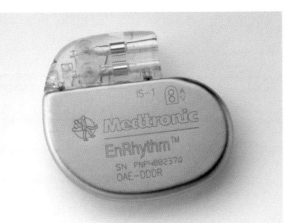

Figure 8-5
An example of a dual chamber pacemaker.

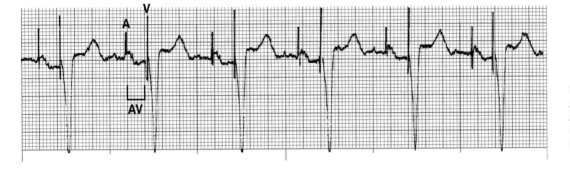

Figure 8-6
AV sequential pacing. A, atrial pacing; V, ventricular pacing; AV, A-V interval.

TRANSCUTANEOUS PACING (TCP)

Indications

TCP is recommended as the initial pacing method of choice in emergency cardiac care because it is effective, quick, safe, and is the least invasive pacing technique available. TCP is indicated for significant bradycardias unresponsive to atropine therapy or when atropine is not immediately available. TCP may be used as a "bridge" until transvenous pacing can be accomplished or the cause of the bradydysrhythmia is reversed (as in cases of drug overdose or hyperkalemia). TCP may be considered in asystolic cardiac arrest (usually less than 10 minutes in duration) and witnessed asystolic arrest.

Technique

Transcutaneous pacing involves attaching two large pacing electrodes to the skin surface of the patient's outer chest wall. The pacing pads used during TCP function as a bipolar pacing system. The electrical signal exits from the negative terminal on the machine (and subsequently the negative electrode) and passes through the chest wall to the heart.

The anterior (negative) chest electrode is placed to the left of the sternum, halfway between the xiphoid process and left nipple (Figure 8-7). The posterior (positive) electrode is placed on the left posterior thorax directly behind the anterior electrode. The electrodes should:

- Fit completely on the patient's chest
- Have a minimum of 1 to 2 inches of space between electrodes
- Not overlap bony prominences of the sternum, spine, or scapula

Studies have evaluated the importance of electrode positioning during TCP and found that, in normal volunteers, electrode placement was not crucial if the anterior electrode was of

Depolarization of the myocardium requires an electric current strong enough to overcome the resistance of the chest wall.

The adhesive pacing electrodes should be applied to clean, dry skin. In women, the anterior electrode should be positioned under the left breast.

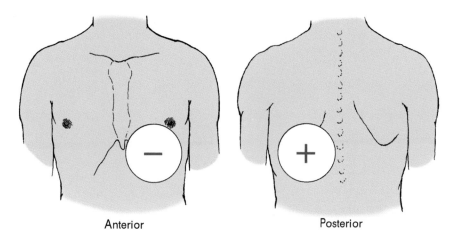

Figure 8-7
Anterior-posterior positioning of transcutaneous electrodes.

Anterior   Posterior

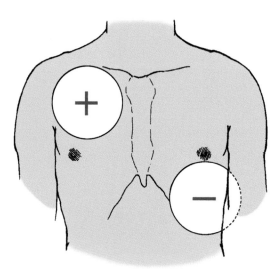

Figure 8-8
Anterior-lateral positioning of transcutaneous electrodes.

negative polarity.[4] However, electrode placement may be more significant in the critically ill patient.

If the anterior-posterior electrode position is contraindicated, the anterior-lateral position may be used. The anterior (negative) electrode is placed on the left anterior chest, just lateral to the left nipple in the midaxillary line. The posterior (positive) electrode is placed on the right anterior upper chest in the subclavicular area (Figure 8-8).

Begin TCP by connecting the patient to an ECG monitor, obtaining a rhythm strip, and verifying the presence of a paceable rhythm. Connect the pacing cable to the adhesive electrodes on the patient and to the pulse generator. After turning on the power to the pulse generator, set the pacing rate. In a patient with a pulse, the rate is generally set at a nonbradycardic rate between 60 and 80 bpm. In an asystolic patient, the rate is typically set between 80 and 100 bpm.

Chest compressions can be performed during pacing without risk of injury to the healthcare provider.

After the rate has been regulated, the stimulating current (output or milliamperes) is set. In a patient with a pulse, increase the current slowly but steadily until capture is achieved. Sedation or analgesia may be needed to minimize the discomfort associated with this procedure (common with currents of 50 mA or more). For the asystolic patient, it is reasonable to increase the current quickly in an attempt to obtain capture.

Watch the cardiac monitor closely for *electrical* capture. This is usually evidenced by a wide QRS and broad T wave. In some patients, electrical capture is less obvious—indicated only as a change in the shape of the QRS. Assess *mechanical* capture by assessing the patient's right upper extremity or right femoral pulses. Avoid assessment of pulses on the patient's left side to help minimize confusion between the presence of an actual pulse and skeletal muscle contractions caused by the pacemaker. Once capture is achieved, continue pacing at an output level slightly higher (approximately 2 mA) than the threshold of initial electrical capture. The patient's blood pressure and level of consciousness should also be assessed. Monitor the patient closely and record the ECG rhythm.

If electrical capture is achieved *without* mechanical capture, the patient should be treated according to the resuscitation guidelines for pulseless electrical activity.

If defibrillation is necessary, the defibrillation paddles should be placed 2 to 3 cm (¾–1 inch) away from the pacemaker electrodes to prevent arcing. Some pacemaker models should be turned off or disconnected before defibrillating.

—— *ECG Pearl*

Documentation should include the date and time pacing was initiated (including baseline and pacing rhythm strips), the current required to obtain capture, the pacing rate selected, the patient's responses to electrical and mechanical capture, medications administered during the procedure, and the date and time pacing was terminated.

Contraindications for TCP

- Children weighing less than 15 kg (33 lb) unless pediatric pacing electrodes are used
- Flail chest
- Bradycardia in the setting of severe hypothermia
- Bradyasystolic cardiac arrest of more than 20 minutes in duration (relative contraindication)

—— *ECG Pearl*

Adult pacing electrodes should not be trimmed or modified in any way because such modifications may alter current distribution.

Limitations of TCP

The primary limitation of TCP is patient discomfort that is proportional to the intensity of skeletal muscle contraction and the direct electrical stimulation of cutaneous nerves (Table 8-2). The degree of discomfort varies with the device used and the stimulating current required to achieve capture. Increased chest wall muscle mass, chronic obstructive pulmonary disease (COPD), or pleural effusions may require increased stimulating current.[5]

PACEMAKER MALFUNCTION

Failure to Pace

Failure to pace is a pacemaker malfunction that occurs when the pacemaker fails to deliver an electrical stimulus or when it fails to deliver the correct number of electrical stimulations per minute. Failure to pace is recognized on the ECG as an absence of pacemaker spikes (even though the patient's intrinsic rate is less than that of the pacemaker) and a return of the underlying rhythm for which the pacemaker was implanted. Patient signs and symptoms may include syncope, chest pain, bradycardia, and hypotension.

Failure to pace is also referred to as *failure to fire.*

Causes of failure to pace include battery failure, fracture of the pacing lead wire, displacement of the electrode tip, pulse generator failure, a broken or loose connection between the pacing lead and the pulse generator, electromagnetic interference, and/or the sensitivity set-

TABLE 8-2	Patient Responses to Current with Transcutaneous Pacing
Output (mA)*	**Patient Response**
20	Prickly sensation on skin
30	Slight thump on chest
40	Definite thump on chest
50	Coughing
60	Diaphragm pacing and coughing
70	Coughing and knock on chest
80	More uncomfortable than 70 mA
90	Strong, painful knock on chest
100	Leaves bed because of pain

*Responses with Zoll-NTP.

ting set too high. Treatment may include adjusting the sensitivity setting, replacing the pulse generator battery, replacing the pacing lead, replacing the pulse generator unit, tightening connections between the pacing lead and pulse generator, performing an electrical check, and/or removing the source of electromagnetic interference.

Failure to Capture

Capture is successful depolarization of the atria and/or ventricles by an artificial pacemaker and is obtained after the pacemaker electrode is properly positioned in the heart. Failure to capture is the inability of the pacemaker stimulus to depolarize the myocardium and is recognized on the ECG by visible pacemaker spikes not followed by P waves (if the electrode is located in the atrium) or QRS complexes (if the electrode is located in the right ventricle) (Figure 8-9). Patient signs and symptoms may include fatigue, bradycardia, and hypotension.

Causes of failure to capture include battery failure, fracture of the pacing lead wire, displacement of pacing lead wire (common cause), perforation of the myocardium by a lead wire, edema or scar tissue formation at the electrode tip, output energy (mA) set too low (common cause), and/or increased stimulation threshold because of medications, electrolyte imbalance, or increased fibrin formation on the catheter tip.

Treatment may include repositioning the patient, slowly increasing the output setting (mA) until capture occurs or the maximum setting is reached, replacing the pulse generator battery, replacing or repositioning of the pacing lead, or surgery.

Failure to Sense (Undersensing)

Sensitivity is the extent to which a pacemaker recognizes intrinsic electrical activity. Failure to sense occurs when the pacemaker fails to recognize spontaneous myocardial depolarization (Figure 8-10). This pacemaker malfunction is recognized on the ECG by pacemaker spikes that follow too closely behind the patient's QRS complexes (earlier than the programmed escape interval). Because pacemaker spikes occur when they should not, this type of pacemaker malfunction may result in pacemaker spikes that fall on T waves (R-on-T phenomenon) and/or competition between the pacemaker and the patient's own cardiac rhythm. The patient may complain of palpitations or skipped beats. R-on-T phenomenon may precipitate VT or VF.

Causes of failure to sense include battery failure, fracture of pacing lead wire, displacement of the electrode tip (most common cause), decreased P wave or QRS voltage, circuitry dysfunction (generator unable to process QRS signal), increased sensing threshold from edema or fibrosis at the electrode tip, antiarrhythmic medications, severe electrolyte disturbances,

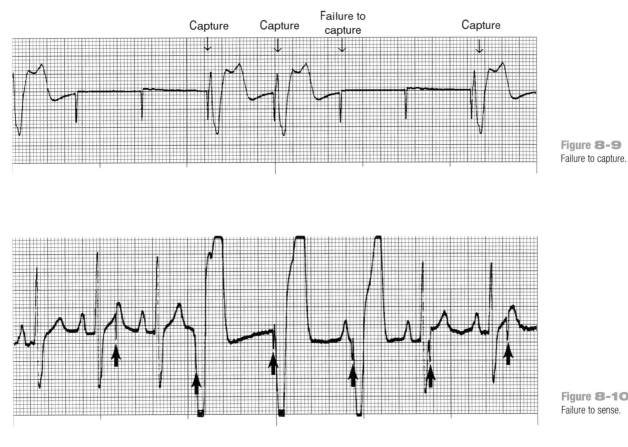

Figure **8-9**
Failure to capture.

Figure **8-10**
Failure to sense.

and myocardial perforation. Treatment may include increasing the sensitivity setting, replacing the pulse generator battery, and/or replacing or repositioning the pacing lead.

Oversensing

Oversensing is a pacemaker malfunction that results from inappropriate sensing of extraneous electrical signals. Atrial sensing pacemakers may inappropriately sense ventricular activity; ventricular sensing pacemakers may misidentify a tall, peaked intrinsic T wave as a QRS complex. Oversensing is recognized on the ECG as pacemaker spikes at a rate slower than the pacemaker's preset rate (paced QRS complexes that come later than the pacemaker's preset escape interval) or no paced beats even though the pacemaker's preset rate is greater than the patient's intrinsic rate.

The patient with a pacemaker should avoid strong electromagnetic fields such as those associated with welding equipment or a magnetic resonance imaging (MRI) machine. Treatment includes adjustment of the pacemaker's sensitivity setting or possible insertion of a bipolar lead if oversensing is caused by unipolar lead dysfunction.

PACEMAKER COMPLICATIONS

Complications of Transcutaneous Pacing

Complications of transcutaneous pacing include pain from electrical stimulation of the skin and muscles, failure to recognize that the pacemaker is not capturing, and failure to recognize the presence of underlying treatable VF. Tissue damage, including third-degree burns, has been reported in pediatric patients with improper or prolonged transcutaneous pacing. Prolonged pacing has been associated with pacing threshold changes, leading to capture failure.

Complications of Temporary Transvenous Pacing

Complications of temporary transvenous pacing include bleeding, infection, pneumothorax, cardiac dysrhythmias, myocardial infarction, lead displacement, fracture of the pacing lead, hematoma at the insertion site, perforation of the right ventricle with or without pericardial tamponade, and perforation of the inferior vena cava, pulmonary artery, or coronary arteries because of improper placement of the pacing lead.

Complications of Permanent Pacing

Complications of permanent pacing associated with the implantation procedure include bleeding, local tissue reaction, pneumothorax, cardiac dysrhythmias, air embolism, and thrombosis. Long-term complications of permanent pacing may include infection, electrode displacement, congestive heart failure, fracture of the pacing lead, pacemaker-induced dysrhythmias, externalization of the pacemaker generator, and perforation of the right ventricle with or without pericardial tamponade.

ANALYZING PACEMAKER FUNCTION ON THE ECG

Identify the Intrinsic Rate and Rhythm

- Are P waves present? At what rate?
- Are QRS complexes present? At what rate?

Is There Evidence of Paced Activity?

- If paced atrial activity is present, evaluate the paced interval.
- Using calipers or paper, measure the distance between two consecutively paced atrial beats.
- Determine the rate and regularity of the paced interval.
- If paced ventricular activity is present, evaluate the paced interval.
- Using calipers or paper, measure the distance between two consecutively paced ventricular beats.
- Determine the rate and regularity of the paced interval.

Evaluate the Escape Interval

- Compare the escape interval to the paced interval measured earlier. The paced interval and escape interval should measure the same.

Analyze the Rhythm Strip

- Analyze the rhythm strip for failure to capture, failure to sense, oversensing, and failure to pace.

REFERENCES

1. Gibler WB: *Emergency cardiac care,* St Louis, 1994, Mosby.
2. Munter DW: Assessment of implanted pacemaker/AICD devices. In Roberts JR III, Hedges JR, editors. *Clinical procedures in emergency medicine,* ed 4, St Louis, 2004, WB Saunders, pp 257-268.
3. Vukmir RB: Emergency cardiac pacing. *Am J Emerg Med* 11:166-176, 1993.
4. Falk RH, Ngai S: External cardiac pacing: influence of electrode placement. *Crit Care Med* 14: 931-932, 1986.
5. Correa LF: Electrical intervention in cardiac disease. In Crawford MV, Spence MI, editors. *Common sense approach to coronary care,* ed 6, St Louis, 1994, Mosby, pp 443-496.

S T O P & REVIEW

Matching

a. Output
b. Threshold
c. Rate modulation
d. Fusion beat
e. Pulse generator
f. Demand pacemaker
g. V-A interval
h. Capture

i. Pacemaker spike
j. Base rate
k. A-V interval
l. Escape interval
m. Atrial pacemaker
n. Dual-chamber pacemaker
o. Inhibition

_____ 1. Rate at which the pulse generator of a pacemaker paces when no intrinsic activity is detected; expressed in pulses per minute

_____ 2. Discharges only when the patient's heart rate drops below the pacemaker's preset rate

_____ 3. The minimum amount of voltage (mA) needed to obtain consistent capture

_____ 4. Successful depolarization of the atria and/or ventricles by an artificial pacemaker

_____ 5. Power source that houses the battery and controls for regulating a pacemaker

_____ 6. Time measured between a sensed cardiac event and the next pacemaker output

_____ 7. Pacemaker response in which the output pulse is suppressed when an intrinsic event is sensed

_____ 8. Pacemaker that stimulates the atrium and ventricle

_____ 9. Electrical stimulus delivered by a pacemaker's pulse generator

_____ 10. In dual-chamber pacing, the length of time between an atrial sensed or atrial paced event and the delivery of a ventricular pacing stimulus; analogous to the P-R interval of intrinsic waveforms

_____ 11. In dual-chamber pacing, the interval between a sensed or ventricular-paced event and the next atrial-paced event

_____ 12. A vertical line on the ECG that indicates the pacemaker has discharged

_____ 13. ECG waveform that results when an intrinsic depolarization and a pacing stimulus occur simultaneously and both contribute to depolarization of that cardiac chamber

_____ 14. Ability of a pacemaker to increase the pacing rate in response to physical activity or metabolic demand

_____ 15. A pacing system with a lead attached to the right atrium designed to correct abnormalities in the SA node

ECG Crossword

Across

3. Pacemaker that stimulates first the atrium, then the ventricle
6. __ __: In pacing, the ECG waveform that results when an intrinsic depolarization and a pacing stimulus occur simultaneously
8. Ability of a pacing stimulus to successfully depolarize the cardiac chamber that is being paced
9. __ rate: Rate at which the pulse generator paces when no intrinsic activity is detected
10. Pacing system with a lead attached to the right atrium
12. Artificial pulse generator that delivers an electrical current to the heart to stimulate depolarization
14. __ pacing: Pacing system with a lead attached in the right ventricle
15. Pacing system __: External testing and measuring device capable of pacing the heart during pacemaker implantation
17. Period, measured in milliseconds, between any two designated cardiac events
19. In dual-chamber pacing, the interval between a sensed or ventricular-paced event and the next atrial-paced event
21. Pacemaker response in which the output pulse is suppressed when an intrinsic event is sensed
22. Electrical stimulus delivered by the pulse generator
23. Another name for a fixed-rate pacemaker

Down

1. Unit of measure of electrical current needed to elicit depolarization of the myocardium
2. Power source that houses the battery and controls for regulating a pacemaker
4. Interval between two ventricular-paced events
5. Another name for demand pacemaker
7. Vertical line on the ECG that indicates the pacemaker has discharged
9. __ __: Pacing lead with two electrical poles that are external from the pulse generator
11. Period, expressed in milliseconds, between two consecutive paced events in the same cardiac chamber without an intervening sensed event
13. Ability of a pacemaker to increase the pacing rate in response to physical activity or metabolic demand
16. __ lead: Pacing lead with a single electrical pole at the distal tip of the pacing lead (negative pole) through which the stimulating pulse is delivered
18. Minimum level of electrical current needed to consistently depolarize the myocardium
20. Ability of a pacemaker to recognize and respond to intrinsic electrical activity; the pacemaker's response to sensed activity depends on its programmed mode and parameters

PRACTICE *Rhythm Strips*

For each of the following rhythm strips, determine the presence of atrial- and ventricular-paced activity, the paced interval rate, and then identify the rhythm. All strips are lead II unless otherwise noted.

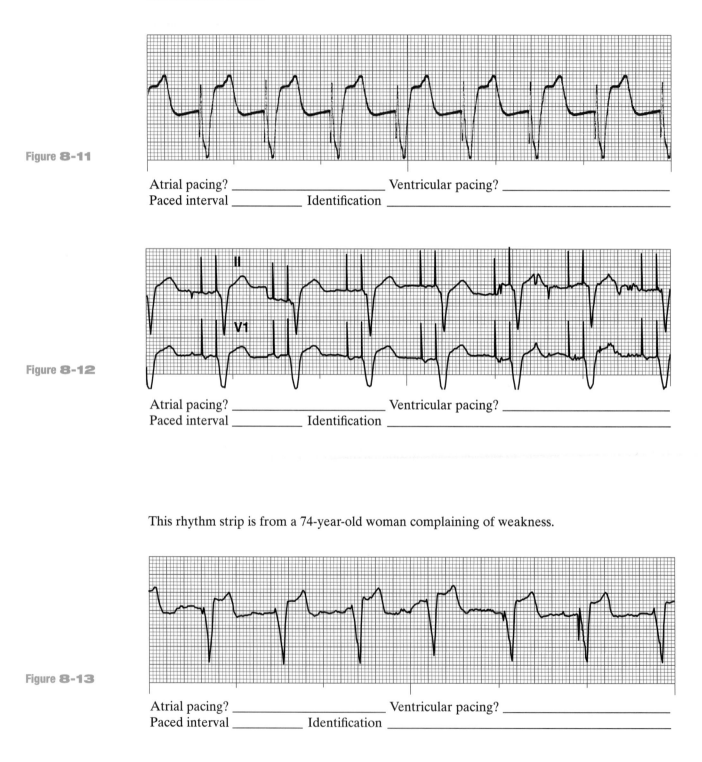

Figure **8-11**

Atrial pacing? _____ Ventricular pacing? _____
Paced interval _____ Identification _____

Figure **8-12**

Atrial pacing? _____ Ventricular pacing? _____
Paced interval _____ Identification _____

This rhythm strip is from a 74-year-old woman complaining of weakness.

Figure **8-13**

Atrial pacing? _____ Ventricular pacing? _____
Paced interval _____ Identification _____

This rhythm strip is from a 52-year-old man with syncope.

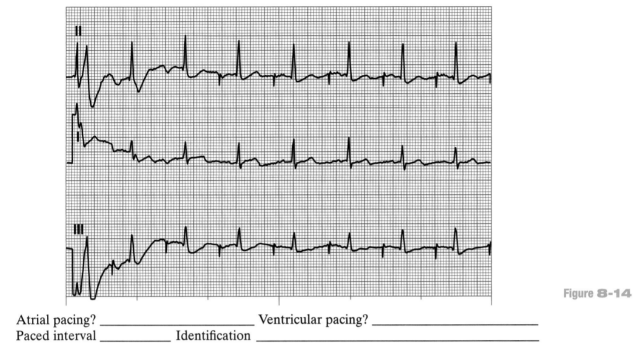

Figure 8-14

Atrial pacing? _____ Ventricular pacing? _____

Paced interval _____ Identification _____

This rhythm strip is from an 80-year-old woman with chest pain. BP 140/78. She states she had a new pacemaker "installed" 13 days ago.

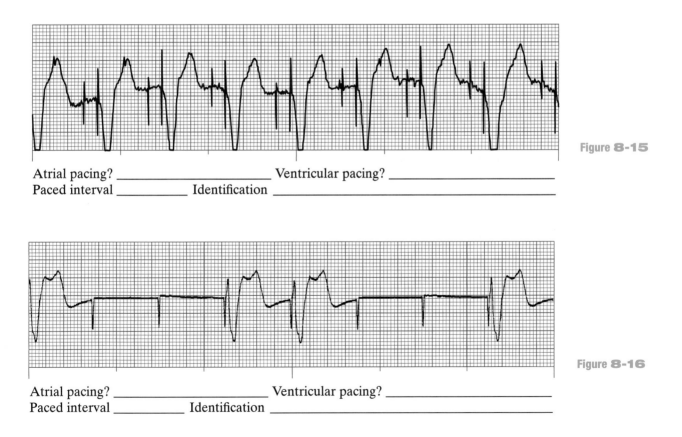

Figure 8-15

Atrial pacing? _____ Ventricular pacing? _____

Paced interval _____ Identification _____

Figure 8-16

Atrial pacing? _____ Ventricular pacing? _____

Paced interval _____ Identification _____

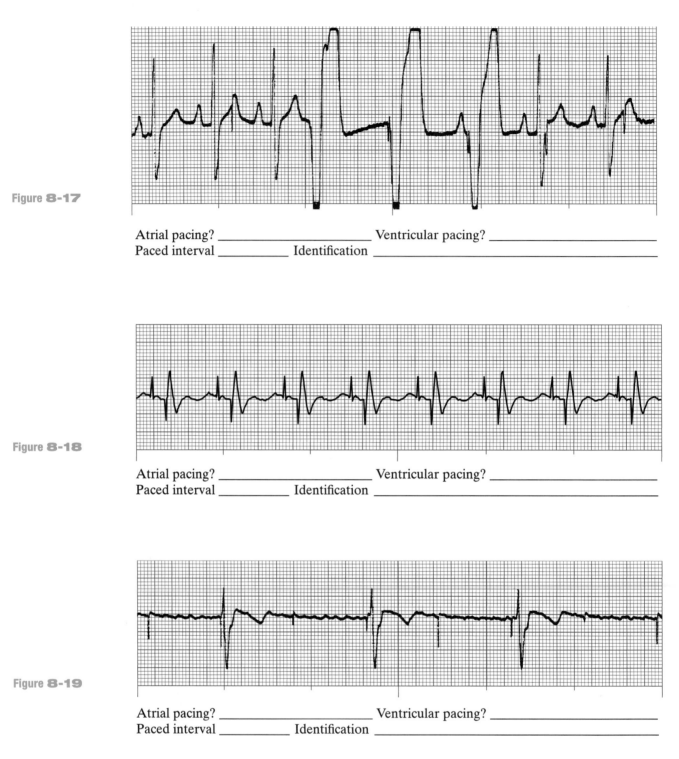

Figure **8-17**

Atrial pacing? _____ Ventricular pacing? _____
Paced interval _____ Identification _____

Figure **8-18**

Atrial pacing? _____ Ventricular pacing? _____
Paced interval _____ Identification _____

Figure **8-19**

Atrial pacing? _____ Ventricular pacing? _____
Paced interval _____ Identification _____

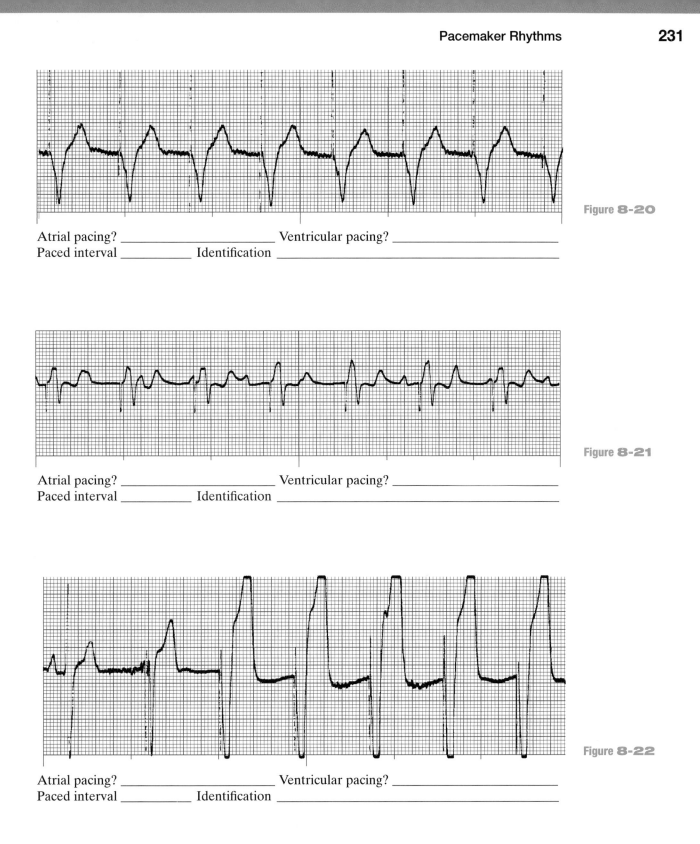

Figure **8-20**

Atrial pacing? _____ Ventricular pacing? _____

Paced interval _____ Identification _____

Figure **8-21**

Atrial pacing? _____ Ventricular pacing? _____

Paced interval _____ Identification _____

Figure **8-22**

Atrial pacing? _____ Ventricular pacing? _____

Paced interval _____ Identification _____

Introduction to the 12-Lead ECG

OBJECTIVES

On completion of this chapter, you should be able to:

1. List the leads that make up the standard 12-lead ECG.
2. Compare bipolar, unipolar, and chest leads.
3. Describe correct anatomic placement of the chest leads.
4. Describe the portion of the heart viewed by each lead of the 12-lead ECG.
5. Explain the term *electrical axis* and its significance.
6. Determine electrical axis using leads I and aVF.
7. Describe ECG changes that may reflect evidence of myocardial ischemia and injury.
8. Identify the ECG changes characteristically seen during the evolution of an acute myocardial infarction.
9. Explain the mechanism of a ST-segment elevation and non–ST-segment elevation myocardial infarction.
10. Describe the sequence of normal R-wave progression.
11. Describe a method for recognizing a posterior wall myocardial infarction.
12. Identify the ECG features of right ventricular myocardial infarction.
13. Describe differentiation of right and left bundle branch block using leads V_1 and V_6.
14. Explain what is meant by the terms *dilatation*, *hypertrophy*, and *enlargement*.
15. Identify the ECG changes characteristically produced by electrolyte imbalances.
16. Describe ECG changes characteristically produced by digitalis toxicity.

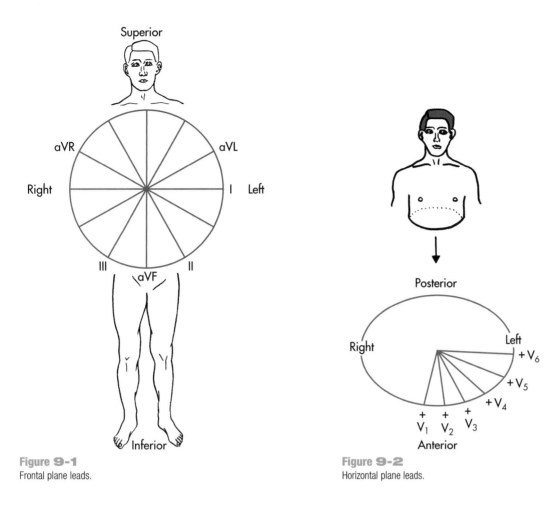

Figure 9-1
Frontal plane leads.

Figure 9-2
Horizontal plane leads.

INTRODUCTION

A standard 12-lead ECG provides views of the heart in both the frontal and horizontal planes and views the surfaces of the left ventricle from 12 different angles. Multiple views of the heart can provide useful information including:

- Recognition of bundle branch blocks
- Identification of ST-segment and T wave changes associated with myocardial ischemia, injury, and infarction
- Identification of ECG changes associated with certain medications and electrolyte imbalances

PLANES

Frontal Plane Leads

Leads allow viewing of the heart's electrical activity in two different planes: frontal (coronal) or horizontal (transverse). Each lead records the average current flow at a specific time in a portion of the heart. Frontal plane leads view the heart from the front of the body. Directions in the frontal plane are superior, inferior, right, and left. Leads I, II, and III (bipolar leads) and leads aVR, aVL, and aVF (unipolar leads) view the heart in the frontal plane (Figure 9-1).

Horizontal Plane Leads

Horizontal plane leads view the heart as if the body were sliced in half. Directions in the horizontal plane are anterior, posterior, right, and left. Six chest (precordial or V) leads view the heart in the horizontal plane, allowing a view of the front and left side of the heart (Figure 9-2).

LEADS

The standard 12-lead comprises six limb leads and six chest leads. Leads I, II, III, aVR, aVL, and aVF are obtained from electrodes placed on the patient's arms and legs. As their names suggest, the six chest leads, V_1 to V_6, are obtained from electrodes placed on the patient's chest. Look at Figure 9-3. Notice that all 12 leads are obtained from only 10 electrodes. This is possible because the four limb electrodes are used for different purposes in different leads. For example, the left arm electrode is used as a negative electrode when lead III is obtained and is used as a positive electrode when lead aVL is obtained.

Standard Limb Leads

Leads I, II, and III make up the standard limb leads. If an electrode is placed on the right arm, left arm, and left leg, three leads are formed. Remember that an imaginary line joining the positive and negative electrodes of a lead is called the axis of the lead. The axes of these three limb leads form an equilateral triangle with the heart at the center (Einthoven's triangle).

Bipolar limb lead: ECG lead consisting of a positive and negative electrode.

Since each of these three leads has a distinct negative pole and a distinct positive pole, they are considered **bipolar** leads. Lead I views the lateral surface of the left ventricle. Leads II and III view the inferior surface of the left ventricle.

Augmented Limb Leads

Unipolar lead: Lead that consists of a single positive electrode and a reference point.

Leads aVR, aVL, and aVF make up the augmented limb leads. The augmented limb leads are unipolar consisting of only one electrode (a positive electrode) on the body surface (Figure 9-4). The electrical potential produced by the augmented leads is normally relatively

Figure 9-3
In a standard 12-lead ECG, all 12 leads are obtained from 10 electrodes positioned as shown here.

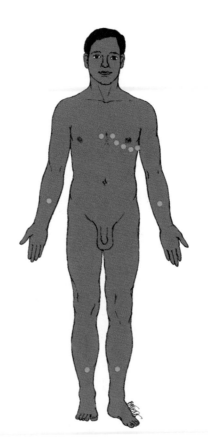

small. The ECG machine augments (magnifies) the amplitude of the electrical potentials detected at each extremity by approximately 50% over those recorded at the bipolar leads. The "a" in aVR, aVL, and aVF refers to augmented. The "V" refers to voltage. The "R" refers to right arm, the "L" to left arm, and the "F" to left foot (leg). The position of the positive electrode corresponds to the last letter in each of these leads. The positive pole in aVR is located on the right arm, aVL has a positive pole at the left arm, and aVF has a positive electrode positioned on the left leg.

Lead aVR views the heart from the right shoulder (the positive electrode) and views the base of the heart (primarily the atria and the great vessels). This lead does not view any wall of the heart. Lead aVL views the heart from the left shoulder (the positive electrode) and is oriented to the lateral wall of the left ventricle. Lead aVF views the heart from the left foot (leg) (positive electrode) and views the inferior surface of the left ventricle.

The relationship between leads aVR, aVL, and aVF can be expressed as aVR + aVL + aVF = 0. When viewing these leads, if the R waves in leads aVR, aVL, and aVF do not appear to equal zero, the leads may have been incorrectly applied.

Chest Leads

The six chest leads are identified as V_1, V_2, V_3, V_4, V_5, and V_6. Because the chest leads (also known as precordial leads) are unipolar, the positive electrode for each lead is placed at a specific location on the chest, and the heart is the theoretical negative electrode (Figure 9-5). The positive electrode for each of the chest leads is positioned as follows:

Each electrode placed in a "V" position is a positive electrode.

- Lead V_1: Right side of sternum, fourth intercostal space
- Lead V_2: Left side of sternum, fourth intercostal space
- Lead V_3: Midway between V_2 and V_4
- Lead V_4: Left midclavicular line, fifth intercostal space
- Lead V_5: Left anterior axillary line at same level as V_4
- Lead V_6: Left midaxillary line at same level as V_4

Leads V_1 and V_2 view the interventricular septum, V_3 and V_4 view the anterior surface of the left ventricle, and V_5 and V_6 view the lateral surface of the left ventricle.

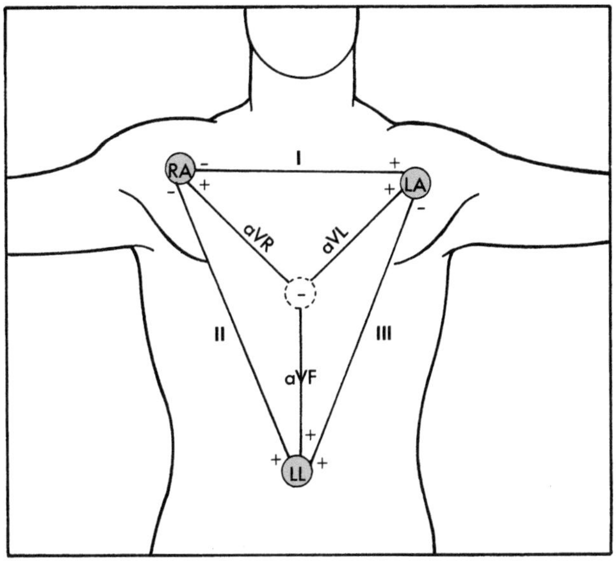

Figure 9-4
View of the standard limb leads and augmented leads.

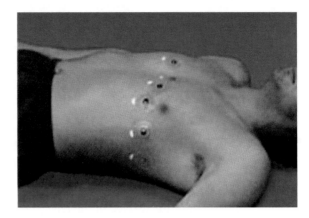

—— *ECG Pearl*

The six-limb leads view the heart in the frontal plane as if the body were flat. The six chest leads view the heart in the horizontal plane allowing a view of the front and left side of the heart.

VECTORS

The position of the positive electrode on the body determines which portion of the left ventricle is seen by each lead.

Because the ECG does not directly measure the heart's electrical activity, it does not "see" all of the current flowing through the heart. What the ECG does see from its vantage point on the body's surface is the net result of countless individual currents competing in a tug-of-war. For example, the QRS complex is not a display of all the electrical activity occurring in the right and left ventricles. It is the net result of a tug-of-war produced by the numerous individual currents in both the right and left ventricles. Since the left ventricle is much more massive than the right, the left overpowers the right. What is seen in the QRS complex is the remaining electrical activity of the left ventricle (i.e., the portion not used to cancel out the right ventricle). Therefore, in a normally conducted beat, the QRS complex represents the electrical activity occurring in the left ventricle. It has been estimated that 80% of the cardiac electrical activity is canceled out by the tug-of-war, leaving only 20% for the ECG to sense. Leads have a negative (−) and positive (+) electrode pole that senses the magnitude and direction of the electrical force caused by the spread of waves of depolarization and repolarization throughout the myocardium. A **vector** (arrow) is a symbol representing this force. Leads that face the tip or point of a vector record a positive deflection on ECG paper.

A vector points in the direction of depolarization.

When "axis" is used by itself, it refers to the QRS axis.

A **mean vector** identifies the average of depolarization waves in one portion of the heart. The mean P vector represents the average magnitude and direction of both right and left atrial depolarization. The mean QRS vector represents the average magnitude and direction of both right and left ventricular depolarization. The average direction of a mean vector is called the **mean axis** and is only identified in the frontal plane. An imaginary line joining the positive and negative electrodes of a lead is called the axis of the lead. **Electrical axis** refers to determining the direction (or angle in degrees) in which the main vector of depolarization is pointed.

Axis

During normal ventricular depolarization, the left side of the interventricular septum is stimulated first. The electrical impulse then traverses the septum to stimulate the right side. The left and right ventricles are then depolarized simultaneously. Because the left ventricle is considerably larger than the right, right ventricular depolarization forces are overshadowed on

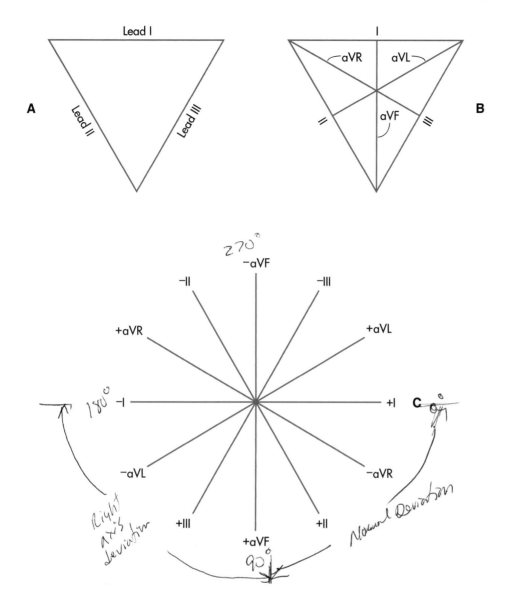

the ECG. As a result, the mean QRS vector points down (inferior) and to the left. The axes of leads I, II, and III form an equilateral triangle with the heart at the center (Einthoven's triangle). If the augmented limb leads are added to this configuration and the axes of the six leads moved in a way in which they bisect each other, the result is the hexaxial reference system (Figure 9-6).

The hexaxial reference system represents all of the frontal plane (limb) leads with the heart in the center and is the means used to express the location of the frontal plane axis. This system forms a 360-degree circle surrounding the heart. The positive end of lead I is designated at 0 degrees. The six frontal plane leads divide the circle into segments, each representing 30 degrees. All degrees in the upper hemisphere are labeled as negative degrees, and all degrees in the lower hemisphere are labeled as positive degrees. The mean QRS vector (normal electrical axis) lies between 0 and +90 degrees.

Current flow to the right of normal is called right axis deviation (+90 to +180 degrees). Current flow in the direction opposite of normal is called indeterminate, "no man's land," northwest, or extreme right axis deviation (−91 to −179 degrees). Current flow to the left of normal is called left axis deviation (−1 to −90 degrees).

TABLE 9-1	Two-Lead Method of Axis Determination			
Axis	Normal	Left	Right	Indeterminate ("No Man's Land")
Lead I QRS Direction	Positive	Positive	Negative	Negative
Lead aVF QRS Direction	Positive	Negative	Positive	Negative

Axis determination can provide clues in the differential diagnosis of wide QRS tachycardia, hemiblocks, and localization of accessory pathways.

In the hexaxial reference system, the axes of some leads are perpendicular to each other. Lead I is perpendicular to lead aVF. Lead II is perpendicular to aVL, and lead III is perpendicular to aVR. If the electrical force moves toward a positive electrode, a positive (upright) deflection will be recorded. If the electrical force moves away from a positive electrode, a negative (downward) deflection will be recorded. If the electrical force is parallel to a given lead, the largest deflection in that lead will be recorded. If the electrical force is perpendicular to a lead axis, the resulting ECG complex will be small or biphasic in that lead.

Leads I and aVF divide the heart into four quadrants. These two leads can be used to quickly estimate electrical axis. In leads I and aVF, the QRS complex is normally positive. If the QRS complex in either or both of these leads is negative, axis deviation is present (Table 9-1).

Right axis deviation may be a normal variant, particularly in the young and in thin individuals. Other causes of right axis deviation include mechanical shifts associated with inspiration or emphysema, right ventricular hypertrophy, chronic obstructive pulmonary disease (COPD), Wolf-Parkinson-White Syndrome (WPW), and pulmonary embolism.

Left axis deviation may be a normal variant, particularly in older individuals and obese individuals. Other causes of left axis deviation include mechanical shifts associated with expiration; a high diaphragm caused by pregnancy, ascites, or abdominal tumors; hyperkalemia; inspiration or emphysema; left atrial hypertrophy; and dextrocardia.

ISCHEMIA, INJURY, AND INFARCTION

The usual cause of an acute coronary syndrome is the rupture of an atherosclerotic plaque.

The processes of ischemia, injury, and infarction are called "the three I's" of an acute coronary event.

The extent of arterial narrowing and reduction in blood flow are critical determinants of coronary artery disease.

Acute coronary syndromes (ACS) are a physiologic continuum of conditions caused by a similar sequence of pathologic events—a transient or permanent obstruction of a coronary artery. ACS include unstable angina, non–ST-segment elevation myocardial infarction (MI), and ST-segment elevation MI. These conditions are characterized by an excessive demand or inadequate supply of oxygen and nutrients to the heart muscle associated with plaque disruption, thrombus formation, and vasoconstriction. Sudden cardiac death can occur with any of these conditions.

The patient's clinical presentation and outcome depend on factors including:

- Amount of myocardium supplied by the affected artery
- Severity and duration of myocardial ischemia
- Electrical instability of the ischemic myocardium
- Degree and duration of coronary obstruction
- Presence (and extent) or absence of collateral coronary circulation

Ischemia

The walls of the ventricles consist of an outer layer (epicardium), a middle layer (myocardium), and an inner layer (endocardium) (Figure 9-7). The myocardium is subdivided

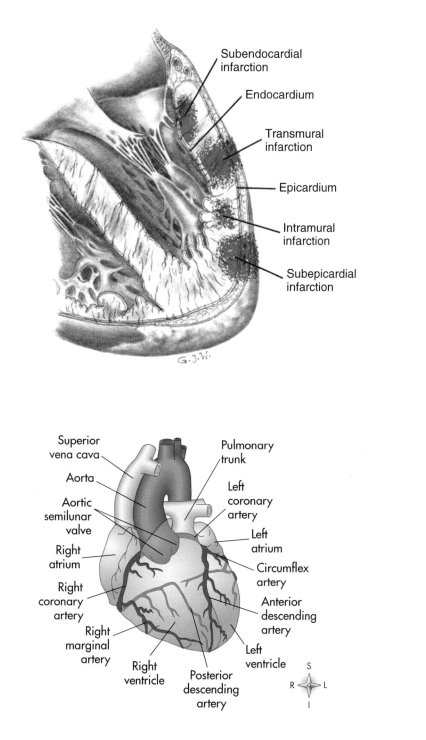

Subendocardial
infarction

Endocardium

Transmural
infarction

Epicardium

Intramural
infarction

Subepicardial
infarction

G.J.W.

Figure 9-7
Possible locations of in-
farctions in the ventricular
wall.

Superior
vena cava

Pulmonary
trunk

Aorta

Left
coronary
artery

Aortic
semilunar
valve

Left
atrium

Right
atrium

Circumflex
artery

Right
coronary
artery

Anterior
descending
artery

Right
marginal
artery

Left
ventricle

Right
ventricle

Posterior
descending
artery

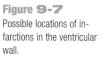

Figure 9-8
Anterior view of the coronary circulation.

into two areas. The innermost half of the myocardium is called the subendocardial area, and the outermost half is called the subepicardial area. The main coronary arteries lie on the epicardial surface of the heart (Figure 9-8) and feed this area first before supplying the heart's inner layers with oxygenated blood. The subendocardium is at greatest risk of ischemia because this area has a high demand for oxygen and is fed by the most distal branches of the coronary arteries.

Myocardial ischemia is the result of an imbalance between the metabolic needs of the myocardium (demand) and the flow of oxygenated blood to it (supply) (Table 9-2). Ischemia can

TABLE 9-2	Possible Causes of Myocardial Ischemia	
Inadequate Oxygen Supply	**Increased Myocardial Oxygen Demand**	
Anemia	Exercise	Cocaine, amphetamines
Hypoxemia	Smoking	Emotional stress
Polycythemia	Eating a heavy meal	Hypertension
Coronary artery narrowing caused by a thrombus, vasospasm, or rapid progression of atherosclerosis	Fever	Exposure to cold weather
	Congestive heart failure	Aortic stenosis
	Tachydysrhythmias	Pheochromocytoma
	Obstructive cardiomyopathy	Thyrotoxicosis

occur as a result of increased myocardial oxygen demand (demand ischemia), reduced myocardial oxygen supply (supply ischemia), or both. For example, demand ischemia may result from physical exertion, tachycardia, sympathetic stimulation, an increase in left ventricular size, or emotional stress. Supply ischemia results from functional or structural abnormalities in the coronary arteries (i.e., coronary vasospasm or coronary artery narrowing as a result of a thrombus) that cause a severe reduction in blood flow and oxygen supply in the area perfused by the vessels. In many cases, ischemia results from both an increase in oxygen demand and a reduction in oxygen supply.

Angina is most commonly caused by atherosclerotic disease of the coronary arteries.

Ischemia affects the heart's cells responsible for contraction, as well as those responsible for generation and conduction of electrical impulses. These effects are related to delays in depolarization and repolarization and can be viewed on the ECG as transient changes in ST-segments and T waves. These ECG changes, as well as the chest pain or discomfort that accompanies myocardial ischemia, usually resolve when the demand for oxygen is reduced (by resting or slowing the heart rate with medications such as beta-blockers) to a level that can be supplied by the coronary artery or increasing blood flow by dilating the coronary arteries with medications such as nitroglycerin (NTG).

In a non–ST-segment elevation MI (NSTEMI), ST-segment and T wave changes are the only ECG changes seen.

Myocardial ischemia delays the process of repolarization; thus, the ECG changes characteristic of ischemia include temporary changes in the ST-segment and T wave. ST-segment depression is suggestive of myocardial ischemia and is considered significant when the ST-segment is more than 0.5 mm (one half of a small box) below the baseline at a point 0.04 seconds (one small box) to the right of the J-point (the point where the QRS ends and the ST-segment begins) (Figure 9-9) and is seen in two or more leads facing the same anatomic area of the heart.

The TP segment begins at the end of the T wave of one cardiac cycle and ends with onset of the P wave of the next cycle.

When looking for ST-segment elevation on a 12-lead ECG, we are particularly interested in the early portion of the ST-segment. Locate the J (junction)-point—the connection between the end of the QRS complex and the beginning of the ST-segment. Locate a QRS complex on the 12-lead ECG and look to see where the end of the QRS complex makes a sudden sharp change in direction. That point identifies the J-point. There is some difference of opinion as to where ST-segment deviation should be measured. Some authorities simply measure deviation at the J-point while others look for deviation 0.04 seconds (one small box) after the J-point. Still others measure ST-segment deviation 0.06 seconds (1 ½ small boxes) after the J-point.[2] Compare the ST-segment deviation to the isoelectric line. The TP segment or PR segment may be used for this comparison.

If ischemia is present through the full thickness of the myocardium, a negative (inverted) T wave will be present in the leads facing the affected area of the ventricle. In leads opposite

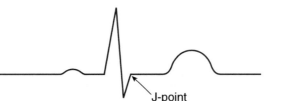

Figure 9-9
The point where the QRS complex and the ST-segment meet is called the "junction" or "J"-point.

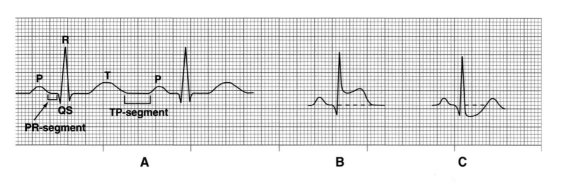

Figure 9-10
The ST-segment. **A,** The PR segment is used as the baseline from which to determine the presence of ST-segment elevation or depression. **B,** ST-segment elevation. **C,** ST-segment depression. The TP segment may also be used as the baseline from which to determine ST-segment deviation.

the affected area, reciprocal (mirror image) changes may be seen. If ischemia is present only in the subendocardial layer, the T wave is usually positive (upright) because the direction of repolarization is unaffected (repolarization normally occurs from epicardium to endocardium) but may be abnormally tall. T wave inversion may be seen in conditions other than myocardial ischemia including pericarditis, bundle branch block, ventricular hypertrophy, shock, electrolyte disorders, and subarachnoid hemorrhage.

Injury

Ischemia prolonged more than just a few minutes results in myocardial **injury**. Injured myocardial cells are still alive but will **infarct** (die) if the ischemia is not quickly corrected. If blood flow is quickly restored, no tissue death occurs. Myocardial injury can be extensive enough to produce a decrease in pump function or electrical conductivity in the affected cells. Injured myocardial cells do not depolarize completely, remaining electrically more positive than the uninjured areas surrounding them. This is viewed on the ECG as ST-segment elevation in the leads facing the affected area. ST-segment elevation is considered significant when the ST-segment is elevated more than 1 mm above the baseline at a point 0.04 seconds (one small box) to the right of the J-point in the limb leads or more than 2 mm in the chest leads, and these changes are seen in two or more leads facing the same anatomic area of the heart (Figures 9-9 and 9-10).

Symptoms of coronary artery disease are often not manifested until blood flow to an area of the heart is compromised by at least 60%.

In leads opposite the affected area, ST-segment depression (reciprocal changes) may be seen. If injury is present only in the subendocardial layer, the ST-segment is usually depressed. A ventricular aneurysm should be suspected if ST-segment elevation persists for more than a few months after MI (Figure 9-11).

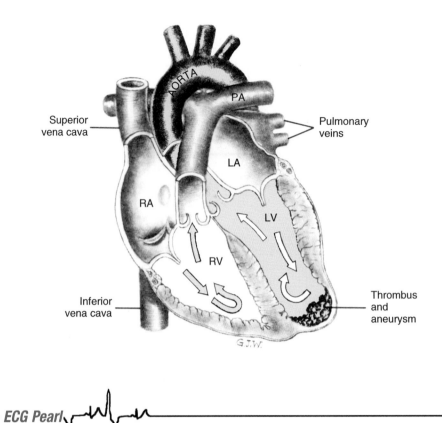

Figure 9-11
Ventricular aneurysm.

—— *ECG Pearl*

Infarction: Recognition Criteria

ST-segment elevation of 1 mm or more in two contiguous limb leads or more than 2 mm in two contiguous chest leads is the primary criteria used for infarct recognition. However, some authorities use a less stringent requirement for ST-segment elevation. In this alternate means of infarct recognition, at least 1 mm of ST-segment elevation is required in two contiguous leads (limb or chest leads) before infarction is suspected. Each method has its advantage: The 1-mm threshold for ST-segment elevation favors sensitivity, and the 2-mm criterion favors specificity.[2]

Early ST-elevation MI may be present with <1 mm of ST-segment elevation. Further, ST-segment elevation may be a normal variant or due to a cause other than infarction. For example, ST-elevation may be present in ventricular hypertrophy, conduction abnormalities, pulmonary embolism, spontaneous pneumothorax, intracranial hemorrhage, hyperkalemia, and pericarditis. In pericarditis, ST-segment elevation is usually present in all leads except aVR. In myocardial injury, ST-segment elevation is more localized and often accompanied by ST-segment depression in the opposite leads.

Infarction

The extent of arterial narrowing and reduction in blood flow is a critical determinant of coronary artery disease.

A **myocardial infarction** occurs when blood flow to the heart muscle stops or is suddenly decreased long enough to cause cell death. Infarcted cells are without function and cannot respond to an electrical stimulus or provide any mechanical function.

In the strictest sense, the term *myocardial infarction* relates to necrosed myocardial tissue. In a practical sense, the term *myocardial infarction* is applied to the *process* that results in the death of myocardial tissue. Consider the "process" of myocardial infarction as a continuum rather than the presence of dead heart tissue. If efforts are made to recognize the process of myocardial infarction, patients may be identified earlier and, if promptly treated, may altogether avoid the loss of myocardial tissue.[2]

The diagnosis for an acute, evolving, or recent myocardial infarction can be made with either of the following criteria[1]:

TABLE 9-3 **Serum Cardiac Markers**		
	Rises	**Duration of Elevation**
Troponin-C	3-4 hours	10-14 days
Troponin-I	4-6 hours	4-7 days
Creatine kinase (CK) –MB	3-4 hours	24-35 hours
Myoglobin	1-3 hours	12-24 hours

1. Typical rise and gradual fall (troponin) or more rapid rise and fall (creatine kinase [CK]-MB) of biochemical markers of myocardial necrosis with at least one of the following:
   a. Ischemic symptoms
   b. Development of pathologic Q waves on the ECG
   c. ECG changes indicative of ischemia (ST-segment elevation or depression)
   d. Or coronary artery intervention (e.g., coronary angioplasty)
2. Pathologic findings of an acute MI

—— *ECG Pearl*

Myocardial Infarction

Terminology	Classification by size
• Acute myocardial infarction (MI) = 6 hours-7 days	• Microscopic: focal necrosis
	• Small: <10% of the left ventricle
• Healing MI = 7-28 days	• Medium: 10%-30% of the left ventricle
• Healed MI = 29 days or more	• Large: >30% of the left ventricle

As myocardial cells die, their cell membranes break and leak substances into the blood-stream. The presence of these substances in the blood can subsequently be measured by means of blood tests to verify the presence of an infarction. These substances (called cardiac markers or serum cardiac markers) include creatine kinase (CK), MB isoforms, troponin, and myoglobin. Troponin T and troponin I are two tests that may be ordered for a patient with a suspected MI. If the level is elevated (positive test), myocardial necrosis (infarction) has almost certainly occurred. The troponin-I test appears to have better specificity than troponin-T (Table 9-3). Serum cardiac markers are useful for confirming the diagnosis of MI when patients present without ST-segment elevation, when the diagnosis may be unclear, and when physicians must distinguish patients with unstable angina from those with a non–ST-segment elevation (non–Q-wave) MI. They are also useful for confirming the diagnosis of MI for patients with ST-segment elevation.

Sensitivity refers to a test's ability to identify true disease. *Specificity* refers to a test that is correctly negative in the absence of disease. A test with high specificity has few false positives.

Non–ST-Segment Elevation Myocardial Infarction (NSTEMI)

In the acute phase of a non–ST-segment elevation MI, the ST-segment may be depressed in the leads facing the surface of the infarcted area. An NSTEMI can only be diagnosed if the ST-segment and T wave changes are accompanied by elevations of serum cardiac markers indicative of myocardial necrosis. Patients with NSTEMI are known to be at higher risk for death, reinfarction, and other morbidity than those with unstable angina. NSTEMIs tend to be smaller and have a better *short-term* prognosis than ST-elevation infarctions; however, overall prognosis is similar to ST-elevation MIs. Recurrence of the infarct is common in the days to weeks after the patient has been sent home. This is referred to as "completion" of the infarction. Recent data suggest the incidence of NSTEMI is increasing as the population of older patients with more advanced disease increases.

ST-Segment Elevation (Q-Wave) Myocardial Infarction

Most patients with ST-segment elevation will develop Q-wave MI. Only a minority of patients with ischemic chest discomfort at rest who do not have ST-segment elevation will develop Q-wave MI. A Q-wave MI is diagnosed by the development of abnormal Q waves in serial ECGs. Q-wave MIs tend to be larger than non–Q-wave MIs, reflecting more damage to the left ventricle, and are associated with a more prolonged and complete coronary thrombosis.

ECG Changes

Recognition of infarction on the ECG relies on the detection of morphologic changes (i.e., changes in shape) of the QRS complex, the T wave, and the ST-segment. These changes occur in relation to certain events during the infarction.

One of the earliest changes that might be detected is the development of a tall (hyperacute) T wave (Figure 9-12, *A*). These T-wave changes may occur within the first few minutes of infarction, during what has been described as the hyperacute phase of infarction. These changes are often not recorded on the ECG because they have typically resolved by the time the patient seeks medical assistance. As time progresses, signs of myocardial injury may develop. ST-segment elevation (Figure 9-12, *B*) provides the primary indication of myocardial injury in progress. The appearance of coved ("frowny face") ST-segment elevation is called an *acute injury pattern*. ST-segment elevation may occur within the first hour or first few hours of infarction and is considered to occur in the early acute phase of infarction. In the later acute phase of the infarction, you may see the presence of T-wave inversion, suggesting the presence of ischemia (Figure 9-12, *C*). In fact, T-wave inversion may precede the development of ST-segment elevation, or they may occur simultaneously. A few hours later, the ECG may give its first evidence that tissue death has occurred. That evidence comes with the development of abnormal Q waves (Figure 9-12, *D*). Remember that a Q wave that is 0.04 seconds or more wide (one small box or more wide) is suggestive of infarction. An abnormal Q wave indicates the presence of dead myocardial tissue and, subsequently, a loss of electrical activity. Abnormal Q waves can appear within hours after occlusion of a coronary artery but more commonly appear several hours or days after the onset of signs and symptoms of an acute MI. When combined with ST-segment or T-wave changes, the presence of abnormal Q waves suggests an acute MI.

In time, the T wave regains its normal contour and the ST-segment returns to the isoelectric line. The Q wave, however, often remains as evidence that an infarct has occurred (Figure 9-12, *E*). When this pattern is seen, establishing the time of the infarct is impossible. It is only possible to recognize the presence of a previous MI.[2]

> Hyperacute T waves may be called "tombstone" T waves. Because of their size, it is often possible to inscribe "RIP" (rest in peace) in the waveform on the ECG. Hyperacute T waves typically measure more than 50% of the preceding R wave.

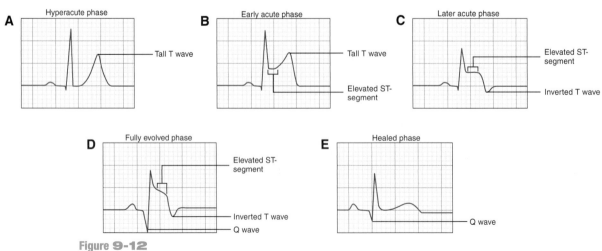

Figure 9-12
The evolving pattern of ST-segment elevation myocardial infarction on the ECG.

The changes just described are referred to as the **indicative changes** of myocardial infarction. Of the indicative changes, ST-segment elevation is especially well-suited for the detection of MI in the early hours. A tall T wave alone is not specific enough to diagnose MI, and T wave inversion may occur in stable angina. Because a pathologic Q wave may take hours to develop to confirm the presence of MI (and not all MIs develop pathologic Q waves), the patient's signs and symptoms, serum cardiac markers, and the presence of ST-segment elevation provides the strongest evidence for the early recognition of MI.[2]

Prinzmetal's angina produces ST-segment elevation without infarction.

—— *ECG Pearl*

ST-segment Elevation (Figure 9-13)

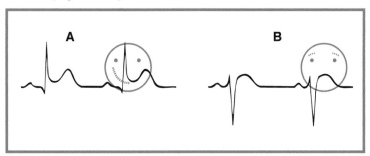

Figure **9-13**
A, ST-segment elevation in the shape of a "smiley" face (upward concavity) is usually benign, particularly when it occurs in an otherwise healthy, asymptomatic patient. **B,** ST-segment elevation in the shape of a "frowny" face (downward concavity) is more often associated with an acute injury pattern.

R-Wave Progression

Depolarization of the interventricular septum normally occurs from left to right and posteriorly to anteriorly. The wave of ventricular depolarization in the major portions of the ventricles is normally from right to left and in an anterior to posterior direction. When viewing the chest leads in a normal heart, the R wave becomes taller and the S wave becomes smaller as the electrode is moved from right to left. This pattern is called *R-wave progression* (Figure 9-14).

In V_1 and V_2, the QRS deflection is predominantly negative (moving away from the positive chest electrode), reflecting depolarization of the septum and right ventricle (small R wave) and the left ventricle (large S wave). As the chest electrode is placed farther left, the wave of depolarization is moving toward the positive electrode. V_3 and V_4 normally record an equiphasic (equally positive and negative) RS complex. The area in which this equiphasic complex occurs is called the transitional zone. V_5 and V_6 normally record a QR complex in which the Q wave is small, reflecting depolarization of the septum, and the R wave is tall, reflecting ventricular depolarization.

Poor R-wave progression (Figure 9-15) is a phrase used to describe R waves that decrease in size from V_1 to V_4. This is often seen in an anteroseptal infarction but may be a normal variant in young persons, particularly in young women. Other causes of poor R-wave progression include left bundle branch block, left ventricular hypertrophy, severe chronic obstructive pulmonary disease (particularly emphysema), and old anteroseptal and anterior infarctions.

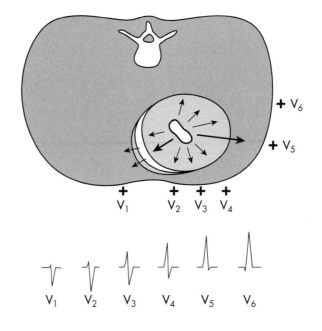

Figure 9-14
Ventricular activation and
R wave progression as
viewed in the chest leads.

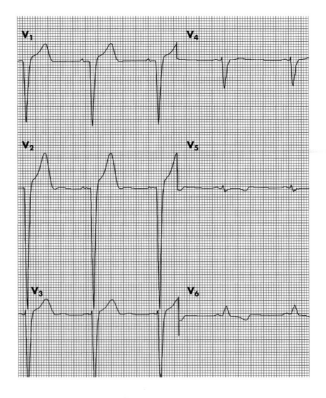

Figure 9-15
Poor R wave progression
in V₁ through V₄; QRS
>0.12 seconds: left bun-
dle branch block.

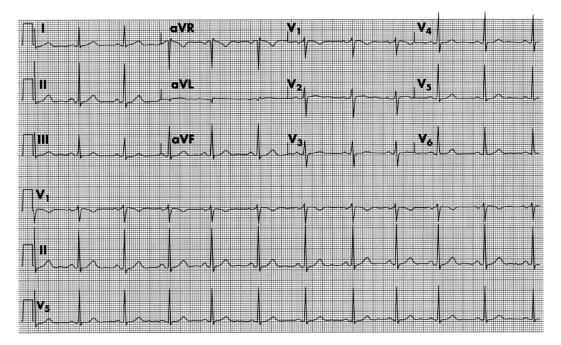

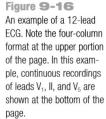

Figure 9-16
An example of a 12-lead ECG. Note the four-column format at the upper portion of the page. In this example, continuous recordings of leads V_1, II, and V_5 are shown at the bottom of the page.

TABLE 9-4	Layout of the 4-Column 12-lead ECG		
Limb Leads		**Chest Leads**	
Standard Leads	Augmented Leads	V_1-V_3	V_4-V_6
Column I	Column II	Column III	Column IV
I: lateral	aVR: none	V_1: septum	V_4: anterior
II: inferior	aVL: lateral	V_2: septum	V_5: lateral
III: inferior	aVF: inferior	V_3: anterior	V_6: lateral

LAYOUT OF THE 12-LEAD ECG

Most 12-lead monitors record all 12 leads simultaneously but display them in a conventional three row–by–four column format. The standard limb leads are recorded in the first column, the augmented limb leads in the second column, and the chest leads in the third and fourth columns (Table 9-4). All of the QRS complexes in a row are consecutive while QRS complexes that are aligned vertically represent a simultaneous recording of the same beat. Because the leads are obtained simultaneously, only 10 seconds of sampling time are required to record all 12 leads.[2]

The 12-lead ECG provides a 2.5-second view of each lead because it is assumed that 2.5 seconds is long enough to capture at least one representative complex. However, a 2.5-second view is not long enough to properly assess rate and rhythm, so at least one continuous rhythm strip is usually included at the bottom of the tracing.[2]

—— *ECG Pearl*

When viewing a 12-lead, keep in mind that leads that line up vertically are simultaneous recordings of the same beat. When you read the 12-lead from left to right, the ECG tracing is continuous. As you switch from one lead to the next, it is still continuous.[2]

A 12-lead ECG is shown in Figure 9-16. When reviewing a 12-lead ECG, intervals and duration are expressed in milliseconds (ms). Seconds can be easily converted to milliseconds by moving the decimal point three places to the right. Measurements are provided by the 12-lead computer's interpretive program, which is usually very accurate when measuring intervals and durations.

LOCALIZATION OF INFARCTIONS

Contiguous Leads

Anatomically contiguous leads refer to those leads that "see" the same area of the heart.

When ECG changes of myocardial infarction occur, they are not found in every lead of the ECG. In fact, they are only present in the leads "looking" directly at the infarct site (indicative changes). Indicative changes are significant when they are seen in two anatomically contiguous leads. Two leads are contiguous if they look at the same area of the heart or they are numerically consecutive *chest* leads (Figure 9-17). Table 9-5 shows the area viewed by each lead of a standard 12-lead ECG. Look at this table and determine the leads that view the inferior region of the left ventricle.

Leads II, III, and aVF are anatomically contiguous because they all look at adjoining tissue in the inferior region of the left ventricle. Figure 9-18 shows ST-segment elevation of more than 1 mm in leads II, III, and aVF. An inferior wall infarction is suspected to be the cause of the ST-segment elevation.

The ECG is nondiagnostic in approximately 50% of patients with chest discomfort. A normal ECG does not rule out an acute MI, particularly in the early hours of a coronary artery occlusion.

To review, look at Table 9-5 again and answer the following questions. Are leads V_2 and V_3 contiguous leads? Are leads II and V_2 contiguous? Leads V_2 and V_3 *are* contiguous. What area of the heart do leads V_1 and V_2 see? They view the septum. What area of the heart do leads V_3 and V_4 see? They view the anterior wall of the left ventricle. V_2 and V_3 are right next to each other on the patient's chest. When their "eyes" or "cameras" look in at tissue, they see adjoining tissue in the heart as well. Leads II and V_2 *are not* contiguous. Remember: Two leads are contiguous if they look at the same area of the heart or they are numerically

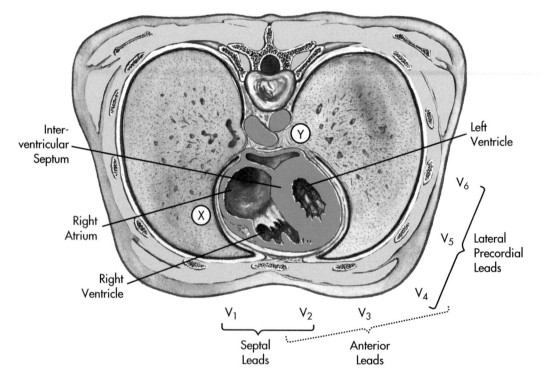

Figure 9-17
This is a schematic view of the areas of the heart visualized by the chest leads. Leads V_1, V_2, and V_3 are contiguous. Leads V_3, V_4, and V_5 are contiguous, as are V_4, V_5, and V_6. Note that neither the right ventricular wall (*X*) nor the posterior wall of the left ventricle (*Y*) is well visualized by any of the usual six chest leads.

consecutive *chest* leads. If ST-segment elevation is noted in leads II and V$_2$, one would not suspect an MI since leads II and V$_2$ are not contiguous (lead II is a *limb* lead that looks at the inferior wall while V$_2$ is a *chest* lead that looks at the septum). This fact demonstrates how infarct recognition and infarct localization are closely tied together: To recognize infarction, it is necessary to know which portion of the heart each lead is viewing. To localize the infarct, note which leads are displaying that evidence and consider which part of the heart that those leads "see."[2]

Reciprocal Changes

We have said that ECG signs of myocardial injury are reflected by the presence of ST-segment *elevation* in the leads looking directly at the affected area. The noninvolved areas of the heart may show ST-segment *depression*. This is called a **reciprocal (*mirror image*) change**. Reciprocal changes are seen in the wall of the heart opposite the location of the infarction (Figure 9-19). Reciprocal changes are usually most readily observed at the onset of an infarction and tend to be short lived. When present, reciprocal changes strongly suggest an acute infarction.[2]

> Reciprocal changes are seen in approximately 75% of inferior wall MIs and approximately 30% of anterior wall MIs.

—— ECG Pearl

Two leads are contiguous if they look at the same area of the heart or they are numerically consecutive *chest* leads.

TABLE 9-5	Localizing ECG Changes		
I: lateral	aVR: none	V$_1$: septum	V$_4$: anterior
II: inferior	aVL: lateral	V$_2$: septum	V$_5$: lateral
III: inferior	aVF: inferior	V$_3$: anterior	V$_6$: lateral

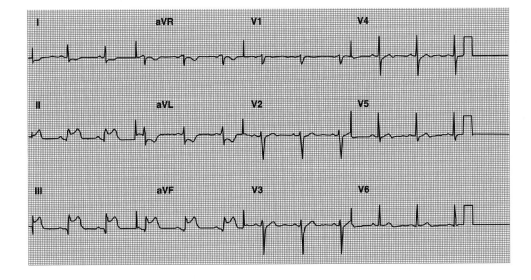

Figure 9-18
ST-segment elevation in leads II, III, and aVF reflect an inferior wall injury pattern.

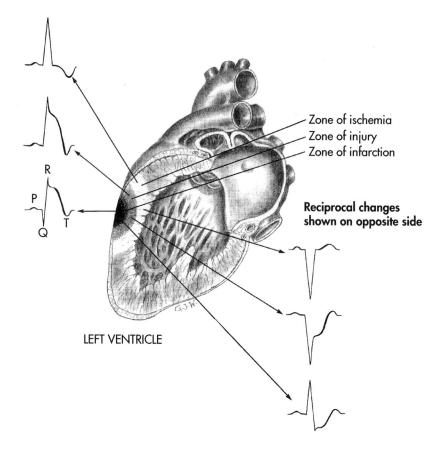

Zone of ischemia
Zone of injury
Zone of infarction

**Reciprocal changes
shown on opposite side**

LEFT VENTRICLE

Figure 9-19
Zones of ischemia, injury, and infarction showing indicative ECG changes and reciprocal changes corresponding to each zone.

PREDICTING THE SITE AND EXTENT OF CORONARY ARTERY OCCLUSION

Since an MI is the result of an occluded coronary artery, it is worthwhile to develop a familiarity with the coronary arteries that supply the heart. Once the infarction has been recognized and localized, an understanding of coronary artery anatomy makes it possible to predict which coronary artery is occluded. In the standard 12-lead ECG, leads II, III, and aVF "look" at tissue supplied by the right coronary artery and eight leads "look" at tissue supplied by the left coronary artery—leads I, aVL, V_1, V_2, V_3, V_4, V_5, and V_6. When evaluating the extent of infarction produced by a left coronary artery occlusion, determine how many of these leads are showing changes consistent with an acute infarction. The more of these eight leads demonstrating acute changes, the larger the infarction is presumed to be (Figure 9-20).[2]

To identify the site of occlusion, compare the infarct location with the coronary anatomy. If an ECG shows changes in leads II, III, and aVF, suspect an inferior wall infarction. Since the inferior wall of the left ventricle is supplied by the right coronary artery in most of the population, it is reasonable to suppose that this infarct is due to a right coronary artery occlusion. When indicative changes are seen in the leads viewing the septal, anterior, and/or lateral walls of the left ventricle (V_1-V_6, I, and aVL), it is reasonable to suspect a left coronary artery occlusion.[2] Table 9-6 summarizes the pattern in which coronary arteries most commonly supply the myocardium.

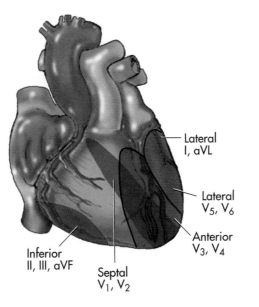

Lateral
I, aVL

Lateral
V₅, V₆

Anterior
V₃, V₄

Inferior
II, III, aVF

Septal
V₁, V₂

Figure 9-20
Multilead assessment of
the heart.

TABLE 9-6	Localization of a Myocardial Infarction		
Location of MI	Indicative Changes (Leads facing affected area)	Reciprocal Changes (Leads opposite affected area)	Affected Coronary Artery
Anterior	V₃, V₄	V₇, V₈, V₉	Left coronary artery • LAD—diagonal branch
Anteroseptal	V₁, V₂, V₃, V₄	V₇, V₈, V₉	Left coronary artery • LAD—diagonal branch • LAD—septal branch
Anterolateral	I, aVL, V₃, V₄, V₅, V₆	II, III, aVF, V₇, V₈, V₉	Left coronary artery • LAD—diagonal branch and/or • Circumflex branch
Inferior	II, III, aVF	I, aVL	Right coronary artery (most common)— posterior descending branch or Left coronary artery—circumflex branch
Lateral	I, aVL, V₅, V₆	II, III, aVF	Left coronary artery • LAD—diagonal branch and/or • Circumflex branch Right coronary artery
Septum	V₁, V₂	V₇, V₈, V₉	Left coronary artery • LAD—septal branch
Posterior	V₇, V₈, V₉	V₁, V₂, V₃	Right coronary or left circumflex artery
Right ventricle	V₁R-V₆R	I, aVL	Right coronary artery • Proximal branches

Specific MI Types

The left ventricle has been divided into regions where an MI may occur—septal, anterior, lateral, inferior, and posterior. A myocardial infarction may not be limited to one of these regions. For example, if the chest leads indicate ECG changes in leads V_3 and V_4, suggestive of an anterior wall MI, and indicative changes are also present in V_5 and V_6, the infarction would be called an anterolateral infarction or an anterior infarction with lateral extension.[2]

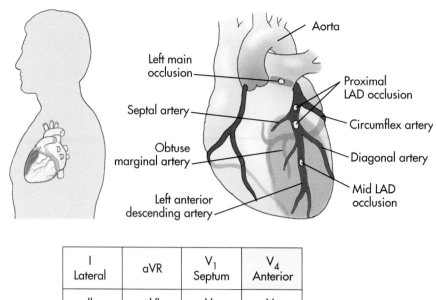

I Lateral	aVR	V₁ Septum	V₄ Anterior
II Inferior	aVL Lateral	V₂ Septum	V₅ Lateral
III Inferior	aVF Inferior	V₃ Anterior	V₆ Lateral

Anterior Wall

Anterior wall MI is abbreviated *AWMI.*

Leads V_3 and V_4 face the anterior wall of the left ventricle. The left main coronary artery supplies the left anterior descending (LAD) artery and the circumflex artery. Occlusion of the left main coronary artery ("widow maker") often leads to cardiogenic shock and death without prompt reperfusion. Occlusion of the midportion of the LAD results in an anterior infarction (Figure 9-21). However, an infarction involving the anterior wall is usually not localized only to this area. For example, proximal occlusion of the LAD may become an anteroseptal infarction if the septal branch is involved or an anterolateral infarction if the marginal branch is involved. If the occlusion occurs proximal to both the septal and diagonal branches, an extensive anterior infarction (anteroseptal-lateral MI) will result. An example of an infarction involving the anterior wall is shown in Figure 9-22.

Inferior Wall

Because the inferior surface of the heart rests on the diaphragm, the presence of ischemia, injury, or infarction in this area may be called "inferior" or "diaphragmatic." Inferior wall MI is abbreviated *IWMI.*

Leads II, III, and aVF view the inferior surface of the left ventricle. In most individuals, the inferior wall of the left ventricle is supplied by the posterior descending branch of the right coronary artery (Figure 9-23). In most individuals, the inferior wall of the left ventricle is supplied by the posterior descending branch of the right coronary artery ("right dominant system"). Occlusion of the RCA proximal to the marginal branch will result in an inferior wall MI and right ventricular infarction. Occlusion of the RCA distal to the marginal branch will result in an inferior infarction, sparing the right ventricle. In some individuals, the circumflex artery supplies the inferior wall through the posterior descending artery ("left dominant system"). Occlusion of the posterior descending artery will result in an inferior infarction; however, a proximal occlusion of the circumflex may result in infarction in the lateral and posterior walls. An example of an inferior wall infarction is shown in Figure 9-24.

Lateral Wall

Lateral wall infarctions often occur as extensions of anterior or inferior infarctions. Lateral wall MI is abbreviated *LWMI.*

Leads I, aVL, V_5, and V_6 view the lateral wall of the left ventricle. The lateral wall of the left ventricle may be supplied by the left circumflex artery, the left anterior descending artery, or a branch of the right coronary artery (Figure 9-25). Isolated lateral wall infarctions usually involve occlusion of the circumflex artery and are frequently missed. More commonly, the lat-

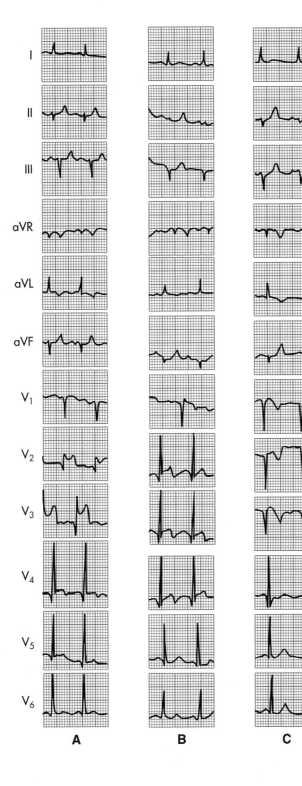

Figure 9-22
Evolutionary changes in anteroseptal myocardial infarction reflected in leads V_2 to V_4. **A,** At admission, hyperacute phase is reflected by ST-segment elevation. **B,** At 24 hours; **C,** At 48 hours, there are abnormal (pathologic) Q waves.

eral wall is involved with proximal occlusion of the LAD artery (anterolateral MI) or a branch of the right coronary artery (inferolateral MI). Occlusion of the marginal branches of the circumflex artery may cause a posterolateral MI. An example of an infarction involving the lateral wall is shown in Figure 9-26.

Septum

Leads V_1 and V_2 face the septal area of the left ventricle. The septum, which contains the bundle of His and bundle branches, is normally supplied by the left anterior descending

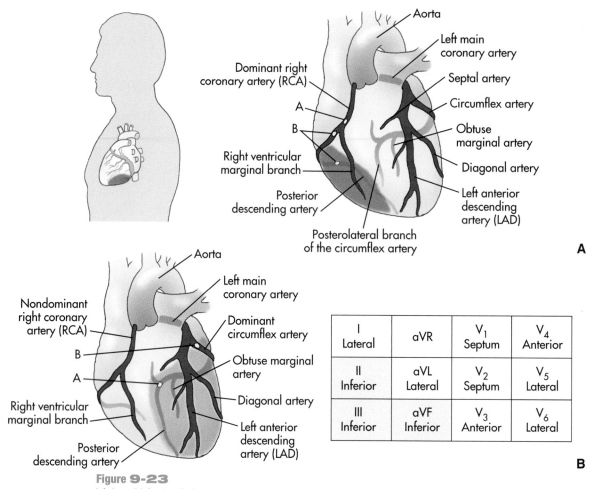

I Lateral	aVR	V$_1$ Septum	V$_4$ Anterior
II Inferior	aVL Lateral	V$_2$ Septum	V$_5$ Lateral
III Inferior	aVF Inferior	V$_3$ Anterior	V$_6$ Lateral

Figure 9-23
Inferior wall infarction. **A,** Coronary anatomy shows a dominant right coronary artery. Occlusion at point *A* results in an inferior and right ventricular infarction. Occlusion at point *B* is limited to the inferior wall, sparing the right ventricle. **B,** Inferior wall infarction. Coronary anatomy shows a dominant left circumflex artery. Occlusion at point *A* results in an inferior infarction. An occlusion at *B* may result in infarction in the lateral and posterior walls.

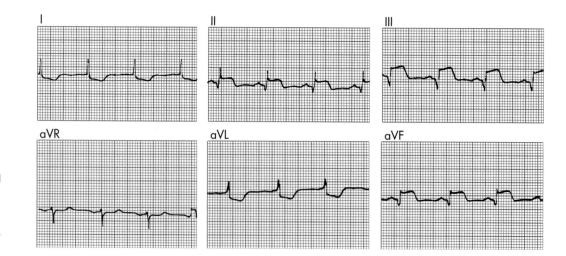

Figure 9-24
Acute inferior wall infarction. Note the ST-segment elevation in leads II, III, and aVF, and the reciprocal ST depression in leads I and aVL. Abnormal Q waves are also present in leads II, III, and aVF.

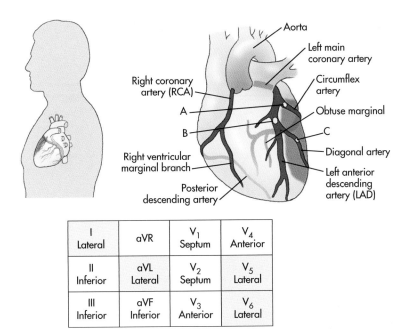

I Lateral	aVR	V$_1$ Septum	V$_4$ Anterior
II Inferior	aVL Lateral	V$_2$ Septum	V$_5$ Lateral
III Inferior	aVF Inferior	V$_3$ Anterior	V$_6$ Lateral

Figure 9-25

Lateral wall infarction. Coronary artery anatomy shows **A** occlusion of the circumflex artery; **B** occlusion of the proximal left anterior descending artery; and **C** occlusion of the diagonal artery.

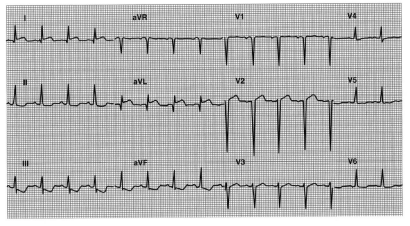

Figure 9-26

Lateral infarction due to occlusion of the first large obtuse marginal branch of the left circumflex artery. Lead I shows a small Q wave with ST-segment elevation. A larger Q wave with ST-segment elevation is present in lead aVL. Reciprocal ST-segment depression is seen in leads II, III, and aVF. This patient had an anterior non–ST-elevation infarction 4 days earlier with ST-segment elevation and T-wave inversion in leads V$_2$ through V$_6$. Coronary arteriogram at that time revealed an occluded left anterior descending artery distal to its first large septal perforator. The ST-segment elevation evolved and the T waves in all of the chest leads had become upright the day before this tracing was recorded when the patient had another episode of chest pain associated with the appearance of signs of acute lateral infarction as shown in this tracing. A repeated coronary arteriogram showed new occlusion of the obtuse marginal branch of the left circumflex artery.

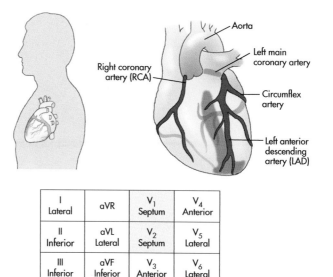

I Lateral	aVR	V₁ Septum	V₄ Anterior
II Inferior	aVL Lateral	V₂ Septum	V₅ Lateral
III Inferior	aVF Inferior	V₃ Anterior	V₆ Lateral

Figure 9-27
Septal infarction.

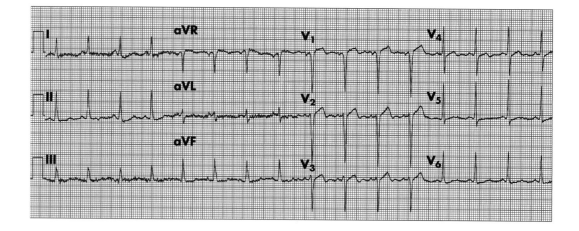

Figure 9-28
Septal infarction. Poor R-wave progression.

artery (Figure 9-27). If the site of infarction is limited to the septum, ECG changes are seen in V_1 and V_2. If the entire anterior wall is involved, ECG changes will be visible in V_1, V_2, V_3, and V_4. An example of a septal infarction is shown in Figure 9-28.

— *ECG Pearl*

Lead aVR is useful in determining if the limb lead electrodes have been correctly positioned. Current normally moves away from aVR. So, under normal conditions you would expect the QRS complex in lead aVR to be predominantly negative (upside down). If the QRS complex is predominantly negative, continue with your interpretation of the 12-lead. If the QRS complex is predominantly positive (upright), there are two possible causes: There has been a change in current flow and the current is now moving toward the patient's right arm (significant axis deviation) or a cable has been incorrectly placed on the wrong limb. If the cables are incorrectly positioned, reposition the cables and run another 12-lead.[2]

Posterior wall MIs occur in 15% to 21% of all acute MIs, usually in conjunction with an inferior or lateral infarction.

Posterior Wall Infarctions

The posterior wall of the left ventricle is supplied by the left circumflex coronary artery in most patients; however, in some patients it is supplied by the right coronary artery (Figure 9-29). Because no leads of a standard 12-lead ECG directly view the posterior wall of the left

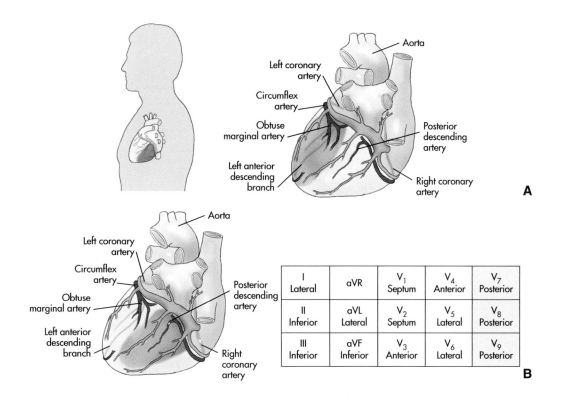

I Lateral	aVR	V$_1$ Septum	V$_4$ Anterior	V$_7$ Posterior
II Inferior	aVL Lateral	V$_2$ Septum	V$_5$ Lateral	V$_8$ Posterior
III Inferior	aVF Inferior	V$_3$ Anterior	V$_6$ Lateral	V$_9$ Posterior

Figure 9-29
A, Posterior infarction. Coronary anatomy shows a dominant right coronary artery (RCA). Occlusion of the RCA commonly results in an inferior and posterior infarction. **B,** Coronary anatomy shows a dominant left circumflex artery. Occlusion of a marginal branch is the cause of most isolated posterior infarctions.

Posterior view

Left

Right

V$_7$ V$_8$ V$_9$ V$_9$R   V$_8$R   V$_7$R

Figure 9-30
Posterior chest lead placement.

ventricle, additional chest leads may be used to view the heart's posterior surface. All of the leads are placed on the same horizontal line (fifth intercostal space) as V$_4$ to V$_6$. Lead V$_7$ is placed at the posterior axillary line. Lead V$_8$ is placed at the angle of the scapula (posterior scapular line), and lead V$_9$ is placed over the left border of the spine (Figure 9-30). Indicative changes of a posterior wall infarction include ST-segment elevation in these leads. An example of an infarction involving the posterior wall is shown in Figure 9-31.

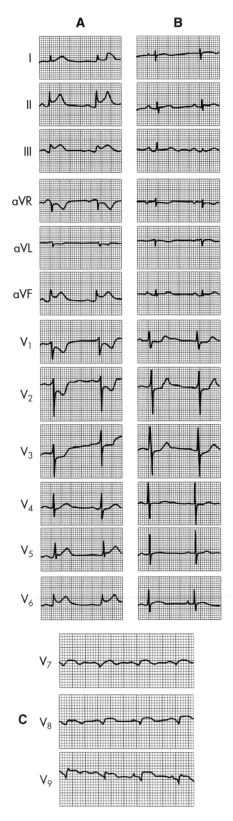

A   B

I

II

III

aVR

aVL

aVF

V₁

V₂

V₃

V₄

V₅

V₆

C   V₇

V₈

V₉

Figure 9-31
Evolutionary changes in inferior and posterior myocardial infarction (MI).
A, Acute inferior and apical injury. **B,** At 24 hours. Note tall R wave in lead V₁ not present in **A,** suggesting posterior MI. **C,** Posterior infarction confirmed.

If placement of posterior chest leads is not feasible, changes in the opposite (anterior) wall of the heart can be viewed as reciprocal changes. A posterior wall MI usually produces tall R waves and ST-segment depression in leads V₁, V₂, and to a lesser extent in lead V₃. To assist in the recognition of ECG changes suggesting a posterior wall MI, the "mirror test" is helpful. Flip over the ECG to the blank side and turn it upside down. When held up to the light,

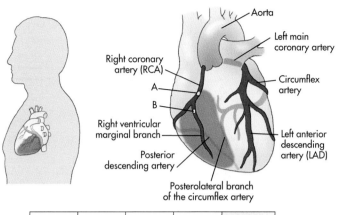

I Lateral	aVR	V₁ Septum	V₄ Anterior	V₄R Rt ventricle
II Inferior	aVL Lateral	V₂ Septum	V₅ Lateral	V₅R Rt ventricle
III Inferior	aVF Inferior	V₃ Anterior	V₆ Lateral	V₆R Rt ventricle

Figure 9-32
Right ventricular infarction. Occlusion of the right coronary artery proximal to the right ventricular marginal branch results in an inferior and right ventricular infarction. An occlusion of the right ventricular marginal branch results in an isolated right ventricular infarction.

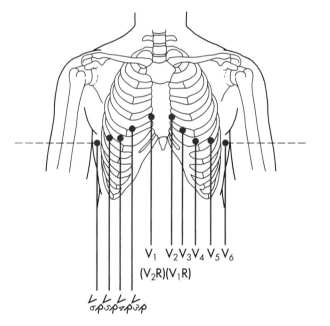

Figure 9-33
Anatomic placement of the left and right chest leads.

the tall R waves become deep Q waves and ST-segment depression becomes ST-segment elevation—the "classic" indicative changes associated with MI.

Right Ventricular Infarction

Approximately 50% of patients with inferior infarction have some involvement of the right ventricle. The right ventricle is supplied by the right ventricular marginal branch of the right coronary artery (Figure 9-32). An occlusion of the right ventricular marginal branch results in an isolated right ventricular infarction. Occlusion of the right coronary artery proximal to the right ventricular marginal branch results in an inferior and right ventricular infarction.

Right ventricular infarction (RVI) should be suspected when ECG changes suggesting an inferior infarction (ST-segment elevation in leads II, III, and/or aVF) are observed. To view the right ventricle, right chest leads are used (Figure 9-33). Placement of right chest leads is iden-

Isolated infarction of the right ventricle is seen in 3% to 5% of autopsy-proven cases of MI.

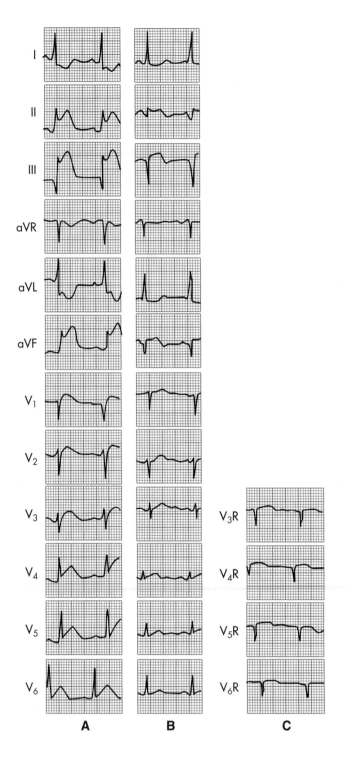

Figure 9-34

Evolutionary changes in inferior and right ventricular infarction. **A,** At admission—acute phase. **B,** At 12 hours. **C,** Right chest leads demonstrating right ventricular infarction.

tical to placement of the standard chest leads except on the right side of the chest. These leads then "look" directly at the right ventricle and can show the ST-segment elevation created by the infarct. If time does not permit the acquisition of all six right-sided chest leads, the lead of choice is V_4R. An example of an infarction involving the right ventricle is shown in Figure 9-34.

—— ECG Pearl

A modification of lead V$_4$R (MC$_4$R) using a standard three-lead system can be used to view the right ventricle. The positive electrode is placed in the fifth intercostal space, right mid-clavicular line. The negative electrode is placed on the left arm and the lead selector on the monitor placed in the lead III position.[2]

A right ventricular MI should be suspected in the patient with an inferior left ventricular MI; unexplained, persistent hypotension; clear lung fields; and jugular venous distention. During right ventricular infarction, the right ventricle dilates acutely and does not effectively pump blood to the pulmonary system. Jugular venous distention occurs because of the backup of blood into the systemic venous vessels. Signs of pulmonary edema are absent because the right ventricle is unable to effectively pump blood into the pulmonary vasculature. Filling of the left ventricle is subsequently decreased, resulting in decreased cardiac output and, ultimately, hypotension.

> Consider the presence of RVI if the patient with an inferior wall infarction becomes hypotensive after administration of nitrates.

INTRAVENTRICULAR CONDUCTION DELAYS

Intraventricular conduction delays are best identified by using leads MCL$_1$, MCL$_6$, V$_1$, and/or V$_6$.

Structures of the Intraventricular Conduction System

After passing through the AV node, the electrical impulse enters the bundle of His (also referred to as the *common bundle* or the *atrioventricular bundle*). The bundle of His is normally the only electrical connection between the atria and the ventricles. It is located in the upper portion of the interventricular septum and connects the AV node with the two bundle branches. The bundle of His conducts the electrical impulse to the right and left bundle branches.

The right bundle branch travels down the right side of the interventricular septum to conduct the electrical impulse to the right ventricle. Structurally, the right bundle branch is long, thin, and more fragile than the left. Because of its structure, a relatively small lesion in the right bundle branch can result in delays or interruptions in electrical impulse transmission.

The left bundle branch begins as a single structure that is short and thick (the left common bundle branch or main stem) and then divides into three divisions (fascicles) called the anterior fascicle, posterior fascicle, and the septal fascicle. The anterior fascicle spreads the electrical impulse to the anterior and lateral walls of the left ventricle. This fascicle is thin and vulnerable to disruptions in electrical impulse transmission. The posterior fascicle relays the impulse to the posterior (inferior) portions of the left ventricle, and the septal fascicle relays the impulse to the midseptum (Figure 9-35). The posterior fascicle is short, thick, and rarely disrupted because of its structure and dual blood supply from both the left anterior descending artery and the right coronary artery. As a rule, only two divisions of the left bundle branch (the anterior and posterior fascicles) are explained when discussing bundle branch blocks, despite the existence of its three distinct divisions.

> The anterior fascicle is also called the superior fascicle. The posterior fascicle is also called the inferior fascicle.

Blood Supply to the Intraventricular Conduction System

The bundle of His receives a dual blood supply from the left anterior and posterior descending coronary arteries, making this portion of the conduction system less vulnerable to ischemic damage. The posterior descending artery is the right coronary artery in 90% of individuals. The right bundle branch and the anterior division of the left bundle branch are supplied by the left anterior descending artery.

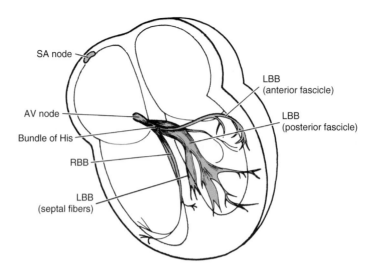

Figure 9-35
Conduction system.

Bundle Branch Activation

The wave of depolarization moves from endocardium to epicardium.

During normal ventricular depolarization, the left side of the interventricular septum (stimulated by the left posterior fascicle) is stimulated first. The electrical impulse (wave of depolarization) then traverses the septum to stimulate the right side. The left and right ventricles are then depolarized simultaneously.

A left anterior hemiblock is also called anterior hemiblock or anterior fascicular block. A left posterior hemiblock is also called posterior hemiblock or posterior fascicular block.

A delay or block can occur in any part of the intraventricular conduction system. A block in only one of the fascicles of the bundle branches is called a **monofascicular block**. A block in any two divisions of the bundle branches is a **bifascicular block**. Although this term may be used to describe a block in both the anterior and posterior branches of the left bundle branch, it is more commonly used to describe a combination of a right bundle branch block and either a left anterior fascicular block (LAFB) or a left posterior fascicular block (LPFB). A **trifascicular block** is a block in the three primary divisions of the bundle branches (i.e., right bundle branch, left anterior fascicle, and left posterior fascicle). A hemiblock is a block in either of the fascicles of the left bundle branch (e.g., left anterior hemiblock, left posterior hemiblock). A hemiblock can be complete or intermittent. Because the right bundle branch has only one fascicle, there is no right hemiblock.

Causes

A bundle branch block is abbreviated *BBB*.

RBBB can occur in individuals with no underlying heart disease but more commonly occurs in the presence of organic heart disease—coronary artery disease being the most common cause. In patients with acute myocardial infarction, complete RBBB is present in 3% to 7% of the cases. In such cases, it is often accompanied by left anterior hemiblock and is the result of an anterior myocardial infarction. RBBB occurring as the result of acute myocardial infarction may require pacemaker intervention. The progression of RBBB to complete AV block occurs twice as often as that of LBBB, especially when RBBB is associated with a fascicular block.

LBBB may be acute or chronic. Acute LBBB may occur secondary to an anteroseptal (more common) or inferior MI, acute congestive heart failure, or acute pericarditis or myocarditis. The most common causes of chronic LBBB are coronary artery disease, hypertensive heart disease, or a combination of the two, and dilated cardiomyopathy.

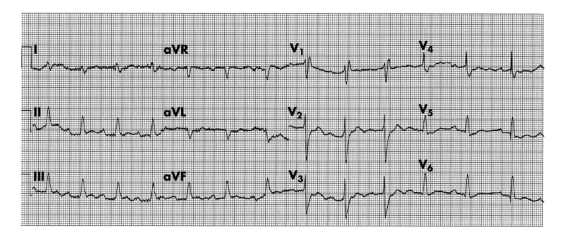

Figure 9-36
The RSR' pattern, characteristic of right bundle branch block.

ECG Characteristics

If a delay or block occurs in one of the bundle branches, the ventricles will be depolarized asynchronously. The impulse travels first down the unblocked branch and stimulates that ventricle. Because of the block, the impulse must then travel from cell to cell through the myocardium (rather than through the normal conduction pathway) to stimulate the other ventricle. This means of conduction is slower than normal, and the QRS complex appears widened on the ECG. The ventricle with the blocked bundle branch is the last to be depolarized.

A QRS measuring 0.10 to 0.12 seconds is called an incomplete right or left bundle branch block. A QRS measuring more than 0.12 seconds is called a complete right or left bundle branch block. If the QRS is wide but there is no BBB pattern, the term *wide QRS* or *intraventricular conduction delay* is used to describe the QRS.

ECG criteria for identification of a right or left BBB are:

- QRS duration of more than 0.12 seconds (if a complete BBB)
- QRS complexes produced by supraventricular activity (i.e., the QRS complex is not a paced beat nor did it originate in the ventricles)

Differentiating RBBB from LBBB

Once the presence of BBB is suspected, an examination of V_1 can reveal whether the block affects the right or the left bundle branch. Following are descriptions of how each type of block affects the direction of electrical current and produces its own, distinct QRS morphology.

In RBBB, the electrical impulse travels through the AV node and down the left bundle branch into the interventricular septum. The septum is activated by the left posterior fascicle and is depolarized in a left-to-right direction (event 1 in Figure 9-36). Thus, septal depolarization moves in a left-to-right direction, which is toward V_1, and produces an initial small R wave. As the left bundle continues to conduct impulses, the entire left ventricle is depolarized from right to left (event 2). This produces movement away from V_1 and results in a negative deflection (S wave). Now, the impulses that depolarized the left ventricle conduct through the myocardial cells and depolarize the right ventricle (event 3). This depolarization creates a movement of electrical activity in the direction of V_1, so a second positive deflection is recorded (R'). The RSR' pattern is characteristic of right bundle branch block. Whenever the two criteria for BBB have been met, and V_1 displays an RSR' pattern, RBBB is suspected. In RBBB, the ECG changes suggestive of an acute MI are normally still visible. Closely monitor the patient with an RBBB in lead II for the development of a hemiblock.[2]

A right bundle branch block is abbreviated *RBBB*.

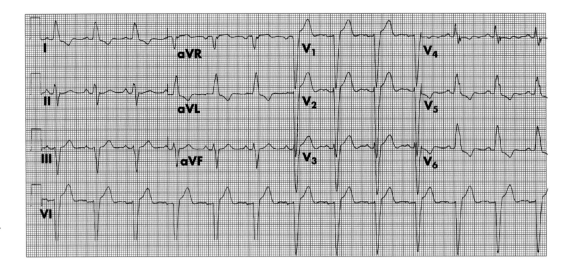

Figure 9-37
A QS pattern in V$_1$, characteristic of left bundle branch block.

Left bundle branch block is abbreviated *LBBB*. When used alone, LBBB implies a *complete* LBBB.

In LBBB, the septum is depolarized by the right bundle branch as is the right ventricle. The septum is part of the left ventricle and, thus, the wave of myocardial depolarization has begun with the net movement of current going away from V$_1$ (event 1 in Figure 9-37). This movement of current continues to move away from V$_1$ as the rest of the left ventricle is depolarized (event 2), and the QRS complex continues in its negative direction. Thus, LBBB produces a QS pattern in V$_1$. When BBB is known to exist and a QS pattern is seen in V$_1$, LBBB is suspected. ST-segment and T wave changes are often present with LBBB, making the diagnosis of acute MI difficult. In LBBB, the ST-segment and T wave are normally of opposite polarity (direction) to the terminal portion of the QRS. If an LBBB pattern is observed in V$_5$ or V$_6$ and the ST-segment and T wave are of the same polarity as the terminal portion of the QRS, ischemia should be suspected.

In BBB, the last ventricle to be depolarized is the ventricle with the blocked bundle branch. Therefore, if it is possible to determine the ventricle that was depolarized last, it becomes possible to determine the bundle branch that was blocked. For example, if the right ventricle was depolarized last, it is because the impulse traveled down the left bundle branch, depolarized the left ventricle first, then marched through and depolarized the right ventricle. It stands to reason that if one ventricle is depolarized late, its depolarization makes up the later portion of the QRS complex. Examination of the terminal force of the QRS complex reveals the ventricle that was depolarized last, and, therefore, the bundle that was blocked.[2]

Two notable exceptions must be mentioned to complete the discussion of BBB. The first involves the criteria used to recognize BBB, while the second relates to differentiating LBBB from RBBB.

The final portion of the QRS complex is referred to as the **terminal force**. To identify the terminal force, first view lead V$_1$ or MCI$_1$ and locate the J-point. From the J-point, move backward into the QRS and determine if the last electrical activity produced an upward or downward deflection. Move from the J-point back into the QRS complex and determine if the terminal portion (last 0.04 seconds) of the QRS complex is a positive (upright) or negative (downward) deflection (Figures 9-38 and 9-39). If the right bundle branch is blocked, then the right ventricle will be depolarized last and the current will be moving from the left ventricle to the right. This will create a positive deflection in the terminal force of the QRS complex in V$_1$. If the left bundle branch is blocked, the left ventricle will be depolarized last, and the current will flow from right to left. This will produce a negative deflection in the terminal force of the QRS complex seen in V$_1$.[2]

The criteria used to recognize BBB are valid, but lack some sensitivity and specificity. The sensitivity can be limited by junctional rhythms because there may be no discernible P waves when the AV junction is the pacemaker site. While the AV junction is a supraventricular

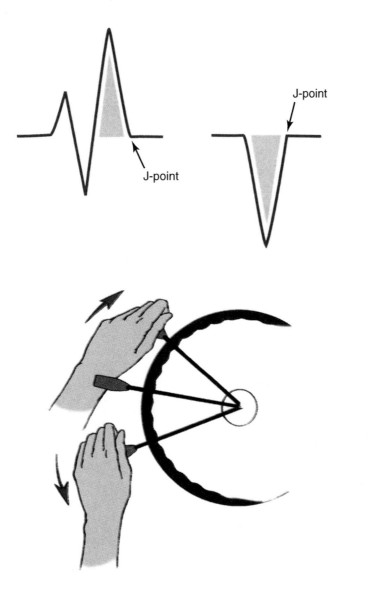

Figure 9-38
Move from the J-point back into the QRS complex and determine if the terminal portion (last 0.04 second) of the QRS complex is a positive (upright) or negative (downward) deflection. If the two criteria for bundle branch block are met and the terminal portion of the QRS is positive, a RBBB is most likely present. If the terminal portion of the QRS is negative, a LBBB is most likely present.

J-point

J-point

Figure 9-39
Differentiating right versus left BBB. The "turn-signal theory": Right is up, left is down.

pacemaker, this presents as an exception to the two-part rule of BBB recognition. Specificity is limited by Wolf-Parkinson-White syndrome (WPW) and other conditions that produce wide QRS complexes resulting from atrial activity. If the characteristic delta wave and shortened PR interval are recognized, then WPW can be suspected. Similarly, hyperkalemia and other conditions that can widen the QRS are relatively infrequent.[2]

As for differentiating LBBB from RBBB, a third category exists—nonspecific intraventricular conduction delay (NSIVCD). These blocks do not display the typical V_1 morphologies generally produced by BBB. Their origin may not be due to a complete BBB but is often the result of several factors, of which incomplete BBB may be one. Atypical patterns of BBB can be attributed to NSIVCD.[2]

CHAMBER ENLARGEMENT

Enlargement of the atrial and/or ventricular chambers of the heart may occur if there is a volume or pressure overload in the heart. **Dilatation** is an increase in the diameter of a chamber of the heart caused by volume overload. Dilatation may be acute or chronic. **Hypertrophy** is

Hypertrophy is commonly accompanied by dilatation.

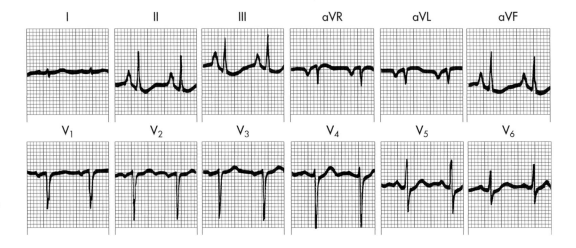

I　II　III　aVR　aVL　aVF

V₁　V₂　V₃　V₄　V₅　V₆

Figure 9-40
When the ECG machine is properly calibrated, a 1-millivolt electrical signal will produce a deflection measuring exactly 10 millimeters tall.

Figure 9-41
Right atrial enlargement. P pulmonale pattern in a 44-year-old woman with chronic obstructive pulmonary disease (COPD). Negative P waves are visible in V₁ and V₂.

an increase in the thickness of a heart chamber because of chronic pressure overload. **Enlargement** is a term that implies the presence of dilatation or hypertrophy, or both.

When evaluating the ECG for the presence of chamber enlargement, it is important to check the standardization marker to make sure it is 10 mm high.

The vertical axis of ECG graph paper represents voltage or amplitude of the ECG waveforms or deflections. The size or amplitude of a waveform is measured in millivolts (mV) or millimeters (mm). The ECG machine's sensitivity must be calibrated so that a 1-mV electrical signal will produce a deflection measuring exactly 10-mm tall (Figure 9-40). Clinically, the height of a waveform is usually stated in millimeters, not millivolts.

Atrial Enlargement

The first half of the P wave is recorded when the electrical impulse that originated in the SA node stimulates the right atrium and reaches the AV node. The downslope of the P wave reflects stimulation of the left atrium. A normal P wave is smooth and rounded, no more than 2.5 mm in height, and no more than 0.11 seconds in duration (width). Normal P waves are positive (upright) in leads I, II, aVF, and V₄ through V₆.

Right Atrium

The presence of right atrial enlargement (RAE) is suggested by the presence of tall, peaked P waves of normal duration on the ECG. RAE = increased amplitude.

Enlargement of the right atrium produces an abnormally tall initial part of the P wave. The P wave is tall (2.5 mm or more in height in leads II, III, and aVF), peaked, and of normal duration. This type of P wave is called P pulmonale because right atrial enlargement (RAE) is usually caused by conditions that increase the work of the right atrium, such as chronic obstructive pulmonary disease with or without pulmonary hypertension, congenital heart disease, or right ventricular failure of any cause (Figure 9-41). The P wave may be biphasic in lead V₁ with a more prominent positive portion.

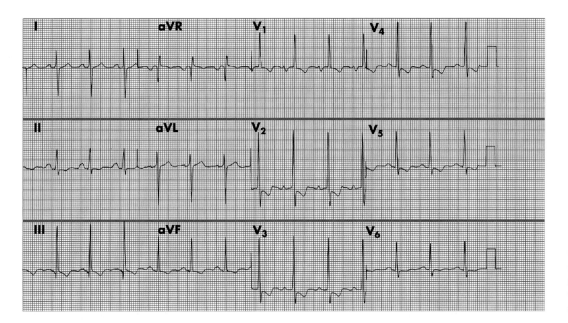

Figure 9-42
Left atrial enlargement. Note the wide, notched P waves in leads II, III, and aVF.

Left Atrium

The latter part of the P wave is prominent in LAE. This is because the impulse starts in the right atrium where the SA node is located and chamber size is normal. The electrical impulse then travels to the left to depolarize the left atrium. The waveform inscribed on the ECG is widened (latter part of the P wave) because it takes longer to depolarize an enlarged muscle. The P wave is more than 0.11 seconds in duration and often notched in leads I, II, aVL, and V_4, V_5, and V_6 (Figure 9-42). The P wave may be biphasic in lead V_1 with a more prominent negative portion. LAE occurs because of conditions that increase left atrial pressure or volume overload, or both. These conditions include mitral regurgitation, mitral stenosis, left ventricular failure, and systemic hypertension. Because of the frequent association of LAE with mitral valve disease, the wide, notched P wave that is usually seen is called *P mitrale*.

The presence of left atrial enlargement (LAE) is suggested by the presence of wide, notched P waves on the ECG. LAE = increased time.

Ventricular Enlargement

Ventricular muscle thickens (hypertrophies) when it sustains a persistent pressure overload. Dilatation occurs because of persistent volume overload. The two often go hand in hand. Hypertrophy increases the QRS amplitude and is often associated with ST-segment depression and asymmetric T-wave inversion. The ST-segment depression and T-wave inversion pattern is called *ventricular strain* or *secondary repolarization changes*.

The amplitude (voltage) of the QRS complex can be affected by various factors, including age, body weight, and lung disease. Increased QRS amplitude may occur normally in thin-chested individuals or young adults because the chest electrodes are closer to the heart in these patients.

Right Ventricle

Because the right ventricle is normally considerably smaller than the left, it must become extremely enlarged before changes are visible on the ECG. Right axis deviation is one of the earliest and most reliable findings of right ventricular hypertrophy (RVH). Further, normal R-wave progression is reversed in the chest leads, revealing taller than normal R waves and small S waves in V_1 and V_2 and deeper than normal S waves and small R waves in V_5 and V_6. Ventricular activation time (VAT) is delayed in V_1. Causes of RVH include pulmonary hypertension and chronic lung diseases, valvular heart disease, and congenital heart disease (Figure 9-43).

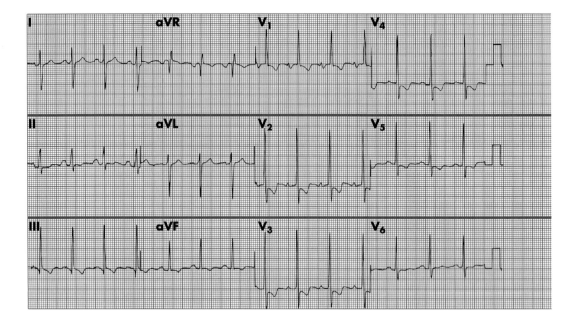

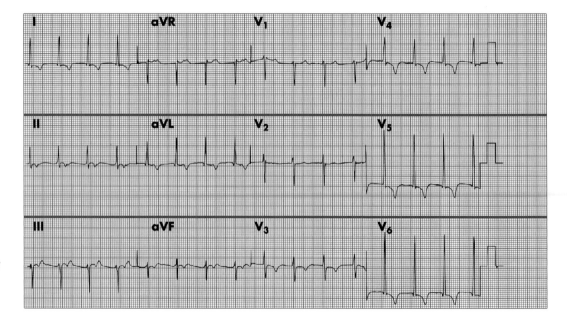

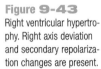

While bundle branch block increases the *width* of the QRS complex, LVH increases the *amplitude* because of the increase in electrical activity.

Left Ventricle

Recognition of left ventricular hypertrophy (LVH) on the ECG is not always obvious, and many methods to assist in its recognition have been suggested. ECG signs of LVH include deeper than normal S waves and small R waves in V_1 and V_2 and taller than normal R waves and small S waves in V_5 and V_6. If S-wave amplitude in lead V_1 added to the R-wave amplitude in V_5 is greater than or equal to 35 mV, LVH should be suspected (Figure 9-44). Causes of LVH include systemic hypertension, hypertrophic cardiomyopathy, aortic stenosis, and aortic insufficiency. LVH may be accompanied by left axis deviation.

TABLE 9-7   ECG Changes Associated with Electrolyte Disturbances

Medication	P wave	PR Interval	QRS Complex	ST-segment	T Wave	QT interval	Heart Rate
Hypocalcemia				Long, flattened		Prolonged	
Hypercalcemia		Prolonged		Shortened		Shortened	
Hypokalemia			Widen as level decreases	Depressed	Flattened; U wave present	Prolonged	
Hyperkalemia	Disappear as level increases	Normal or prolonged	Widen as level increases	Disappear as level increases	Tall, peaked/tented		Slows
Hypomagnesemia	Diminished voltage (amplitude)		Widen as level decreases; diminished voltage	Depressed	Flattened; U wave present	Prolonged	
Hypermagnesemia		Prolonged	Widened		Tall/elevated		

ECG CHANGES ASSOCIATED WITH ELECTROLYTE DISTURBANCES

The primary ions involved in propagation of impulses from cell to cell in the myocardium are sodium, potassium, and calcium.

There are two types of action potentials in the heart: fast and slow. This classification is based on the rate of voltage change during depolarization of cardiac cells. Fast-response action potentials occur in the cells of the atria, ventricles, and Purkinje fibers. The fast-response action potential occurs because of the presence of many voltage-sensitive sodium channels that allow a rapid influx of sodium when these channels are open and prevent influx when they are closed. Myocardial fibers with a fast-response action potential can conduct impulses at relatively rapid rates.

Slow-response action potentials normally occur in cells such as the SA and AV nodes. These cells do not have fast sodium channels but have slow calcium and slow sodium channels that result in a slower rate of depolarization compared to the depolarization of cardiac cells with fast sodium channels. Slow-response action potentials can occur abnormally anywhere in the heart, usually secondary to ischemia, injury, or an electrolyte imbalance (Table 9-7).

Sodium

Causes of hypernatremia (sodium excess) include hypertonic parenteral fluid administration, significantly deficient water intake, excessive salt ingestion, high-protein liquid diets without adequate fluid intake, severe watery diarrhea, or severe insensible water losses (e.g., heat stroke, prolonged high fever). Hypernatremia does not cause any significant changes on the ECG.

Normal values: 135-145 mEq/L

Hyponatremia (sodium deficit) may occur because of prolonged diuretic therapy, excessive diaphoresis, and excessive loss of sodium from trauma (e.g., burns); adrenal insufficiency; severe gastrointestinal fluid losses from gastric suctioning or lavage; prolonged vomiting or diarrhea or laxative use; and an insufficient intake of sodium. Hyponatremia does not cause any significant changes on the ECG.

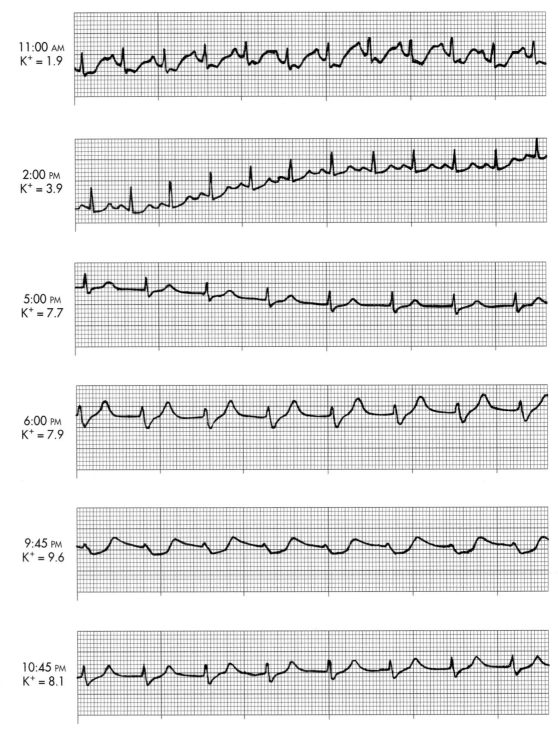

Figure 9-45
Serial ECG tracings in a patient with marked changes in the serum potassium (K+) level. In the 11 AM tracing, the depressed ST-segment and low-amplitude T-wave blending into a probable U wave (this cannot be seen with clarity because of the superimposed P waves) indicate the presence of hypokalemia. After administration of K+, the 2 PM tracing becomes relatively normal. Continued K+ administration results in hyperkalemia with the disappearance of atrial activity on the ECG and some prolongation of the QRS complex. By 6 PM, the QRS complex is more prolonged, and by 9:45 PM, the QRS complex is greatly prolonged. Secondary ST–T-wave changes are present. Improvement follows the administration of bicarbonate, glucose, and insulin at 10:45 PM with reduction in the serum K+ level; improvement in the ECG results.

Calcium

Normal values: 4.5-5.5 mEq/L or 9-11 mg/dL

Causes of hypercalcemia (calcium excess) include prolonged immobility, excessive vitamin D intake, thyrotoxicosis, metastatic carcinoma, excessive use of calcium-containing antacids, and an excessive intake of calcium supplements. ECG changes include a prolonged PR interval, prolonged QRS complex, and shortened QT interval (because of shortening of the ST-segment).

TABLE 9-8   Classification of Antiarrhythmic Medications

Classification	Action	Medication Examples
Class I	Fast sodium channel blockers	
Class Ia	Moderately depress conduction and usually prolong repolarization	Disopyramide, procainamide, quinidine
Class Ib	Modestly slow conduction and usually shorten repolarization	Lidocaine, mexiletine, phenytoin, tocainide
Class Ic	Markedly depress conduction and have little effect on repolarization	Encainide, flecainide, propafenone, moricizine
Class II	Beta-adrenergic blockers; indirectly affect electrophysiologic parameters by blocking beta-adrenergic receptors	Acebutolol, esmolol, metoprolol, atenolol, timolol, pindolol, carvedilol
Class III	Potassium channel blockers; prolong the duration of refractoriness by delaying membrane repolarization	Amiodarone, ibutilide, dofetilide, sematilide, N-acetylprocainamide, bretylium
Class IV	Calcium channel blockers	Verapamil, diltiazem

Hypocalcemia (calcium deficit) may occur because of acute or chronic renal failure, vitamin D deficiency, hyperphosphatemia, hypomagnesemia, and inadequate exposure to ultraviolet light. ECG changes include a long, flattened ST-segment and prolonged QT interval.

Magnesium

Causes of hypermagnesemia (magnesium excess) include renal failure, excessive use of parenteral magnesium, and excessive use of magnesium-containing antacids or laxatives. ECG changes include a prolonged PR interval, prolonged QRS complex, and elevated T wave.

Normal values: 1.2-2.6 mEq/L

Hypomagnesemia (magnesium deficit) may occur because of prolonged or excessive diuretic therapy, excessive calcium or vitamin D intake, administration of intravenous fluids or total parenteral nutrition without magnesium replacement, hypercalcemia, high-dose steroid use, cancer chemotherapy, and sepsis. ECG changes include diminished voltage of P waves and QRS complexes, flattened T waves, slightly widened QRS complexes, and prominent U waves.

Potassium

Hyperkalemia (potassium excess) may occur because of an excessive administration of potassium supplements, excessive use of salt substitutes, potassium-sparing diuretics (e.g., spironolactone), widespread cell damage (e.g., crush injuries, burns), metabolic or respiratory acidosis, and acute or chronic renal failure. ECG changes include tall, peaked (tented) T waves; widened QRS complexes, prolonged PR intervals, flattened ST-segments, and flattened or absent P waves. Hyperkalemia may lead to ventricular dysrhythmias and asystole if not reversed.

Normal values: 3.5-5.0 mEq/L

Hypokalemia (potassium deficit) may be the result of prolonged diuretic therapy with thiazide diuretics or furosemide, an inadequate dietary intake of potassium, administration of potassium-deficient parenteral fluids, severe gastrointestinal fluid losses from gastric suctioning or lavage, prolonged vomiting or diarrhea, or laxative use without replacement of potassium. ECG changes include a depressed ST-segment, flattened T wave, and prominent U wave (Figure 9-45). Hypokalemia may increase the patient's sensitivity to digitalis toxicity.

A summary of antiarrhythmic medication classifications and the ECG changes associated with the medications can be found in Tables 9-8 and 9-9.

TABLE 9-9 ECG Changes Associated with Medications

Medication	Classification	Indications	ECG Characteristics					Comments
			Heart Rate	PR Interval	QRS Duration	QT Interval		
Adenosine (Adenocard)	Endogenous nucleoside	PSVT involving the AV node	Slows	Prolongs				May result in brief period of bradycardia or asystole after IV bolus administration
Amiodarone (Cordarone)	Class III antiarrhythmic	VT, VF, polymorphic VT, SVT, atrial fibrillation, atrial flutter	Slows	Prolongs	May prolong	Prolongs		May cause AV block, hypotension, bradycardia
Atenolol (Tenormin)	Class II antiarrhythmic (Beta-blocker)	SVT, angina, hypertension	Slows	Prolongs				Possible AV block
Atropine sulfate	Parasympatholytic	Symptomatic bradycardia, asystole	Increases	Shortens				May result in tachycardia with higher doses
Digoxin (Lanoxin)	Cardiac glycoside	PSVT, uncontrolled atrial fibrillation or flutter, CHF	Slows	Prolongs		Shortens		Downward sloping of ST-segment ("dig dip"); T-wave inversion or flattening
Diltiazem (Cardizem)	Class IV antiarrhythmic (calcium channel blocker)	PSVT, uncontrolled atrial fib or flutter, angina	Slows	Prolongs				Possible AV block
Disopyramide (Norpace)	Class IA antiarrhythmic	Ventricular dysrhythmias, atrial fibrillation or flutter with WPW	Variable	Prolongs	Prolongs	Prolongs		May precipitate torsades de pointes, possible AV block
Epinephrine (Adrenaline)	Sympathomimetic, natural catecholamine	VT, VF, PEA, asystole (IV bolus); symptomatic bradycardia (IV infusion)	Increases	Decreases				May result in tachycardia
Esmolol (Brevibloc)	Class II antiarrhythmic (Beta-blocker)	SVT, angina, hypertension	Slows	Prolongs		May shorten		Possible AV block
Flecainide (Tambocor)	Class IC antiarrhythmic	Ventricular & supraventricular dysrhythmias	May slow	Prolongs	Prolongs	Prolongs		Possible SA block, AV block, BBB
Ibutilide (Corvert)	Class III antiarrhythmic	For rapid conversion of recent onset atrial fibrillation or atrial flutter to sinus rhythm	Slows	Prolongs		Prolongs		Can induce or worsen ventricular dysrhythmias, including TdP

Drug	Classification	Indications	Heart rate				Other effects
Lidocaine (Xylocaine)	Class IB antiarrhythmic	VF, VT			May prolong		Possible AV block
Magnesium sulfate	Electrolyte	Torsades de pointes	May increase	Prolongs		May shorten	
Metoprolol (Lopressor)	Class II antiarrhythmic (Beta-blocker)	SVT, angina, hypertension	Slows	Prolongs			Possible AV block
Norepinephrine (Levophed)	Sympathomimetic	Significant hypotension not due to hypovolemia	Increases	Shortens			Increases ventricular irritability
Procainamide (Pronestyl)	Class IA antiarrhythmic	Ventricular & supraventricular tachydysrhythmias	Variable	Prolongs	Prolongs	Prolongs	May precipitate torsades de pointes, possible AV block
Propafenone (Rythmol)	Class IC antiarrhythmic	Prevention of recurrence of chronic or paroxysmal atrial fibrillation; WPW syndrome (stable patient), life-threatening ventricular rhythms	Slows or no change	Prolongs	Prolongs	Usually not affected	
Propranolol (Inderal)	Class II antiarrhythmic (beta-blocker)	Angina, hypertension, supraventricular & ventricular dysrhythmias	Slows	Prolongs		May shorten	May worsen existing AV block
Quinidine (Duraquin, Quinaglute)	Class IA antiarrhythmic	Supraventricular and ventricular dysrhythmias	Variable	Prolongs	Prolongs	Prolongs	May precipitate torsades de pointes; BBB sign of toxicity; wide, notched P waves
Sotalol (Betapace)	Beta-blocker with Class III antiarrhythmic activity	Supraventricular & serious ventricular dysrhythmias	Slows	Prolongs		Prolongs	Possible AV block
Verapamil (Isoptin, Calan)	Class IV antiarrhythmic (calcium channel blocker)	PSVT, MAT, angina	Slows	Prolongs			Possible SA and AV block

AV, atrioventricular; BBB, branched bundle block; CHF, congestive heart failure; ECG, electrocardiogram; IV, intravenous; MAT, multifocal atrial tachycardia; PEA, pulseless electrical activity; PSVT, paroxysmal supraventricular tachycardia; SA, sinoatrial; SVT, supraventricular tachycardia; VF, ventricular fibrillation; VT, ventricular tachycardia; WPW, Wolff-Parkinson-White.

ANALYZING THE 12-LEAD ECG

When analyzing a 12-lead ECG, it is important to use a systematic method. Findings suggestive of an acute MI are considered significant if viewed in two or more leads looking at the same area of the heart. If these findings are viewed in leads that look directly at the affected area, they are called *indicative changes*. If findings are observed in leads opposite the affected area, they are called *reciprocal changes*.

1. Assess the quality of the tracing. If baseline wander or artifact is present to any significant degree, note it. If the presence of either of these conditions interferes with the assessment of any lead, use a modifier such as "possible" or "apparent" in your interpretation.
2. Identify the rate and underlying rhythm.
3. Evaluate intervals: PR interval, QRS duration, QT interval.
4. Evaluate waveforms: P waves, Q waves, R waves (R wave progression), T waves, U waves. If a Q wave is present, express the duration in milliseconds.
5. Examine each lead for the presence of ST-segment displacement (elevation or depression). If ST-segment elevation is present, express it in millimeters. Assess the areas of ischemia or injury by assessing lead groupings. Examine the T waves for any changes in orientation, shape, and size.
6. Determine axis.
7. Look for evidence of hypertrophy/chamber enlargement.
8. Look for effects of medications and electrolyte imbalances.
9. Interpret your findings.

REFERENCES

For additional information regarding the 12-lead ECG, please pick up a copy of *The 12-Lead ECG in Acute Coronary Syndromes,* second edition, by Tim Phalen.

1. Alpert JS and others: Myocardial infarction redefined: a consensus document of the Joint European Society of Cardiology/American College of Cardiology Committee for the redefinition of myocardial infarction. *J Am Coll Cardiol* 36(3):959-969, 2000.
2. Phalen T and Aehlert B: *The 12-lead ECG in acute coronary syndromes,* 2006, Mosby.

STOP & REVIEW

True/False

Indicate whether the sentence or statement is true or false.

____ 1. Placement of right precordial leads is identical to the standard precordial leads except on the right side of the chest.

____ 2. In a patient experiencing an acute coronary syndrome, ST-segment elevation in the shape of a "smiley" face (upward concavity) is usually associated with an acute injury pattern.

Completion

Complete each sentence or statement.

3. Each electrode placed on the chest in a "V" position is a _____ (positive/negative) electrode.

4. 0.12 seconds = _____ milliseconds

Matching

a. Lead II
b. aVR
c. Vector
d. Chest
e. V_1-V_2
f. Inferior
g. Electrical axis
h. Injury
i. V_1
j. I, aVL, V_5, V_6

k. Anterior
l. Infarction
m. aVF
n. Tall, tented T waves
o. II, III, aVF
p. V_2
q. Limb
r. aVL
s. V_1R-V_6R
t. V_4

____ 5. Lead located at the fourth intercostal space, left sternal border
____ 6. Common ECG finding in hyperkalemia
____ 7. The zone of __ is typically characterized by ST-segment elevation.
____ 8. Lead I + lead III = __
____ 9. Occlusion of the left anterior descending coronary artery may result in a(n) __ myocardial infarction.
____ 10. Leads that view the heart in the horizontal plane
____ 11. Leads that view the inferior wall of the heart
____ 12. Lead I is perpendicular to lead __.
____ 13. Occlusion of the right coronary artery may result in a(n) __ myocardial infarction.
____ 14. Leads used to view the right ventricle
____ 15. Lead located at the fourth intercostal space, right sternal border
____ 16. Lead II is perpendicular to lead __.
____ 17. Leads that view the heart in the frontal plane
____ 18. Lead located at the fifth intercostal space, left midclavicular line
____ 19. Direction of the mean QRS vector
____ 20. Lead III is perpendicular to lead __.
____ 21. Leads that view the lateral wall of the heart
____ 22. The zone of __ is typically characterized by Q waves.
____ 23. Indicator of the magnitude and direction of current flow
____ 24. Leads that view the septum

25. The axes of leads I, II, and III form an equilateral triangle with the heart at the center (Einthoven's triangle). If the augmented limb leads are added to this configuration and the axes of the six leads moved in a way in which they bisect each other, the result is the _____ _____ _____.

26. The area supplied by an obstructed coronary artery goes through a characteristic sequence of events that have been identified as zones of _____, _____, and _____.

27. Complete the following.

Lead	Heart Surface Viewed
V_1	_____
V_2	_____
V_3	_____
V_4	_____
V_5	_____
V_6	_____

28. List two other names for the "chest" leads.
    1.

    2.

29. Complete the following table.

Axis	Normal	Left	Right	Indeterminate
Lead I QRS direction	_____	_____	_____	_____
Lead aVF QRS direction	_____	_____	_____	_____

30. List three (3) acute coronary syndromes.
    1.

    2.

    3.

31. List the "three I's" of an acute coronary event.
    1.

    2.

    3.

32. List four (4) causes of ST-segment elevation other than myocardial infarction.
    1.

    2.

    3.

    4.

33. Explain what is meant by the phrase, "Poor R-wave progression."

34. In a 12-lead ECG, how long (in seconds) is the view of each lead?

PRACTICE *Rhythm Strips*

This 12-lead ECG is from a 48-year-old woman complaining of substernal chest pain that radiates to her back. Her symptoms began while driving to work. She has a history of hypertension and asthma. She takes a blood pressure medication but cannot recall the name. BP 132/84, R 16.

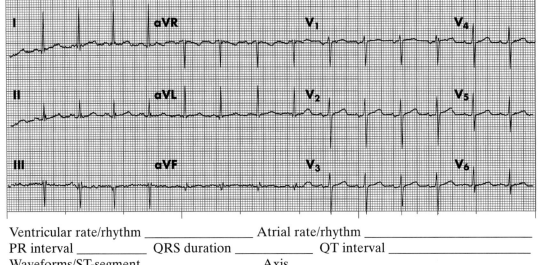

Figure 9-46

Ventricular rate/rhythm _____ Atrial rate/rhythm _____
PR interval _____ QRS duration _____ QT interval _____
Waveforms/ST-segment _____ Axis _____
Chamber enlargement _____
Ischemia/injury/infarction _____ Medication effects _____
Identification: _____

This 12-lead ECG is from an 83-year-old woman complaining of substernal chest pain that has been present for the past 6 hours. She had a myocardial infarction 5 years ago and has a history of emphysema. The patient is on home oxygen. She has taken one nitroglycerin tablet with no relief of pain. BP 162/108.

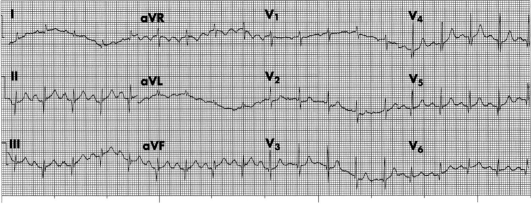

Figure 9-47

Ventricular rate/rhythm _____ Atrial rate/rhythm _____
PR interval _____ QRS duration _____ QT interval _____
Waveforms/ST-segment _____ Axis _____
Chamber enlargement _____
Ischemia/injury/infarction _____ Medication effects _____
Identification: _____

This 12-lead ECG is from a 72-year-old man complaining of chest pain. BP 138/72, R 28. The patient has a history of angina, two prior myocardial infarctions, coronary artery bypass surgery 3 years ago, abdominal aortic aneurysm repair 5 years ago, atrial fibrillation, and emphysema. Medications include aspirin, lorazepam, nitroglycerin, and dexamethasone.

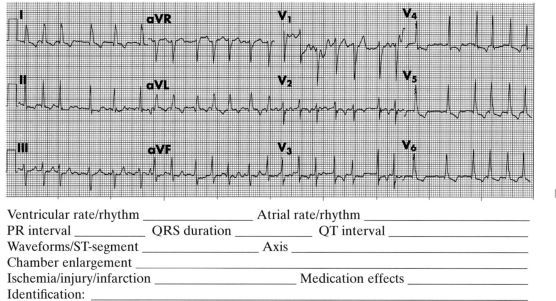

Figure 9-48

Ventricular rate/rhythm _____ Atrial rate/rhythm _____

PR interval _____ QRS duration _____ QT interval _____

Waveforms/ST-segment _____ Axis _____

Chamber enlargement _____

Ischemia/injury/infarction _____ Medication effects _____

Identification: _____

This 12-lead ECG is from a 58-year-old man complaining of a headache, nausea, and a burning sensation in his chest. He states the pain radiates to his jaw and tongue. BP 140/90, R16. Skin is warm and dry.

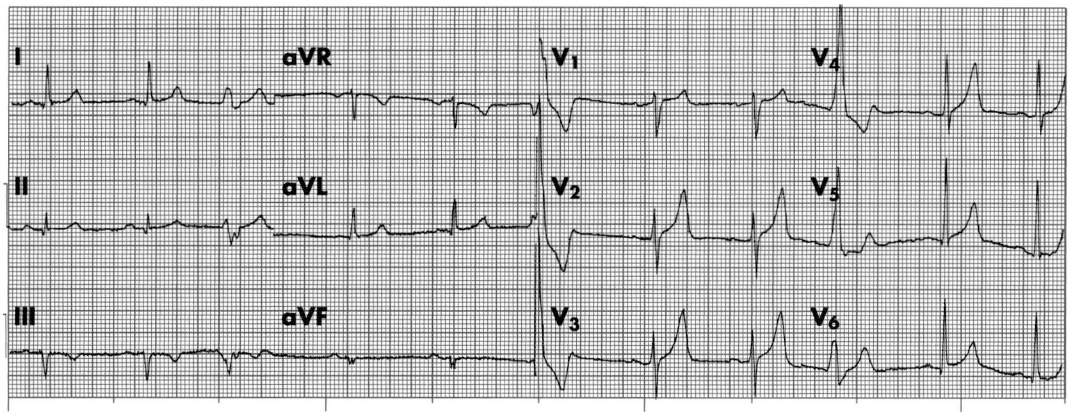

Figure 9-49

Ventricular rate/rhythm _____ Atrial rate/rhythm _____

PR interval _____ QRS duration _____ QT interval _____

Waveforms/ST-segment _____ Axis _____

Chamber enlargement _____

Ischemia/injury/infarction _____ Medication effects _____

Identification: _____

Post-Test

True/False

Indicate whether the sentence or statement is true or false.

_____ 1. A macroreentrant circuit is one that involves a small area of heart tissue, usually a few centimeters or less.

_____ 2. Depolarization is the same as contraction.

_____ 3. Proper positioning of the electrodes for leads I, II, and III requires placement on the patient's torso.

Multiple Choice

Identify the letter of the choice that best completes the statement or answers the question.

_____ 4. The anterior surface of the heart consists primarily of the:
   a. Left atrium
   b. Right atrium
   c. Left ventricle
   d. Right ventricle

_____ 5. The _____ supplies the right atrium and ventricle with blood.
   a. Right coronary artery
   b. Left main coronary artery
   c. Left circumflex artery
   d. Left anterior descending artery

_____ 6. How do you determine whether the atrial rhythm on an ECG tracing is regular or irregular?
   a. Compare QT intervals
   b. Compare PR intervals
   c. Compare R-R intervals
   d. Compare P-P intervals

_____ 7. The absolute refractory period:
   a. Begins with the onset of the P wave and terminates with the end of the QRS complex
   b. Begins with the onset of the QRS complex and terminates at approximately the peak of the T wave
   c. Begins with the onset of the QRS complex and terminates with the end of the T wave
   d. Begins with the onset of the P wave and terminates with the beginning of the QRS complex

_____ 8. Which of the following ECG leads are bipolar leads?
   a. Leads aVR, aVL, and aVF
   b. Leads V_4, V_5, and V_6
   c. Leads V_1, V_2, and V_3
   d. Leads I, II, and III

_____ 9. _____ cells are specialized cells of the electrical conduction system responsible for the spontaneous generation and conduction of electrical impulses.
   a. Working
   b. Pacemaker
   c. Mechanical
   d. Contractile

10. When the cardiac muscle cell is stimulated, the cell is said to:
    a. Polarize
    b. Depolarize
    c. Repolarize
    d. Recover

11. Which of the following are chest leads?
    a. Leads I, II, and III
    b. Leads I and aVL
    c. Leads V_1, V_2, V_3, V_4, V_5, V_6
    d. Leads I, II, III, aVR, aVL, and aVF

12. U waves are thought to represent:
    a. Repolarization of the Purkinje fibers
    b. Repolarization of the bundle of His
    c. Ventricular depolarization
    d. Atrial depolarization

13. Tall, peaked T waves observed on the ECG are most commonly seen in patients with:
    a. Hyperkalemia
    b. Hypokalemia
    c. Hypernatremia
    d. Hyponatremia

14. In sinus arrhythmia, a gradual decreasing of the heart rate is usually associated with:
    a. Expiration
    b. Inspiration
    c. Excessive caffeine intake
    d. Early signs of congestive heart failure

15. An ECG rhythm strip shows a ventricular rate of 46, a regular rhythm, a PR interval of 0.14 seconds, a QRS duration of 0.06, and one upright P wave before each QRS. This rhythm is:
    a. Sinus rhythm
    b. Sinus bradycardia
    c. Sinus arrest
    d. Sinoatrial block

16. What is meant by the term *uncontrolled* atrial fibrillation?
    a. The overall ventricular rate is less than 100 bpm.
    b. The atrial rate is less than 100 bpm.
    c. The overall ventricular rate is greater than 100 bpm.
    d. The atrial rate is greater than 100 bpm.

17. Which of the following correctly describes multifocal atrial tachycardia?
    a. Atrial rhythm is regular.
    b. Ventricular rhythm is irregular.
    c. Atrial and ventricular rhythms are regular.
    d. Atrial and ventricular rhythms are irregular.

18. The most common type of supraventricular tachycardia (SVT) is:
    a. Atrial tachycardia
    b. Atrial flutter
    c. AV reentrant tachycardia (AVRT)
    d. AV nodal reentrant tachycardia (AVNRT)

19. Wolff-Parkinson-White syndrome is associated with a:
    a. Long PR interval, delta wave, and wide QRS complex
    b. Short PR interval, flutter waves, and narrow QRS complex
    c. Long PR interval, flutter waves, and narrow QRS complex
    d. Short PR interval, delta wave, and wide QRS complex

20. Signs and symptoms experienced during a tachydysrhythmia are usually primarily related to:
    a. Slowed conduction through the AV node
    b. Vasoconstriction
    c. Atrial irritability
    d. Decreased ventricular filling time and stroke volume

21. How are frequent premature atrial complexes (PACs) usually managed?
    a. Synchronized cardioversion
    b. Defibrillation
    c. Administration of medications such as atropine or epinephrine
    d. Correcting the underlying cause

22. Which of the following ECG characteristics distinguishes atrial flutter from other atrial dysrhythmias?
    a. The presence of fibrillatory waves
    b. The presence of delta waves before the QRS
    c. The "saw-tooth" or "picket-fence" appearance of waveforms before the QRS
    d. P waves of varying size and amplitude

23. In a junctional rhythm viewed in lead II, where is the location of the P wave on the ECG if atrial and ventricular depolarizations occur simultaneously?
    a. Before the QRS complex
    b. During the QRS complex
    c. After the QRS complex

24. The usual rate of nonparoxysmal junctional tachycardia is:
    a. 50-80 bpm
    b. 80-120 bpm
    c. 101-140 bpm
    d. 150-300 bpm

25. Depending on the severity of the patient's signs and symptoms, management of slow rhythms originating from the AV junction may require intervention including:
    a. Defibrillation
    b. Vagal maneuvers and/or adenosine
    c. Atropine and/or transcutaneous pacing
    d. Synchronized cardioversion

26. The term for three or more premature ventricular complexes (PVCs) occurring in a row at a rate of more than 100 per minute is:
    a. Ventricular trigeminy
    b. A run of ventricular tachycardia
    c. A run of ventricular escape beats
    d. Ventricular fibrillation

27. The PR interval of a first-degree AV block:
    a. Is constant and greater than 0.20 seconds in duration
    b. Is completely variable in duration
    c. Gradually decreases in duration until a P wave appears without a QRS complex
    d. Gradually lengthens until a P wave appears without a QRS complex

____ 28. In 2:1 AV block, the PR interval:
   a. Is completely variable
   b. Shortens
   c. Remains the same
   d. Lengthens

____ 29. Capture is:
   a. The time measured between a sensed cardiac event and the next pacemaker output
   b. A vertical line on the ECG that indicates the pacemaker has discharged
   c. The ability of a pacing stimulus to successfully depolarize the cardiac chamber that is being paced
   d. The electrical stimulus delivered by a pacemaker's pulse generator

____ 30. Myocardial ischemia delays the process of repolarization. Thus, the ECG changes characteristic of ischemia include:
   a. Changes in the ST segment and T wave
   b. Widening of the QRS complex
   c. Changes in the QRS complex and ST segment
   d. Prolongation of the PR interval

____ 31. Poor R wave progression is a phrase used to describe R waves that decrease in size from V_1 to V_4. This is often seen in a(n) _____ infarction.
   a. Anteroseptal
   b. Anterolateral
   c. Anterolateral
   d. Inferoposterior

____ 32. The basic contractile unit of a myofibril is the:
   a. Sinoatrial (SA) node
   b. Action potential
   c. Sarcomere
   d. Intercalated disk

____ 33. The QT interval is measured from the:
   a. Beginning of the QRS complex to the beginning of the T wave
   b. End of the Q wave to the beginning of the P wave
   c. Beginning of the QRS complex to the end of the T wave
   d. End of the T wave to the beginning of the P wave

Completion

Complete each sentence or statement.

34. A beat originating from the AV junction that appears later than the next expected sinus beat is called a _____ _____ _____.

35. A rapid, wide-QRS rhythm associated with pulselessness, shock, or congestive heart failure should be presumed to be _____ _____.

36. PACs associated with a wide QRS complex are called _____ _____ PACs, indicating that conduction through the ventricles is abnormal.

37. The right atrium receives deoxygenated blood from the _____ _____ _____ (which carries blood from the head and upper extremities), the _____ _____ _____ (which carries blood from the lower body), and the _____ _____ (which receives blood from the intracardiac circulation).

38. _____ is the period of relaxation during which a heart chamber is filling.

39. The thick, muscular middle layer of the heart wall that contains the atrial and ventricular muscle fibers necessary for contraction is the _____.

40. An ECG lead that has a positive and negative electrode is called a(n) _____ lead.

41. The appearance of coved ("frowny face") ST-segment elevation is called a(n) _____ _____ _____.

42. Delivery of an electrical current timed for delivery during the QRS complex is called _____ _____.

43. Sometimes, when a PAC occurs very prematurely and close to the T wave of the preceding beat, only a P wave may be seen with no QRS after it (appearing as a pause). This type of PAC is termed a _____ PAC.

44. If the AV junction paces the heart, the electrical impulse must travel in a(n) _____ direction to activate the atria.

45. A _____ _____ occurs as a result of an electrical impulse from a supraventricular site (such as the SA node) discharging at the same time as an ectopic site in the ventricles.

46. A _____ _____ is a vertical line on the ECG that indicates the pacemaker has discharged.

47. A demand pacemaker is also known as a _____ pacemaker.

48. A _____ bundle branch block produces an RSR' pattern in lead V_1.

49. Indicate the heart surface viewed by each of the following.

    Leads II, III, aVF: _____

    Leads V_1, V_2: _____

    Leads V_3, V_4: _____

    Leads I, aVL, V_5, V_6: _____

Short Answer

50. Indicate the inherent rates for each of the following pacemaker sites:

    Sinoatrial (SA) node: _____

    Atrioventricular (AV) junction: _____

    Ventricles: _____

51. List four (4) properties of cardiac cells.

    1.

    2.

    3.

    4.

52. List four (4) reasons why the AV junction may assume responsibility for pacing the heart.

    1.

    2.

    3.

    4.

53. List four (4) common causes of premature ventricular complexes.

    1.

    2.

    3.

    4.

54. List five (5) signs or symptoms of hemodynamic compromise.

    1.

    2.

    3.

    4.

    5.

55. What is the name given to polymorphic ventricular tachycardia (VT) that occurs in the presence of a long QT interval?

56. List five (5) possible causes of asystole or pulseless electrical activity.

    1.

    2.

    3.

    4.

    5.

57. Indicate the ECG criteria for the following dysrhythmias.

	Second-Degree AV Block Type I	Third-Degree AV Block
Ventricular rhythm	_____	_____
PR interval	_____	_____
QRS width	_____	_____

58. The axes of leads I, II, and III form an equilateral triangle with the heart at the center (Einthoven triangle). If the augmented limb leads are added to this configuration and the axes of the six leads moved in a way in which they bisect each other, the result is the

    _____ _____ _____.

59. Complete the following ECG criteria for second-degree AV block type II.

    Rate _____

    Rhythm _____

    P waves _____

    PR interval _____

    QRS duration _____

60. The area supplied by an obstructed coronary artery goes through a characteristic sequence of events that have been identified as zones of _____,
    _____, and _____.

61. What is the most important difference between sinus rhythm and sinus tachycardia?

62. Explain the Frank-Starling law of the heart.

63. List the four (4) major electrolytes that influence cardiac function.

    1.

    2.

    3.

    4.

64. On the ECG, what do the ST-segment and T wave represent?

65. What is a biphasic waveform?

66. List three (3) causes of artifact on an ECG tracing.

    1.

    2.

    3.

67. Your patient has a VVI pacemaker. Briefly explain the meaning of each of these letters.

68. Explain what is meant by the phrase, "anatomically contiguous leads."

69. Describe the appearance of a pathologic Q wave.

70. List three (3) uses for ECG monitoring.

    1.

    2.

    3.

TEST *Rhythm Strips*

For each of the following rhythm strips, determine the atrial and ventricular rates, measure the PR interval and QRS duration, and identify the rhythm. All strips are lead II unless otherwise noted.

This ECG is from a 1-year-old girl. Mom says the infant suddenly went limp and her limbs began shaking. The episode lasted about 45 seconds. Temperature is normal.

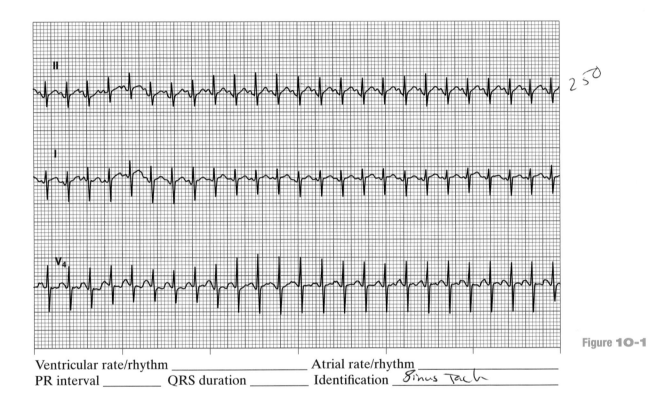

250

Figure 10-1

Ventricular rate/rhythm _____ Atrial rate/rhythm _____
PR interval _____ QRS duration _____ Identification _Sinus Tach_

This ECG is from an 89-year-old man complaining of weakness and nausea for 3 to 4 days. BP 122/82. He has a history of diabetes.

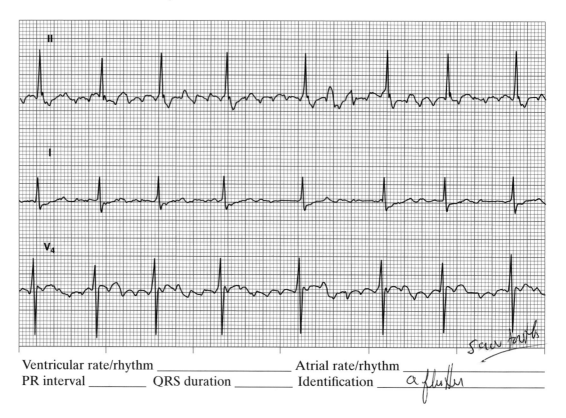

Figure **10-2**

Ventricular rate/rhythm _____ Atrial rate/rhythm _____
PR interval _____ QRS duration _____ Identification _____ a flutter _____

This ECG is from a 69-year-old man who is disoriented. He knows his name but has no idea where he is or how he got there. BP 172/98, R 20, and serum glucose 127 mg/dL.

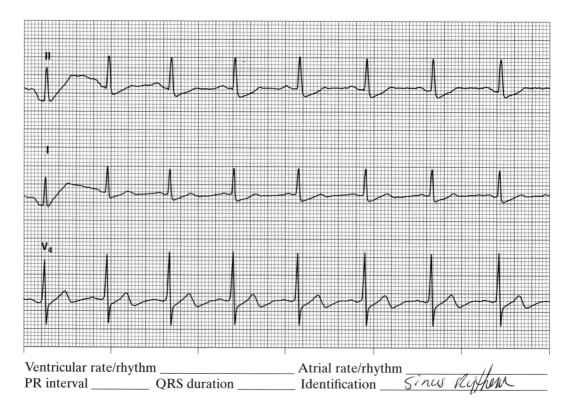

Figure **10-3**

Ventricular rate/rhythm _____ Atrial rate/rhythm _____
PR interval _____ QRS duration _____ Identification ____ Sinus Rhythm ____

This ECG strip is from a 79-year-old man after choking on a piece of meat. The foreign body was removed. BP 119/83, R 20.

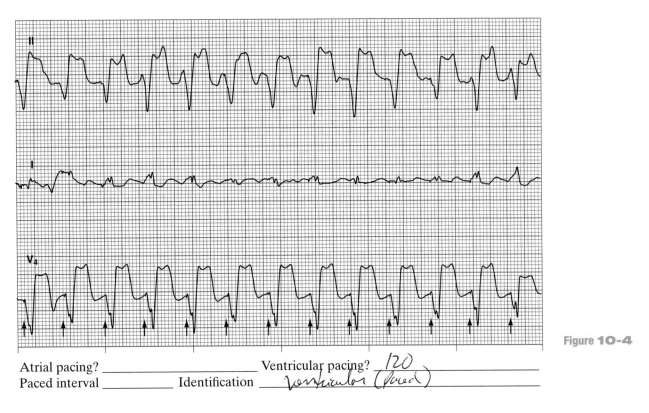

Figure 10-4

Atrial pacing? _____ Ventricular pacing? _120_____

Paced interval _____ Identification __Ventricular (paced)_____

This ECG is from an 81-year-old woman complaining of weakness. BP 122/59, R 12, and serum glucose 109 mg/dL.

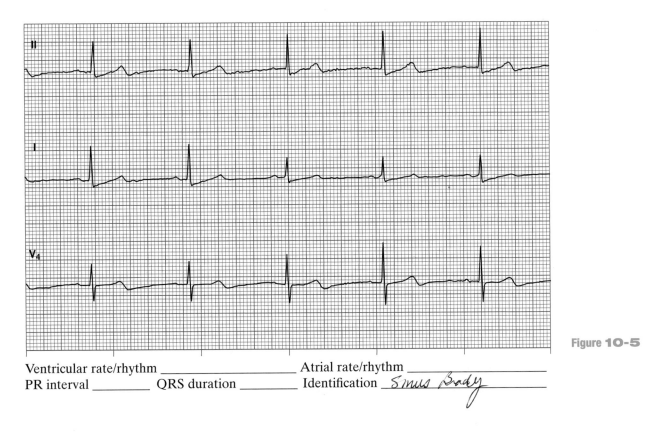

Figure 10-5

Ventricular rate/rhythm _____ Atrial rate/rhythm _____

PR interval _____ QRS duration _____ Identification __Sinus Brady_____

This ECG is from a 69-year-old man complaining of substernal chest pain. He rates his discomfort 9/10.

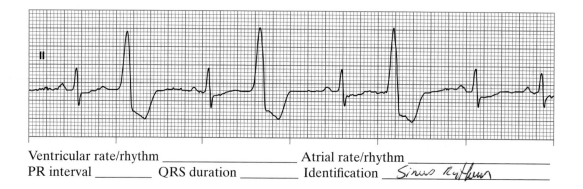

Ventricular rate/rhythm _____ Atrial rate/rhythm _____
PR interval _____ QRS duration _____ Identification _Sinus Rythum_

This ECG is from a 51-year-old man complaining of "dull chest pain" that began about 2 hours ago. He rates his discomfort 6/10. BP 70/48, R 24. His skin is cool, pale, and diaphoretic.

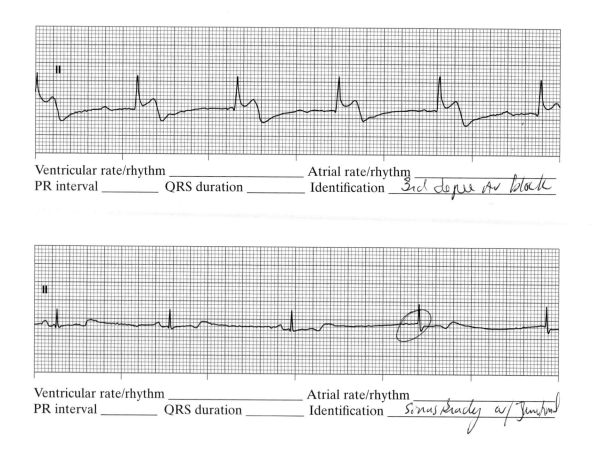

Ventricular rate/rhythm _____ Atrial rate/rhythm _____
PR interval _____ QRS duration _____ Identification _3rd degree AV block_

Ventricular rate/rhythm _____ Atrial rate/rhythm _____
PR interval _____ QRS duration _____ Identification _Sinus Brady w/ Junctional_

This ECG is from an 82-year-old man complaining of chest pain.

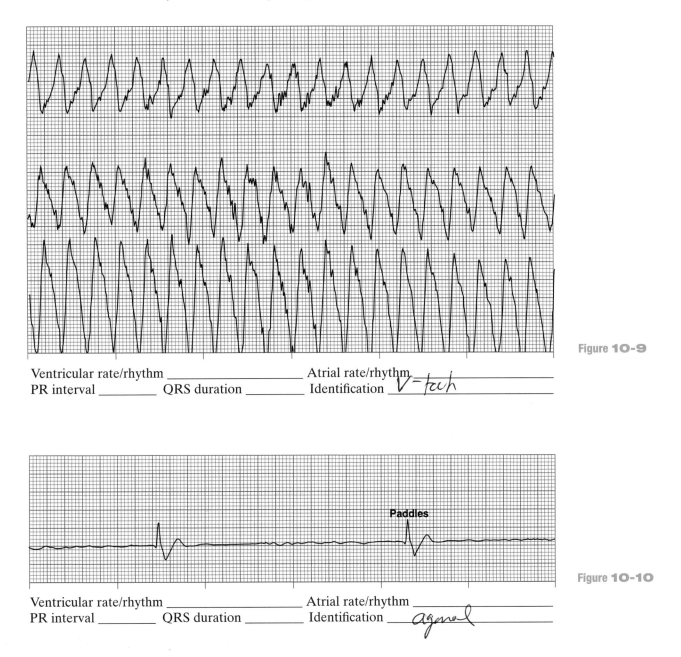

Figure 10-9

Ventricular rate/rhythm _____ Atrial rate/rhythm _____
PR interval _____ QRS duration _____ Identification _V-tach_____

Figure 10-10

Ventricular rate/rhythm _____ Atrial rate/rhythm _____
PR interval _____ QRS duration _____ Identification _agonal_____

This ECG is from a 52-year-old man complaining of weakness.

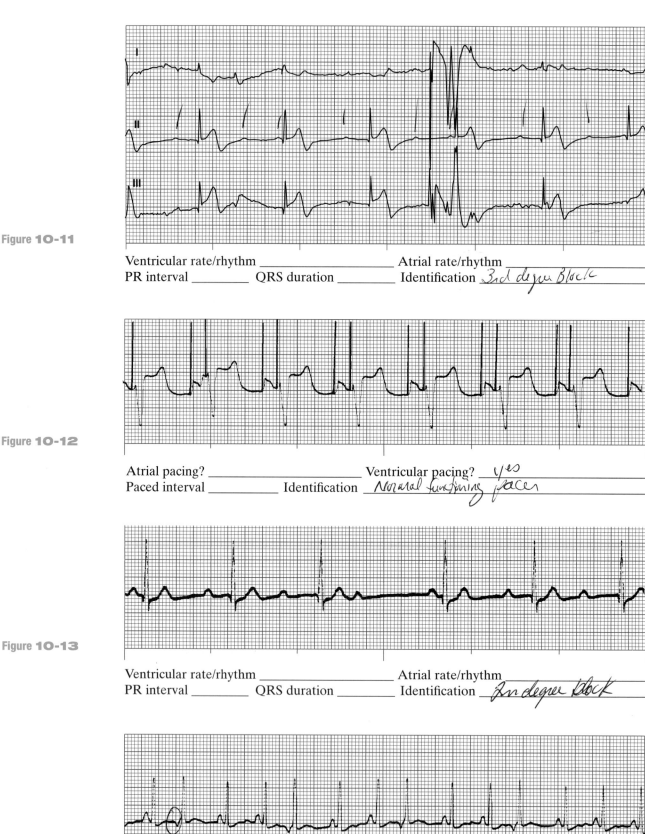

Figure **10-11**

Ventricular rate/rhythm _____ Atrial rate/rhythm _____
PR interval _____ QRS duration _____ Identification _3rd degree Block_

Figure **10-12**

Atrial pacing? _____ Ventricular pacing? _Yes_
Paced interval _____ Identification _Normal functioning pacer_

Figure **10-13**

Ventricular rate/rhythm _____ Atrial rate/rhythm _____
PR interval _____ QRS duration _____ Identification _2nd degree Block_

Figure **10-14**

Ventricular rate/rhythm _____ Atrial rate/rhythm _____ Takes a/R
PR interval _____ QRS duration _____ Identification _Sinus rhythm_ 1/R

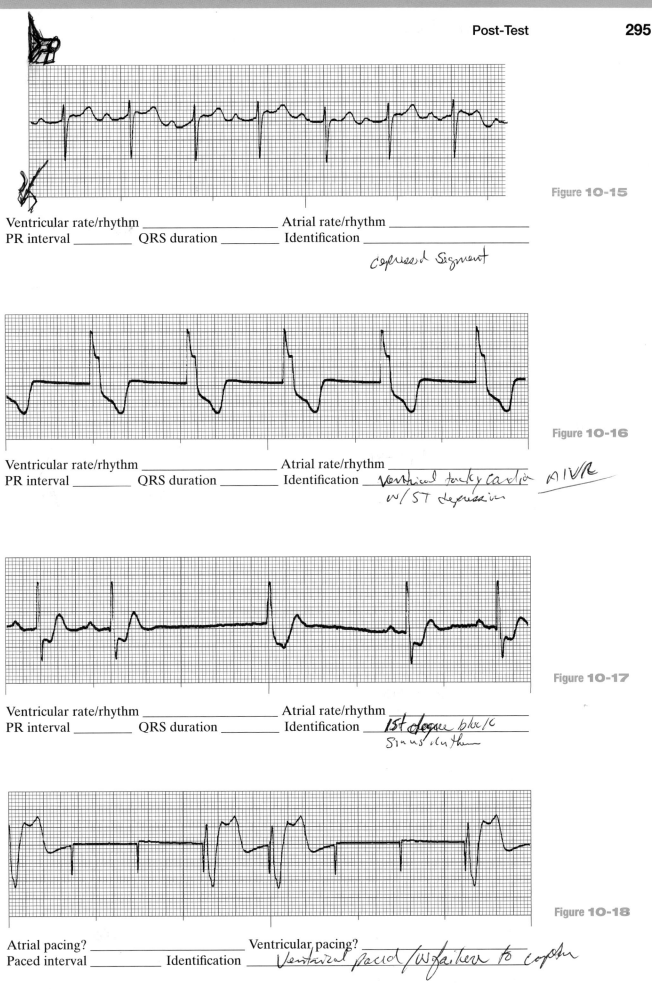

Figure 10-15

Ventricular rate/rhythm _____ Atrial rate/rhythm _____
PR interval _____ QRS duration _____ Identification _____
depressed Segment

Figure 10-16

Ventricular rate/rhythm _____ Atrial rate/rhythm _____
PR interval _____ QRS duration _____ Identification Ventricular tacky cardia AIVR
w/ ST depression

Figure 10-17

Ventricular rate/rhythm _____ Atrial rate/rhythm _____
PR interval _____ QRS duration _____ Identification 1st degree block
Sinus rhythm

Figure 10-18

Atrial pacing? _____ Ventricular pacing? _____
Paced interval _____ Identification Ventricular paced /w failure to capture

Figure **10-19**

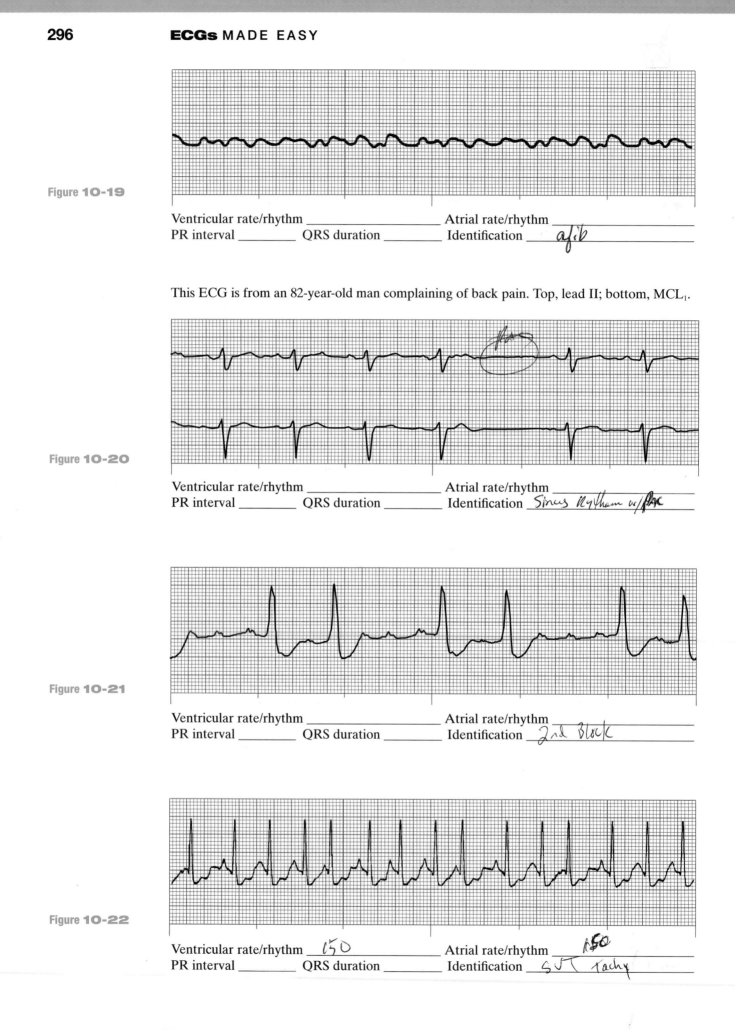

Ventricular rate/rhythm _____ Atrial rate/rhythm _____
PR interval _____ QRS duration _____ Identification _*afib*_

This ECG is from an 82-year-old man complaining of back pain. Top, lead II; bottom, MCL₁.

Figure **10-20**

Ventricular rate/rhythm _____ Atrial rate/rhythm _____
PR interval _____ QRS duration _____ Identification _Sinus Rythom w/PAC_

Figure **10-21**

Ventricular rate/rhythm _____ Atrial rate/rhythm _____
PR interval _____ QRS duration _____ Identification _2nd Block_

Figure **10-22**

Ventricular rate/rhythm _150_ Atrial rate/rhythm _150_
PR interval _____ QRS duration _____ Identification _SVT Tachy_

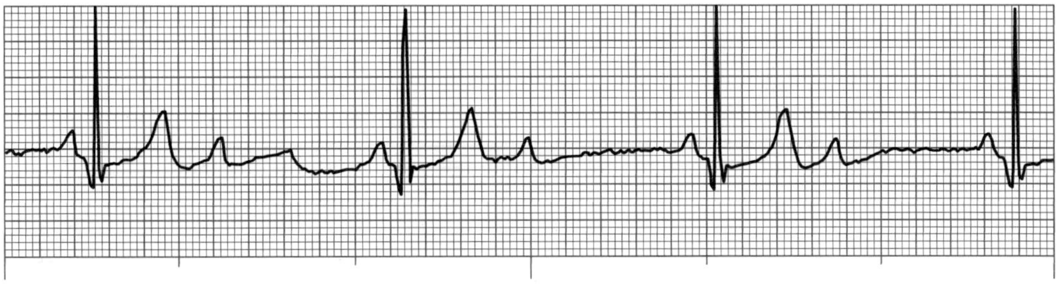

Figure **10-23**

Ventricular rate/rhythm _____   Atrial rate/rhythm _____
PR interval _____ QRS duration _____   Identification _2nd degree block Type I_
? :1 conduction

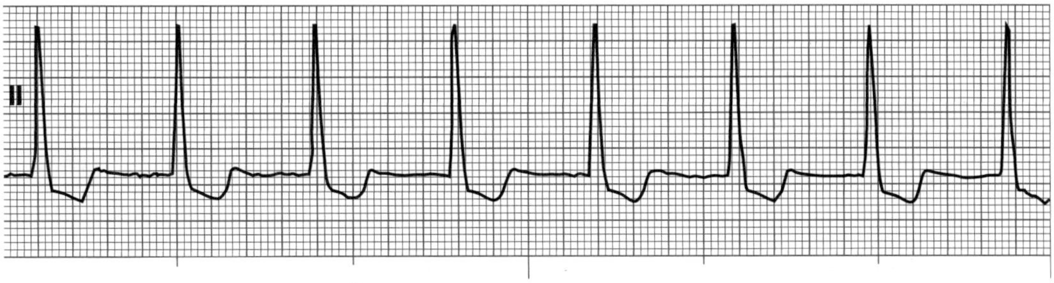

Figure **10-24**

Ventricular rate/rhythm ___80___   Atrial rate/rhythm _____
PR interval _____ QRS duration _____   Identification _accelerated junctional_

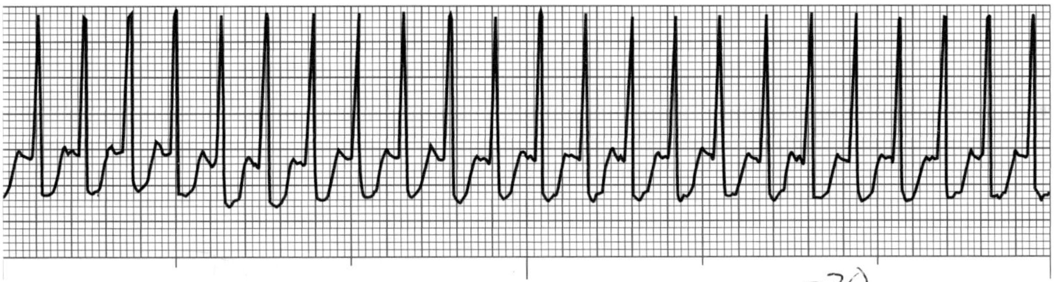

Figure **10-25**

Ventricular rate/rhythm _____   Atrial rate/rhythm _230_
PR interval _____ QRS duration _____   Identification _V tach_

This ECG is from an 83-year-old woman with shortness of breath. Top, lead II; bottom, lead V$_1$.

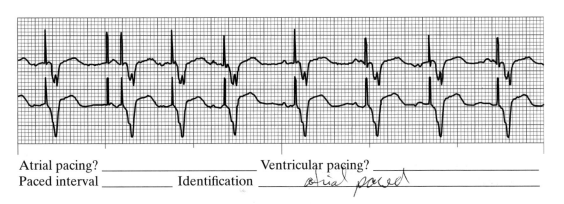

Figure **10-26**

Atrial pacing? _____   Ventricular pacing? _____
Paced interval _____   Identification _atrial paced_

Figure **10-27**

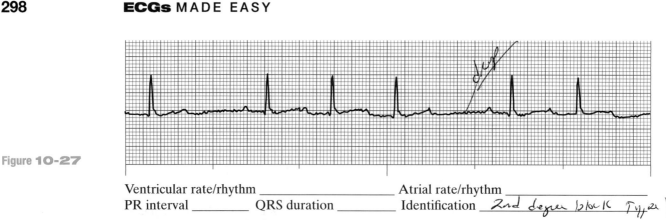

Ventricular rate/rhythm _____ Atrial rate/rhythm _____

PR interval _____ QRS duration _____ Identification _2nd degree block Type 1_

This ECG is from a 58-year-old man complaining of palpitations.

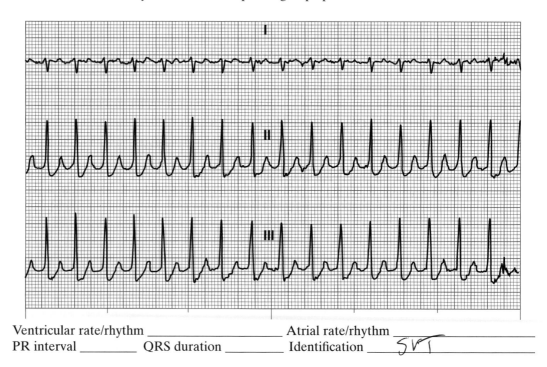

Figure **10-28**

Ventricular rate/rhythm _____ Atrial rate/rhythm _____

PR interval _____ QRS duration _____ Identification _SVT_

This ECG is from a 44-year-old construction worker with a sudden onset of chest pressure.

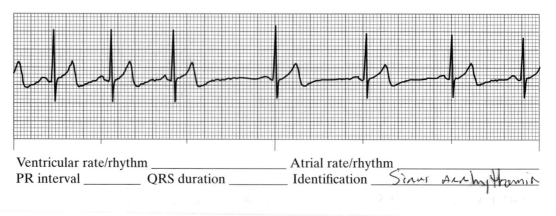

Figure **10-29**

Ventricular rate/rhythm _____ Atrial rate/rhythm _____

PR interval _____ QRS duration _____ Identification _Sinus Arrhythmia_

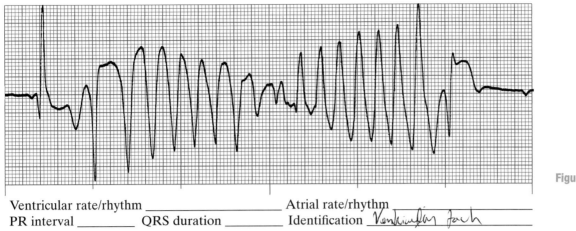

Figure **10-30**

Ventricular rate/rhythm _____ Atrial rate/rhythm _____
PR interval _____ QRS duration _____ Identification _Ventricular tach_

This ECG is from a 52-year-old man with syncope.

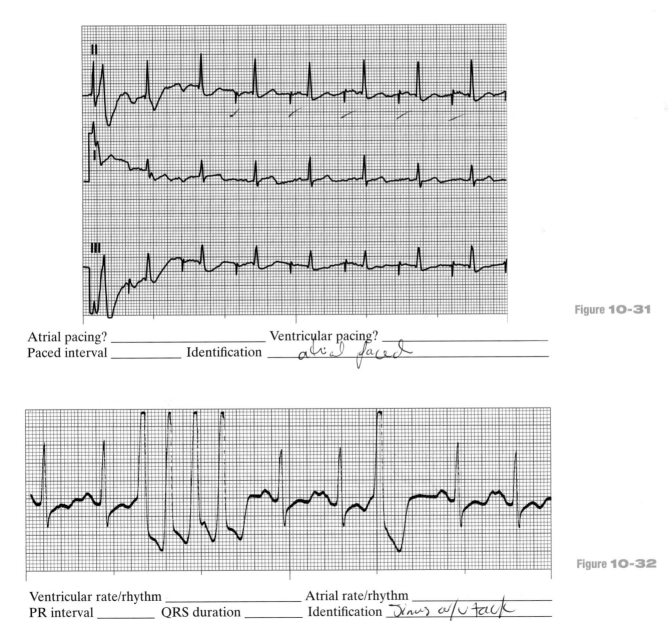

Figure **10-31**

Atrial pacing? _____ Ventricular pacing? _____
Paced interval _____ Identification _atrial paced_

Figure **10-32**

Ventricular rate/rhythm _____ Atrial rate/rhythm _____
PR interval _____ QRS duration _____ Identification _Sinus w/u tach_

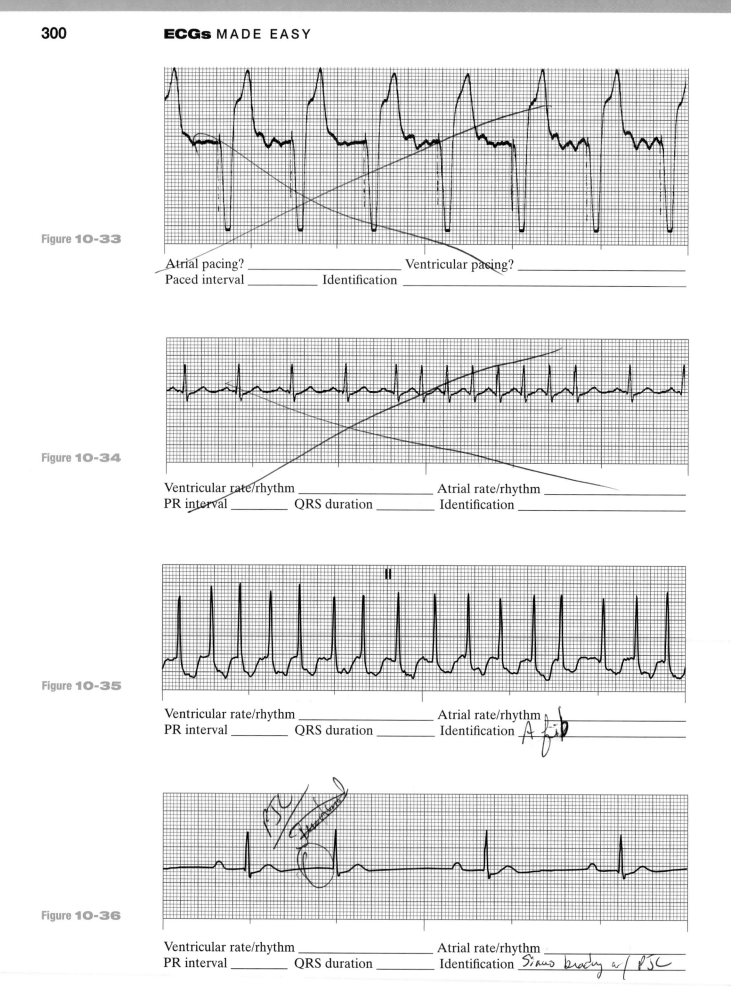

Figure 10-33

Atrial pacing? _____ Ventricular pacing? _____

Paced interval _____ Identification _____

Figure 10-34

Ventricular rate/rhythm _____ Atrial rate/rhythm _____

PR interval _____ QRS duration _____ Identification _____

Figure 10-35

Ventricular rate/rhythm _____ Atrial rate/rhythm _____

PR interval _____ QRS duration _____ Identification A fib

Figure 10-36

Ventricular rate/rhythm _____ Atrial rate/rhythm _____

PR interval _____ QRS duration _____ Identification Sinus brady w/ PJC

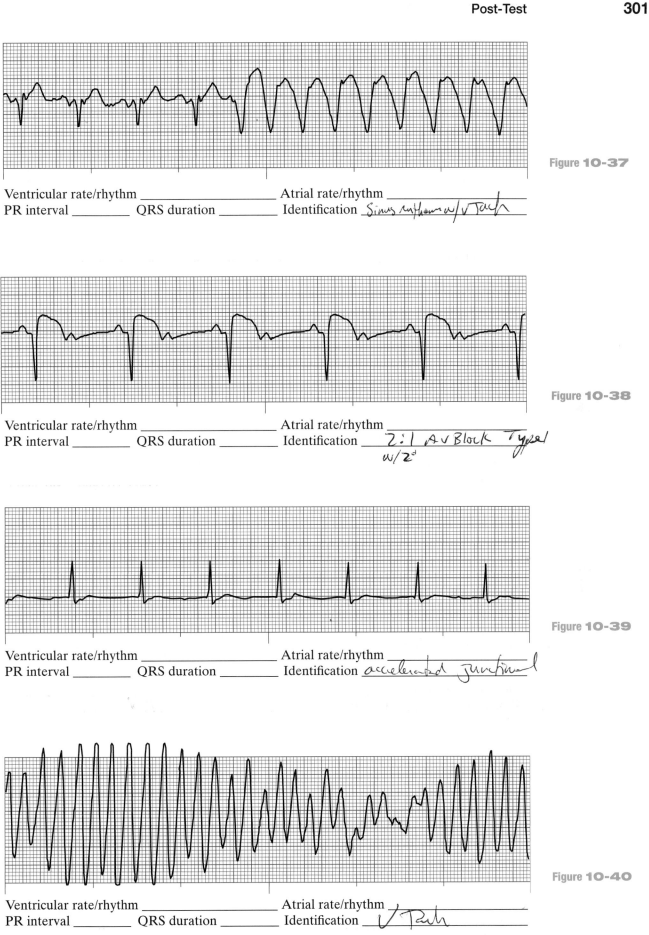

Figure **10-37**

Ventricular rate/rhythm _____ Atrial rate/rhythm _____
PR interval _____ QRS duration _____ Identification _Sinus rhythm w/ vTach_

Figure **10-38**

Ventricular rate/rhythm _____ Atrial rate/rhythm _____
PR interval _____ QRS duration _____ Identification _2:1 AV Block Type I w/2°_

Figure **10-39**

Ventricular rate/rhythm _____ Atrial rate/rhythm _accelerated junctional_
PR interval _____ QRS duration _____ Identification _accelerated junctional_

Figure **10-40**

Ventricular rate/rhythm _____ Atrial rate/rhythm _____
PR interval _____ QRS duration _____ Identification _VTach_

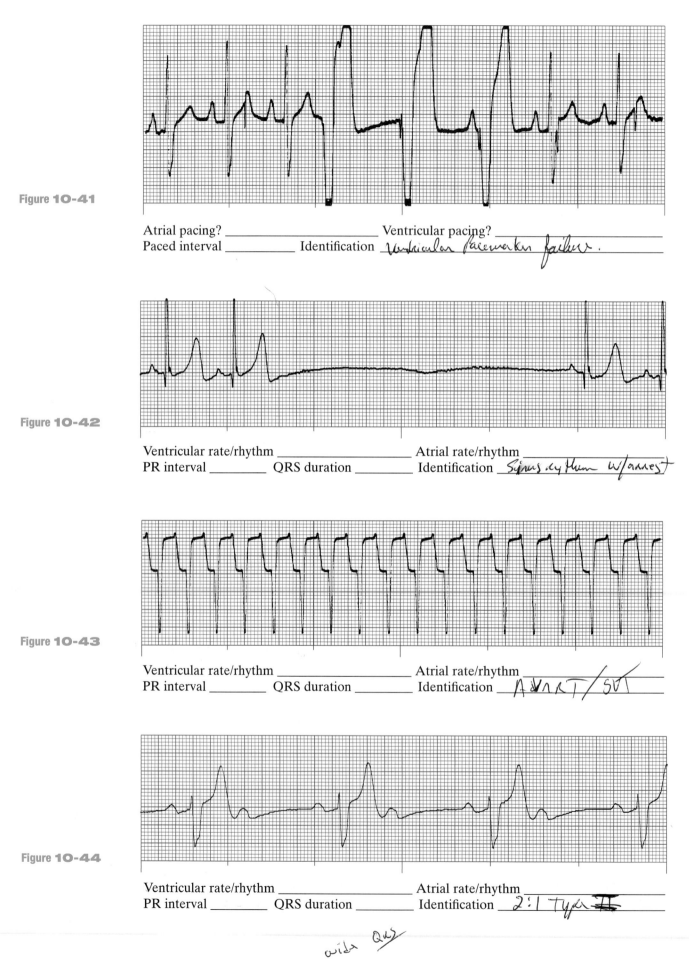

Figure **10-41**

Atrial pacing? _____ Ventricular pacing? _____
Paced interval _____ Identification _Ventricular Pacemaker failure._

Figure **10-42**

Ventricular rate/rhythm _____ Atrial rate/rhythm _____
PR interval _____ QRS duration _____ Identification _Sinus rhythm w/arrest_

Figure **10-43**

Ventricular rate/rhythm _____ Atrial rate/rhythm _____
PR interval _____ QRS duration _____ Identification _AVNRT / SVT_

Figure **10-44**

Ventricular rate/rhythm _____ Atrial rate/rhythm _____
PR interval _____ QRS duration _____ Identification _2:1 Type II_

wide QRS

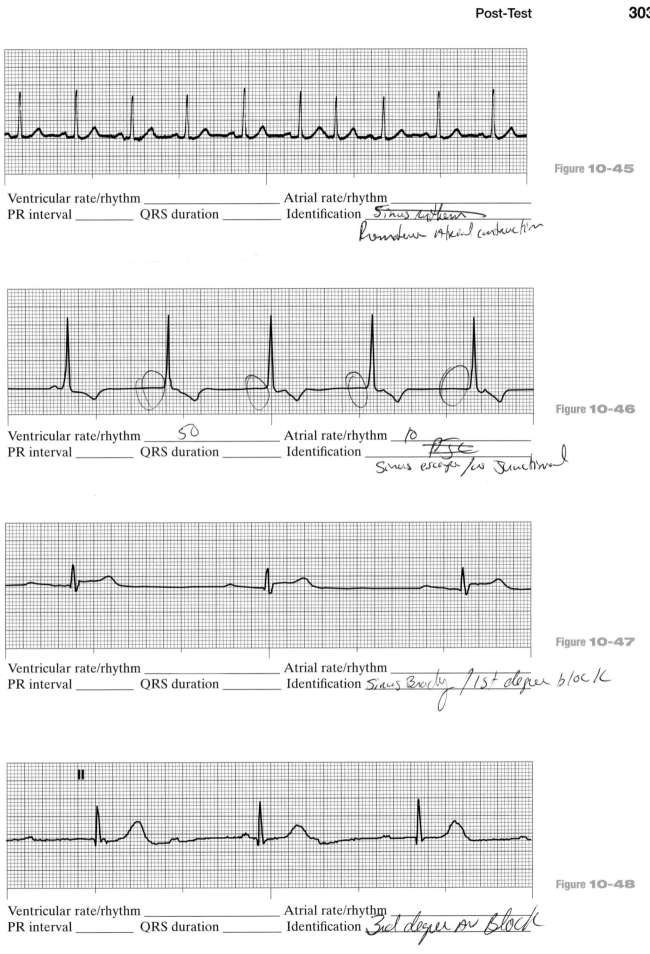

Figure 10-45

Ventricular rate/rhythm _____ Atrial rate/rhythm _____
PR interval _____ QRS duration _____ Identification *Sinus rythem*
Premature atrial contraction

Figure 10-46

Ventricular rate/rhythm *50* Atrial rate/rhythm *10*
PR interval _____ QRS duration _____ Identification *PJC*
Sinus escape /w Junctional

Figure 10-47

Ventricular rate/rhythm _____ Atrial rate/rhythm _____
PR interval _____ QRS duration _____ Identification *Sinus Brady / 1st degree block*

Figure 10-48

Ventricular rate/rhythm _____ Atrial rate/rhythm _____
PR interval _____ QRS duration _____ Identification *3rd degree AV Block*

This ECG is from a 76-year-old woman complaining of back pain. Her medical history includes a myocardial infarction 2 years ago.

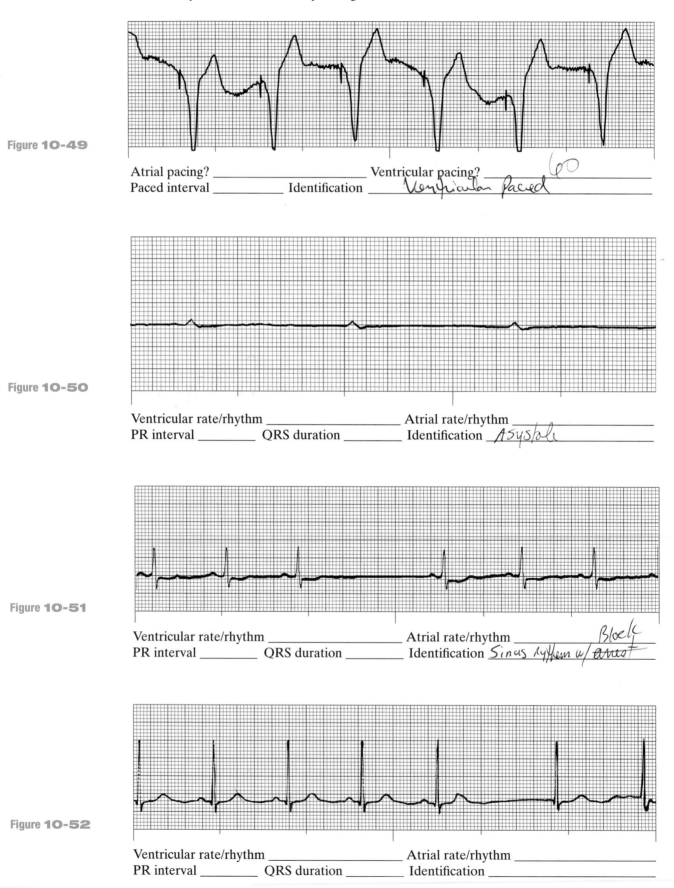

Figure 10-49

Atrial pacing? _____ Ventricular pacing? _____ 60
Paced interval _____ Identification ___Ventricular Paced___

Figure 10-50

Ventricular rate/rhythm _____ Atrial rate/rhythm _____
PR interval _____ QRS duration _____ Identification _Asystole_

Figure 10-51

Ventricular rate/rhythm _____ Atrial rate/rhythm _____ Block
PR interval _____ QRS duration _____ Identification _Sinus rhythm w/ arrest_

Figure 10-52

Ventricular rate/rhythm _____ Atrial rate/rhythm _____
PR interval _____ QRS duration _____ Identification _____

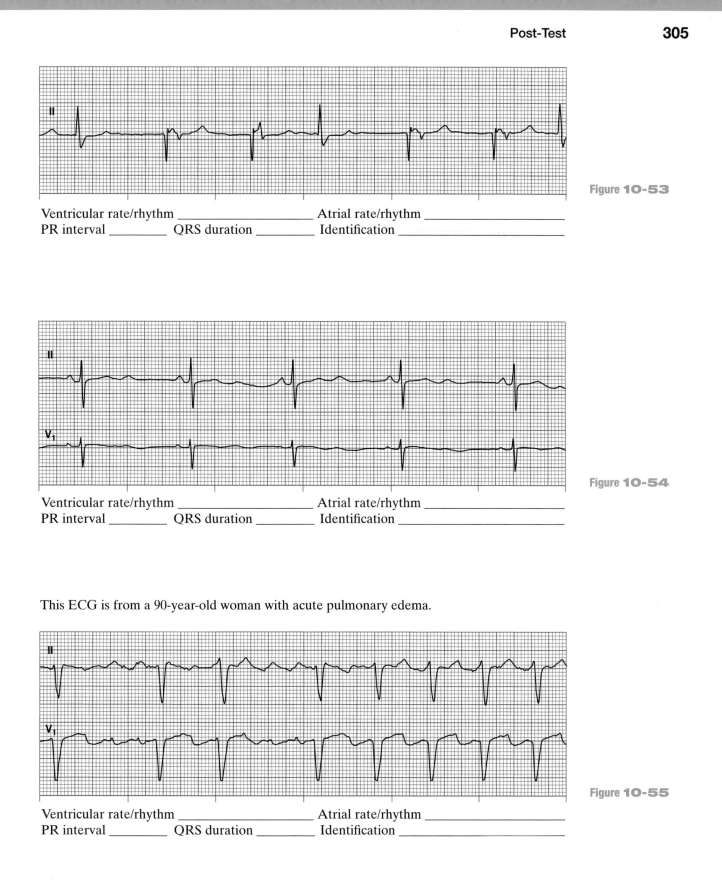

Figure 10-53

Ventricular rate/rhythm _____ Atrial rate/rhythm _____
PR interval _____ QRS duration _____ Identification _____

Figure 10-54

Ventricular rate/rhythm _____ Atrial rate/rhythm _____
PR interval _____ QRS duration _____ Identification _____

This ECG is from a 90-year-old woman with acute pulmonary edema.

Figure 10-55

Ventricular rate/rhythm _____ Atrial rate/rhythm _____
PR interval _____ QRS duration _____ Identification _____

This ECG is from a 26-year-old man with end-stage cardiomyopathy. His condition was apparently the result of chronic methamphetamine use.

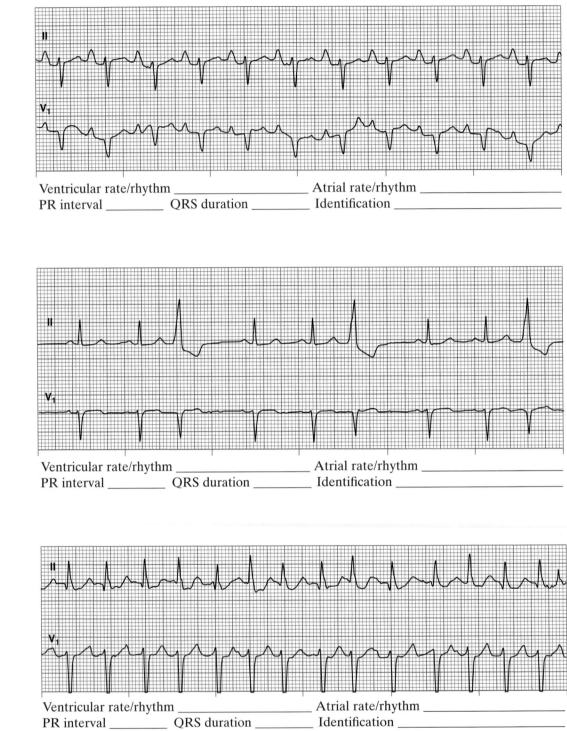

Figure 10-56

Ventricular rate/rhythm _____ Atrial rate/rhythm _____
PR interval _____ QRS duration _____ Identification _____

Figure 10-57

Ventricular rate/rhythm _____ Atrial rate/rhythm _____
PR interval _____ QRS duration _____ Identification _____

Figure 10-58

Ventricular rate/rhythm _____ Atrial rate/rhythm _____
PR interval _____ QRS duration _____ Identification _____

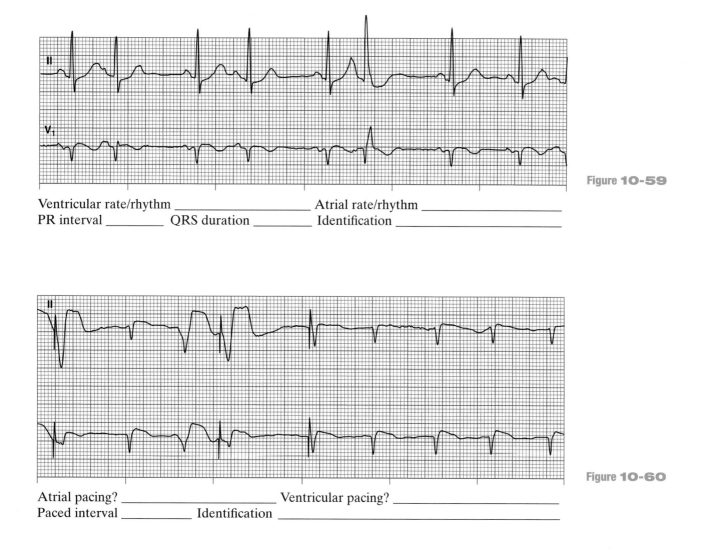

Figure 10-59

Ventricular rate/rhythm _____ Atrial rate/rhythm _____
PR interval _____ QRS duration _____ Identification _____

Figure 10-60

Atrial pacing? _____ Ventricular pacing? _____
Paced interval _____ Identification _____

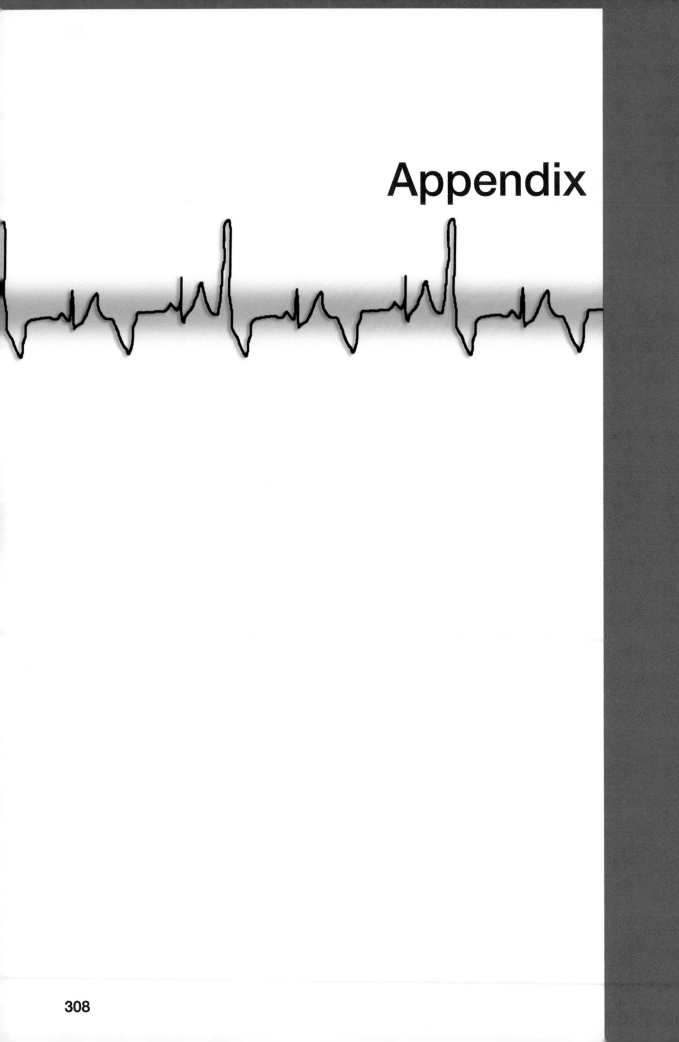

Appendix

CHAPTER 1 STOP & REVIEW ANSWERS

MULTIPLE CHOICE

1. B
2. A
3. D

COMPLETION

4. The <u>atria</u> are the heart chambers that receive blood.
5. The <u>ventricles</u> are the heart chambers that pump blood.
6. The thick, muscular middle layer of the heart wall that contains the atrial and ventricular muscle fibers necessary for contraction is the <u>myocardium</u>.

SHORT ANSWER

7. Sympathetic (adrenergic) receptor sites are divided into alpha, beta, and dopaminergic receptors.
8. The right atrium receives deoxygenated blood from the superior vena cava (which carries blood from the head and upper extremities), the inferior vena cava (which carries blood from the lower body), and the coronary sinus (which receives blood from the intracardiac circulation). Blood passes through the tricuspid valve to the right ventricle.
9. At the end of ventricular diastole, both atria simultaneously contract to eject 10% to 30% more blood into the ventricles.

MATCHING

10. O
11. H
12. I
13. P
14. L
15. A
16. N
17. M
18. J

19. F
20. C
21. D
22. G
23. B
24. E
25. K

26. Labeling exercise

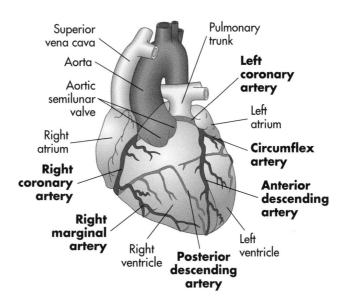

ECG Crossword Chapter 1 Solution

CHAPTER 2 STOP & REVIEW ANSWERS

MULTIPLE CHOICE

1. B
2. D
3. B

COMPLETION

4. The appearance of coved ("frowny face") ST-segment elevation is called an <u>acute injury pattern</u>.
5. A line between waveforms is called a <u>segment</u>.
6. <u>Reentry</u> is the spread of an impulse through tissue already stimulated by that same impulse.

SHORT ANSWER

7. SA node: <u>60-100 beats per minute (bpm)</u>
   AV junction: <u>40-60 bpm</u>
   Ventricles: <u>20-40 bpm</u>
8. The four properties of cardiac cells are (1) automaticity, (2) excitability (or irritability), (3) conductivity, and (4) contractility.
9. ECG monitoring may be used to (1) monitor a patient's heart rate, (2) evaluate the effects of disease or injury on heart function, (3) evaluate pacemaker function, (4) evaluate the response to medications (e.g., antiarrhythmics), and (5) obtain a baseline recording before, during, and after a medical procedure.
10.

Lead	Positive Electrode	Negative Electrode	Heart Surface Viewed
Lead I	Left arm	Right arm	Lateral
Lead II	Left leg	Right arm	Inferior
Lead III	Left leg	Left arm	Inferior

11. Artifact may be due to loose electrodes, broken wires or ECG cables, muscle tremor, patient movement, external chest compressions, or 60-cycle interference.
12. 1. Assess the rate.
    2. Assess rhythm/regularity.
    3. Identify and examine P waves.
    4. Assess intervals; evaluate conduction (PR interval, QRS duration, QT interval).
    5. Evaluate the overall appearance of the rhythm (ST-segments, T waves).
    6. Interpret the rhythm and evaluate its clinical significance.

MATCHING

13. I	22. G
14. Q	23. A
15. N	24. B
16. O	25. F
17. J	26. M
18. E	27. C
19. L	28. D
20. P	29. K
21. R	30. H

ECG Crossword Chapter 2 Solution

Practice Rhythm Strips

Note: WNL, within normal limits; UTD, unable to determine (strips shown for labeling).

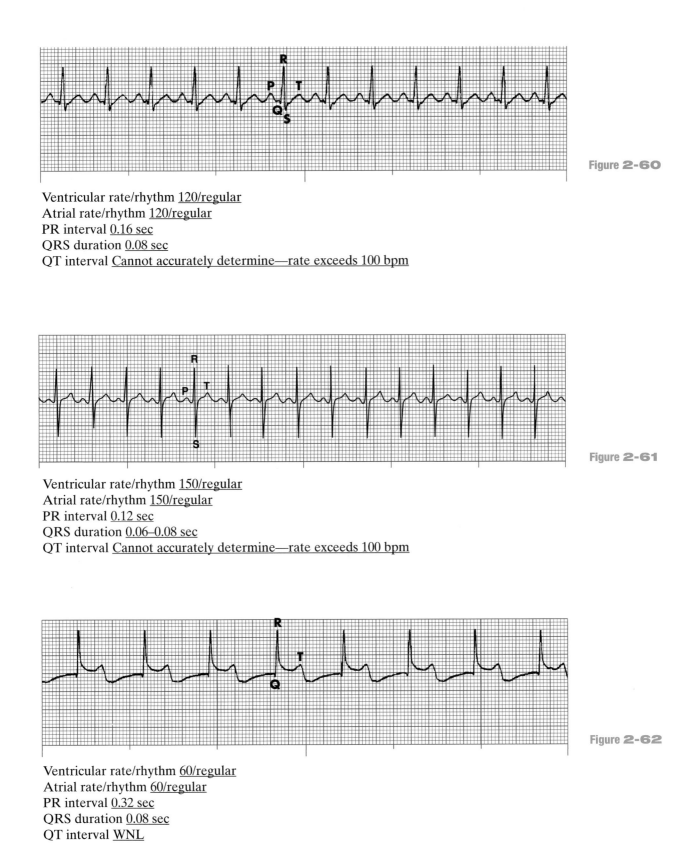

Figure **2-60**

Ventricular rate/rhythm 120/regular
Atrial rate/rhythm 120/regular
PR interval 0.16 sec
QRS duration 0.08 sec
QT interval Cannot accurately determine—rate exceeds 100 bpm

Figure **2-61**

Ventricular rate/rhythm 150/regular
Atrial rate/rhythm 150/regular
PR interval 0.12 sec
QRS duration 0.06–0.08 sec
QT interval Cannot accurately determine—rate exceeds 100 bpm

Figure **2-62**

Ventricular rate/rhythm 60/regular
Atrial rate/rhythm 60/regular
PR interval 0.32 sec
QRS duration 0.08 sec
QT interval WNL

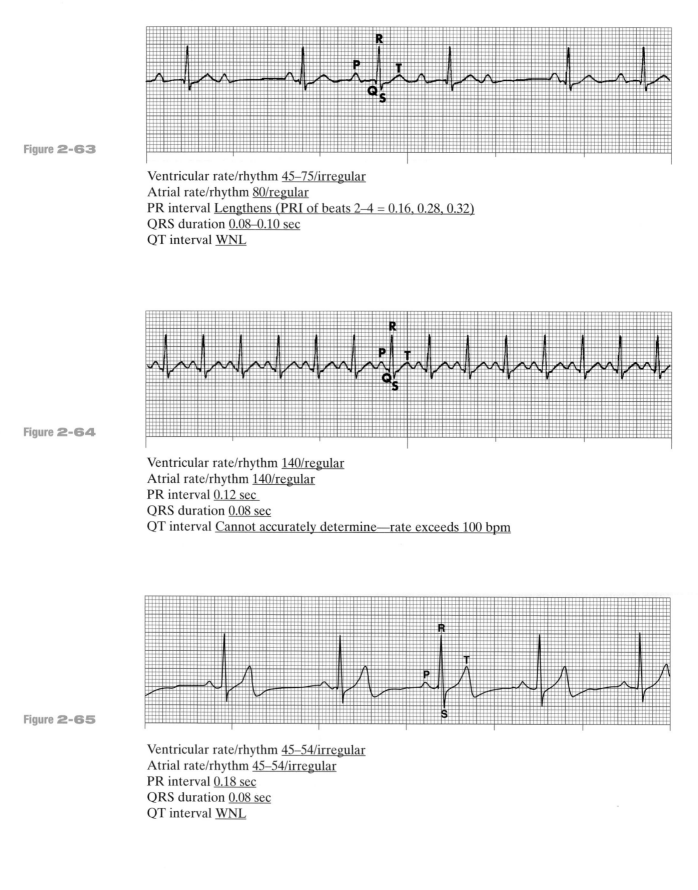

Figure **2-63**

Ventricular rate/rhythm <u>45–75/irregular</u>
Atrial rate/rhythm <u>80/regular</u>
PR interval <u>Lengthens (PRI of beats 2–4 = 0.16, 0.28, 0.32)</u>
QRS duration <u>0.08–0.10 sec</u>
QT interval <u>WNL</u>

Figure **2-64**

Ventricular rate/rhythm <u>140/regular</u>
Atrial rate/rhythm <u>140/regular</u>
PR interval <u>0.12 sec</u>
QRS duration <u>0.08 sec</u>
QT interval <u>Cannot accurately determine—rate exceeds 100 bpm</u>

Figure **2-65**

Ventricular rate/rhythm <u>45–54/irregular</u>
Atrial rate/rhythm <u>45–54/irregular</u>
PR interval <u>0.18 sec</u>
QRS duration <u>0.08 sec</u>
QT interval <u>WNL</u>

CHAPTER 3 STOP & REVIEW ANSWERS

MULTIPLE CHOICE

1. B
2. D

MATCHING

3. J	11. C
4. K	12. D
5. F	13. E
6. M	14. L
7. I	15. A
8. O	16. B
9. P	17. H
10. N	18. G

SHORT ANSWER

19.
Rate	60–100 bpm
Rhythm	Regular
P waves	Uniform in appearance, positive (upright) in lead II, one precedes each QRS complex
PR interval	0.12–0.20 sec and constant from beat to beat
QRS duration	0.10 sec or less

20. A sinus rhythm has a rate of 60 to 100 bpm. A sinus bradycardia has a rate of < 60 bpm.
21. A sinus rhythm has a rate of 60 to 100 bpm. A sinus tachycardia has a rate of 101 to 180 bpm.
22. A sinus rhythm has a regular atrial and ventricular rhythm. A sinus arrhythmia occurs when the SA node fires irregularly, resulting in an irregular atrial and ventricular rhythm.
23. Signs and symptoms of hemodynamic compromise
    - Changes in mental status (restlessness, confusion, possible loss of consciousness)
    - Low blood pressure
    - Chest pain
    - Shortness of breath
    - Signs of shock
    - Congestive heart failure
    - Pulmonary congestion
    - Fall in urine output
    - Cold, clammy skin

24. Causes of sinus tachycardia
    - Exercise
    - Fever
    - Pain
    - Fear and anxiety
    - Hypoxia
    - Congestive heart failure
    - Acute myocardial infarction
    - Infection
    - Sympathetic stimulation
    - Shock
    - Dehydration, hypovolemia
    - Pulmonary embolism
    - Hyperthyroidism
    - Medications such as epinephrine, atropine, dopamine, and dobutamine
    - Caffeine-containing beverages
    - Nicotine
    - Drugs such as cocaine and amphetamines

ECG Crossword Chapter 3 Solution

Practice Rhythm Strips

Figure 3-7

Ventricular rate/rhythm	71 bpm, regular
Atrial rate/rhythm	71 bpm, regular
PRI:	0.12 sec
QRS:	0.08 sec
Identification:	Sinus rhythm at 71 bpm

Figure 3-8

Ventricular rate/rhythm	85 bpm, regular
Atrial rate/rhythm	85 bpm, regular
PRI:	0.16 sec
QRS:	0.08 sec
Identification:	Sinus rhythm at 85 bpm

Figure 3-9

Ventricular rate/rhythm	95 bpm, regular
Atrial rate/rhythm	95 bpm, regular
PRI:	0.16 sec
QRS:	0.08 sec
Identification:	Sinus rhythm at 95 bpm

Figure 3-10

Ventricular rate/rhythm	44 bpm, regular
Atrial rate/rhythm	44 bpm, regular
PRI:	0.16 sec
QRS:	0.06 sec
Identification:	Sinus bradycardia at 44 bpm, ST-segment depression Note the upright U waves following each T wave

Figure 3-11

Ventricular rate/rhythm	94 bpm, regular
Atrial rate/rhythm	94 bpm, regular
PRI:	0.18 sec
QRS:	0.12 sec
Identification:	Sinus rhythm at 94 bpm with a wide (and notched) QRS, ST-segment depression

Figure 3-12

Ventricular rate/rhythm	60 bpm, regular
Atrial rate/rhythm	60 bpm, regular
PRI:	0.20 sec
QRS:	0.06 sec
Identification:	Sinus rhythm at 60 bpm

Figure 3-13

Ventricular rate/rhythm	71 bpm, regular
Atrial rate/rhythm	71 bpm, regular
PRI:	0.16-0.20 sec
QRS:	0.12-0.14 sec
Identification:	Sinus rhythm at 71 bpm with a wide QRS, ST-segment depression

Figure 3-14

Ventricular rate/rhythm	75 bpm, regular
Atrial rate/rhythm	75 bpm, regular
PRI:	0.14 sec
QRS:	0.08 sec
Identification:	Sinus rhythm at 75 bpm, ST-segment depression

Figure 3-15

Ventricular rate/rhythm	130 bpm, regular
Atrial rate/rhythm	130 bpm, regular
PRI:	0.16 sec
QRS:	0.12 sec
Identification:	Sinus tachycardia at 130 bpm with a wide-QRS and ST-segment depression

Figure 3-16

Ventricular rate/rhythm	67-83 bpm, irregular
Atrial rate/rhythm	67-83 bpm, irregular
PRI:	0.16 sec
QRS:	0.06-0.08 sec
Identification:	Sinus arrhythmia at 67-83 bpm

Figure 3-17

Ventricular rate/rhythm	65 bpm, regular
Atrial rate/rhythm	65 bpm, regular
PRI:	0.20 sec
QRS:	0.10 sec
Identification:	Sinus rhythm at 65 bpm with ST-segment depression

Figure 3-18

Ventricular rate/rhythm	64-94 bpm, irregular
Atrial rate/rhythm	64-94 bpm, irregular
PRI:	0.16 sec
QRS:	0.06-0.08 sec
Identification:	Sinus arrhythmia at 64-94 bpm

Figure 3-19

Ventricular rate/rhythm	0-75 bpm, irregular
Atrial rate/rhythm	0-75 bpm, irregular
PRI:	0.16 sec
QRS:	0.08 sec
Identification:	Sinus rhythm at 0-75 bpm with an episode of sinus arrest; tall T waves

Figure 3-20

Ventricular rate/rhythm	167 bpm, regular
Atrial rate/rhythm	167 bpm, regular
PRI:	0.12 sec
QRS:	0.06 sec
Identification:	Sinus tachycardia at 167 bpm

CHAPTER 4 STOP & REVIEW ANSWERS

TRUE/FALSE

1. T
2. F
3. F

MATCHING

4. G	12. A
5. L	13. E
6. O	14. K
7. F	15. D
8. M	16. I
9. J	17. B
10. N	18. C
11. H	

SHORT ANSWER

19. Tachycardias may cause syncope because the rapid ventricular rate decreases cardiac output and blood flow to the brain. Syncope is most likely to occur just after the onset of a rapid atrial tachycardia or when the rhythm stops abruptly.
20. AV nodal reentrant tachycardia (AVNRT) is the most common type of SVT.
21. The term "paroxysmal" is used to describe a rhythm that starts or ends suddenly. Some physicians use this term to describe the sudden onset or end of a patient's symptoms.
22. • Short PR interval
    • Delta wave
    • Widening of the QRS
23. Different types of dysrhythmias occur in WPW syndrome. The most common is AVRT, followed by atrial fibrillation and atrial flutter.
24. There are two types (subclasses) of AVRT: orthodromic (narrow QRS) AVRT and antidromic (wide QRS) AVRT.
25. Because the atria do not contract effectively and expel all of the blood within them, blood may pool within the atria and form clots. A clot may dislodge on its own or because of conversion to a sinus rhythm. A stroke can result if a clot moves from the atria and lodges in an artery in the brain.

ECG Crossword Chapter 4 Solution

Practice Rhythm Strips

Figure 4-23

Ventricular rate/rhythm	188 bpm, regular
Atrial rate/rhythm	Unable to determine
PRI:	Unable to determine
QRS:	0.06 sec
Identification:	Narrow-QRS tachycardia (AVNRT) with ST-segment depression

Figure 4-24

Ventricular rate/rhythm	83 bpm (sinus beats), regular except for events
Atrial rate/rhythm	83 bpm (sinus beats), regular except for events
PRI:	0.16 sec
QRS:	0.04-0.08 sec
Identification:	Sinus rhythm at 83 bpm with frequent PACs (atrial bigeminy), ST-segment depression, inverted T waves (beats 3, 5, 7, and 9 are PACs)

Figure 4-25

Ventricular rate/rhythm	98 bpm, regular
Atrial rate/rhythm	98 bpm, regular
PRI:	0.16 sec
QRS:	0.04-0.06 sec
Identification:	Sinus rhythm at 98 bpm; ST-segment elevation

Figure 4-26

Ventricular rate/rhythm	88-130 bpm, irregular
Atrial rate/rhythm	Unable to determine
PRI:	Unable to determine
QRS:	0.08 sec
Identification:	Atrial fibrillation at 88-130 bpm

Figure 4-27

Ventricular rate/rhythm	93 bpm, regular except for the event
Atrial rate/rhythm	93 bpm, regular except for the event
PRI:	0.16 sec
QRS:	0.04 sec
Identification:	Sinus rhythm at 93 bpm with a PAC (PAC is the seventh complex from the left)

Figure 4-28

Ventricular rate/rhythm	111 bpm, regular except for event
Atrial rate/rhythm	111 bpm, regular except for event
PRI:	0.18 sec
QRS:	0.08 sec
Identification:	Sinus tachycardia at 111 bpm with a nonconducted PAC

Figure 4-29

Ventricular rate/rhythm	75-107 bpm, irregular
Atrial rate/rhythm	Unable to determine
PRI:	Unable to determine
QRS:	0.08 sec
Identification:	Atrial flutter at 75-107 bpm

Figure 4-30

Ventricular rate/rhythm	115 bpm, regular except for events
Atrial rate/rhythm	115 bpm, regular except for events
PRI:	0.12 sec (sinus beats)
QRS:	0.08 sec (sinus beats)
Identification:	Sinus tachycardia at 115 bpm with PACs and ST-segment elevation

Figure 4-31

Ventricular rate/rhythm	180 bpm, regular
Atrial rate/rhythm	Unable to determine
PRI:	Unable to determine
QRS:	0.04 sec
Identification:	AVNRT at 180 bpm, ST-segment elevation

Figure 4-32

Ventricular rate/rhythm	75 bpm, regular except for event
Atrial rate/rhythm	75 bpm, regular except for event
PRI:	0.20 sec
QRS:	0.12 sec
Identification:	Sinus rhythm at 75 bpm with a wide QRS and a nonconducted PAC

Figure 4-33

Ventricular rate/rhythm	88 bpm, regular
Atrial rate/rhythm	Unable to determine
PRI:	Unable to determine
QRS:	0.06 sec
Identification:	Atrial flutter at 88 bpm with ST-segment depression

Figure 4-34

Ventricular rate/rhythm	70 bpm, regular
Atrial rate/rhythm	70 bpm (sinus beats), Unable to determine
PRI:	Varies
QRS:	Varies
Identification:	Underlying rhythm is sinus but pacemaker site varies; ventricular rate approximately 70 bpm; patient with known WPW; note delta waves

Figure 4-35

Ventricular rate/rhythm	55-94 bpm, irregular
Atrial rate/rhythm	Unable to determine
PRI:	Unable to determine
QRS:	0.10 sec
Identification:	Controlled atrial fibrillation at 55-94 bpm

Figure 4-36

Ventricular rate/rhythm	29 bpm, regular
Atrial rate/rhythm	Unable to determine
PRI:	Unable to determine
QRS:	0.10 sec
Identification:	Controlled atrial fibrillation at 29 bpm; this patient was diagnosed with digitalis toxicity

Figure 4-37

Ventricular rate/rhythm	186 bpm, regular
Atrial rate/rhythm	Unable to determine
PRI:	Unable to determine
QRS:	0.06 sec
Identification:	AVNRT at 186 bpm with ST-segment depression

Figure 4-38

Ventricular rate/rhythm	170 bpm, regular
Atrial rate/rhythm	170 bpm, regular
PRI:	0.08 sec
QRS:	0.06 sec
Identification:	Atrial tachycardia at 170 bpm

Figure 4-39

Ventricular rate/rhythm	78 bpm, regular except for the event
Atrial rate/rhythm	78 bpm, regular except for the event
PRI:	0.16 sec
QRS:	0.06 sec
Identification:	Sinus rhythm at 78 bpm with a PAC, ST-segment elevation (PAC is the third complex from left)

CHAPTER 5 STOP & REVIEW ANSWERS

TRUE/FALSE

1. F
2. F
3. F

COMPLETION

4. If the AV junction paces the heart, the electrical impulse must travel in a backward direction to activate the atria. This is called <u>retrograde</u> conduction.
5. A beat originating from the AV junction that appears later than the next expected sinus beat is called a <u>junctional</u> <u>escape</u> <u>beat</u>.

MATCHING

6. H	11. E
7. I	12. A
8. G	13. F
9. D	14. I
10. B	15. C

SHORT ANSWER

16.
1.	Junctional bradycardia	Less than 40 bpm
2.	Junctional tachycardia	101-180 bpm
3.	Accelerated junctional rhythm	61-100 bpm
4.	Junctional rhythm	40-60 bpm

17. The AV junction may assume responsibility for pacing the heart if:
   * The SA node fails to discharge (such as sinus arrest)
   * An impulse from the SA node is generated but blocked as it exits the SA node (such as SA block)
   * The rate of discharge of the SA node is slower than that of the AV junction (such as a sinus bradycardia or the slower phase of a sinus arrhythmia)
   * An impulse from the SA node is generated and is conducted through the atria but is not conducted to the ventricles (such as an AV block)

ECG Crossword Chapter 5 Solution

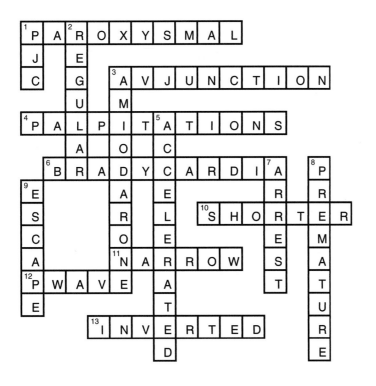

Practice Rhythm Strips

Figure 5-9

Ventricular rate/rhythm	75 bpm, regular
Atrial rate/rhythm	None
PRI:	None
QRS:	0.08 sec
Identification:	Accelerated junctional rhythm at 75 bpm; ST-segment depression

Figure 5-10

Ventricular rate/rhythm	45 bpm, regular
Atrial rate/rhythm	None
PRI:	None
QRS:	0.08 sec
Identification:	Junctional rhythm at 45 bpm; ST-segment elevation

Figure 5-11

Ventricular rate/rhythm	75 bpm, regular
Atrial rate/rhythm	75 bpm, regular
PRI:	0.16 sec
QRS:	0.08 sec
Identification:	Accelerated junctional rhythm at 75 bpm

Figure 5-12

Ventricular rate/rhythm	70 bpm, regular except for the event
Atrial rate/rhythm	70 bpm, regular except for the event
PRI:	0.16 sec
QRS:	0.08 sec
Identification:	Sinus rhythm at 70 bpm with a nonconducted PAC (note distortion of the T wave of the beat preceding the pause) and a junctional escape beat

Figure 5-13

Ventricular rate/rhythm	115 bpm (sinus beats), regular except for the event
Atrial rate/rhythm	115 bpm (sinus beats), regular except for the event
PRI:	0.16 sec (sinus beats)
QRS:	0.06 sec (sinus beats)
Identification:	Sinus tachycardia at 115 bpm with a PJC (fifth beat is the PJC)

Figure 5-14

Ventricular rate/rhythm	79 bpm, regular (junctional beats)
Atrial rate/rhythm	Not measurable in junctional beats
PRI:	Not measurable in junctional beats
QRS:	0.06 sec
Identification:	Sinus rhythm changing to an accelerated junctional rhythm at 79 bpm, back to a sinus rhythm

Figure 5-15

Ventricular rate/rhythm	71 bpm, regular
Atrial rate/rhythm	71 bpm, regular
PRI:	0.14 sec
QRS:	0.08 sec
Identification:	Accelerated junctional rhythm at 71 bpm; ST-segment elevation

Figure 5-16

Ventricular rate/rhythm	32 bpm, regular
Atrial rate/rhythm	None
PRI:	None
QRS:	0.06-0.08 sec
Identification:	Junctional bradycardia at 32 bpm; ST-segment depression, inverted T waves

Figure 5-17

Ventricular rate/rhythm	30 bpm (junctional beats), irregular
Atrial rate/rhythm	None (junctional beats), irregular
PRI:	0.16 sec (sinus beats); none (junctional beats)
QRS:	0.06-0.08 sec
Identification:	Sinus beat, two junctional beats, sinus beat; ST-segment depression

Figure 5-18

Ventricular rate/rhythm	138 bpm, regular
Atrial rate/rhythm	Unable to determine
PRI:	Unable to determine
QRS:	0.10 sec
Identification:	Narrow-QRS tachycardia, probably junctional tachycardia, at 138 bpm

Figure 5-19

Ventricular rate/rhythm	44 bpm, regular
Atrial rate/rhythm	44 bpm, regular
PRI:	0.14 sec
QRS:	0.08 sec
Identification:	Junctional rhythm at 44 bpm; ST-segment elevation

Figure 5-20

Ventricular rate/rhythm	52 bpm, regular
Atrial rate/rhythm	None
PRI:	None
QRS:	0.06 sec
Identification:	Sinus beat to junctional rhythm at 52 bpm; inverted T waves

Figure 5-21

Ventricular rate/rhythm	100 bpm, regular
Atrial rate/rhythm	None
PRI:	None
QRS:	0.08 sec
Identification:	Accelerated junctional rhythm at 100 bpm; inverted T waves

Figure 5-22

Ventricular rate/rhythm	63 bpm (sinus beats)/regular except for events (every third beat is a PJC)
Atrial rate/rhythm	63 bpm (sinus beats)/regular except for events (every third beat is a PJC)
PRI:	0.12-0.16 sec (sinus beats)
QRS:	0.06 sec (sinus beats)
Identification:	Sinus rhythm at 63 bpm with PJCs (junctional trigeminy)

Figure 5-23

Ventricular rate/rhythm	64 bpm (sinus beats)/regular except for the event
Atrial rate/rhythm	64 bpm (sinus beats)/regular except for the event
PRI:	0.16-0.18 sec
QRS:	0.08 sec
Identification:	Sinus rhythm at 64 bpm with an episode of sinus arrest and a junctional escape beat

CHAPTER 6 STOP & REVIEW ANSWERS

MATCHING

1. G
2. J
3. D
4. B
5. H

6. I
7. F
8. C
9. E
10. A

SHORT ANSWER

11. A PVC is premature and occurs before the next expected sinus beat. A ventricular escape beat is late, occurring after the next expected sinus beat.
12. Common causes of PVCs include normal variant, hypoxia, stress/anxiety, exercise, digitalis toxicity, acid-base imbalance, myocardial ischemia, electrolyte imbalance (hypokalemia, hypocalcemia, hypercalcemia, hypomagnesemia), congestive heart failure, increased sympathetic tone, acute myocardial infarction, stimulants (alcohol, caffeine, tobacco), and medications (sympathomimetics, cyclic antidepressants, phenothiazines).
13. Coarse ventricular fibrillation (VF) is 3 mm or more in amplitude. Fine VF is less than 3 mm in amplitude.
14. Polymorphic VT that occurs in the presence of a long QT interval is called torsades de pointes.
15. The ventricles may assume responsibility for pacing the heart if the:
    - SA node fails to discharge
    - Impulse from the SA node is generated but blocked as it exits the SA node
    - Rate of discharge of the SA node is slower than that of the ventricles
    - Irritable site in either ventricle produces an early beat or rapid rhythm
16. **PATCH-4-MD**
    - **P**ulmonary embolism
    - **A**cidosis
    - **T**ension pneumothorax
    - **C**ardiac tamponade
    - **H**ypovolemia (most common cause of PEA)
    - **H**ypoxia
    - **H**eat/cold (hypo-/hyperthermia)
    - **H**ypo-/hyperkalemia (and other electrolytes)
    - **M**yocardial infarction
    - **D**rug overdose/accidents

ECG Crossword Chapter 6 Solution

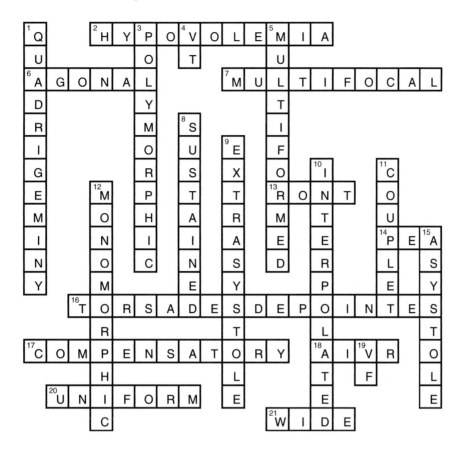

Practice Rhythm Strips

Figure 6-22
Ventricular rate/rhythm:	94 (sinus beats), irregular
Atrial rate/rhythm:	94 (sinus beats), irregular
PRI:	0.16 sec (sinus beats)
QRS:	0.08 sec (sinus beats)
Identification:	Sinus rhythm at 94 bpm with an episode of couplets and a run of VT

Figure 6-23
Ventricular rate/rhythm	150 bpm, regular
Atrial rate/rhythm	Unable to determine
PRI:	Unable to determine
QRS:	0.16 sec
Identification:	Monomorphic ventricular tachycardia at 150 bpm

Figure 6-24
Ventricular rate/rhythm	54 bpm, regular (sinus beats)
Atrial rate/rhythm	54 bpm, regular (sinus beats)
PRI:	0.12 sec (sinus beats)
QRS:	0.06-0.08 sec (sinus beats)
Identification:	Sinus bradycardia at 54 bpm with ventricular bigeminy; ventricular rate approximately 100 bpm if PVCs counted in the rate

Figure 6-25
Ventricular rate/rhythm	250-333 bpm, irregular
Atrial rate/rhythm	Unable to determine
PRI:	Unable to determine
QRS:	0.16 sec
Identification:	Polymorphic VT at 250-333 bpm

Figure 6-26
Ventricular rate/rhythm	150 bpm, essentially regular
Atrial rate/rhythm	Unable to determine
PRI:	Unable to determine
QRS:	0.12-0.16 sec
Identification:	Monomorphic VT at 150 bpm

Figure 6-27
Ventricular rate/rhythm	125 bpm, essentially regular except for events
Atrial rate/rhythm	125 bpm, essentially regular except for events
PRI:	0.12 sec (sinus beats)
QRS:	0.06 sec (sinus beats)
Identification:	Sinus tachycardia at 125 bpm with multiform PVCs

Figure 6-28
Ventricular rate/rhythm	230-300 bpm, irregular
Atrial rate/rhythm	Unable to determine
PRI:	Unable to determine
QRS:	Varies
Identification:	Polymorphic VT at 230-300 bpm

Figure 6-29
Ventricular rate/rhythm	62 bpm, essentially regular
Atrial rate/rhythm	62 bpm, essentially regular
PRI:	0.20 sec
QRS:	0.10 sec
Identification:	Sinus rhythm at 62 bpm with an interpolated PVC; inverted T waves

Figure 6-30
Ventricular rate/rhythm	71 bpm, regular
Atrial rate/rhythm	Unable to determine
PRI:	Unable to determine
QRS:	0.12 sec
Identification:	Accelerated idioventricular rhythm (AIVR) at 71 bpm; ST-segment elevation

Figure 6-31
Ventricular rate/rhythm	Unable to determine
Atrial rate/rhythm	None
PRI:	None
QRS:	None
Identification:	Coarse ventricular fibrillation

Figure 6-32
Ventricular rate/rhythm	60 bpm, regular
Atrial rate/rhythm	60 bpm, regular
PRI:	0.20 sec (sinus beats)
QRS:	0.08 sec (sinus beats)
Identification:	Sinus rhythm at 60 bpm with R-on-T interpolated PVC; tall T waves

Figure 6-33
Ventricular rate/rhythm	88 bpm (sinus beats), regular except for the events
Atrial rate/rhythm	88 bpm (sinus beats), regular except for the events
PRI:	0.20 sec (sinus beats)
QRS:	0.08 sec (sinus beats)
Identification:	Sinus rhythm at 88 bpm with a PVC and run of VT, ST-segment depression, inverted T waves

Figure 6-34

Ventricular rate/rhythm	Two ventricular complexes to none
Atrial rate/rhythm	None
PRI:	None
QRS:	0.14 sec-none
Identification:	Agonal rhythm/asystole

Figure 6-35

Ventricular rate/rhythm	None-40 bpm, irregular to regular
Atrial rate/rhythm	None
PRI:	None
QRS:	None-0.16 sec
Identification:	Ventricular fibrillation; shock (defibrillation); idioventricular rhythm at 40 bpm

Figure 6-36

Ventricular rate/rhythm	150-250 bpm, irregular
Atrial rate/rhythm	None
PRI:	None
QRS:	0.06 sec (atrial beats)
Identification:	Atrial fibrillation with a rapid ventricular response of 150-250 bpm and a run of VT

Figure 6-37

Ventricular rate/rhythm	42 bpm, regular
Atrial rate/rhythm	None
PRI:	None
QRS:	0.24 sec
Identification:	Accelerated idioventricular rhythm (AIVR) at 42 bpm

Figure 6-38

Ventricular rate/rhythm	83 bpm (sinus beats), regular except for events (PVCs)
Atrial rate/rhythm	83 bpm (sinus beats), regular except for events (PVCs)
PRI:	0.16 sec (sinus beats)
QRS:	0.08 sec (sinus beats)
Identification:	Sinus rhythm at 83 bpm with ventricular trigeminy, ST-segment depression, inverted T waves

Figure 6-39

Ventricular rate/rhythm	30 bpm (sinus beats), regular except for the events
Atrial rate/rhythm	30 bpm (sinus beats), regular except for the events
PRI:	0.12-0.16 sec (sinus beats)
QRS:	0.06 sec (sinus beats)
Identification:	Sinus bradycardia at 30 bpm with ventricular bigeminy (ventricular rate approximately 60 if PVCs counted), inverted T waves, horizontal ST-segments

CHAPTER 7 STOP & REVIEW ANSWERS

TRUE/FALSE

1. F
2. F

MATCHING

3. G		11. A	
4. L		12. F	
5. O		13. H	
6. J		14. B	
7. N		15. C	
8. I		16. E	
9. D		17. K	
10. M			

SHORT ANSWER

18.

	Second-Degree AV Block Type I	Third-Degree AV Block
Ventricular rhythm	Irregular	Regular
PR interval	Progressively lengthening	None
QRS width	Usually narrow	Narrow or wide

19.

Rate	Atrial rate is greater than the ventricular rate
Rhythm	Atrial regular (Ps plot through); ventricular irregular
P waves	Normal in size and shape; some P waves are not followed by a QRS complex (more Ps than QRSs)
PR interval	Lengthens with each cycle (although lengthening may be very slight), until a P wave appears without a QRS complex; the PR interval after the nonconducted beat is shorter than the interval preceding the nonconducted beat
QRS duration	Usually 0.10 sec or less but is periodically dropped

20. Second-degree AV block type II

ECG Crossword Chapter 7 Solution

Practice Rhythm Strips

Figure 7-10

Ventricular rate/rhythm	38 bpm, regular
Atrial rate/rhythm	68 bpm, regular
PRI:	Varies
QRS:	0.06 sec
Identification:	Third-degree AV block at 38 bpm with ST-segment depression and inverted T waves

Figure 7-11

Ventricular rate/rhythm	36 bpm, regular
Atrial rate/rhythm	72 bpm, regular
PRI:	0.20-0.22 sec
QRS:	0.06-0.08 sec
Identification:	2:1 AV block at 36 bpm, probably type I

Figure 7-12

Ventricular rate/rhythm	88 bpm, regular
Atrial rate/rhythm	88 bpm, regular
PRI:	0.28 sec
QRS:	0.08 sec
Identification:	Sinus rhythm at 88 bpm with first-degree AV block; ST-segment elevation

Figure 7-13

Ventricular rate/rhythm	<20-94 bpm, irregular
Atrial rate/rhythm	94 bpm, regular
PRI:	lengthening
QRS:	0.08 sec
Identification:	Second-degree AV block type I at <20-94 bpm (leads II and III)

Figure 7-14

Ventricular rate/rhythm	68 bpm, regular
Atrial rate/rhythm	68 bpm, regular
PRI:	0.28 sec
QRS:	0.06 sec
Identification:	Sinus rhythm with first-degree AV block at 68 bpm, ST-segment depression

Figure 7-15

Ventricular rate/rhythm	48-83 bpm, irregular
Atrial rate/rhythm	167 bpm, regular
PRI:	0.24 sec
QRS:	0.12 sec
Identification:	Second-degree AV block type II at 48-83 bpm; ST-segment depression

Figure 7-16

Ventricular rate/rhythm	34 bpm, regular
Atrial rate/rhythm	68 bpm, regular
PRI:	0.14-0.16 sec
QRS:	0.10 sec
Identification:	2:1 AV block at 34 bpm, probably type I; ST-segment depression; tall T waves

Figure 7-17

Ventricular rate/rhythm	60-98 bpm, irregular
Atrial rate/rhythm	111 bpm, regular
PRI:	Lengthens
QRS:	0.08 sec
Identification:	Second-degree AV block type I at 68-90 bpm; ST-segment depression

Figure 7-18

Ventricular rate/rhythm	40 bpm, regular
Atrial rate/rhythm	83 bpm, regular
PRI:	0.24 sec
QRS:	0.10 sec
Identification:	2:1 AV block at 40 bpm, probably type I; ST-segment depression

Figure 7-19

Ventricular rate/rhythm	50 bpm, regular
Atrial rate/rhythm	167 bpm, regular
PRI:	Varies
QRS:	0.06 sec
Identification:	Third-degree AV block at 50 bpm, ST-segment elevation

Figure 7-20

Ventricular rate/rhythm	30 bpm, regular
Atrial rate/rhythm	68 bpm, regular
PRI:	0.28 sec
QRS:	0.16 sec
Identification:	2:1 AV block, probably type II at 30 bpm; ST-segment elevation

Figure 7-21

Ventricular rate/rhythm	45 bpm, regular
Atrial rate/rhythm	115 bpm, regular
PRI:	Varies
QRS:	0.16 sec
Identification:	Third-degree AV block at 45 bpm

Figure **7-22**

Ventricular rate/rhythm	50-94 bpm, irregular
Atrial rate/rhythm	94 bpm, regular
PRI:	Lengthens
QRS:	0.10 sec
Identification:	Second-degree AV block type I at 50-94 bpm, ST-segment elevation

Figure **7-23**

Ventricular rate/rhythm	<20-60 bpm, irregular
Atrial rate/rhythm	60 bpm, regular
PRI:	0.16 sec
QRS:	0.12 sec
Identification:	Second-degree AV block type II at <20-60 bpm, ST-segment depression

Figure **7-24**

Ventricular rate/rhythm	36 bpm, regular
Atrial rate/rhythm	72 bpm, regular
PRI:	0.32 sec
QRS:	0.10 sec
Identification:	2:1 AV block, probably type 1 at 36 bpm

Figure **7-25**

Ventricular rate/rhythm	107 bpm, regular
Atrial rate/rhythm	107 bpm, regular
PRI:	0.24 sec
QRS:	0.08 sec
Identification:	Sinus tachycardia at 107 bpm with first-degree AV block

CHAPTER 8 STOP & REVIEW ANSWERS

MATCHING

1. J
2. F
3. B
4. H
5. E
6. L
7. O
8. N

9. A
10. K
11. G
12. I
13. D
14. C
15. M

ECG Crossword Chapter 8 Solution

Practice Rhythm Strips

Figure 8-11

Atrial pacing?	No
Ventricular pacing?	Yes
Paced interval:	79
Identification:	100% ventricular-paced rhythm

Figure 8-12

Atrial pacing?	Yes
Ventricular pacing?	Yes
Paced interval:	71
Identification:	100% paced rhythm—AV sequential pacemaker

Figure 8-13

Atrial paced activity?	No
Ventricular paced activity?	Yes
Paced interval rate?	68
Identification:	Ventricular-demand pacemaker

Figure 8-14

Atrial pacing?	Yes
Ventricular pacing?	No
Paced interval:	79
Identification:	Atrial pacemaker

Figure 8-15

Atrial paced activity?	Yes
Ventricular paced activity?	Yes
Paced interval rate?	83
Identification:	100% paced rhythm—AV sequential pacemaker

Figure 8-16

Atrial pacing?	No
Ventricular pacing?	Yes
Paced interval:	80
Identification:	Ventricular-paced rhythm with failure to capture

Figure 8-17

Atrial pacing?	No
Ventricular pacing?	Yes
Paced interval:	71
Identification:	Pacemaker malfunction (failure to sense); underlying rhythm is a sinus rhythm at 88 bpm with a PVC; note the pacer spikes in the T waves of the sec and eighth beats from the left

Figure 8-18

Atrial paced activity?	Yes
Ventricular paced activity?	Yes
Paced interval rate?	79
Identification:	100% paced rhythm—AV sequential pacemaker

Figure 8-19

Atrial pacing?	No
Ventricular pacing?	Yes
Paced interval:	72
Identification:	Malfunctioning ventricular-demand pacemaker—failure to capture; underlying rhythm appears to be atrial flutter

Figure 8-20

Atrial pacing?	No
Ventricular pacing?	Yes
Paced interval:	74
Identification:	100% ventricular-paced rhythm

Figure 8-21

Atrial pacing?	No
Ventricular pacing?	Yes
Paced interval:	71
Identification:	100% ventricular-paced rhythm; underlying rhythm is a complete AV block

Figure 8-22

Atrial pacing?	No
Ventricular pacing?	Yes
Paced interval:	71
Identification:	Normal pacemaker function—ventricular-demand pacer

CHAPTER 9 STOP & REVIEW ANSWERS

TRUE/FALSE

1. T
2. F

COMPLETION

3. Each electrode placed on the chest in a "V" position is a <u>positive</u> electrode.
4. 0.12 sec = <u>120</u> milliseconds

MATCHING

5. P	15. I
6. N	16. R
7. H	17. Q
8. A	18. T
9. K	19. G
10. D	20. B
11. O	21. J
12. M	22. L
13. F	23. C
14. S	24. E

SHORT ANSWER

25. The axes of leads I, II, and III form an equilateral triangle with the heart at the center (Einthoven's triangle). If the augmented limb leads are added to this configuration and the axes of the six leads moved in a way in which they bisect each other, the result is the <u>hexaxial</u> <u>reference</u> <u>system</u>.
26. The area supplied by an obstructed coronary artery goes through a characteristic sequence of events that have been identified as zones of <u>ischemia</u>, <u>injury</u>, and <u>infarction</u>.
27. <u>Lead   Heart Surface Viewed</u>

Lead	Heart Surface Viewed
V_1	Septum
V_2	Septum
V_3	Anterior
V_4	Anterior
V_5	Lateral
V_6	Lateral

28. The chest leads are also known as precordial or V leads.
29.

Axis	Normal	Left	Right	Indeterminate ("No Man's Land")
Lead I QRS Direction	Positive	Positive	Negative	Negative
Lead aVF QRS Direction	Positive	Negative	Positive	Negative

30. ACS include unstable angina, non–ST-segment elevation myocardial infarction (MI), and ST-segment elevation MI.
31. The processes of ischemia, injury, and infarction are called "the three I's" of an acute coronary event.
32. ST-segment elevation may be present in ventricular hypertrophy, conduction abnormalities, pulmonary embolism, spontaneous pneumothorax, intracranial hemorrhage, hyperkalemia, and pericarditis.
33. "Poor R-wave progression" is a phrase used to describe R waves that decrease in size from V_1 to V_4.
34. The 12-lead ECG provides a 2.5-sec view of each lead because it is assumed that 2.5 sec is long enough to capture at least one representative complex. However, a 2.5-sec view is not long enough to properly assess rate and rhythm, so at least one continuous rhythm strip is usually included at the bottom of the tracing.

Practice Rhythm Strips

Figure 9-46
Heart rate:	99 bpm
PRI:	0.15 sec
QRS:	0.08 sec
QT:	0.36 sec
Interpretation:	Sinus rhythm; minimal voltage criteria for LVH, may be normal variant; borderline ECG

Figure 9-47
Heart rate:	110 bpm
PRI:	0.19 sec
QRS:	0.08 sec
QT:	0.31 sec
Interpretation:	Sinus tachycardia; possible right atrial enlargement; cannot rule out lateral infarct, age undetermined; inferior infarct, age undetermined with posterior extension; abnormal ECG

Figure 9-48
Heart rate:	153 bpm
PRI:	0 sec
QRS:	0.96 sec
QT:	0.31 sec
Interpretation:	Atrial fibrillation with rapid ventricular response; ST and T wave abnormality, possible anterolateral ischemia or digitalis effect; abnormal ECG

Figure 9-49
Heart rate:	63 bpm
PRI:	0.18 sec
QRS:	0.96 sec
QT:	0.39 sec
Interpretation:	Sinus rhythm with frequent PVCs; tall T waves, possible hyperkalemia; abnormal ECG

CHAPTER 10 POST-TEST ANSWERS

TRUE/FALSE

1. F
2. F
3. F

MULTIPLE CHOICE

4. D	19. D
5. A	20. D
6. D	21. C
7. B	22. C
8. D	23. B
9. B	24. C
10. B	25. C
11. C	26. B
12. A	27. A
13. A	28. C
14. A	29. C
15. B	30. A
16. C	31. A
17. D	32. C
18. D	33. C

COMPLETION

34. A beat originating from the AV junction that appears later than the next expected sinus beat is called a junctional escape beat.
35. A rapid, wide-QRS rhythm associated with pulselessness, shock, or congestive heart failure should be presumed to be ventricular tachycardia.
36. PACs associated with a wide QRS complex are called aberrantly conducted PACs, indicating conduction through the ventricles is abnormal.
37. The right atrium receives deoxygenated blood from the superior vena cava (which carries blood from the head and upper extremities), the inferior vena cava (which carries blood from the lower body), and the coronary sinus (which receives blood from the intracardiac circulation).
38. Diastole is the period of relaxation during which a heart chamber is filling.
39. The thick, muscular middle layer of the heart wall that contains the atrial and ventricular muscle fibers necessary for contraction is the myocardium.
40. An ECG lead that has a positive and negative electrode is called a bipolar lead.
41. The appearance of coved ("frowny face") ST-segment elevation is called an acute injury pattern.
42. Delivery of an electrical current timed for delivery during the QRS complex is called synchronized cardioversion.
43. Sometimes, when a PAC occurs very prematurely and close to the T wave of the preceding beat, only a P wave may be seen with no QRS after it (appearing as a pause). This type of PAC is termed a "nonconducted" (or "blocked") PAC.
44. If the AV junction paces the heart, the electrical impulse must travel in a backward (retrograde) direction to activate the atria.
45. A fusion beat occurs as a result of an electrical impulse from a supraventricular site (such as the SA node) discharging at the same time as an ectopic site in the ventricles.
46. A pacemaker spike is a vertical line on the ECG that indicates the pacemaker has discharged.

47. A demand pacemaker is also known as a <u>synchronous</u> or <u>noncompetitive</u> pacemaker.
48. A <u>right</u> bundle branch block produces an RSR' pattern in lead V$_1$.
49.

Leads	**Heart Surface Viewed**
II, III, aVF	Inferior
V$_1$, V$_2$	Septal
V$_3$, V$_4$	Anterior
I, aVL, V$_5$, V$_6$	Lateral

SHORT ANSWER

50.

SA node:	<u>60-100 bpm</u>
AV junction:	<u>40-60 bpm</u>
Ventricles:	<u>20-40 bpm</u>

51. The four properties of cardiac cells are (1) automaticity, (2) excitability (or irritability), (3) conductivity, and (4) contractility.
52. The AV junction may assume responsibility for pacing the heart if:
   - The SA node fails to discharge (such as sinus arrest)
   - An impulse from the SA node is generated but blocked as it exits the SA node (such as SA block)
   - The rate of discharge of the SA node is slower than that of the AV junction (such as a sinus bradycardia or the slower phase of a sinus arrhythmia)
   - An impulse from the SA node is generated and is conducted through the atria but is not conducted to the ventricles (such as an AV block)
53. Common causes of PVCs include normal variant, hypoxia, stress/anxiety, exercise, digitalis toxicity, acid-base imbalance, myocardial ischemia, electrolyte imbalance (hypokalemia, hypocalcemia, hypercalcemia, hypomagnesemia), congestive heart failure, increased sympathetic tone, acute myocardial infarction, stimulants (alcohol, caffeine, tobacco), and medications (sympathomimetics, cyclic antidepressants, phenothiazines).
54. Signs and symptoms of hemodynamic compromise
   - Changes in mental status (restlessness, confusion, possible loss of consciousness)
   - Low blood pressure
   - Chest pain
   - Shortness of breath
   - Signs of shock
   - Congestive heart failure
   - Pulmonary congestion
   - Fall in urine output
   - Cold, clammy skin
55. Polymorphic VT that occurs in the presence of a long QT interval is called torsades de pointes.
56. **PATCH-4-MD**
   - **P**ulmonary embolism
   - **A**cidosis
   - **T**ension pneumothorax
   - **C**ardiac tamponade
   - **H**ypovolemia (most common cause of PEA)
   - **H**ypoxia
   - **H**eat/cold (hypo-/hyperthermia)
   - **H**ypo-/hyperkalemia (and other electrolytes)
   - **M**yocardial infarction
   - **D**rug overdose/accidents
57.

	Second-Degree AV Block Type I	Third-Degree AV Block
Ventricular rhythm	Irregular	Regular
PR interval	Progressively lengthening	None
QRS width	Usually narrow	Narrow or wide

58. The axes of leads I, II, and III form an equilateral triangle with the heart at the center (Einthoven triangle). If the augmented limb leads are added to this configuration and the axes of the six leads moved in a way in which they bisect each other, the result is the hexaxial reference system.

59. Rate   Atrial rate is greater than the ventricular rate; ventricular rate is often slow

    Rhythm   Atrial regular (Ps plot through); ventricular irregular

    P waves   Normal in size and shape; some P waves are not followed by a QRS complex (more Ps than QRSs)

    PR interval   Within normal limits or slightly prolonged but constant for the conducted beats; there may be some shortening of the PR interval that follows a non-conducted P wave

    QRS duration   Usually 0.10 sec or greater, periodically absent after P waves

60. The area supplied by an obstructed coronary artery goes through a characteristic sequence of events that have been identified as zones of ischemia, injury, and infarction.

61. A sinus rhythm has a rate of 60 to 100 bpm. A sinus tachycardia has a rate of 101 to 180 bpm.

62. According to the Frank-Starling law of the heart, to a point, the greater the volume of blood in the heart during diastole, the more forceful the cardiac contraction, and the more blood the ventricle will pump (stroke volume). This is important so that the heart can adjust its pumping capacity in response to changes in venous return, such as during exercise. If, however, the ventricle is stretched beyond its physiological limit, cardiac output may fall due to volume overload and overstretching of the muscle fibers.

63. The four major electrolytes that influence cardiac function are sodium, potassium, calcium, and chloride.

64. On the ECG, the ST-segment represents early ventricular repolarization and the T wave presents ventricular repolarization.

65. A biphasic waveform is partly positive and partly negative and is recorded when the wave of depolarization moves perpendicularly to the positive electrode.

66. Artifact may be due to loose electrodes, broken wires or ECG cables, muscle tremor, patient movement, external chest compressions, or 60-cycle interference.

67. A ventricular-demand (VVI) pacemaker is a common type of pacemaker. With this device, the pacemaker electrode is placed in the right ventricle (V); the ventricle is sensed (V) and the pacemaker is inhibited (I) when spontaneous ventricular depolarization occurs within a preset interval. When spontaneous ventricular depolarization does not occur within this preset interval, the pacemaker fires and stimulates ventricular depolarization at a preset rate.

68. Anatomically contiguous leads refers to those leads that "see" the same area of the heart. Two leads are contiguous if they look at the same area of the heart or they are numerically consecutive *chest* leads.

69. A Q wave that is 40 millisec or more wide (one small box or more wide) or more than one third of the amplitude of the R wave in that lead is suggestive of infarction.

70. ECG monitoring may be used to (1) monitor a patient's heart rate, (2) evaluate the effects of disease or injury on heart function, (3) evaluate pacemaker function, (4) evaluate the response to medications (e.g., antiarrhythmics), and/or (5) obtain a baseline recording before, during, and after a medical procedure.

Test Rhythm Strips

Figure 10-1
Ventricular rate/rhythm:	215 bpm, regular
Atrial rate/rhythm:	215 bpm, regular
PR interval:	0.10 sec
QRS duration:	0.08 sec
Identification:	Sinus tachycardia at 215 bpm

Figure 10-2
Ventricular rate/rhythm:	64-83 bpm/irregular
Atrial rate/rhythm:	Unable to determine
PR interval:	Unable to determine
QRS duration:	0.08 sec
Identification:	Atrial flutter at 64-83 bpm

Figure 10-3
Ventricular rate/rhythm	79 bpm, regular
Atrial rate/rhythm	79 bpm, regular
PR interval	0.18 sec
QRS duration	0.06-0.08 sec
Identification:	Sinus rhythm at 79 bpm

Figure 10-4
Atrial pacing?	No
Ventricular pacing?	Yes
Paced interval:	115
Identification:	Normal functioning ventricular pacemaker

Figure 10-5
Ventricular rate/rhythm	52 bpm, regular
Atrial rate/rhythm	52 bpm, regular
PR interval	0.16-0.20 sec
QRS duration	0.06 sec
Identification:	Sinus bradycardia at 52 bpm

Figure 10-6
Ventricular rate/rhythm	86 bpm, irregular
Atrial rate/rhythm	86 bpm, irregular
PR interval	0.18 sec (sinus beats)
QRS duration	0.10 sec (sinus beats)
Identification:	Sinus rhythm at 86 bpm with uniform PVCs

Figure 10-7
Ventricular rate/rhythm	48 bpm, regular
Atrial rate/rhythm	71 bpm, slightly irregular
PR interval	Varies
QRS duration	0.08-0.10 sec
Identification:	Third-degree AV block at 48 bpm with ST-segment elevation

Figure 10-8
Ventricular rate/rhythm	33 bpm (sinus beats); 32 bpm (junctional beats)
Atrial rate/rhythm	33 bpm (sinus beats); unable to determine (junctional beats)
PR interval	0.20 sec (sinus beats)
QRS duration	0.04-0.06 sec
Identification:	Sinus bradycardia at 33 bpm to junctional bradycardia at 32 bpm

Figure 10-9
Ventricular rate/rhythm	245 bpm, regular
Atrial rate/rhythm	245 bpm, regular
PR interval	None
QRS duration	0.28 sec
Identification:	Monomorphic ventricular tachycardia at 245 bpm

Figure 10-10
Ventricular rate/rhythm	20 bpm, regular
Atrial rate/rhythm	None
PR interval	None
QRS duration	0.14 sec
Identification:	Idioventricular/agonal rhythm at 20 bpm

Figure 10-11
Ventricular rate/rhythm	36 bpm, regular
Atrial rate/rhythm	94 bpm, regular
PR interval	Varies
QRS duration	0.14 sec
Identification:	Third-degree AV block at 36 bpm

Figure 10-12
Atrial pacing?	Yes
Ventricular pacing?	Yes
Paced interval:	71
Identification:	Normal functioning AV sequential pacemaker

Figure 10-13
Ventricular rate/rhythm	43-60 bpm, irregular
Atrial rate/rhythm	68 bpm, regular
PR interval	Lengthens
QRS duration	0.06 sec
Identification:	Second-degree AV block type I at 43-60 bpm

Figure 10-14

Ventricular rate/rhythm	136 bpm (sinus beats), regular except for the event(s)
Atrial rate/rhythm	136 bpm (sinus beats), regular except for the event(s)
PR interval	0.10 sec
QRS duration	0.06 sec
Identification:	Sinus tachycardia at 136 bpm with frequent PJCs (the PJCs are beats 2, 5, 8, and 11 from the left)

Figure 10-15

Ventricular rate/rhythm	85 bpm, regular
Atrial rate/rhythm	85 bpm, regular
PR interval	0.28 sec
QRS duration	0.06-0.08 sec
Identification:	Sinus rhythm at 85 bpm with first-degree AV block, ST-segment elevation

Figure 10-16

Ventricular rate/rhythm	56 bpm, regular
Atrial rate/rhythm	None
PR interval	None
QRS duration	0.12 sec
Identification:	Accelerated idioventricular rhythm (AIVR) at 56 bpm; ST-segment depression

Figure 10-17

Ventricular rate/rhythm	71 bpm (sinus beats)/regular except for the event
Atrial rate/rhythm	71 bpm (sinus beats)/regular except for the event
PR interval	0.24 sec
QRS duration	0.08 sec
Identification:	Sinus rhythm at 71 bpm with a first-degree AV block, an episode of sinus arrest and a junctional escape beat; ST-segment depression

Figure 10-18

Atrial pacing?	No
Ventricular pacing?	Yes
Paced interval:	80
Identification:	Ventricular-paced rhythm with pacemaker malfunction (failure to capture)

Figure 10-19

Ventricular rate/rhythm	Unable to determine
Atrial rate/rhythm	None
PR interval	None
QRS duration	Unable to determine
Identification:	Ventricular fibrillation

Figure 10-20

Ventricular rate/rhythm	41-73 bpm, irregular
Atrial rate/rhythm	56-125 bpm, irregular
PR interval	0.20 sec
QRS duration	0.12 sec
Identification:	Sinus rhythm at 41-73 bpm with a nonconducted PAC

Figure 10-21

Ventricular rate/rhythm	48-83 bpm, irregular
Atrial rate/rhythm	167 bpm, regular
PR interval	0.24 sec
QRS duration	0.12 sec
Identification:	Second-degree AV block type II at 48-83 bpm with ST-segment depression

Figure 10-22

Ventricular rate/rhythm	115-215 bpm, irregular
Atrial rate/rhythm	Unable to determine, irregular
PR interval	Varies
QRS duration	0.04-0.06 sec
Identification:	Multifocal atrial tachycardia at 115-215 bpm with ST-segment depression

Figure 10-23

Ventricular rate/rhythm	34 bpm, regular
Atrial rate/rhythm	68 bpm, regular
PR interval	0.14-0.16 sec
QRS duration	0.10 sec
Identification:	2:1 AV block, probably type I at 34 bpm

Figure 10-24

Ventricular rate/rhythm	75 bpm, regular
Atrial rate/rhythm	None
PR interval	None
QRS duration	0.08 sec
Identification:	Accelerated junctional rhythm at 75 bpm; ST-segment depression

Figure 10-25

Ventricular rate/rhythm	231 bpm, regular
Atrial rate/rhythm	Unable to determine
PR interval	Unable to determine
QRS duration	0.06 sec
Identification:	AV nodal reentrant tachycardia (AVNRT) at 231 bpm with ST-segment depression

Figure 10-26

Atrial paced activity?	Yes
Ventricular paced activity?	Yes
Paced interval rate?	Atrial = 79, ventricular = 85
Identification:	AV sequential demand pacemaker

Figure 10-27

Ventricular rate/rhythm	51-83 bpm, irregular
Atrial rate/rhythm	88 bpm, regular
PR interval	Lengthens
QRS duration	0.06 sec
Identification:	Second-degree AV block type I at 51-83 bpm

Figure 10-28

Ventricular rate/rhythm	167 bpm, regular
Atrial rate/rhythm	Unable to determine
PR interval	Unable to determine
QRS duration	0.06 sec
Identification:	AV nodal reentrant tachycardia (AVNRT) at 167 bpm with ST-segment depression

Figure 10-29

Ventricular rate/rhythm	52-94 bpm, irregular
Atrial rate/rhythm	52-94 bpm, irregular
PR interval	0.12 sec
QRS duration	0.08 sec
Identification:	Sinus arrhythmia at 52-94 bpm

Figure 10-30

Ventricular rate/rhythm	230-300 bpm, irregular
Atrial rate/rhythm	Unable to determine
PR interval	Unable to determine
QRS duration	Varies
Identification:	Supraventricular beat followed by polymorphic ventricular tachycardia at 230-300 bpm

Figure 10-31

Atrial pacing?	Yes
Ventricular pacing?	No
Paced interval:	79
Identification:	Atrial pacemaker

Figure 10-32

Ventricular rate/rhythm	88 (sinus beats), regular except for the events
Atrial rate/rhythm	88 (sinus beats), regular except for the events
PR interval	0.20 sec (sinus beats)
QRS duration	0.08 sec (sinus beats)
Identification:	Sinus rhythm at 88 bpm with a PVC and run of VT, ST-segment depression, inverted T waves

Figure 10-33

Atrial pacing?	No
Ventricular pacing?	Yes
Paced interval:	74
Identification:	100% ventricular-paced rhythm; underlying rhythm is atrial flutter

Figure 10-34

Ventricular rate/rhythm	96-214 bpm, irregular
Atrial rate/rhythm	96-214 bpm, irregular
PR interval	0.16 sec (sinus beats)
QRS duration	0.08 sec
Identification:	Sinus rhythm at 96 bpm with a PAC precipitating a run of PSVT at 214 bpm, back to a sinus rhythm at 96 bpm

Figure 10-35

Ventricular rate/rhythm	125-158 bpm, irregular
Atrial rate/rhythm	Unable to determine
PR interval	Unable to determine
QRS duration	0.06 sec
Identification:	Atrial fibrillation (uncontrolled) at 125-158 bpm with ST-segment depression

Figure 10-36

Ventricular rate/rhythm	40 bpm (sinus beats), regular except for the event
Atrial rate/rhythm	40 bpm (sinus beats), regular except for the event
PR interval	0.36 sec (sinus beats)
QRS duration	0.06 sec (sinus beats)
Identification:	Sinus bradycardia at 40 bpm with first-degree AV block and a PJC

Figure 10-37

Ventricular rate/rhythm	94 bpm (sinus beats)-150 bpm (VT)/regular (sinus beats), regular (VT)
Atrial rate/rhythm	94 bpm (sinus beats)/regular (sinus beats) to unable to determine (VT)
PR interval	0.16 sec (sinus beats)
QRS duration	0.10 sec (sinus beats)-0.14 sec (VT)
Identification:	Sinus rhythm at 94 bpm to monomorphic ventricular tachycardia (VT) at 150 bpm

Figure 10-38

Ventricular rate/rhythm	55 bpm, regular
Atrial rate/rhythm	107 bpm, regular
PR interval	0.16 sec
QRS duration	0.06 sec
Identification:	2:1 AV block, probably type I at 55 bpm, with ST-segment elevation

Figure 10-39

Ventricular rate/rhythm	76 bpm, regular
Atrial rate/rhythm	None
PR interval	None
QRS duration	0.06 sec
Identification:	Accelerated junctional rhythm at 76 bpm

Figure 10-40

Ventricular rate/rhythm	300-375 bpm, irregular
Atrial rate/rhythm	None
PR interval	None
QRS duration	Varies
Identification:	Polymorphic ventricular tachycardia at 300-375 bpm

Figure 10-41

Atrial pacing?	No
Ventricular pacing?	Yes
Paced interval:	71
Identification:	Pacemaker malfunction (failure to sense); underlying rhythm is a sinus rhythm at 88 bpm; note the pacer spikes in the T waves of the second and eighth beats from the left

Figure 10-42

Ventricular rate/rhythm	0-75 bpm, irregular
Atrial rate/rhythm	0-75 bpm, irregular
PR interval	0.16 sec
QRS duration	0.08 sec
Identification:	Sinus rhythm at approximately 75 bpm with an episode of sinus arrest

Figure 10-43

Ventricular rate/rhythm	180 bpm, regular
Atrial rate/rhythm	Unable to determine
PR interval	Unable to determine
QRS duration	0.04 sec
Identification:	AV nodal reentrant tachycardia (AVNRT) at 180 bpm with ST-segment elevation

Figure 10-44

Ventricular rate/rhythm	30 bpm, regular
Atrial rate/rhythm	68 bpm, regular
PR interval	0.28 sec
QRS duration	0.16 sec
Identification:	2:1 AV block, probably type II at 30 bpm; ST-segment elevation, hyperacute T waves

Figure 10-45

Ventricular rate/rhythm	93 bpm (sinus beats), regular except for the event
Atrial rate/rhythm	93 bpm (sinus beats), regular except for the event
PR interval	0.16 sec (sinus beats)
QRS duration	0.04 sec (sinus beats)
Identification:	Sinus rhythm at 93 bpm with a PAC (PAC is the seventh beat from the left)

Figure 10-46

Ventricular rate/rhythm	52 bpm, regular
Atrial rate/rhythm	None
PR interval	None
QRS duration	0.06 sec
Identification:	Sinus beat to a junction escape rhythm at 52 bpm; inverted T waves

Figure 10-47

Ventricular rate/rhythm	23 bpm, regular
Atrial rate/rhythm	23 bpm, regular
PR interval	0.44 sec
QRS duration	0.08 sec
Identification:	Sinus bradycardia at 23 bpm with first-degree AV block, ST-segment elevation

Figure 10-48

Ventricular rate/rhythm	32 bpm, regular
Atrial rate/rhythm	79 bpm, regular
PR interval	Varies
QRS duration	0.10-12 sec
Identification:	Third-degree AV block at 32 bpm

Figure 10-49

Atrial pacing?	No
Ventricular pacing?	Yes
Paced interval:	65
Identification:	100% ventricular paced rhythm

Figure 10-50

Ventricular rate/rhythm	None
Atrial rate/rhythm	40 bpm, regular
PR interval	None
QRS duration	None
Identification:	P-wave asystole at 40 bpm

Figure 10-51

Ventricular rate/rhythm	36-71 bpm, regular except for the event
Atrial rate/rhythm	36-71 bpm, regular except for the event
PR interval	0.16 sec
QRS duration	0.06 sec
Identification:	Sinus rhythm at a rate of 36 to 71 bpm with an episode of sinoatrial (SA) block

Figure 10-52

Ventricular rate/rhythm	70 bpm, regular except for the event
Atrial rate/rhythm	70 bpm, regular except for the event
PR interval	0.16 sec
QRS duration	0.08 sec
Identification:	Sinus rhythm at 70 bpm with a nonconducted PAC (note distortion of the T wave of the beat preceding the pause) and a junctional escape beat

Figure 10-53

Ventricular rate/rhythm	21 bpm, irregular
Atrial rate/rhythm	21 bpm, irregular
PR interval	0.36 sec
QRS duration	0.08-0.10 sec
Identification:	Sinus bradycardia at 21 bpm with junctional escape beats

Figure 10-54

Ventricular rate/rhythm	44 bpm, regular
Atrial rate/rhythm	83 bpm, regular
PR interval	0.16 sec
QRS duration	0.08 sec
Identification:	2:1 AV block, probably type I at 44 bpm

Figure 10-55

Ventricular rate/rhythm	54-94 bpm, irregular
Atrial rate/rhythm	Unable to determine
PR interval	Unable to determine
QRS duration	0.10-0.12 sec
Identification:	Atrial flutter at 54-94 bpm

Figure 10-56

Ventricular rate/rhythm	96 bpm, regular
Atrial rate/rhythm	96 bpm, regular
PR interval	0.22 sec
QRS duration	0.10 sec
Identification:	Sinus rhythm at 96 bpm with first-degree AV block; tall P waves

Figure 10-57

Ventricular rate/rhythm	91 bpm (sinus beats), regular except for the event(s)
Atrial rate/rhythm	91 bpm (sinus beats), regular except for the event(s)
PR interval	0.16 sec
QRS duration	0.06 sec
Identification:	Sinus rhythm at 91 bpm with ventricular trigeminy

Figure 10-58

Ventricular rate/rhythm	125-230 bpm, irregular
Atrial rate/rhythm	Unable to determine
PR interval	Unable to determine
QRS duration	0.06 sec
Identification:	Atrial fibrillation at 125-230 bpm (rapid ventricular response)

Figure 10-59

Ventricular rate/rhythm	75 bpm (sinus beats)/regular except for the event(s)
Atrial rate/rhythm	75 bpm (sinus beats)/regular except for the event(s)
PR interval	0.16 sec
QRS duration	0.06-0.08 sec
Identification:	Sinus rhythm at 75 bpm with frequent PACs

Figure 10-60

Atrial pacing?	No
Ventricular pacing?	Yes
Paced interval:	60
Identification:	Atrial fibrillation with a ventricular demand pacemaker

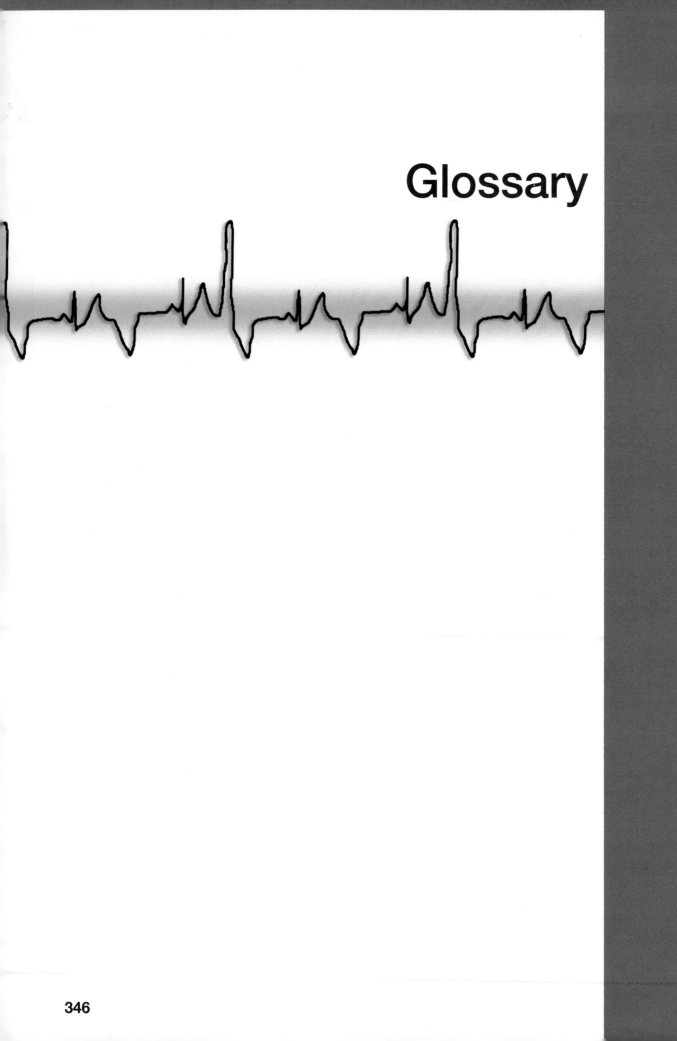

Glossary

a wave: Atrial-paced event; the atrial stimulus or the point in the intrinsic atrial depolarization (P wave) at which atrial sensing occurs; analogous to the P wave of intrinsic waveforms

AA interval: Interval between two consecutive atrial stimuli, with or without an interceding ventricular event; analogous to the P-P interval of intrinsic waveforms

AV interval: In dual-chamber pacing, the length of time between an atrial-sensed or atrial-paced event and the delivery of a ventricular pacing stimulus; analogous to the PR interval of intrinsic waveforms

aberrant: Abnormal

absolute refractory period: Corresponds with the onset of the QRS complex to approximately the peak of the T wave; cardiac cells cannot be stimulated to conduct an electrical impulse, no matter how strong the stimulus

accelerated idioventricular rhythm (AIVR): Dysrhythmia originating in the ventricles with a rate between 41 and 100 bpm

accelerated junctional rhythm: Dysrhythmia originating in the AV junction with a rate between 61 and 100 bpm

accessory pathway: Extra muscle bundle consisting of working myocardial tissue that forms a connection between the atria and ventricles outside the normal conduction system

action potential: Reflection of the difference in the concentration of ions across a cell membrane at any given time

acute coronary syndromes (ACS): Term used to describe a physiologic continuum of conditions caused by a similar sequence of pathologic events—a transient or permanent obstruction of a coronary artery; ACS include unstable angina, non-ST-segment elevation myocardial infarction (NSTEMI), and ST-segment elevation MI (STEMI)

adrenergic: Having the characteristics of the sympathetic division of the autonomic nervous system

afterload: Pressure or resistance against which the ventricles must pump to eject blood

agonal rhythm: Dysrhythmia similar in appearance to an idioventricular rhythm but occurring at a rate of less than 20 bpm; dying heart

amplitude: Height (voltage) of a waveform on the ECG

angina pectoris: Chest discomfort or other related symptoms of sudden onset that may occur because the increased oxygen demand of the heart temporarily exceeds the blood supply

aortic valve: Semilunar valve located between the left ventricle and aorta

apex of the heart: Lower portion of the heart, tip of the ventricles (approximately the level of the fifth left intercostal space); points leftward, downward, and forward

arrhythmia: Term often used interchangeably with dysrhythmia; any disturbance or abnormality in a normal rhythmic pattern; any cardiac rhythm other than a sinus rhythm

artifact: Distortion of an ECG tracing by electrical activity that is noncardiac in origin (e.g., electrical interference, poor electrical conduction, patient movement)

asynchronous pacemaker: Fixed-rate pacemaker that continuously discharges at a preset rate regardless of the patient's intrinsic activity

asystole: Absence of cardiac electrical activity viewed as a straight (isoelectric) line on the ECG

atria: Two upper chambers of the heart (singular, atrium)

atrial kick: Blood pushed into the ventricles because of atrial contraction

atrial pacing: Pacing system with a lead attached to the right atrium, designed to correct abnormalities in the SA node (sick sinus syndrome)

atrial tachycardia: Three or more sequential premature atrial complexes (PACs) occurring at a rate of more than 100 bpm

atrioventricular (AV) valve: Valve located between each atrium and ventricle; the tricuspid separates the right atrium from the right ventricle, the mitral (bicuspid) separates the left atrium from the left ventricle

augmented lead: Leads aVR, aVL, and aVF; these leads record the difference in electrical potential at one location relative to zero potential rather than relative to the electrical potential of another extremity, as in the bipolar leads

automatic interval: Period, expressed in milliseconds, between two consecutively paced events in the same cardiac chamber without an intervening sensed event (e.g., AA interval, VV interval); also known as the demand interval, basic interval, or pacing interval

automaticity: Ability of cardiac pacemaker cells to spontaneously initiate an electrical impulse without being stimulated from another source (such as a nerve)

AV dissociation: Any dysrhythmia in which the atria and ventricles beat independently (e.g., ventricular tachycardia, complete AV block)

AV junction: AV node and the bundle of His

AV node: Specialized cells located in the lower portion of the right atrium; delays the electrical impulse in order to allow the atria to contract and complete filling of the ventricles

AV sequential pacemaker: Type of dual-chamber pacemaker that stimulates first the atrium, then the ventricle, mimicking normal cardiac physiology

axis: Imaginary line joining the positive and negative electrodes of a lead

base of the heart: Top of the heart located at approximately the level of the second intercostal space

baseline: Straight line recorded on ECG graph paper when no electrical activity is detected

base rate: Rate at which the pulse generator of a pacemaker paces when no intrinsic activity is detected; expressed in pulses/min (ppm)

bifascicular block: Block in two divisions of the bundle branches; although this term may be used to describe a block in both the anterior and posterior branches of the left bundle branch, it is more commonly used to describe a combination of a right bundle branch block and either a left anterior fascicular block (LAFB) or a left posterior fascicular block (LPFB)

bigeminy: Dysrhythmia in which every other beat is a premature ectopic beat

biphasic: Waveform that is partly positive and partly negative

bipolar limb lead: ECG lead consisting of a positive and negative electrode; a pacing lead with two electrical poles that are external from the pulse generator; the negative pole is located at the extreme distal tip of the pacing lead; the positive pole is located several millimeters proximal to the negative electrode; the stimulating pulse is delivered through the negative electrode

blocked PAC (nonconducted PAC): Premature atrial complex that is not followed by a QRS complex

blood pressure: Force exerted by the circulating blood volume on the walls of the arteries; blood pressure is equal to cardiac output times peripheral resistance

bpm: Beats/min; the abbreviation bpm usually refers to an intrinsic heart rate, whereas pulses/min (ppm) usually refers to a paced rate

bradycardia: Heart rate slower than 60 bpm (brady, slow)

bundle branch block (BBB): Abnormal conduction of an electrical impulse through either the right or left bundle branches

bundle of His: Cardiac fibers located in the upper portion of the interventricular septum; connects the AV node with the two bundle branches

burst: Three or more sequential ectopic beats; also referred to as a "salvo" or "run"

bypass tract: Term used when one end of an accessory pathway is attached to normal conductive tissue

calibration: Regulation of an ECG machine's stylus sensitivity so that a 1 mV electrical signal will produce a deflection measuring exactly 10 mm

capacitor: Device that can store an electrical charge

capture: Ability of a pacing stimulus to successfully depolarize the cardiac chamber that is being paced; with one-to-one capture, each pacing stimulus results in depolarization of the appropriate chamber

cardiac arrest: Clinical death characterized by cessation of pulse and respiration

cardiac cycle: Period from the beginning of one heart beat to the beginning of the next one; normally consisting of PQRST waves, complexes, and intervals

cardiac index: Measure of a patient's cardiac output per square meter of body surface area (BSA)

cardiac output: Amount of blood pumped into the aorta each minute by the heart

carotid sinus pressure: Type of vagal maneuver in which pressure is applied to the carotid sinus for a brief period to slow conduction through the AV node

catecholamines: Natural chemicals produced by the body that have sympathetic actions; epinephrine, norepinephrine, dopamine

cholinergic: Having the characteristics of the parasympathetic division of the autonomic nervous system

chordae tendineae: Thin strands of fibrous connective tissue that extend from the AV valves to the papillary muscles that prevent the AV valves from bulging back into the atria during ventricular systole (contraction)

chronotropism: Refers to a change in heart rate; a positive chronotropic effect refers to an increase in heart rate; a negative chronotropic effect refers to a decrease in heart rate

circumflex artery: Division of the left coronary artery

coarse ventricular fibrillation: Ventricular fibrillation with fibrillatory waves greater than 3 mm in height

compensatory pause: Pause is termed "compensatory" (or complete) if the normal beat following a premature complex occurs when expected

complex: Several waveforms

conductivity: Ability of a cardiac cell to receive an electrical stimulus and conduct that impulse to an adjacent cardiac cell

contractility: Ability of cardiac cells to shorten, causing cardiac muscle contraction in response to an electrical stimulus

coronary sinus: Outlet that drains five coronary veins into the right atrium

couplet: Two consecutive premature complexes

coupling interval: Interval between an ectopic beat and the preceding beat of the underlying rhythm

current: The flow of electrical charge from one point to another

cycle length: Term used for the period between any one type of event and the next event of the same type, usually expressed in milliseconds

defibrillation: Therapeutic use of electric current to terminate lethal cardiac dysrhythmias

delta wave: Slurring of the beginning portion of the QRS complex, caused by preexcitation

demand interval: Period, expressed in milliseconds, between two consecutively paced events in the same cardiac chamber without an intervening sensed event (e.g., AA interval, VV interval); also known as the basic interval or pacing interval

demand pacemaker: Synchronous pacemaker that discharges only when the patient's heart rate drops below the preset rate for the pacemaker

depolarization: Movement of ions across a cell membrane, causing the inside of the cell to become more positive; an electrical event expected to result in contraction

dextrocardia: Location of the heart in the right thorax because of a congenital defect or displacement by disease

diastole: Phase of the cardiac cycle in which the atria and ventricles relax between contractions and blood enters these chambers; when the term is used without reference to a specific chamber of the heart, the term implies ventricular diastole

dilatation: Increase in the diameter of a chamber of the heart caused by volume overload

diphasic: Waveform that is partly positive and partly negative

dual-chamber pacemaker: Pacemaker that stimulates the atrium and ventricle

dyspnea: Shortness of breath or difficulty breathing

dysrhythmia: Any disturbance or abnormality in a normal rhythmic pattern; any cardiac rhythm other than a sinus rhythm

ectopic: Impulse(s) originating from a source other than the sinoatrial node

ejection fraction: The percentage of blood pumped out of a heart chamber with each contraction

electrical axis: Direction (or angle in degrees) in which the main vector of depolarization is pointed

electrodes: Adhesive pads that contain a conductive gel, applied at specific locations on the patient's chest wall and extremities and connected by means of cables to an electrocardiograph

electrolyte: Element or compound that, when melted or dissolved in water or another solvent, breaks into ions (atoms able to carry an electric charge)

endocardium: Innermost layer of the heart that lines the inside of the myocardium and covers the heart valves

enhanced automaticity: Abnormal condition in which cardiac cells not normally associated with the property of automaticity begin to depolarize spontaneously or when escape pacemaker sites increase their firing rate beyond that considered normal

enlargement: Term that implies the presence of dilatation or hypertrophy, or both

epicardium: Also known as the visceral pericardium; the external layer of the heart wall that covers the heart muscle

escape: Term used when the sinus node slows down or fails to initiate depolarization and a lower pacemaker site spontaneously produces electrical impulses, assuming responsibility for pacing the heart

escape interval: Time measured between a sensed cardiac event and the next pacemaker output

excitability: Ability of cardiac muscle cells to respond to an outside stimulus

extrasystole: Premature complex

extreme right axis deviation: Current flow in the direction opposite of normal (−91 to −179 degrees)

fascicle: Small bundle of nerve fibers

fine ventricular fibrillation: Ventricular fibrillation with fibrillatory waves less than 3 mm in height

fixed-rate pacemaker: Asynchronous pacemaker that continuously discharges at a preset rate regardless of the patient's heart rate

fusion beat: Beat that occurs because of simultaneous activation of one cardiac chamber by two sites (foci); in pacing, the ECG waveform that results when an intrinsic depolarization and a pacing stimulus occur simultaneously and both contribute to depolarization of that cardiac chamber

great vessels: Pulmonary arteries, pulmonary veins, aorta, superior, and inferior vena cavae

ground electrode: Third ECG electrode (the first and second are the positive and negative electrodes), which minimizes electrical activity from other sources

His-Purkinje system: Portion of the conduction system consisting of the bundle of His, bundle branches, and Purkinje fibers

hypertrophy: Increase in the thickness of a heart chamber because of chronic pressure overload

incomplete compensatory pause: Pause is termed incomplete (or noncompensatory) if the normal beat following the premature complex occurs before it was expected

indeterminate axis deviation: Current flow in the direction opposite of normal (−91 to −179 degrees)

infarction: Necrosis of tissue because of an inadequate blood supply

inherent: Natural, intrinsic

inhibition: Pacemaker response in which the output pulse is suppressed (inhibited) when an intrinsic event is sensed

inotropic effect: Refers to a change in myocardial contractility

interpolated PVC: PVC that occurs between two normal QRS complexes and that does not interrupt the underlying rhythm

interval: Waveform and a segment; in pacing, the period, measured in milliseconds, between any two designated cardiac events

intrinsic rate: Rate at which a pacemaker of the heart normally generates impulses

ion: Electrically charged particle

ischemia: Decreased supply of oxygenated blood to a body part or organ

isoelectric line: Absence of electrical activity observed on the ECG as a straight line

J-point: Point where the QRS complex and ST segment meet

junctional bradycardia: a rhythm that begins in the AV junction with a rate of less than 40 bpm

junctional escape rhythm: a rhythm that begins in the AV junction; characterized by a very regular ventricular rate of 40 to 60 bpm

junctional tachycardia: a rhythm that begins in the AV junction with a ventricular rate of more than 100 bpm

KVO: Abbreviation meaning "keep the vein open"; also known as TKO, "to keep open"

LBBB: Left bundle branch block

lead: Electrical connection attached to the body to record electrical activity

left anterior descending artery: Division of the left coronary artery

left axis deviation: Current flow to the left of normal (−1 to −90 degrees)

Lown-Ganong-Levine syndrome (LGL): Type of pre-excitation syndrome in which part or all of the AV conduction system is bypassed by an abnormal AV connection from the atrial muscle to the bundle of His; characterized by a short PR interval (usually less than 0.12 sec) and a normal QRS duration

mean axis: Average direction of a mean vector; the mean axis is only identified in the frontal plane

mean P vector: Average magnitude and direction of both right and left atrial depolarization

mean vector: Average of depolarization waves in one portion of the heart

mean QRS vector: Average magnitude and direction of both right and left ventricular depolarization

mediastinum: Located in the middle of the thoracic cavity; contains the heart, great vessels, trachea, and esophagus, among other structures; extends from the sternum to the vertebral column

membrane potential: Difference in electrical charge across the cell membrane

milliampere (mA): Unit of measure of electrical current needed to elicit depolarization of the myocardium

mitochondria: energy-producing elements of a cell

monofascicular block: Block in only one of the fascicles of the bundle branches

monomorphic: Having the same shape

multiformed atrial rhythm: Cardiac dysrhythmia that occurs because of impulses originating from various sites, including the sinoatrial node, the atria, and/or the AV junction; requires at least three different P waves, seen in the same lead, for proper diagnosis

mV: Abbreviation for millivolt

myocardial cells: Working cells of the myocardium that contain contractile filaments and form the muscular layer of the atrial walls and the thicker muscular layer of the ventricular walls

myocardial infarction (MI): Necrosis of some mass of the heart muscle caused by an inadequate blood supply

myocardium: Middle and thickest layer of the heart; contains the cardiac muscle fibers that cause contraction of the heart and contains the conduction system and blood supply

myofibril: Slender striated strand of muscle tissue

nodal: Term formerly used for junctional beats or rhythms

no man's land (extreme right axis deviation): Current flow in the direction opposite of normal (−91 to −179 degrees)

noncompensatory pause: Pause is termed "noncompensatory" (or incomplete) if the normal beat following the premature complex occurs before it was expected

nonconducted PAC (blocked PAC): Premature atrial complex that is not followed by a QRS complex

nontransmural infarction: Myocardial infarction that is classified as either subendocardial, involving the endocardium and the myocardium, or subepicardial, involving the myocardium and the epicardium

output: Electrical stimulus delivered by a pacemaker's pulse generator, usually defined in terms of pulse amplitude (volts) and pulse width (milliseconds)

overdrive pacing: Pacing the heart at a rate faster than the rate of the tachycardia

PAC: Abbreviation for premature atrial complex

pacemaker: Artificial pulse generator that delivers an electrical current to the heart to stimulate depolarization

pacemaker cells: Specialized cells of the heart's electrical conduction system, capable of spontaneously generating and conducting electrical impulses

pacemaker generator (pulse generator): Power source that houses the battery and controls for regulating a pacemaker

pacemaker spike: Vertical line on the ECG that indicates the pacemaker has discharged

pacemaker syndrome: Adverse clinical signs and symptoms that limit a patient's everyday functioning, occurring in the setting of an electrically normal pacing system; pacemaker syndrome is most commonly associated with a loss of AV synchrony (e.g., VVI pacing) but may also occur because of an inappropriate AV interval or inappropriate rate modulation

pacing interval: Period, expressed in milliseconds, between two consecutively paced events in the same cardiac chamber without an intervening sensed event (e.g., AA interval, VV interval); also known as the demand interval or basic interval

pacing system analyzer (PSA): External testing and measuring device capable of pacing the heart during pacemaker implantation and used to determine appropriate pulse generator settings for the individual patient (e.g., pacing threshold, lead impedance, pulse amplitude)

paired beats: Two consecutive premature complexes

papillary muscles: Projections of myocardium found on the ventricular walls; during ventricular contraction the papillary muscles contract, pulling on the chordae tendineae, preventing inversion of the AV valves into the atria

parameter: Value that can be measured and sometimes changed, either indirectly or directly; in pacing, parameter refers to a value that influences the function of the pacemaker (e.g., sensitivity, amplitude, mode)

paroxysmal: Term used to describe the sudden onset or cessation of a dysrhythmia

Paroxysmal atrial tachycardia (PAT): Atrial tachycardia that starts or ends suddenly

paroxysmal supraventricular tachycardia (PSVT): Term used to describe supraventricular tachycardia that starts and ends suddenly

pericardiocentesis: Procedure in which a needle is inserted into the pericardial space and excess fluid is sucked out (aspirated) through the needle

pericardium: Protective sac that surrounds the heart

peripheral resistance: Resistance to the flow of blood determined by blood vessel diameter and the tone of the vascular musculature

PJC: Premature junctional complex

polarized state: Period of time following repolarization of a myocardial cell (also called the resting state) when the outside of the cell is positive and the interior of the cell is negative

polymorphic: Varying in shape

potential difference: Difference in electrical charge between two points in a circuit; expressed in volts or millivolts

ppm: Abbreviation for pulses/min; ppm usually refers to a paced rate, while beats/min (bpm) refers to an intrinsic heart rate

preexcitation: Term used to describe rhythms that originate from above the ventricles but in which the impulse travels via a pathway other than the AV node and bundle of His; thus the supraventricular impulse excites the ventricles earlier than normal

preload: Force exerted by the blood on the walls of the ventricles at the end of diastole

premature complex: Early beat occurring before the next expected beat

PR interval: P wave plus the PR segment; reflects depolarization of the right and left atria (P wave) and the spread of the impulse through the AV node, bundle of His, right and left bundle branches, and the Purkinje fibers (PR segment)

prophylaxis: Preventive treatment

pulmonary circulation: flow of unoxygenated (venous) blood from the right ventricle to the lungs and oxygenated blood from the lungs to the left atrium

pulse generator: Power source that houses the battery and controls for regulating a pacemaker

pulseless electrical activity (PEA): Organized electrical activity observed on a cardiac monitor (other than VT or VF) without the patient having a palpable pulse

Purkinje fibers: Elaborate web of fibers distributed throughout the ventricular myocardium

PVC: Premature ventricular complex

P wave: The first wave in the cardiac cycle; represents atrial depolarization and the spread of the electrical impulse throughout the right and left atria

QRS complex: Several waveforms (Q wave, R wave, and S wave) that represent the spread of an electrical impulse through the ventricles (ventricular depolarization)

quadrigeminy: Dysrhythmia in which every fourth beat is a premature ectopic beat

R wave: On an EGG, the first positive deflection in the QRS complex, representing ventricular depolarization; in pacing, R wave refers to the entire QRS complex, denoting an intrinsic ventricular event

rate modulation: Ability of a pacemaker to increase the pacing rate in response to physical activity or metabolic demand; some type of physiologic sensor is used by the pacemaker to determine the need for an increased pacing rate; also known as rate adaptation or rate response

RBBB: Right bundle branch block

reciprocal change: "Mirror image" ECG changes seen in the wall of the heart opposite the location of an infarction

reentry: Propagation of an impulse through tissue already activated by that same impulse

refractoriness: Term used to describe the period of recovery that cells need after being discharged before they are able to respond to a stimulus

relative refractory period: Corresponds with the downslope of the T wave; cardiac cells can be stimulated to depolarize if the stimulus is strong enough

repolarization: Movement of ions across a cell membrane in which the inside of the cell is restored to its negative charge

retrograde: Moving backward; moving in the opposite direction to that which is considered normal

right axis deviation: Current flow to the right of normal (190 to 1180 degrees)

run: Three or more sequential ectopic beats; also referred to as a "salvo" or "burst"

RV interval: Period from the intrinsic ventricular event and the ventricular-paced event that follows; the pacemaker's escape interval

salvo: Three or more sequential ectopic beats; also referred to as a "run" or "burst"

sarcolemma: Membrane that covers smooth, striated, and cardiac muscle fibers

sarcomere: Smallest functional unit of a myofibril

sarcoplasm: Semi-fluid cytoplasm of muscle cells

sarcoplasmic reticulum: Network of tubules and sacs that plays an important role in muscle contraction and relaxation by releasing and storing calcium ions

segment: Line between waveforms; named by the waveform that precedes or follows it

semilunar valves: Valves shaped like half moons that separate the ventricles from the aorta and pulmonary artery

sensing: Ability of a pacemaker to recognize and respond to intrinsic electrical activity

septum: Partition

sick sinus syndrome: Term used to describe a sinus node dysfunction that may be manifested as severe sinus bradycardia, sinus arrest or sinus block, or bradycardia-tachycardia syndrome

sinoatrial node: Normal pacemaker of the heart that normally discharges at a rhythmic rate of 60 to 100 bpm

sinus arrhythmia: Dysrhythmia originating in the sinoatrial node that occurs when the SA node discharges irregularly; sinus arrhythmia is a normal phenomenon associated with the phases of respiration and changes in intrathoracic pressure

sinus bradycardia: Dysrhythmia originating in the sinoatrial node with a ventricular response of less than 60 bpm

sinus tachycardia: Dysrhythmia originating in the sinoatrial node with a ventricular response between 101 and 180 bpm

splanchnic: Pertaining to internal organs; visceral

ST-segment: Portion of the ECG representing the end of ventricular depolarization (end of the R wave) and the beginning of ventricular repolarization (T wave)

stroke volume: Amount of blood ejected by either ventricle during one contraction; can be calculated as cardiac output divided by heart rate

subendocardial infarction: Myocardial infarction involving the endocardium and myocardium

subepicardial infarction: Myocardial infarction involving the myocardium and epicardium

sulcus: Groove

supraventricular: Originating from a site above the bifurcation of the bundle of His, such as the sinoatrial node, atria, or AV junction

supraventricular arrhythmias (SVA): Rhythms that begin in the SA node, atrial tissue, or the AV junction

syncope: Fainting; usually resulting from cardiac or neurologic conditions, including seizure disorders, vasodepressor syncope (the simple faint), and cardiac dysrhythmias

syncytium: Unit of combined cells

systole: Contraction of the heart (usually referring to ventricular contraction) during which blood is propelled into the pulmonary artery and aorta; when the term is used without reference to a specific chamber of the heart, the term implies ventricular systole

tachycardia: Heart rate greater than 100 bpm (tachy, fast)

threshold: Membrane potential at which the cell membrane will depolarize and generate an action potential

TKO: Abbreviation meaning "to keep open"; also known as KVO, "keep the vein open"

torsades de pointes (TdP): Type of polymorphic VT associated with a prolonged QT interval; the QRS changes in shape, amplitude, and width and appears to "twist" around the isoelectric line, resembling a spindle

transmural infarction: Myocardial infarction in which the entire thickness of the ventricular wall (endocardium to epicardium) is involved

trifascicular block: Block in the three primary divisions of the bundle branches (i.e., right bundle branch, left anterior fascicle, and left posterior fascicle)

trigeminy: Dysrhythmia in which every third beat is a premature ectopic beat

T wave: Waveform that follows the QRS complex and represents ventricular repolarization

unipolar lead: Lead that consists of a single positive electrode and a reference point; a pacing lead with a single electrical pole at the distal tip of the pacing lead (negative pole) through which the stimulating pulse is delivered; in a permanent pacemaker with a unipolar lead, the positive pole is the pulse generator case

VA interval: In dual-chamber pacing, the interval between a sensed- or ventricular-paced event and the next atrial-paced event

VV interval: Interval between two ventricular-paced events

V wave: Ventricular-paced event; the ventricular stimulus or the point in the intrinsic ventricular depolarization (R wave) during which ventricular sensing occurs

vagal maneuver: Methods used to stimulate the vagus nerve in an attempt to slow conduction through the AV node, resulting in slowing of the heart rate

vector: Quantity having direction and magnitude, usually depicted by a straight arrow whose length represents magnitude and whose head represents direction

venous return: Amount of blood flowing into the right atrium each minute from the systemic circulation

ventricle: Either of the two lower chambers of the heart

ventricular activation time (VAT): Interval it takes for depolarization of the interventricular septum, right ventricle, and most of the left ventricle; VAT is measured on the ECG from the beginning of the QRS complex to the onset of the peak of the R wave

ventricular pacing: Pacing system with a lead attached in the right ventricle

ventricular tachycardia (VT): Dysrhythmia originating in the ventricles with a ventricular response greater than 100 bpm

wandering atrial pacemaker (multiformed atrial rhythm): Cardiac dysrhythmia that occurs because of impulses originating from various sites, including the sinoatrial node, the atria, and/or the AV junction; requires at least three different P waves, seen in the same lead, for proper diagnosis.

waveform: Movement away from the baseline in either a positive or negative direction

Wolff-Parkinson-White syndrome: Type of preexcitation syndrome, characterized by a slurred upstroke of the QRS complex (delta wave) and wide QRS

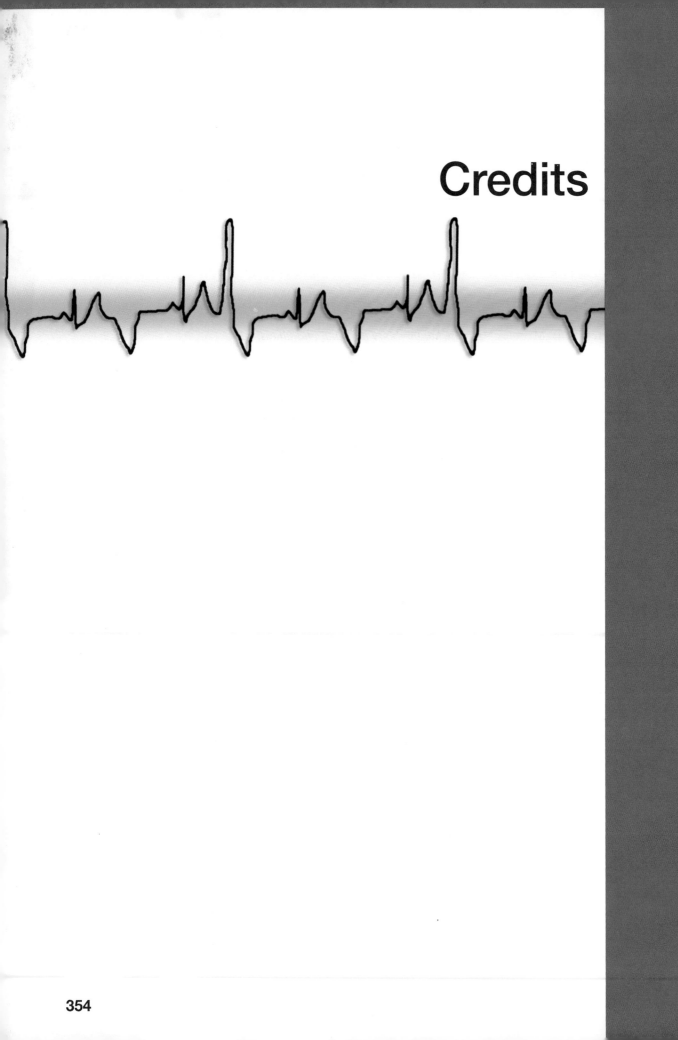

Credits

CHAPTER 1

Figure 1-1: Herlihy B, Maebius NK: *The human body in health and illness,* ed 2, St Louis, 2003, WB Saunders.

Figure 1-2: Thibodeau GA, Patton KT: *Anatomy and physiology,* ed 5, St Louis, 2003, Mosby.

Figure 1-3: Canobbio MM: *Cardiovascular disorders, Mosby's Clinical Nursing Series,* vol. 1, St Louis, 1990, Mosby.

Figure 1-4: Herlihy B, Maebius NK: *The human body in health and illness,* ed 2, St Louis, 2003, WB Saunders.

Figure 1-5: *Managing major diseases: cardiac disorders* (Butler HA, Caplin M, McCaully E, et al eds) vol 2, St Louis, 1999, Mosby.

Figures 1-6, 1-7: Thibodeau GA, Patton KT: *Anatomy and physiology,* ed 5, St Louis, 2003, Mosby.

Figures 1-8, 1-9: Canobbio MM: *Cardiovascular disorders, Mosby's Clinical Nursing Series,* vol. 1. St Louis, 1990, Mosby.

Figure 1-10: Thibodeau GA, Patton KT: *Anatomy and physiology,* ed 5, St Louis, 2003, Mosby.

Figures 1-11, 1-12: Herlihy B, Maebius NK: *The human body in health and illness,* ed 2, WB Saunders.

Figure 1-13: Canobbio MM: *Cardiovascular disorders, Mosby's Clinical Nursing Series,* vol. 1. St Louis, 1990, Mosby.

Figure 1-14: Thibodeau GA, Patton KT: *Anatomy and physiology,* ed 5, St Louis, 2003, Mosby.

Figure 1-15: Modified from Sanders MJ: *Mosby's paramedic textbook,* ed 2, St Louis, 2000, Mosby.

Figure 1-17: Thibodeau GA, Patton KT: *Anatomy and physiology,* ed 5, St Louis, 2003, Mosby.

CHAPTER 2

Figure 2-1: Thibodeau GA, Patton KT: *Anatomy and physiology,* ed 5, St Louis, 2003, Mosby.

Figures 2-2, 2-3, 2-4: Herlihy B, Maebius NK: *The human body in health and illness,* ed 2, St Louis, 2003, WB Saunders.

Figure 2-5: Sanders MJ: *Mosby's paramedic textbook,* ed 3, St Louis, 2005, Mosby.

Figures 2-6, 2-7, 2-8: Canobbio MM: *Cardiovascular disorders, Mosby's Clinical Nursing Series,* vol. 1, St Louis, 1990, Mosby.

Figure 2-9: Goldman L, Ausiello D: *Cecil textbook of medicine,* ed 22, Philadelphia, 2004, WB Saunders.

Figures 2-10, 2-11: Crawford MV, Spence MI: *Commonsense approach to coronary care,* rev ed 6, St Louis, 1994, Mosby.

Figure 2-12: Herlihy B, Maebius NK: *The human body in health and illness,* ed 2, St Louis, 2003, WB Saunders.

Figure 2-14: Thelan L, Urden LD, Lough ME, Stacy KM: *Critical care nursing,* ed 3, St Louis, 1998, Mosby.

Figure 2-15: Guyton A, Hall J: *Textbook of medical physiology,* ed 11, Philadelphia, 2006, WB Saunders.

Figure 2-16: Modified from Marriot H, Conover M: *Advanced concepts in arrhythmias,* ed 3, St. Louis, 1998, Mosby.

Figure 2-17: Guyton A, Hall J: *Textbook of medical physiology,* ed 11, Philadelphia, 2006, WB Saunders.

Figure 2-18: Crawford MV, Spence MI: *Commonsense approach to coronary care,* rev ed 6, St Louis, 1994, Mosby.

Figure 2-19: Courtesy Medtronic, Inc.

Figure 2-20: Phalen T, Aehlert B: *The 12-lead ECG in acute coronary syndromes,* ed 2, St Louis, 2006, Mosby.

Figure 2-21: Urden LD, Stacy KM, Lough ME: *Thelan's critical care nursing: diagnosis and management,* ed 4, St Louis, 2002, Mosby.

Figures 2-22, 2-23: Goldberger A: *Clinical electrocardiography: a simplified approach,* ed 6, St Louis, 1999, Mosby.

Figure 2-24: Methodist Hospital: *Basic electrocardiography: a modular approach,* St Louis, 1986, Mosby.

Figure 2-26: Phillips RE, Feeney MK: *The cardiac rhythms: a systematic approach to interpretation,* ed 3, Philadelphia, 1990, WB Saunders.

Figure 2-27: Urden LD, Stacy KM, Lough ME: *Thelan's critical care nursing: diagnosis and management,* ed 4, St Louis, 2002, Mosby.

Figure 2-28: Phalen T, Aehlert B: *The 12-lead ECG in acute coronary syndromes,* ed 2, St Louis, 2006, Mosby.

Figure 2-29: Clochesy J, Breau C, Cardin S, et al: *Critical care nursing,* ed 2, Philadelphia, 1996, WB Saunders.

Figure 2-30: Lounsbury P, Frye SE: *Cardiac rhythm disorders: a nursing process approach,* ed 2, St Louis, 1991, Mosby.

Figures 2-31: Urden LD, Stacy KM, Lough ME: *Thelan's critical care nursing: diagnosis and management,* ed 4, St Louis, 2002, Mosby.

Figure 2-33: Goldberger A: *Clinical electrocardiography: a simplified approach,* ed 6, St Louis, 1999, Mosby.

Figure 2-34: Modified fromThibodeau GA, Patton KT: *Anatomy and physiology,* ed 5, St Louis, 2003, Mosby.

Figure 2-35: Goldberger A: *Clinical electrocardiography: a simplified approach,* ed 6, St Louis, 1999, Mosby.

Figure 2-37: Modified from Thibodeau GA, Patton KT: *Anatomy and physiology,* ed 5, St Louis, 2003, Mosby.

Figure 2-38: Goldberger A: *Clinical electrocardiography: a simplified approach,* ed 6, St Louis, 1999, Mosby.

Figure 2-39: Modified from Thibodeau GA, Patton KT: *Anatomy and physiology,* ed 5, St Louis, 2003, Mosby.

Figure 2-41: Goldberger AL: *Myocardial infarction: electrocardiographic differential diagnosis,* ed 4, St Louis, 1991, Mosby.

Figure 2-42: Surawicz B, Knilans TK: *Chou's electrocardiography in clinical practice: adult and pediatric,* ed 5, Philadelphia, 2001, WB Saunders.

Figure 2-44: Modified from Thibodeau GA, Patton KT: *Anatomy and physiology,* ed 5, St Louis, 2003, Mosby.

Figure 2-45: Urden LD, Stacy KM, Lough ME: *Thelan's critical care nursing: diagnosis and management,* ed 4, St Louis, 2002, Mosby.

Figure 2-46: Grauer K: *A practical guide to ECG interpretation,* ed 2, St Louis, 1998, Mosby.

Figures 2-47, 2-48: Goldberger A: *Clinical electrocardiography: a simplified approach,* ed 6, St Louis, 1999, Mosby.

Figure 2-51: Modified from Thibodeau GA, Patton KT: *Anatomy and physiology,* ed 5, St Louis, 2003, Mosby.

Figure 2-52: Grauer K: *A practical guide to ECG interpretation,* ed 2, St Louis, 1998, Mosby.

Figures 2-53, 2-54: Modified from Thibodeau GA, Patton KT: *Anatomy and physiology,* ed 5, St Louis, 2003, Mosby.

Figures 2-55, 2-56, 2-57: Sanders MJ: *Mosby's paramedic textbook,* ed 3, St Louis, 2005, Mosby.

Figure 2-58: Urden LD, Stacy KM, Lough ME: *Thelan's critical care nursing: diagnosis and management,* ed 4, St Louis, 2002, Mosby.

Figure 2-59: Crawford MV, Spence MI: *Commonsense approach to coronary care,* rev ed 6, St Louis, 1994, Mosby.

CHAPTER 4

Figure 4-1: Crawford MV, Spence MI: *Commonsense approach to coronary care,* rev ed 6, St Louis, 1994, Mosby.

Figure 4-3: Kinney MP, Packa DR: *Andreoli's comprehensive cardiac care,* ed 8, St Louis, 1996, Mosby.

Figure 4-5: Goldberger A: *Clinical electrocardiography: a simplified approach,* ed 6, St Louis, 1999, Mosby.

Figure 4-6: Zipes DP, Libby P, Bonow RO, Braunwald E (hon): *Braunwald's heart disease: a textbook of cardiovascular medicine,* ed 7, Philadelphia, 2005, WB Saunders.

Figure 4-7: Conover MB: *Understanding electrocardiography,* ed 8, St Louis, 2003, Mosby.

Figures 4-8, 4-9: Goldberger A*: Clinical electrocardiography: a simplified approach,* ed 6, St Louis, 1999, Mosby.

Figure 4-10: Kinney MP, Packa DR: *Andreoli's comprehensive cardiac care,* ed 8, St Louis, 1996, Mosby.

Figure 4-11: Goldman L, Braunwald E: *Primary cardiology,* Philadelphia, 1998, WB Saunders.

Figure 4-13: Urden LD, Stacy KM, Lough ME: *Thelan's critical care nursing: diagnosis and management,* ed 4, St Louis, 2002, Mosby.

Figure 4-14: Crawford MV, Spence MI: *Commonsense approach to coronary care,* rev ed 6, St Louis, 1994 Mosby.

Figure 4-15: Surawicz B, Knilans TK: *Chou's electrocardiography in clinical practice: adult and pediatric,* ed 5, Philadelphia, 1996, WB Saunders.

Figure 4-16: Grauer K: *A practical guide to ECG interpretation,* ed 2, St Louis, 1998, Mosby.

Figure 4-17: Zipes DP, Jalife J: *Cardiac electrophysiology: from cell to bedside,* ed 4, Philadelphia, 2004, WB Saunders.

Figure 4-18: Behrman RE, Kliegman RM, Jenson HB: *Nelson textbook of pediatrics,* ed 17, Philadelphia, 2004, WB Saunders.

Figure 4-19: Grauer K: *A practical guide to ECG interpretation,* ed 2, St Louis, 1998, Mosby.

Figure 4-22: Goldberger A*: Clinical electrocardiography: a simplified approach,* ed 6, St Louis, 1999, Mosby.

CHAPTER 5

Figures 5-2, 5-3: Grauer K: *A practical guide to ECG interpretation,* ed 2, St Louis, 1998, Mosby.

CHAPTER 6

Figure 6-1: Grauer K: *A practical guide to ECG interpretation,* ed 2, St Louis, 1998, Mosby.

Figure 6-2: Crawford MV, Spence MI: *Commonsense approach to coronary care,* rev ed 6, St Louis, 1994, Mosby.

Figure 6-3: Kinney MP, Packa DR: *Andreoli's comprehensive cardiac care,* ed 8, St Louis, 1996, Mosby.

Figure 6-9: Surawicz B, Knilans TK: *Chou's electrocardiography in clinical practice: adult and pediatric,* ed 5, Philadelphia, 1996, WB Saunders.

Figure 6-12: Crawford MV, Spence MI: *Commonsense approach to coronary care,* rev ed 6, St Louis, 1994, Mosby.

Figure 6-18: Grauer K: *A practical guide to ECG interpretation,* ed 2, St Louis, 1998, Mosby.

CHAPTER 7

Figure 7-7: Grauer K: *A practical guide to ECG interpretation,* ed 2, St Louis, 1998, Mosby.

CHAPTER 8

Figure 8-5: Courtesy Medtronic, Inc.

Table 8-2: From Flynn JB: *Introduction to critical care skills,* St Louis, 1993, Mosby.

CHAPTER 9

Figures 9-1, 9-2: Goldberger A*: Clinical electrocardiography: a simplified approach,* ed 6, St Louis, 1999, Mosby.

Figure 9-3: Phalen T, Aehlert B: *The 12-lead ECG in acute coronary syndromes,* ed 2, St Louis, 2006, Mosby.

Figure 9-4: Urden LD, Stacy KM, Lough ME: *Thelan's critical care nursing: diagnosis and management,* ed 4, St Louis, 2002, Mosby.

Figure 9-5: Phalen T, Aehlert B: *The 12-lead ECG in acute coronary syndromes,* ed 2, St Louis, 2006, Mosby.

Figure 9-6: Surawicz B, Knilans TK: *Chou's electrocardiography in clinical practice: adult and pediatric,* ed 5, Philadelphia, 1996, WB Saunders.

Figure 9-7: Urden LD, Stacy KM, Lough ME: *Thelan's critical care nursing: diagnosis and management,* ed 4, St Louis, 2002, Mosby.

Figure 9-8: Thibodeau GA, Patton KT: *Anatomy and physiology,* ed 5, St Louis, 2003, Mosby.

Figure 9-9: Urden LD, Stacy KM, Lough ME: *Thelan's critical care nursing: diagnosis and management,* ed 4, St Louis, 2002, Mosby.

Figure 9-10: Grauer K: *A practical guide to ECG interpretation,* ed 2, St Louis, 1998, Mosby.

Figure 9-11: Urden LD, Stacy KM, Lough ME: *Thelan's critical care nursing: diagnosis and management,* ed 4, St Louis, 2002, Mosby.

Figure 9-12: *Managing major diseases: cardiac disorders* (Butler HA, Caplin M, McCaully E, et al eds) vol 2, St Louis, 1999, Mosby.

Figure 9-13: Grauer K: *A practical guide to ECG interpretation,* ed 2, St Louis, 1998, Mosby.

Figures 9-14: Conover MB: *Understanding electrocardiography,* ed 8, St Louis, 2003, Mosby.

Figure 9-15: Khan MG: *Rapid ECG interpretation,* Philadelphia, 1997, WB Saunders.

Figure 9-16: Phalen T, Aehlert B: *The 12-lead ECG in acute coronary syndromes,* ed 2, St Louis, 2006, Mosby.

Figure 9-17: Grauer K: *A practical guide to ECG interpretation,* ed 2, St Louis, 1998, Mosby.

Figure 9-18: Johnson R, Schwartz M: *A simplified approach to electrocardiography,* Philadelphia, 1986, WB Saunders.

Figure 9-19: Urden LD, Stacy KM, Lough ME: *Thelan's critical care nursing: diagnosis and management,* ed 4, St Louis, 2002, Mosby.

Figure 9-20: Sanders MJ: *Mosby's paramedic textbook,* ed 3, St Louis, 2005, Mosby.

Figure 9-21: Phalen T, Aehlert B: *The 12-lead ECG in acute coronary syndromes,* ed 2, St Louis, 2006, Mosby.

Figure 9-22: Kinney MP, Packa DR: *Andreoli's comprehensive cardiac care,* ed 8, St Louis, 1996, Mosby.

Figure 9-23: Phalen T, Aehlert B: *The 12-lead ECG in acute coronary syndromes,* ed 2, St Louis, 2006, Mosby.

Figure 9-24: Goldberger A: *Clinical electrocardiography: a simplified approach,* ed 6, St Louis, 1999, Mosby.

Figure 9-25: Phalen T, Aehlert B: *The 12-lead ECG in acute coronary syndromes,* ed 2, St Louis, 2006, Mosby.

Figure 9-26: Surawicz B, Knilans TK: *Chou's electrocardiography in clinical practice: adult and pediatric,* ed 5, Philadelphia, 1996, WB Saunders.

Figures 9-27, 9-28, 9-29: Phalen T, Aehlert B: *The 12-lead ECG in acute coronary syndromes,* ed 2, St Louis, 2006, Mosby.

Figure 9-30: Lounsbury P, Frye SE: *Cardiac rhythm disorders: a nursing process approach,* ed 2, St Louis, 1991, Mosby.

Figure 9-31: Kinney MP, Packa DR: *Andreoli's comprehensive cardiac care,* ed 8, St Louis, 1996, Mosby.

Figure 9-32: Phalen T, Aehlert B: *The 12-lead ECG in acute coronary syndromes,* ed 2, St Louis, 2006, Mosby.

Figure 9-33: Thelan L, Urden LD, Lough ME, Stacy KM: *Critical care nursing,* ed 3, St. Louis, 1998, Mosby.

Figure 9-34: Kinney MP, Packa DR: *Andreoli's comprehensive cardiac care,* ed 8, St Louis, 1996, Mosby.

Figure 9-35: Urden LD, Stacy KM, Lough ME: *Thelan's critical care nursing: diagnosis and management,* ed 4, St Louis, 2002, Mosby.

Figures 9-36, 9-37, 9-38, 9-39: Phalen T, Aehlert B: *The 12-lead ECG in acute coronary syndromes,* ed 2, St Louis, 2006, Mosby.

Figure 9-40: Goldberger A: *Clinical electrocardiography: a simplified approach,* ed 6, St Louis, 1999, Mosby.

Figure 9-41: Surawicz B, Knilans TK: *Chou's electrocardiography in clinical practice: adult and pediatric,* ed 5, Philadelphia, 1996, WB Saunders.

Figures 9-42, 9-43, 9-44: Johnson R, Schwartz M: *A simplified approach to electrocardiography,* Philadelphia, 1986, WB Saunders.

Figure 9-45: Kinney MP, Packa DR: *Andreoli's comprehensive cardiac care,* ed 8, St Louis, 1996, Mosby.

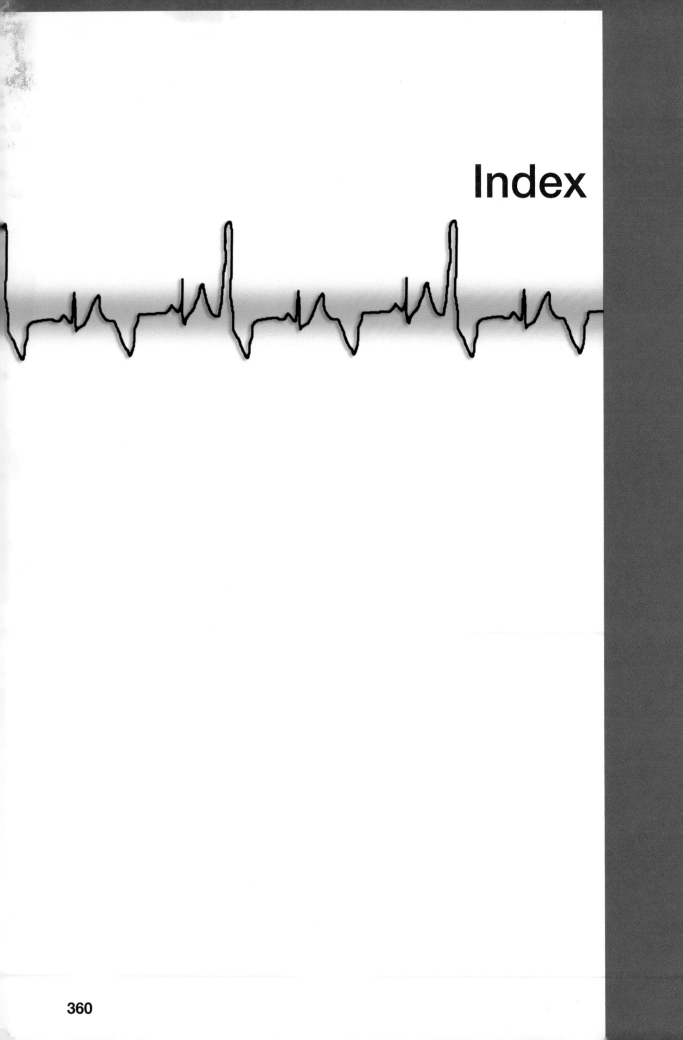

Index

b denotes box, f denotes figure, t denotes table